Fatherhood in the Borderlands

Joe R. and Teresa Lozano Long Series
in Latin American and Latino Art and Culture

Fatherhood in the Borderlands

A DAUGHTER'S SLOW APPROACH

DOMINO RENEE PEREZ

University of Texas Press

AUSTIN

Copyright © 2022 by the University of Texas Press
All rights reserved
Printed in the United States of America
First edition, 2022

Requests for permission to reproduce material from this work should be sent to:
 Permissions
 University of Texas Press
 P.O. Box 7819
 Austin, TX 78713-7819
 utpress.utexas.edu/rp-form

♾ The paper used in this book meets the minimum requirements of ANSI/NISO Z39.48-1992 (R1997) (Permanence of Paper).

Library of Congress Cataloging-in-Publication Data

Names: Perez, Domino Renee, 1967– author.
Title: Fatherhood in the borderlands : a daughter's slow approach / Domino Renee Perez.
Other titles: Joe R. and Teresa Lozano Long series in Latin American and Latino art and culture.
Description: First edition. | Austin : University of Texas Press, 2022. | Series: Joe R. and Teresa Lozano Long series in Latin American and Latino art and culture | Includes bibliographical references and index.
Identifiers: LCCN 2022002746
 ISBN 978-0-292-74553-7 (cloth)
 ISBN 978-1-4773-2634-3 (paperback)
 ISBN 978-1-4773-2635-0 (PDF)
 ISBN 978-1-4773-2636-7 (ePub)
Subjects: LCSH: Perez, Domino Renee, 1967– | Mexican Americans in literature—Case studies. | Mexican Americans in motion pictures—Case studies. | Fathers in literature—Case studies. | Fathers in motion pictures—Case studies. | Fatherhood in literature—Case studies. | Fatherhood in motion pictures—Case studies.
Classification: LCC PS173.M39 P47 2022 | DDC 810.9/352510896872—dc23/eng/20220518
LC record available at https://lccn.loc.gov/2022002746

doi:10.7560/745537

*For the Big Grandpa,
who understood me
from the very beginning.*

*Para el Big Grandpa,
que me entendió
desde el principio.*

CONTENTS

PREFACE The Slow Lowdown *1*

INTRODUCTION A Slow Approach to Fathers and Other Fictions *13*

PART I **Sourcing Authority** *37*

FILM *Ancianos* not *Abuelos*: Making Space and Mediating Male Power *45*

PERSONAL NARRATIVE "No, I Am Your Father" *77*

LITERATURE Fathers and Racialized Masculinities in Luis Alberto Urrea's *In Search of Snow* *84*

PART II **Instrumentalizing Indigeneity** *111*

PERSONAL NARRATIVE Nobody Ever Said We Were Aztecs *119*

FILM Fatherhood, Chicanismo, and the Cultural Politics of Healing in *La Mission* *128*

LITERATURE New Tribalism and Chicana/o Indigeneity in the Work of Gloria Anzaldúa *154*

PART III *Fantasmas* **and** *Fronteras* *175*

LITERATURE Fathers, Sons, and Other (Short) Fictions *183*

FILM Meta and Mutant Fathers *217*

PERSONAL NARRATIVE Family Fictions and Other Lies about the Truth *252*

CONCLUSION Fathers and Futurity *257*

PARTING SHOT *270*

ACKNOWLEDGMENTS *272*

NOTES *275*

WORKS CITED AND CONSULTED *300*

INDEX *316*

Fatherhood in the Borderlands

PREFACE

THE SLOW LOWDOWN

During the 1920s and 1930s, in the shadow of downtown Houston, a steel mill, an oil field, and a railroad yard served as the center of economic life for the tiny city of Cottage Grove, Texas. Working class and surprisingly diverse for the pre–civil rights era, the neighborhood—named for the cottages built to house workers—included Anglo, Mexican, Czech, and Chinese residents. Around 1950, much of my family on both sides made their way from the rural communities of Beeville and Lockhart, Texas, to live there. In the late 1960s, my parents would eventually take up residence in their own home at 5633 Petty, the house where I spent the first six years of my life. Grandparents, aunts, uncles, and cousins, who watched over and looked out for us kids, were minutes away on Larkin and Leroy. But during the mid-1970s, as families fled Cottage Grove to pursue decidedly middle-class lives away from their working-class roots, the area began to fall into decline. We were the first ones in our family to leave. The steel mill had long closed, and the remaining business owners suspiciously eyed their customers in ways they never had before. In the 1980s, crime finally pushed people off their porches and behind locked doors. By that time, we were settled in the suburbs of northwest Houston, twenty-five minutes away.

Built in 1973, with its black trim and scalloped façade, ours was the only mission-style home in the Candlelight Forest West neighborhood. The brand new four-bedroom, two-bathroom house, 1,376 square feet on a corner lot, with its wood-paneled living room and multicolored shag carpeting, and our old icebox in the kitchen, was walking distance from good schools but twelve miles from the nearest relative. Early on, friends and family members regularly traveled the distance to help us lay sod, dig fence postholes, and plant shrubbery, including the trees my father would repeatedly nick with the lawnmower. As time passed, we saw folk from the old neighborhood less frequently and slowly began to settle into our new lives. Our house sat on the last street in the back of a neighborhood where we, along with the Sicilian family and the Mexican and Anglo couple, constituted the only ethnic or racial diversity. No one stopped by to *chismear*, drop off food, or borrow/return something or the other. There were no outdoor parties or celebrations that lingered long into the night. Everyone in this new neighborhood seemed to withdraw into their homes and only occasionally offer up a wave to passersby.

My barrio-to-middle-class suburban family was television perfect, a long-running episode in which my parents embraced in the kitchen and talked about their day, family members would gather at Christmastime for tamale and menudo making, and we once held a wedding reception for my cousin in the backyard and danced barefoot in the grass. We took modest family vacations, sleeping in the bed of my father's truck covered in a camper. All around us, as families disintegrated, we knew with certainty that would never happen to us, until it did, when my father left years later. Back then, to afford this middle-class existence, both my parents had to work, so my brother and I learned to take care of ourselves; our biggest responsibility included getting to and from school on our own. In the morning, my brother, who was five years older, caught the middle school bus less than a block away. He regularly stayed after school playing sports until my mom picked him up on her way home from work. For me, the last school bell of the day signaled the familiar task of going through a gauntlet of crowded hallways, past the parents outside waiting in cars, and back home again, safely, on foot.

Like so many in Generation X, I was a latchkey kid, though not tragically so.[1] Secret pockets sewn into dresses and jeans, oversized safety pins, grimy yarn necklaces. These safeguarded the instruments of latchkey kids' independence. Alone or in packs, we were an army of children who made our way from home to school and home again each day unsupervised. The ritual was repeated every afternoon across the country as keys were fished out of hiding places or taken from around necks to let ourselves into empty homes, where we were expected to remain until our parents or guardians arrived later in the evening, or sometimes not until the next morning.

In elementary school, my walk was a quarter of a mile and took only about ten minutes: out my door at 7302 Battlewood Drive, left onto Deanwood, and right onto Woodsman Trail, I joined a whole herd of children in the early morning hours moving in the same direction toward Willie B. Ermel Elementary School. (Go Ermel Jets!) In the afternoon, I simply took the same route in reverse and made it home in plenty of time before my mother's first phone call at 3:30, followed by two others, one at 4:15 and another at about 5:00 before she left work to collect my brother at Hoffman Middle School. Daddy did not arrive home until around 5:45 p.m. So it was mostly just me, Gilligan, the Skipper, and the Brady or Munster families at home while I sat at the kitchen table, ate a snack, and did my homework. Under no circumstances could I leave the locked and latched house or open the door to anyone other than my parents. As I waited for my family to return after completing my schoolwork, I usually watched TV, listened to the radio, and read comic books or other treasured Scholastic Book Fair acquisitions. Sometimes I talked on the avocado-green rotary phone that was mounted on the kitchen wall—its twenty-foot cord, a dingy off-white and coiled in an impossibly tangled nest, allowing me free movement around at least two rooms but only after I performed a practiced maneuver that both untwisted the jumbled knot and in the process caused the phone receiver to spin wildly.

During the summers, with longer hours to fill, my day was ordered by soap operas, *Ryan's Hope, All My Children, One Life to Live*, and *General Hospital*, followed by the Million Dollar Movie (1972–1992), a title that belied the quality of many of the selections. When the gold-plated, bejeweled film reel container spun onto the screen, I knew I had about an hour before it was time to start cooking dinner. Dramas, comedies, westerns, and sci-fi movies filled my late afternoons, the titles of which were mostly forgettable (except for the ones about Sinbad or Godzilla). The lessons they conveyed were not. In those afternoon hours, I traveled the globe or into outer space learning about conflict, goodness, duty, loyalty, love, and adventure, without ever leaving home. The indiscriminate variety of films that aired from 3 to 5 p.m. each day provided a breadth and depth of exposure to motion pictures that, under different circumstances, I would not have chosen or been allowed to watch. Still, the Million Dollar Movie films were a form of companionship and a way to order my afternoons.

Sometimes, to break up the summer monotony, my mother would take me with her to work. These were some of the best days. I did not sit at my mother's elbow at the bank teller counter in some nascent version of take-your-daughter-to-work day. In fact, the only thing I ever remember about the inside of the bank is the break room because it had an "honor" snack box, a low-tech version of a vending machine, where customers could deposit the "suggested price" for each item in a small cutout in the cardboard labeled with the words "Deposit Coins Here." Candy bars, potato chips, crackers, and nuts were propped up like soldiers, standing at attention in perfect rows, all waiting to be selected as I held tight to the two coins in my pocket. For me, the real prizes were down the street in a building filled with treasure that I could claim with a little card bearing my name.

One block away from the bank, at 1349 W. 43rd Street, stood the Oak Forest Library, a branch of the Houston Public Library. Since opening in 1960, the library and its mid-century modern architecture had woven its way into the fabric of the community, despite, or perhaps because of, its odd location, nestled among the trees at the far end of an outdoor shopping center. The steel and masonry exterior was very much a product of its time. But I did not care about any of that. To this day, when looking at the building in photographs, I still feel a twinge of excitement at the sight of the façade, with its thin metal brow cutting across vertical mosaic stripes, a cascade of blues and greens streaming down the front, working together to create an illusion of uniformity. Only upon closer inspection do the different parts of the mosaics come into view, each tile carefully placed to enhance the one beside it and create form and structure. Flanked on either side by doors of steel and glass, this was the threshold of adventure.

Within the walls of this magical place, I would remain for the entirety of the day. My mother would drop me off in the morning a little after 9 a.m., always walking me inside and settling me at an out-of-the-way table. This ritual was accompanied by the "under-no-circumstances-do-you-leave-the-building-or-talk-to-strangers" speech. Before exiting, she would stop at the circulation desk to exchange a few words with the on-duty librarian, who would turn in my direction and offer a small wave. I always felt obliged to respond in kind. For the next three hours, until my mom returned at lunch, I would wander through the stacks. Unaccompanied, I explored, letting my mind and imagination settle upon whatever caught my eye: titles, colors, book covers under crinkly plastic, gilded lettering on a spine. In this way, I encountered the Money Pit on Oak Island, Bigfoot, UFOs, men in black, Easter Island, Area 51, the Nazca Lines, Machu Picchu, Devil's Tower, Coral Castle, vampires, *Dracula*, and the Warren Report. Thinking back on that time, I am reminded of eccentric mythology professor Hector Cyr (Oliver Platt) in *Lake Placid* (1999). In response to a local sheriff's disbelief that crocodiles can cross oceans, Professor Cyr quips, "Well, they conceal information like that in books."

I was never interested in semiaquatic reptiles, although I did feel that a world of important information was being concealed from me, small pieces of which I glimpsed each time I opened a book. I believed that if only I read enough, I could learn about the world and discover facts not even my parents knew about.

With my tendency toward solitude, the public library was a haven where I could wander for hours, traveling over oceans or under them, across galaxies into nebulas, through time—backward and into the future. During these treasured outings, I mastered my use of the card catalogue and developed a tendency to plop down in the stacks, where I would sit and read until my mother came to collect me. I wonder what I must have looked like then, a lone nine-year-old (shocking by today's sensibilities), sometimes the only person, other than the librarians, in the building, seated on the floor in between shelves, books arranged around me in a circle like friends that would share their secrets if only I opened them up.

Movies and books, my refuge and my teachers. They filled the very long summer days and afternoons. Sometimes they also taught me the things that my parents thought I should know. ABC Afterschool Specials, movies that covered such issues as substance abuse, sexual violence, teen pregnancy, disability, and fascism (*The Wave* [1983], anyone?), were required viewing.[2] Unsurprisingly, instead of one of my parents giving me a sex education talk, *The Life Cycle Library for Young People* (1969), an illustrated four-volume set that covered everything from menstruation to naked petting, appeared inexplicably one day in my room. The books embarrassed, terrified, and enthralled me, so I hid them in the bottom drawer of my dresser. Though I have lost and given away many things over the years, I still have these books. They are carefully tucked away with stacks of miniature *Empire Strikes Back* (1980) movie posters, clipped from newspapers, that I collected in anticipation of seeing the film. These material remnants tell the truth of my childhood. Books and movies always fit together in my mind because they were always with me.

This relationship was solidified after I fractured my pelvis and L5 vertebra in a car accident at the age of eleven. For four long months I was forced to lie supine with a hideous dusky blue corset laced around my hips to keep the bones in place. Buckles, laces, and bits of steel were always digging into some body part, antagonizing me to no end. Various ties and straps were held in place with an oversized Velcro flap that nipped at my skin. Metal stays constantly jabbed into my back. That horrible contraption became my enemy, but without it, the doctors told my parents, I would never walk again. With nothing to do except read and watch movies, I devoured both. Even if I was reading the same comics or books again and again or watching a movie I had seen dozens of times, they gave me a purpose and a place to go beyond the confines of my bed, which had been moved to the center of the living room. A string of paid caregivers turned me to prevent bedsores, changed the channel on the TV, prepared and served me meals, and on occasion read to me—until the insurance benefits ran out. When they did, my mother left her job to care for me. Having her home would have been the one good thing to come out of these prolonged circumstances, except she spent all her time on the phone with insurance companies and lawyers. She was scared and worried. I understand that now. At the time, I thought she was angry. More specifically, I thought she was angry with me, so I retreated further into books and movies.

A few years later, when I was thirteen, cable arrived with a knock on the door, an offer of free installation, and the promise of *all* the premium movie channels for one guaranteed low price for six months. The salesman believed he had sealed the deal with my parents by making them see that cable television was something the whole family could enjoy, but I knew what my overprotective parents were really thinking: sixty channels would keep me occupied *and* inside throughout the day. Cable allowed me to graduate from limited UHF and VHF offerings to a different world with twenty-four-hour music and movies. Rob Halford of Judas Priest, bobbing on and off screen as he sang "Hot Rockin'" while his shirtless, scrawny bandmates lifted weights in the background, served as my introduction to MTV. It was godawful and mesmerizing all at once.

With the help of the Movie Channel, I added well-known classic and contemporary films, including ones with R ratings, to my growing catalogue of knowledge. I consumed movies, without commercial interruption, around the clock. Even when I was not intently watching, especially if I was home alone, they were always on in the background, a habit of mine that endures to this day. I can still vividly recall the first time I saw Zeffirelli's *Romeo and Juliet* (1968); the O'Neal father-daughter duo of *Paper Moon* (1973); Jodie Foster in the family con caper *Candleshoe* (1977), a mere one year after her turn as a child prostitute in *Taxi Driver* (1976); the time-traveling, terribly romantic *Somewhere in Time* (1980); the hypersexual animated dystopia *Heavy Metal* (1981); and the literary stylings of the soft-core porn classic *Lady Chatterley's Lover* (1981).

All of these films made an impression, though none quite as much as a black comedy featuring swingers and cannibalism. I did not understand what *Eating Raoul* (1982) was satirizing through its Anglo protagonists

Paul and Mary Bland (Paul Bartel and Mary Waronov), aspiring restauranteurs who have been killing swingers in their building and taking their money to raise enough to start their dream business. I did think the hustler named Raoul (played by Robert Beltran) was handsome, though I found his proclamation of being a "hot-blooded, crazy, emotional Chicano" confusing because I had never heard the term before and thought it might have something to do with sex. Once Raoul turned on his criminal partners Paul and Mary, the latter of whom Raoul had been having an affair with, I knew something bad was going to happen. I did not anticipate, however, that they would kill and serve him up as a "Spanish" dish to a dinner guest as a way of disposing of the body. Impressed by the flavor of such "cheap meat," the guest advises the couple to make the dish a staple at their new restaurant. Mexicans on the menu did not seem funny; in fact, it scared me. Although I did not have the words for it at the time, I was watching Chicano bodies being remade into palatable cuisine for white consumption, literally.[3] At the same time, I was getting an education in how certain types of people—namely, those who looked like me—were treated in film. The cannibalization of Raoul was played for laughs. His killers were not sorry for what they had done, and keeping "cheap meat" on the menu meant more Chicanos would have to die. The experience taught me that there was a lot about movies and the world that I still did not understand, some of which was frightening. In retrospect, this fear seems odd given that in elementary school, we had regularly practiced "duck and cover drills" that involved huddling beneath our desks or against a brick wall, in preparation for a nuclear attack.

Though as a child I lived in palpable fear of global thermonuclear war, in no small part exacerbated by the nightmare-inducing television movie *The Day After* (1983) and the feature film *War Games* (1983), I never could have imagined a pandemic—a plague, really—where thousands of people die each day. While at first minimized, ignored, and at times denied, the novel coronavirus COVID-19 has killed hundreds of thousands of people in the United States alone. In the early days, starting in March 2020, those of us with certain privileges retreated into our residences, where books, movies, and Netflix, or rather any available streaming service, became a way to sustain us. I returned unironically to beloved films such as the original *Star Wars* trilogy (1977; 1980; 1983); the *Lord of the Rings* series (2001; 2002; 2003); John Hughes's catalogue, which has not held up well; and television shows about those places that fascinated me as a child, including Oak Island. *The Curse of Oak Island* (2014–present) focuses on current exploration efforts to solve the island's mystery. The central explorers, brothers Rick Lagina and Marty Lagina, are captivated by the same *Reader's Digest* story I read all those years ago about an elusive treasure buried on an island off the coast of Nova Scotia that has been sought after for more than two hundred years.[4] Beyond the treasure and the occasional artifacts, it is the narrative that captivates me, not about what is or is not buried on the island but about what people believe is there and the lengths they are willing to go to uncover it. These ideas about the power of stories, how and where we encounter them and fit them together, have tugged at me throughout the ongoing COVID-19 pandemic, especially as misinformation, "fake news," and lies became the lingua franca of the times.

For me, it has also been a return to my childhood and the skills I acquired during it: "[W]hen faced with the prospect of sheltering in place for an unspecified number of weeks, Generation X knows for sure that we got this. Heck, we've been training for a moment like this all our lives" (Dabney). Like sleeper agents, former latchkey kids across the country were activated into service. This time, we stayed indoors for our own safety and the safety of others as we waited for a vaccine and an outcome to the presidential election that many of us hoped would bring about an administration change, thereby signaling that the "grown-ups" were on their way to "fix" the pandemic problems. Whereas some people refused to stay put and others resisted or struggled with early-onset cabin fever, I settled in. Life around me began to slow down, and I began to think about the parallels between my childhood and the pandemic shelter-in-place orders. As I reflected on that earlier period in my life, I realized that books and movies had sustained me. More than this, they had also *made* me, not biologically (volume 1 of *The Life Cycle Library* made that very clear), but intellectually. Books and film, in large part, are the knowledge base for how I know what I know.

The culmination of time, age, experience, and enduring devotion has resulted in this deeply personal "slow" research project. From its application in food, arts, and exercise to parenting and educational practices, "slow," as a multivalent ideology, has taken shape over the last thirty years. In each instance, it encourages us to think about the generative possibility of cultural or structural transformation. Rather than a temporal designation or an assessment of the rate of output, specifically within the context of the neoliberal academy slow *research* emphasizes the interconnectedness of research and knowledge formation, particularly when derived from sources that are gendered, classed, and racialized. Stated another way, slow research strives to lay bare how research is "made." The approach furthers the ideas central to the global grassroots organization Slow Food, part of an Italian movement started in the mid-1980s. Slow Food works "to prevent the disappearance of local food cultures and traditions, counteract the rise of fast life and combat people's dwindling interest in the food they eat, *where it comes from* and how our food choices affect the world around us" ("Good"; emphasis added). In the performing arts, Lisa Schlesinger brings similar ideas to her concept "slow theatre," which is theatre that is "not necessarily slow but it does allow time to do its work" (70). "Slow," as a practice or approach, can take on any number of forms, though its transformative potential is rooted in the relationality of ideas, people, places, and environments.

Slow as an approach presents opportunities for innovation, but the concept is not a new one. Long before the theatre or Italian-based slow movements, Indigenous lifeways, for example, epitomized what we now understand as slow in the contemporary. As Rohina Katoch Sehra points out, "'Slow fashion' has been practiced by Indigenous communities for centuries. Painstaking beadwork, sewing and weaving, attention to material and detail, and small-batch production are consistent hallmarks." To this day, creative expressions and practices rooted in cultures and traditions are seen as legitimate objects of study but are not valued as historical or contemporary sources of knowledge. American Indian activist Zitkála-Šá/Gertrude Simmons Bonnin (Yankton Dakota) reflects on the generational and gendered knowledge of the textile arts she learned from her mother in "Impressions of an Indian Childhood" (1900). Zitkála-Šá recounts how her mother crafted beadwork designs on buckskin in the late 1800s: "On a lapboard she smoothed out a double sheet of soft white buckskin; and drawing from a beaded case that hung on the left of her wide belt a long, narrow blade, she trimmed the buckskin into shape" (40). Eventually Zitkála-Šá, as she spent "many a sunny hour" working on her own design, learned the value of intricate designs done slowly rather than simplistic ones completed quickly. Design is only one aspect of Zitkála-Šá's education among her people, which also included storytelling, legends, hospitality, caring for one's community, and the importance of play. At the age of eight, she attended White's Indian Manual Labor Institute, a Quaker Christian missionary school in Wabash, Indiana, where children were beaten, forced to pray, and also had their culture stripped by what Zitkála-Šá refers to as "the civilizing machine" ("School Days" 190). Her slow life on the reservation contrasts sharply with the regimented existence she experienced in boarding school, where the main objective was to teach Indian children how not to be Indians so that they might someday become Americans.

Various forms of slow living and culture have long been practiced by Black, Indigenous, and people of color (BIPOC) communities. Slow is how things were done, until they were not. The only difference now is the value placed on those traditions and ideals by the groups that once sought to eradicate slow lifeways through settler colonialism, enslavement, and other genocidal practices. This is a history that slow movements need to acknowledge, especially since most center on the experiences of white, middle- to upper-class individuals who neither recognize nor contend with their own privilege. In their efforts to "restore" or "reclaim" what has been lost or to "return" to an earlier time when slowness was valued, people participating in slow movements engage in a form of what cultural theorist Renato Rosaldo calls "imperialist nostalgia." As Rosaldo explains, "Imperialist nostalgia revolves around a paradox: . . . In a more attenuated form, someone deliberately alters a form of life, and then regrets that things have not remained as they were prior to the intervention. At one more remove, people destroy their environment, and then they worship nature" (69–70). The result is a continued erasure and at the same time a veneration of a culture or worldview that was intentionally destroyed and then remade anew in a more idealized way.

Historically, Black and Indigenous communities used temporal slowness as a disruptive action, dating as far back as the early colonial period in the US. Although colonizers and settler colonials saw these actions as inherent racial or cultural flaws, slowness was one method of resistance available to people with limited power. They used it to disrupt labor and/or work flow. Black, Indigenous, and later Mexican people were often derided as "lazy" for these actions. Slowness has long been antithetical to being American. Identifying a group of people as lazy was the equivalent of calling them un-American or anti-American.

In the mid-twentieth century, Mexican American and Chicanx youth began exercising a different kind of slowness, one that counters what Rosaldo identifies as the American ethic of "fast and efficient" (qtd. in Burciaga 68). Emerging as a post–World War II cultural form, "low riding originated as a conscious rebellion against the stereotypic hot-rodding middle-class Anglo American of the 1940s and 1950s" (Gradante 29). For lowriding communities, "low and slow" represents both an aesthetic and an ethos. With their signature dropped-down bodies, these classic cars, preferably of the Detroit steel variety, called lowriders often feature straight-lace chrome spoke wheels; velvet or crushed-velour top-to-bottom interiors; and candy, pearl, or metallic paint finishes sometimes adorned with elaborate images or scenes from Chicanx culture, such as *soldaderas*, Aztec royalty, women *ranchera* singers in traditional attire, or the Virgen de Guadalupe, but also of family members and loved ones. Lowriders represent years of (slow) dedication to rebuilding, refurbishing, and creative design. American-made automobiles are remade into Chicanx works of art. Participation in the cultural practice requires specific skills and various forms of technical, or in some cases generational, knowledge ranging from auto mechanics and design to hydraulics and engineering. These rolling masterpieces can best be appreciated when the vehicles are driven slowly, thereby allowing onlookers to see the skill and creative work of the artist, though they may not necessarily understand how the lowrider was made. Yet when these vehicles cruise at a leisurely pace down highways and main streets, they disrupt the hurrying principles of the mainstream and in the process center Chicanx culture as a site and source of knowledge production: low and slow.

Fatherhood in the Borderlands: A Daughter's Slow Approach is a product of slow research, a work that offers something familiar in a newly imagined way, one I did not know was possible for me. But a pandemic can change things and people. It touches every part of my life, from work and parenting to social interaction and well-being to procuring food. Even my understanding of temporalities has changed. Any day that is not today, however long in the past, is simply yesterday. There is "the before" the virus, and there is "the after" we were vaccinated. Time feels both fleeting and interminable. The slippage between the two has created a permeability of boundaries that has allowed me to see my childhood in a way I might not have otherwise. In so doing I arrived at a simple truth. My mother gave me books and unfettered access to them, though she did take away my copy of *Forever* . . . (1975), by Judy Blume. Books became a way for her to communicate what she wanted me to know, which was everything, except about teen sex. My mother wanted to give me the world. And my father helped to cultivate my nascent understanding of film. We learned side by side. Movie theatres became our holy place of communion. Looking back, one might say that I was nurtured under the twin cultural pillars of books and popular film.

Revisiting the primary early sites of my knowledge formation, I learned that they no longer exist, seem haunted, or have been remade. Our house in Cottage Grove, along with almost all the other modest homes, was razed to give way to "revitalization," which sounds nicer than tear-ing down memories or out-taxing longtime residents—frequently BIPOC or seniors on fixed incomes—in order to build three-story, quadra-plex, gated "community residences." My childhood home on Battlewood was flooded during Hurricane Harvey, the deadly category 4 storm that devastated much of Houston in 2017. Online photos show that the structure is intact though the insides, still recognizable to me, are gutted. The once scrappy trees, now impervious to lawnmower blades, provide a towering canopy over the front yard. And my beloved library? In 2011, after two years of renovation and construction, the Oak Forest Library, which added 4,500 square feet to its original 7,500, reopened with greater accessibility, new brick-and-glass wings, an outdoor reading area, and an added second entrance, all while preserving its iconic mid-century modern façade.[5] Regardless of the current conditions of these structures, their foundations remain solid within me. It was in and around them that I learned about culture, community, and the joys of intellectual inquiry, sources of knowledge that sustained me long before there was a viral pandemic and will continue to do so in the after.

INTRODUCTION

A SLOW APPROACH TO FATHERS AND OTHER FICTIONS

The bright pink pullover and sneakers belie the darkness of the image. Wisps of hair plastered against the tiny girl's brown cheek suggest that only moments earlier that same cheek had rested against the shoulder or neck of someone cradling her securely in their arms. But the child's expression remains unforgettable, mouth frozen open somewhere between opposition and abject terror, as she reacts to something we cannot see but can only imagine.[1] Less than a month later, on 2 July 2018, a cut-out photo of little Yanela Hernández appeared on the cover of *Time*. Rather than the little girl staring up at a scene visible only to her, in this instance a smirking Donald Trump looms over the tearful Yanela, along with the caption "Welcome to America" (Vick). The image became a powerful condemnation of the Trump administration's cruel, xenophobic zero-tolerance policy that separated, sometimes permanently, parents and children seeking asylum at the US-Mexico border.[2]

Against the backdrop of rolled razor wire atop a border fence, a mother, Maria Meza, is running with her twin daughters, their bodies twisted away from a smoking tear-gas canister.[3] The mother's expression conveys an unmistakable determination. In flight, the five-year-old girls' arms and legs cut sharp angles, in contrast to the curved lines of the mother's muscled body as she grips an arm of each daughter. Behind them, an American flag flies high. Individuals and families flee in all directions. Amidst the chaos, Elsa and Anna from Disney's *Frozen* (2013) form the scene's focal point. Featured on the mother's merry blue and pink graphic T-shirt, the Disney siblings appear to exchange knowing looks. The effect is twofold: as representatives of the US culture industry, the sisters stand indifferently in the middle of this turmoil; at the same time, when juxtaposed with the poor Brown sisters, the wealthy white Disney princesses highlight the disparity between the allure of US culture and the fact that some will forever be excluded, at times violently, from its promises.

Throughout the press conference in New York City, Javier Garrido Martínez continually hugs and kisses his little boy (Associated Press). Only after making the trek from Honduras and entering the US did Martínez learn that US policies had changed and he would be separated from his son. For fifty-five days, Martínez waited and worried. At one point, the father was told by an official that someone might have adopted his child. Martínez pauses and tearfully expresses his fears that he would never see his boy again. At a reunion at the Los Angeles International Airport of a few parents with the children from whom they had been separated, another father, David Xol, sobs as he holds fast to his son Byron. David and Byron had been apart for over eighteen months: "Xol was one of nine parents who won the exceedingly rare chance to return to the US after being deported under family separation" (Merchant and Spagat). Having been unable to prevent their separation, the father pleads for his son's forgiveness. In Puerto Cortes, Honduras, 2,776 miles away, Denis Javier Varela Hernández reacts to seeing his daughter Yanela in the image that was circulating widely on the internet and in news outlets: "You can imagine how I felt when I saw that photo of my daughter. It broke my heart. It's difficult as a father to see that . . ." (Bates and Ruiz). Varela Hernández reports that his wife had made the decision, one he did not support, to travel north with their daughter. The first time he saw anything of them after they departed was when he saw the published image of his daughter, three weeks later, crying by the roadside in the dark.

Snapshots of children, mothers, fathers become an authoritative means of capturing Brown families at the border.[4] Media stories that circulate about Latinx (primarily Brown and Indigenous) families emphasize division, lack of documentation, and negligence or irresponsibility on the part of the parents for knowingly putting their children at risk by making the perilous journey to the border. Photos and images offer up Brown affect, primarily tears and terror, to readers/viewers ambivalent about immigrants, regardless of whether they are asylum-seeking parents entering the US "the right way" and their children have been taken from them. In contrast to these emotional displays, benevolent white people (foster parents, social workers, and sometimes missionaries involved in reuniting families) hover stoically in the backgrounds of these images. Their presence reinforces a "white savior" narrative that underscores both their power and the powerlessness of Brown parents, who alone cannot save or reunite with their children.

These images, which demonstrate two powerful discourses about Brown families, are one beginning for this book, though no single beginning exists. There are, instead, multiple beginnings that have floated around me in various forms, waiting to be organized and put into words. The stories of families at the border, along with an Arizona gas station, aging X-Men, a California vineyard, mythic animals, a fireworks stand in Brownsville, Texas, and my own childhood are all connected, though not necessarily in any one particular order, in this slow-research assemblage, *Fatherhood in the Borderlands: A Daughter's Slow Approach*. Each location, character, novel, film, or artifact, significant on its own, accrues meaning in proximity to the entities around it. Until recently, how these ideas all fit together remained part of a larger, unseen whole.

Research does not materialize out of thin air.[5] Sometimes ideation starts with an observation or question that will not leave us alone, an itch at the back of the brain. Maybe critical inquiry is a response to events that have touched us personally. Perhaps we conduct studies because we are best equipped to do so based on who we are, where we come from, and what we know. Or maybe research is all or none of these, ideas constantly shifting back and forth in our minds until they find a way out or take root and grow. Regardless of how we arrive at the questions, the ways of presenting our findings in the academy, overdetermined historically by affluent white cisgender heterosexual men, have been prescribed in the forms of poster presentations, conference papers, journal articles, edited chapter collections, and scholarly monographs. By design, then, these forms ensure that the academy largely reproduces itself as white and male. The constant creep of neoliberalism compounds these issues.[6] As an organizational approach that emphasizes meritocracy, neoliberalism is indifferent to the racist or insular nature of the academy because those with the greatest advantages in a competitive market are already poised to succeed and often do. Neoliberalism has further codified these acceptable modes of research and demanded that academics increase our rate of output, resulting in what the Great Lakes Feminist Geography Collective (GLFGC), a group of US and Canadian feminists in geography interested in identifying the disparities in their field and addressing them through collective action, identifies as a "counting imperative" (1241). For these and other reasons, the GLFGC advocates for slow scholarship as a way to countermand the entrenchment of neoliberal priorities. Medievalist Catherine E. Karkov echoes these sentiments in her own slow research, stressing that "[t]hinking cannot be counted, nor depth of thought measured" (6). Whereas historically professors could ponder and ruminate, now as knowledge workers or laborers we must produce: it is publish or perish. As a result, quantity of research, along with a fungible definition of "quality," becomes the primary metric for measuring "success" or determining one's place in academe. Institutional refusal to make transparent the criteria for what constitutes quality research allows room for scholars to be punished professionally and financially for not meeting an invisible standard.

Neoliberalism exacerbates the structural inequities that undergird higher education, which affect how much and what kinds of research get produced, as well as the value placed on it. Although slow scholarship alone cannot disrupt or transform institutions that increasingly prioritize the monetizing of research or promote academic entrepreneurship, it can represent one site of important change. Accordingly, the GLFGC proposes ten strategies that can "facilitate slowness," including openly discussing and supporting slow strategies, organizing, caring for one's self and others, turning off or writing fewer emails, and making time to think and write, among others (1249–1253). In her reflections on slow theatre, written in a style that itself instantiates slow *criticism* (in this case, she begins and ends with the potentiality of bread), Lisa Schlesinger urges us to think: "How do we break through old structures, borders, territories? How do we go beyond what we imagined for ourselves and for each other?" (70). The questions she asks of theatre resonate with me. They pushed me to think more broadly about what "going beyond" might look like in my own scholarship. To make that determination, I would need to answer the query, as Schlesinger pointedly asks, "How do we give what we most need?" (70). For many of us, what we need does not exist, has yet to be imagined, or is unavailable for reasons ranging from the need to secure a job to career vulnerability. Innovation represents one way to "break through" and "go beyond" in our scholarship. Still, legibility in the academy remains paramount; only innovation that does not dislodge but reinforces the status quo of how things get done and by whom is allowed. Changing what kinds of scholarship we produce without altering how that work gets read in an institution deeply invested in reproducing itself represents a professional risk, especially for BIPOC scholars seeking employment, attempting to maintain it, or pursuing a promotion.

Not all research is treated equally or seen as having the same value, an assessment often complicated by the race, class, and/or gender (and politics) of the academic. A study rooted in slow research can easily be read as an alibi for limited professional output. Slow research is not strictly about temporality, but that can be a component of it. For example, the "slow" in slow writing means "collaps[ing] a product-process duality and offer[ing] a different pace than either fast and efficient or 'as long as it takes'" (Tremmel 114). Thus, time does become a consideration in slow writing. In lieu of a set of techniques or strategies, "slow writing shares with other 'slow' movements (like slow foods) a savoring of time and local context that allows students to practice as writers while they build proficiency" (115). The key is for students to find pleasure as they build proficiency. Slow research, therefore, can be thought about as a shifting of our priority from producing quantifiable output to creating meaningful connections to our work. It provides a means of "reclaiming time, time to think, read, talk, collaborate about and around what is of value to scholars and scholarly communities" (Karkov 6). In other words, slow research is about how we put things together in the ways we need; it also means taking ownership of manifested forms of—and pleasure in—research.

Critics and colleagues might say (and have said) that research, slow or otherwise, conducted by BIPOC and other underrepresented groups in the academy lacks rigor no matter how it is crafted or which academic journal or press publishes it. Across disciplines and fields, we do produce rigorous work, though we do so at great cost. Intellectual assembly takes time, and "good scholarship requires time to think, write, read, research, analyze, edit, organize, and resist the growing administrative and professional demands that disrupt these crucial processes of intellectual growth and personal freedom" (GLFGC 1236). For many of us, time is a luxury we do not have for any number of reasons: limited access to resources, eldercare, parenting, and personal health issues, to name but a few. We often produce research under duress or at the very least under tremendous stress; while these conditions may benefit some, they do harm to others.[7] To add, academia goes through the motions of contending with its own moral and ethical failures regarding its history of ongoing systemic racism and sexism, and shifts responsibility to individuals (e.g., diversity officers) as opposed to acknowledging its own political failings.

Slow research encourages us to account for both the factors and the conditions that go into academic research practices and presentation. Galina Kallio and Eeva Houtbeckers brought similar considerations to their work in food studies, advocating that "researchers [should] turn to examining their own research practice" for the ways that "it advances knowledge production" in their field and beyond (1). Knowledge production ("research publications, teaching and advising, practical engagement, popular publications, and engagement in societal and political discussions") at the individual level is not static (3). Expressions of knowledge production should not be either. In addition, the social, economic, and institutional conditions, for instance, in which research is conducted or made are not equitable. Whereas Schlesinger encourages us to think about the creative possibility of slow, the Slow Food movement encourages us to think about how something is made and where it comes from. As outlined in Slow Food's manifesto, the organization, along with its commitment to sustainability, focuses on three key ideas: good (quality), clean (method of production and level of harm), and fair (in terms of conditions for producers) ("Good"). These same concepts can shed light on how BIPOC scholars navigate extra sets of expectations and standards. For example, when BIPOC scholars in the academy produce work of good quality, rarely is such work clean, for it often comes at great personal and physical costs, "individual emotional and embodied effects of the neoliberal university that are often overlooked or deemed insignificant" (GLFGC 1239). Similarly, the conditions in which we produce research are hardly fair, overburdened as we are with committee work, often as the singular representatives of diversity on our campuses. There are ever-increasing service obligations and expectation from students, colleagues, and administrators that we be available 24/7, and "these often overwhelming demands exact an isolating psychic and physical toll that is neither reasonable nor sustainable" (GLFGC 1237). And if we are woman-identified BIPOC, we encounter misogyny or sexism from within and without our own communities.[8] As volumes such as *Presumed Incompetent: The Intersections of Race and Class for Women in Academia* (2012; Gutiérrez y Muhs et al.) and *Presumed Incompetent II: Race, Class, Power, and Resistance of Women in Academia* (2020; Flores Niemann et al.) demonstrate with firsthand accounts and empirical data, women faculty from diverse intersectional identities at all levels of the academy face systemic biases, ranging from overt racism, including the questioning of intellectual competency, to the sabotaging of tenure, promotion, or reappointment. Too often, BIPOC scholars are held to completely different standards than their white colleagues or are denied tenure after doing exactly what was expected of them, though in some cases double or triple the amount of their white fellows in terms of research and service.

If we are continually held to a different standard, as we try to make ourselves and our work legible in the academy, then slow research represents an opportunity to strengthen our commitment to pushing against that difference by "break[ing] through old structures, borders, territories" (Schlesinger 70). The creation of new expressions of knowledge that do not fit antiquated paradigms (ones predicated on the absence or exclusion of people of color) can promote previously undervalued or ignored ways of knowing. In addition to the fact that slow research practices breach existing institutional borders, they also highlight epistemic disregard for racialized or other intersectional knowledge formulations. Most importantly, slow research encourages us to think, write, and present our work in a way that not only gives us what we most need professionally and creatively but also plots for future scholars a sustainable and ethical pathway for how research is made and the generative possibilities of raced, classed, and gendered epistemologies.

Slow approaches or methodologies, however, do present certain problems. Slow movements rarely acknowledge or contend with the privilege at their core. As political sociologist Luke Martell asks, who can go slow? Martell surmises, for instance, that "slow food may be as much an issue of displaying a liberal middle class identity as about food itself" (par. 36). A scholarly approach emerging from a bourgeois sensibility seems incredibly limited and limiting for analyzing Mexican American fathers in borderlands narratives, especially given the connotation of "slow" in relation to Latinx populations. "Slow" is interchangeable with "lazy." "Slow" is also used as an insult to speak about perceived mental capacity. The perpetually lethargic, sometimes confused, often Tequila-drunk, and pistol-packing Slowpoke Rodriguez, the counterpart and "cousin" to Speedy Gonzales, represents an example of both of these negative traits, and more, in one Latinx character.[9] And then there is "Despacito," the ear worm of 2019 by Luis Fonsi and Daddy Yankee, which offers a Latinx man's slow approach to sex. All reinforce well-worn tropes about Latinx men entangled with ideas of slowness: they are unintelligent, lazy, and oversexualized. However, that does not mean that slow in relation to Mexican American populations always has a negative value. For example, lowriders use slow as a means of interruption to call attention to, and thereby center, Chicanx cultural productions and practices—and the people themselves. Slow, for lowriders, as highlighted in the preface, represents both an aesthetic and a practice that disrupts hurried mainstream life. To add, lowriders' low and slow cultural practices predate contemporary slow movements by approximately forty years. Slow, therefore, provides a distinct avenue for analyzing power relations among and between groups.

Fatherhood in the Borderlands: A Daughter's Slow Approach takes inspiration from such diverse genre-bending creative/scholarly works as *The Borderlands/La Frontera: The New Mestiza* (1987), by Gloria Anzaldúa; *The Phantom Empire: Movies in the Mind of the Twentieth Century* (1993), by Geoffrey O'Brien; *Gaga Feminism: Sex, Gender, and the End of Normal* (2012), by J. Jack Halberstam; and *Decolonizing Academia: Poverty, Oppression, and Pain* (2018), by Clelia O. Rodríguez. Anzaldúa's exegesis of life in the borderlands manifests as prose, poetry, dichos, semiautobiography, history, and memoir—all while code switching along a continuum between English and Spanish, sometimes blending the two. The book is divided into two sections, prose and poetry; the division between them is both artificial and intentional, underscoring Anzaldúa's idea of the border as an "unnatural boundary" (3). *The Phantom Empire*, on the other hand, invites readers on O'Brien's personal journey through film by "[w]eaving observations on more than 600 mostly pre-1980 films into . . . [a] second-person narrative" (Review of *The Phantom Empire*, *Publishers Weekly*). His highly stylized narration of film genre and history "presents cinema as contemporary religion, history, and epistemology rolled into one" (Review of *The Phantom Empire*, *Kirkus*). The book was on the reading list for my comprehensive exam in film, and I found it insufferable. I wanted O'Brien to tell me, through conventional academic signposting, why his work matters. Looking back, I can see that I did not know how to read his work. Despite that fact, it has stayed with me for more than twenty-five years.[10] Whereas O'Brien's work does present certain frustrations, reviewer Ariel Levy, in a blurb that appears on the cover, calls Halberstam's book "fun," a word not often used in regard to academic writing in any genre. Described on the inside book jacket flap as "a provocative manifesto," "part handbook, part guidebook, and part sex manual," and "creative mayhem," *Gaga Feminism* analyzes the downfall of heterosexuality and the role pop superstar Lady Gaga, feminist icon, plays in the shifting gender and cultural politics. And finally, through prose, poetry, epistles, footnotes, and stories of personal experience, alongside a "research and education" contract, Rodríguez mobilizes these different forms to critique systemic racism in the academy, at all levels.

These books are not necessarily my favorites, nor are they the only mixed-genre or genre-bending works that have made their way into the academy. Still, in the dynamic process of my knowledge formation, they do represent touchstones for thinking about an array of creative possibilities for presenting academic research, whether through order, arrangement, form, style, genre, documents, or documentation. Chicanx writers, from Norma E. Cantú to Nina Marie Martínez, and Latinx authors, more broadly, have made structural use of mixed-genre writing, primarily in fiction and memoir, to tell multilayered, multifaceted, and at times polyvocal narratives.[11] As critics, Anzaldúa, O'Brien, Halberstam, and Rodríguez, in their own work, go beyond what we expect of or imagine for academic publications in terms of form and dispel the idea that, as Kallio and Houtbeckers state in a different context, "[a]cademic research practice ... carries the expectation of objectivity" (8). By drawing upon their personal connections to borders, film, popular culture, literature, and the academy, these authors, who have influenced my book, reject the idea that the subjective or personal cannot be critical. Each of these authors and their works dislodge ideas about academic conventions and critique, though it is noteworthy that the ones who take the greatest risks are the BIPOC authors. In doing so, they call attention to disruptive practices, not as a novelty but as an imbrication of theory *and* practice.

Fatherhood in the Borderlands: A Daughter's Slow Approach extends the work of the aforementioned genre-bending authors, and others, by laying bare both how and why this research production was made. Epistemically rooted and inquiry driven, my book, which includes ephemera, lists, and narrative interruptions, sits at the intersection of slow research, personal narrative, and literature, and of film, cultural, ethnic, and gender studies. My book emphasizes not only the epistemic value of creative inquiry but also the role such an approach can play in academic research practices. In an effort to break through "old structures," as Schlesinger calls them, namely, how we think about "serious academic inquiry," the book is organized as a series of dialogues, featuring personal narrative, literary, and film components. These sites of inquiry grate against each other, revealing the shifting tension in the literal and figurative borderlands of popular narratives, nuanced reflection, and cultural critique. Anzaldúa in *The Borderlands/La Frontera* avers, "The U.S-Mexican border *es una herida abierta* where the Third World grates against the first and bleeds" (3). The idea is useful for thinking about how particular forms of knowledge production and presentation can become sites of wounding in the academy. In some cases, though certainly not all, wounding can also be generative. But scholars of color should not have to bleed to belong.

This study focuses on Mexican American and/or Chicanx fathers, an understudied group largely perceived as static in the US cultural imaginary. In both literature and film, Mexican American fathers, when represented at all, exist under a type of cultural patrimony, one foisted upon them, that positions these men as either absent or overbearing and frequently with an undercurrent of anger or frustration. Mexican American fathers, often lacking any nuance, alternate between oppressed and oppressive, the latter usually a response to the former. As a result, the family emerges as one of the few sites where these fathers can and do exert authority, but as this book demonstrates, Mexican American patriarchs in borderlands narratives must actively work to maintain, reinforce, or in some cases substantiate their power, which is constantly in peril because of the changing historical, cultural, social, or political landscape.

PRESIDENTS, PANDEMICS, AND THE INCANTATORY POWER OF NAMING

> Thought woman, the spider,
> named things and
> as she named them
> they appeared.
> Leslie Marmon Silko, *Ceremony*

~~The Papi Problem: Shifting Mexican American Masculinities~~
~~Machos, Myths, and Men: Mexican American Masculinities~~
~~Brown In, Brown Out: Screening Mexican American Fatherhood~~
~~Family Comes First: Screening Mexican American Father~~
~~Fatherhood in the Cinematic Borderlands~~
~~Genre and Gender: Fatherhood in the Borderlands~~
~~Patrimonial Papás in Literature and Film~~
~~Fatherhood in the Borderlands of Literature and Film~~
~~Slow Approaches to Fatherhood in the Borderlands of Literature and Film~~
~~Fatherhood in the Borderlands: A Slow Approach~~
~~Fatherhood in the Borderlands and the Slow Making of a Brown Academic~~
Fatherhood in the Borderlands: A Daughter's Slow Approach

Names have power. For thirteen years I have tried to call versions of this project into existence, but it has resisted my attempts, refusing both shape and substance. Concomitantly, none of the names I gave my nebulous ideas inspired any sustained interest on my part. Gaining momentum or making progress on the project was elusive, so I turned my attention elsewhere, always with the promise (lie?) that I would return. After all, I had signed an advance contract with the press in 2008 and pledged to deliver the work within a year. Thirteen years went by. Although I now hold the dubious honor of authoring the second-longest overdue book at the press, I long feared that I would never fulfill my contract because life (and death) kept getting in the way. But Donald Trump and the pandemic shifted something in me.

Long before his administration's abhorrent zero-tolerance policies sought to criminally prosecute anyone who crossed into the US without proper documentation, Trump had set his sights on villainizing Mexicans. On 16 June 2015, when he announced he was running for president, he characterized Mexicans as drug dealers, criminals, and rapists—"people that have lots of problems" (Reilly). Trump raised the specter of bandidos stealing across the border, thereby increasing the necessity, by his narrative fallacy, of building a border wall. Such a barrier would keep out, as he stated on 19 October 2016, during the third presidential debate, the "bad hombres," meaning drug lords and criminals. The wall became the cornerstone of Trump's campaign and a focal point for his administration.

After winning the presidential election, Trump targeted Mexicans and Mexican Americans, along with Latinxs more generally, for attacks. Not since George H. W. Bush, as the Republican nominee in 1988, stoked racial fears through his infamous Willie Horton campaign has a racial or ethnic group been attacked so explicitly by a presidential candidate.[12] Approximately four months into his term, Trump accused federal judge Gonzalo Curiel of being a "hater" and biased because he was "Mexican." Born in Indiana, where he also attended law school, the judge, who is of Mexican descent, oversaw the fraud case against Trump University in San Diego, California.[13] Trump asserted that Curiel harbored animus related to the border wall and publicly attacked the judge for being partial. From 2015 to 2020, racist narratives about the border and the moral character of the Latinx and Indigenous people trying to cross it or being detained there circulated widely. They were not mothers, fathers, children, grandparents, sisters, brothers, or, at times, people, who were risking everything to seek out a different life. In Trump's view, they were rapists, liars, haters, and murderers. Not thinking about the people and their stories, for me, seemed impossible if not immoral. The situation felt related to my own work, though I struggled to make an explicit connection.

Then COVID-19 happened. With barely a moment to adjust, everything shifted to online: teaching, mentoring, committee work, research, and social interactions, which then often resembled the opening sequence from the television show *The Brady Bunch* (1969–1974), with each person, inevitably looking off in different directions, confined to his/her/their own square. Suddenly we were all waving goodbye into a camera to signal the end of a class or meeting. As dystopian scenarios unspooled around us (wildfires, droughts, the virus, death, Snovid-21, near economic collapse . . .), some of us tried to order the chaos in whatever ways possible.[14] At first, I tried puzzling, putting together thousand-piece challenges that called out to be assembled and ordered to reveal an image of a famous painting, a scenic locale, a movie poster, a book cover, some bit of nostalgia, or various sundries arranged in piles or glass jars. I soon began to experience an undeniable satisfaction as pieces fit together, and even more upon a puzzle's completion.

During this same time, I also revisited familiar books and films, including *Star Wars: Episode V—The Empire Strikes Back* (1980), one of the greatest sequels of all time. As Luke Skywalker was struggling with revelations about his father, I reflected on my own—the good and the bad. My father was complex, though I have no idea whether this quality endures because I have not spoken to or seen him in over twenty-five years. He was loving and present but also never satisfied. There was always something only he could see, just beyond his grasp, something my mother, my brother, and I—and our middle-class life—could not provide, so he left, remarried, and started a new family as his father had before him, fulfilling his own kind of familial patrimony. What I had never realized was that these facts and feelings overshadowed an important truth: *The Empire Strikes Back* meant something to me *because* of my father. The impact of seeing that film, in the way he and I saw it, and what the film inspired in me remain a significant part of who I am as a person and a scholar. So I sat with that knowledge, and then I decided to write through it to see where it would lead. I had discovered a piece of what I wanted to say about Mexican American fathers. The finished version appears in part 1.

Soon, I began puzzling in my professional life, though in a different form. I was moving a few pieces around, the same ones each time, trying to make connections among and between ideas in my work, but I was not motivated to write. Never mind that picking up a large writing project during a pandemic felt impossible and certainly not like a priority until two things changed: (1) I found a writing buddy; and (2) I updated my curriculum vitae (CV).

Writing is a solitary act. Or is it? We tell our graduate students to join or start a writing group, one that can provide accountability and support as they tackle a thesis, dissertation, article, or any other major writing project. And then we ignore our own advice, telling ourselves we have neither the time to meet about our work nor the time to write, despite the latter's centrality to who we are as thinkers: "Writing is a fundamental mark we make in the world as academics and should reflect values inherent in the life of the mind: rigor, engagement, nuance, critique, making a difference" (GLFGC 1252). For me, writing had come to mean repeating a familiar pattern of composing articles or book chapters in a series of midnight marathons, a method that served me effectively but exacted a noticeable toll on my health. A few years ago, I had an extraordinary writing collaborator with whom I coedited a book. We finished each other's thoughts and sentences. We were so in tune that I found it difficult to write without her once the project was completed. Finding the right writing partner is like finding the right therapist: she must be someone who understands where the patient is at that moment, meets her where she is, and plots a course forward.

Three months into the pandemic, I had little energy to think about my overdue book project. Although we were still very much in the early stages of a virus that has since gone on to kill more than five million people worldwide, I was already exhausted and could not have identified any particular help I might have needed at the time. Then again, no one had asked, that is, until a friend and senior colleague in another college on campus reached out. Over the course of 2014–2015, we both had participated in the OpEd Project, a program aimed at amplifying the voices of underrepresented groups in the media and creating thought leaders on campus and in the public at large. Whenever she and I worked together in peer-review groups, I always admired how she could pack a textbook's worth of knowledge into a few paragraphs. Although we occasionally crossed paths, we came into contact with greater frequency after I was elected the incoming chair of the Faculty Council, a democratic, university-wide shared-governance body. Having previously held the leadership role that I was soon to occupy, my colleague offered to help and share advice about the position should I need it. We made plans and met over Zoom. We talked about pandemic-induced anxieties, our children, and inevitably work. She had two books that needed completing, and I had an overdue, uncooked project that was going nowhere.

Given our outstanding obligations, she offered collaboration of a different sort, describing how we could work alongside each other on our projects with weekly sessions to discuss our work or whatever else we needed to lay down to lighten our loads. She proposed a loose set of guidelines: "Whether it's an outline, five pages, a paragraph, one sentence, or nothing, we meet. No guilt, no apologies. And then we do it again the next week." I agreed to the terms and we became writing buddies. That a feminist-informed, slow-scholarship practice revolving around the idea of "care" would jump-start my work seems fitting. As one of ten strategies to create meaningful and substantive scholarship, the Great Lakes Feminist Geography Collective recommends that we "[f]ind concrete ways to support and find support in someone else who might be struggling to move a project forward or just wants to talk through ideas. Take time to meet with a colleague to discuss ideas, slow work, projects that have been relegated to the back burner but are burning to come to the fore" (1251). My writing buddy and I began meeting virtually every week, with few exceptions.

At first, I tried to pick up my project where I had left off. Too soon, I encountered the familiar feeling best described as trying to run while waist deep in wet cement. Writing was a trudge. Still, I wrote and showed up to our meetings. Writing the piece about my father was a turning point. One week, when I produced nothing for our session, my writing buddy read aloud portions of *There Was a Woman: La Llorona from Folklore to Popular Culture* (2008), my first monograph, as a way to talk about my work. She observed, "I can see that this book is very much influenced by your mother. It's interesting, then, that your current project seems to have a strong connection to your father." What seemed obvious after she said this had never occurred to me. I began to think about why that was the case and what it meant (figure 1).

In *Harry Potter and the Deathly Hallows: Part 2* (2011), the final film in the series, when the goblin Griphook asks the titular hero how he came into possession of the jeweled Sword of Gryffindor, the boy wizard replies, "It's complicated." The *Harry Potter* films played a substantial role in my son's early film literacy. Long ago we reached a point where we could discuss the many problems the films (and later the author's own views) posed concerning the racialization of certain characters/creatures. Even so, some things in those films stick with us, so when either my son or I do not wish to answer a question, we reply, "It's complicated." Such would be my initial retort about the suggested connection this project has to my father. The truth is as knotty as it is simple. I dearly loved my father. My love did not change the fact that I found it difficult to forgive him for what he took from me—our unified family. Given the rage I felt at the time, I needed to find a way forward past my anger and grief. As I often did, I connected my life to movies, and in this case I took inspiration from Diane Court (Ione Skye) in *Say Anything* (1989). Before flying off to England with her aspiring kickboxer boyfriend, the lovable Lloyd Dobler (John Cusack), Diane writes to her incarcerated father that she cannot forgive him for what he has done (embezzling money from seniors under

FIGURE 1. *My father and me in the living room of our house in Cottage Grove, Texas. This picture has always been one of my favorites. According to the date on the border (February 1969), I am twenty months old.*

his direct care), though she eventually confesses that she does love him. I wrote a similar letter and sent it to my father, though I did not feel any better. I cannot remember what I said exactly or whether he replied. I do know that the betrayal and anger I felt had everything to do with the connection we had forged over the years. My father was my home, and then he was gone. He made a new home with a new wife and child, and I had no idea where I fit into any of it or whether I wanted to at all. From a distance, I can see the messiness of our relationship, tinged as it was by race, class, ethnicity, and my father's deep sense of dissatisfaction with everything. No movie, book, or piece of writing will ever fix what is broken between us.

The second significant event in the development of my project occurred when I updated my CV in anticipation of my annual review. The CV is not a readily apparent source of knowledge production. Rarely do I take the time to reflect on all I have done in my career. How many of us do? Usually, I simply drag and drop: throughout the year I keep a running list of my professional activities and then transfer them to my CV when departmental annual reports are due. In the summer of 2020, when I received a new computer while campus was almost completely shut down, I was left to my own devices for the data transfer from one machine to the other. Things did not go smoothly: files were duplicated, sometimes quadrupled, or transferred without names. So when it came time to update my CV, I could not find the most current version of it. (This was the actual name I had given the file: "Current CV." I have since amended this egregious practice to include a file name and month or year.) As I tried to update the document from a number of sources, I had to *read* it, all twenty pages, carefully. At first, I was merely annoyed. Then I was struck by and more than a little proud of the amount of work I had done across the areas of publication, teaching, and especially service. As I moved between documents and subheaded sections, an infinitesimal shot of adrenaline made my fingers and the top of my head tingle, an intuition perhaps. Words and phrases caught my attention: *Myth and Men Racialized Masculinities Mexican Masculinity Fatherhood Gender, Class, and Ethnicity in Literature and Film Transnational Masculinities in Mexican American Literature Popular Culture Mexican American Family Fathers, Sons, and Fictions "Bless Me, Papi."* The failed attempts to kick-start my project were all there, yet something else was there too—an idea that carried across syllabi, topics courses, presentations, a book chapter, and an article. I learned that I had been substantively working through the central questions of *Fatherhood in the Borderlands: A Daughter's Slow Approach* in a number of locales (classrooms, conferences, journals, and edited collections) and from different vantage points (as a teacher and as a literature, film, and ethnic studies scholar) for almost twenty years.

Through re-creating and updating my CV, I was confronted with a puzzle of a different sort, one in which I had in my possession the individual pieces but no image of the whole from which to work. So I asked for help. Again, a little louder for the folx in the back of the room: I ASKED FOR HELP. Doing so was an important step in breaking down old structures and boundaries, particularly the belief that ideation and knowledge production are solitary acts. Care (for ourselves and each other) and collaboration, as proposed by the GLFGC, are key strategies associated with facilitating slow research. As scholars, we do not ask for help enough. In fact, we should ask for it more, but bootstrapping is an enduring myth in the academy, one that regularly prioritizes individual achievement over collaboration.

A most trusted colleague (my partner) and I sifted through my CV and computer files. In an effort to track down conference papers in document files, I came across completed drafts of essays that, for whatever

FIGURE 2. *My father dressed for work. 1971.*

reason, had been abandoned. As we grouped and regrouped related ideas and themes, they fell into three distinct categories: Mexican American fathers, literature, and film. Knowing that I am a tactile, visually inclined thinker, my partner suggested that printing out everything—all the related materials—might be useful. Indeed it was, for through the process of physically spreading out and moving around drafts and other materials on the floor, I began to imagine a way to organize these pieces. I also learned, in the final tally, that I had a book sitting on my computer.

Still, I had yet to determine the "why" of a book-length work on Mexican American fatherhood in the borderlands. To be sure, I am the daughter of a Mexican American father in the borderlands. But this book is not about that. I am not interested in pathologizing my relationship with my own Mexican American father. The simple truth is that families—Black, Indigenous, white, straight, queer, or mixed race—fall apart or disintegrate for any number of reasons. My relationship with my father helped me to identify the stakes of this argument (figure 2). As previously stated, he was a complicated individual; most people are in some way or another. My subjective understanding of this fact and how it impacted our relationship helped me to see what was not present elsewhere, explicitly that Mexican American fathers (and families) in literature and film bore little resemblance to my own experiences, though some cultural aspects did resonate. This is as true now as it was in the 1970s and 1980s. My father was a former sergeant in the Marine Corps who became an electrical engineer, through apprenticeships, years of on-the-job training, and a few junior college classes. In literature, film, journalism, and other popular media, the stories being told about Mexican, Mexican American, Chicanx, and Latinx fathers in the borderlands were not about men like my father or the others I grew up knowing. Instead, the men were repeatedly raced, classed, and gendered in ways that solidified a singular way of being a Mexican American father in the borderlands (read: mestizo, manual laborer, and hypermasculine) at the expense of more nuanced or complicated depictions. Within the spaces that Mexican American fathers occupied, I was interested in what they were allowed to do and could do in these environments.

PRACTICES AND EXPECTATIONS

> I keep waiting for the lit review to appear, but now I kind of don't want it.
> Writing Buddy, "Feedback"

An anecdote, a historical contextualization, or a quotation from a relevant work: these features often launch, depending on the proclivity of an author, the results of scholarly research (books, conference presentations, articles, or chapters). These are followed, preferably somewhere in the initial three pages, by a statement of the problem or argument. In the introduction to a scholarly book, readers are most certain to also encounter a literature review, where authors dutifully demonstrate that they have read widely and responsibly enough to join or intervene in a particular conversation. Liana Darren, on the popular writing website *Grammarly*, describes the literature review as

> essentially a survey of scholarly articles, books, dissertations, conference proceedings, and/or other published material. The review provides a summary, description, and critical evaluation of a topic, issue, or area of research. . . . The author of a literature review is usually giving feedback on published works.

Convention in scholarly writing dictates that such a review be done. Even if done thoroughly and thoughtfully, inevitably a critic or Anonymous Reader #2 will, nevertheless, note that the author, in an egregious oversight, has not cited the work of scholars X, Y, Z and that this omission represents a serious problem. This sort of name checking or roll call of relevant or preferred scholars gets replicated across disciplines and fields, rarely being questioned. But why? *Because that's the way things are done.* I was taught the importance of literature reviews by my professors, have included them in my work, and have taught my own students how to do them. *And literature reviews are necessary for evaluating research quality.* The form is akin to building an entrance in a wall, the archway of which must be assembled stone by stone, in the right way, and in the correct order before the author is allowed to pass through and present her views on a given subject or topic. *This is the correct way to structure research.* As such, literature reviews represent yet another border, another old structure meant to maintain the status quo in the academy. *They're also necessary for citation indexing.* Flash the right credentials, say the right names, and one may proceed. Instead, we should "seek out unfamiliar names that may be attached to high quality, original work, names we do not recognize because they have been mapped as marginal to the field by gendered, racialized, classed, heteronormative, and ableist power relations" (GLFGC 1250). Reproducing without reflecting on the purposes and origins of certain writing practices can further entrench systemic disparities in the academy.

In large part, literature reviews are done to uphold the idea that knowledge formation and presentation are objective, and most of all that they are replicable. In other words, that when presented with the same evidence, any reasonably intelligent person might reach a similar conclusion. Literature reviews serve to mark the work and the author as being objective: "The objective point of view held by the expert has to be (and often it is enough that it is) in stark contrast with the subjectivity of questions that are important for 'opinion'" (Stengers, *Another Science* 31). The subjective, on the other hand, in its specific contours or conditions, is not always knowable or replicable. In its capacity to convey emotions, thoughts, and beliefs embodied by an individual, the subjective is often viewed as uncritical or biased. However, the subjective can be used as a means for disrupting academic conventions and expectations to produce nuanced and community-based scholarship rooted in the real world. I am not advocating for abandoning critical knowledge of disciplinary research relevant to new analyses or arguments. *It sure sounds like it.* Through these methods, we "extend," "engage," or "refute" analyses and theories to move them in new directions. As scholars, we need to rethink and reimagine how this knowledge can be used to invite people in rather than keep people out. Doing so involves a risk, one I am prepared to take in this long-form study because this is my book, though the press might have other ideas. I am not sure it would pass muster in a peer-review journal article, yet meaningful ways do exist for engaging with scholarly work in similar areas beyond formulating walls of knowledge as an intellectual rite and requirement.

One such way of engaging with scholars and scholarship is to recognize those intellectual antagonists and kin, though some have already been identified, who have contributed to my knowledge creation with this book. Such a recognition is not some circumscribed attempt to re-create the literature review under another name. These scholars and their work accompanied me, most unknowingly, through the various iterations of my project. Sonia Saldívar-Hull provided a frame for thinking about gender and the border in literature; her effective use of personal narrative in her chapter section "Transfrontera Memorias," as a place from which to theorize, continues to inspire (ch. 1). I find something new each time I read *Latino Images in Film: Stereotypes, Subversion, and Resistance* (2002), by Charles Ramírez Berg. His analysis of the six Latinx stereotypes in film and his insights, in another work, on Mexican family integrity in social-problem films served as my foundation for determining what Brown men can do and why.[15] Rosa Linda Fregoso offers a crucial avenue for scrutinizing Mexican American fatherhood through her work on "*familia* romances."[16] Her ideas, more than any other, framed my initial path of critical inquiry about Mexican American fathers. And finally, Stella Bruzzi, author of *Bringing Up Daddy: Fatherhood and Masculinity in Post-War Hollywood* (2005), the first book focusing exclusively on cinematic depictions of fathers in film, showed me the work that needed to be done in this area as not one single Latinx father appears in her study. These scholars laid the groundwork for building the interdisciplinary architecture necessary for my thinking critically about fathers in the borderlands of literature and film.

More recently, however, Arturo J. Aldama and Frederick Luis Aldama, in the introduction to their edited collection *Decolonizing Latinx Masculinities* (2020), offer a historiography of the multivalent conversations around gender and masculinities that have been made more complex by the work done on numerous scholarly, intellectual, and personal fronts. The Aldamas provide a strikingly comprehensive catalogue of knowledge production by feminist and queer Latinx scholars and activists. Not only does their research highlight the deep-seated sexism and homophobia in the political activism of the 1960s and 1970s but also it demonstrates how scholars and activists have moved conversations about masculinities in vital new directions. The first section of their collection also includes hybrid forms of scholarship that feature personal narrative, autoethnography, and a "multigenre, autoethnographic semio-text" (10). The edited collection realizes two of my central aims with this book: to support and make a space for alternate expressions of knowledge production and to analyze systems and structures of male power.[17]

Old habits die hard. Along with a literature review, readers have an expectation of finding, in an introduction, detailed outlines for the organizational structure of a book. I have decided not to include such a map, except to say that I convey the main ideas of the book in a series of interrelated conversations about sourcing authority, instrumentalizing Indigeneity, and *fantasmas* and *fronteras*, as related to Mexican American fathers. So leaf through the book. Pick a spot or an image and start there. Read the "Parting Shot" first. Comb through the index or table of contents. Pay attention only to the personal narratives in each section or to none of those. Ways of engaging with written works as part of the process of individual knowledge formation is as varied as the people who read them. I remember in graduate school trying to understand a theoretically dense book that frustrated me at every turn until I flipped to the end and read the final chapter. Then I read the penultimate chapter, and then the one before that, and so on. In a reverse engineering of thought, I needed to see the end result to make sense of the individual parts (how it was made). During class discussion, I proudly shared how this strategy opened a productive avenue into the work for me. To this day, I can hear the professor's disapproval of such a strategy being necessary for a student doing *graduate*-level work. The incident taught me two things to advise others to do in their knowledge production: learn strategies that work on an individual level and then keep quiet about them.

"THIS IS THE WAY"

Sometimes we search and struggle to find answers. And sometimes, the answers are sent to us directly via a newsfeed link on our smartphones. Before getting out of bed one morning, I watched a story that appeared in my news alert feed with the headline "Father Shares Family Reunification Story as Lawyers Search for Parents of More than Five Hundred Children" (G. King). The video featured Daniel Paz, who had been detained and separated from his daughter Angie for two months after reaching the Texas border in 2018. When faced with the reality of separation, Paz recounts, he found a pen and desperately began writing the telephone numbers of family members and relatives back in Honduras all over his daughter's body, telling her, "I'm gonna look for you. I'm gonna find you. It's gonna be OK." Paz says in the video that he considers himself fortunate, especially given the number of children whose parents' whereabouts remain unknown. Through tears he explains that the fear of being disappeared in Honduras motivated him to make the trek north with Angie. In the moment, he switches from English to Spanish: "Por eso yo luché para llegar aquí."[18] After viewing this story, I felt the last pieces of the puzzle fall into place.

Yanela and her mother, Sandra; Maria and her twin daughters; Javier and his son; David and Byron; Daniel and Angie. Based on the small sample with which I was working, the stories about the families and the border fell into two groups: women who did not make it across the border and men who made it across the border but had their children taken away. None included both parents either being separated from or reunited with their children; all the families were broken, which carried an implicit value judgment. Not a single news story addressed how for two hundred years the US has actively worked to destabilize Central America, from the Monroe Doctrine (1823), which imagined the US as the guardian of the Western Hemisphere, to the deportation in the early 1990s of MS-13 gang members, who are now largely responsible for the violence in El Salvador, Guatemala, and Honduras from which people are fleeing to the US.[19] Instead, these stories featured details about the lives of the women, including that Sandra left behind her husband and other children, choosing to bring along only Yanela, and that Maria was mother to twelve children. As someone who has written about La Llorona, a folkloric figure perceived as the ultimate bad mother, I recognized how these women's stories were being told. The subtext was that these were bad mothers who had abandoned husbands and children or knowingly placed their large broods in peril.

For the men, a different narrative emerged, one made clear by the reporter's steely resolve juxtaposed with Daniel Paz's unguarded affective display. The stories featuring weeping fathers were as much about them being reunited with their children as they were about the spectacle of Latinx male vulnerability. While such positioning seemingly contradicts the tough Latinx masculine type, it nevertheless remains rooted in the politics of affective Latinx excess. This emotionality marks them as other, especially in comparison to the flat affect of the white observers in attendance at reunion events between fathers and children. According to José Esteban Muñoz, "Whiteness claims affective normativity and neutrality, but for that fantasy to remain in place one must only view it from the vantage point of US cultural and political hegemony" ("Feeling Brown" 70). Through their affective displays and tears, these Latinx fathers are marked as outside of US cultural and political hegemony even as they take up residence inside those same borders, serving as a reminder that "mainstream depictions of Latino affect serve to reduce, simplify, and *contain* ethnic difference" (69; emphasis added). Moreover, they serve to characterize these men as incapable of protecting their own children. Their affective distress is simultaneously on display and contained, a practice that consistently limits the characterizations of Latinx men.

Recognizing the parameters within which depictions of Latinx men are so often confined, I extrapolated out toward popular culture, specifically the relationship between Mando (Pedro Pascal) and Grogu from the Disney+ series *The Mandalorian* (2019–present). In this stylized space western, bounty hunter Mando is hired to retrieve the child Grogu (referred to by fans as "Baby Yoda") and turn him over to Imperial forces for nefarious purposes. When Mando chooses to go on the run with Grogu, the duo form an attachment, "a clan of two," and eventually a father-son bond.[20] The laconic bounty hunter lives by a strict moral code expressed in the much-memed saying "This is the way." With his people scattered or in exile after being the targets of genocide, cultural practices are some of the few things that Mando has left that tie him to a larger community. Part of this code involves the cultural practice of never removing one's helmet in front of others, especially enemies. Viewers see Mando's face only twice in two seasons, once when he is on the verge of death and again when he relinquishes Grogu to the Jedi Luke Skywalker. For most of the series, Mando's helmet shields his expressions and reactions from the audience.

The shield also acts as a form of restraint that contains Mando's emotions. His affect, therefore, is expressed through other means—body posture, vocal intonation, and other physical actions. In a true testament to Pascal's ability as an actor, audiences know Mando to be rigid, selfish, and a loner who does not form attachments. He is also quick tempered. This latter quality alone is not uncharacteristic of a gunslinger or bounty hunter, but it takes on additional significance when factoring in Pascal's Chilean ancestry. No Latinx designation exists in the *Star Wars* storyverse, nor does any other racial or ethnic group, for that matter (difference appearing to be based in species and culture).[21] Given Pascal's Latinx identity, Mando could easily have lapsed into a familiar bandido type: a vicious, murdering pistolero. Mando is as much a bounty hunter as he is a reluctant yet ultimately devoted father. His love for Grogu is such that Mando sacrifices his moral code by removing his helmet so that the child can see and touch the face of his father before they are separated. Mando chooses to abandon tradition to let Grogu (and audiences) see a father's vulnerability and heartbreak. When Mando makes the decision to remove his helmet, he embodies a complexity rarely afforded to Latinx men in any genre. The show is not about a Latinx father, but it nevertheless represents one of the most striking depictions of legible Latinx fatherhood.

In the borderlands between the white US cultural mainstream and Mexican American cultural productions, *Fatherhood in the Borderlands: A Daughter's Slow Approach* concerns itself not with the liberation but with the legibility of Mexican American fathers in literature and film. Few works focus exclusively on Brown fathers in the borderlands. This slow study focuses on the interplay of form, genre, and subject that determines the roles Mexican American fathers are allowed to occupy in the cultural imaginary. An analysis of the kinds of positions Mexican American fathers occupy is essential for understanding the agency or power, mitigated by race or class, they actually possess and its derivation. Doing such an analysis calls attention to what Mexican American fathers do with this power, however limited, in a cultural landscape that has historically worked to contain racialized bodies and families. Ultimately, my slow work on Brown fathers is as much an undoing as it is a doing of something. This book represents the truest version of how I think and make meaning. It is beyond anything I could have imagined for myself; it is what I always needed but did not have. Now others will have it too. This is the way.

PART I
Sourcing Authority

IN PERHAPS ONE OF THE MOST QUOTED PASSAGES from *Three Guineas* (1938), a collection of essays, modernist writer and feminist icon Virginia Woolf proposes setting fire to a women's college, if the institution's only purpose is to serve the interests of men by reinforcing patriarchy and its attendant combative practices:

> No guinea of earned money should go to rebuilding the college on the old plan; just as certainly none could be spent upon building a college upon a new plan; therefore the guinea should be earmarked "Rags. Petrol. Matches." And this note should be attached to it. "Take this guinea and with it burn the college to the ground. Set fire to the old hypocrisies. . . . And let the daughters of educated men dance round the fire and heap armful upon armful of dead leaves upon the flames. And let their mothers lean from the upper windows and cry, 'Let it blaze! Let it blaze! For we have done with this "education"!'" (36)[1]

Burning it all down is one approach to reforming higher education. But even Woolf thought better of doing so because she valued the sociocultural influence college education provided "the daughters of educated men." Indeed, she self-identifies in this way and uses the phrase repeatedly throughout *Three Guineas*.[2] Still, Woolf opposed modeling women's higher education "on the same lines as others," especially if "it followed that the college for the daughters of educated men must also make Research produce practical results which will induce bequests and donations from rich men; it must encourage competition; . . . it must accumulate great wealth; [and] it must exclude other people from a share of its wealth" (35). Rather than replicate existing structures to the same oppressive ends, Woolf believed women required different approaches to education and training for the professions than men so as not to continue patriarchal practices.[3] Her argument anticipates current critiques about the rise of the neoliberal university and the transactional economy that characterizes it.

These and other observations are part of a response to three requests Woolf received for donations of one guinea each to various causes.[4] The author uses the appeals as opportunities to comment on social and gender inequalities of the time and to illustrate how institutions of male power—domestic relationships, the church, and politics—work in conjunction to oppress women. Woolf envisioned her three responses as part of a "novel-essay" *The Pargiters*, with alternating fiction and nonfiction chapters, addressing the topics of war, underfunding of women's colleges, and professional opportunities for women. She intended the book to reflect back on ideas brought up in her influential essay "A Room of One's Own" (1929), in which she argues that women need money and the physical space to write. In its imagined form, *The Pargiters* would have been a notable contribution, through its mixing of genres, to modernist experimentations with literary style and form.[5] Woolf's decision to separate the work into a collection of nonfiction essays and the novel *The Years* (1939) represents an aesthetic choice to retreat within generic boundaries. The decision seems contrary to the author's advocating for women to advance outside of traditional confines, expressly, the home, in order to pursue university education and professional training: "Behind us lies the patriarchal system; the private house, with its nullity, its immorality, its hypocrisy, its servility. Before us lies the public world, the professional system, with its possessiveness, its jealousy, its pugnacity, its greed" (74). In women's move from one patriarchal realm of influence (private) to another (public), Woolf worried about what might happen to them in the professional sphere. More directly, she wondered about the transformations women might undergo: "Are we not right then in thinking that if we enter the same professions, we shall acquire the same qualities?" (66). She wanted to support women in their pursuits of access and equity, but she did not want women to adopt the attitudes or postures of men. As a result, Woolf was not content to simply fund efforts that helped women; she wanted to help women transform institutions and the practices that governed them.

Belgian philosopher of science and trained chemist Isabelle Stengers, in *Another Science Is Possible: A Manifesto for Slow Science* (2018), combines philosophy, science, personal experience, feminism, and portions of Woolf's *Three Guineas*, including the quotation above about burning the college to the ground, to envision a *slow* science (28–29, 41). In the process, Stengers critiques the shaping and reshaping of scientific research by a knowledge economy (meaning producing work in/for market- or economy-driven problems). The push to problem solve accelerates and, in some cases, predetermines outcomes, thereby emphasizing the transactional nature of the model. Furthermore, it leaves little room either for error, which can undermine public trust, or for thinking about science for the sake of science, as in, *We discovered this thing, and it could be useful, though we don't yet know how.* Katalin Kariko, for example, devoted her career to the study of messenger RNA while "clinging to the fringes of academia" (Kolata). Arriving from Hungary to Philadelphia in the mid-1980s, as a researcher, she never had a permanent position or made more than sixty thousand dollars a year. Kariko did, however, believe that mRNA "could be used to instruct cells to make their own medicines, including vaccines," and now she is celebrated as "one of the heroes of Covid-19 vaccine development" (Kolata). Stengers's manifesto urges the discipline to grapple with what science does and can actually do, as opposed to what public or private interests would like for it to do. Stated another way, science can solve some, but not all, problems, as well as create problems of its own.

The contributions to *Slow Scholarship: Medieval Research and the Neoliberal University* (2019), edited by Catherine E. Karkov, demonstrate the kinds of transformative work that slow research makes possible. Within the context of medieval literary studies as practiced in the neoliberal academy, the collection offers philosophical reflections on knowledge production and, in particular, research. Each of the authors included chooses to emphasize, for instance, how they cope, escape, advocate, engage in self-care, and/or find time for meaningful work as medieval scholars. These matters are unexpected or perceived as out of place in serious research or scholarship. "Only by upsetting the status quo," Karkov underscores, "can [we] create a space for change" (6). When scholars have opportunities to determine the scope and forms of their knowledge production, dynamic sites of innovation or change open up across disciplines and fields. This is the potential of slow research and what excites me about it. Slow scholarship, in theory and in practice, "is a means of experiencing time, place and the things we study differently" (Karkov 6). But this also means that we should *think* slowly about slow approaches so that our differences do not replicate or enhance structural barriers. A careful consideration of what slow does or does not account for theoretically or practically, alongside Woolf's and Stengers's appraisals and proposed initiatives, is central to my work, as I think through sourcing authority for fathers in borderlands narratives, a process that involves identifying and selecting sites and/or individuals based on their proximity to economic, social, or political power. Stated differently, I analyze how power is obtained from a particular source and what one does with that power.

> **orthogonal,** *adj.*
> *Forms:* 1500s–1600s *orthogonall*, 1600s–1800s *orthogonal*.
> *Origin:* A borrowing from French. *Etymon*: French *orthogonal*. *Etymology:* < Middle French, French *orthogonal* having a right angle (1520) . . .
> Oxford English Dictionary, "orthogonal"

Common use, a way to say that someone's work or analysis veers off in different directions.
Sentence: "The *orthogonal* structuring of the book made its focus seem convoluted."

When I applied to graduate school, my application materials included a writing sample on Joseph Conrad's *Heart of Darkness* (1899) and a statement of purpose that focused on how *René* (1802), a novella by François-René de Chateaubriand, shaped my thinking about the roles of American Indians in literary history. To my mind, Marlow's account of the native people in the jungles of Africa was not far removed from Chateaubriand's imaginings of Indigenous people in the forests of the Americas, except that the latter was more romantic. As a first-year graduate student, I wanted to study British modernism, American Indian literature, and film. A faculty advisor asked me to explain how those three interests fit together. When I could not produce an answer that satisfied her, she told me to drop the modernism and pursue comparative ethnic literatures of the US instead. So I did. My fields and I were not yet "up to the challenge of developing a collective awareness of the particularity and selective character of [our] own thought-style" (Stengers, *Another Science* 100). I was not encouraged to do the slow work of finding how my interests fit together in a way that was meaningful or sustainable for me. Instead I was "redirected." But I have never been one to stay in my lane.

Consequently, when my first book, which focused on folklore, included poetry, fiction, painting, sculpture, drama, music, film, and commercial products, the expansive scope was not terribly surprising. The archive I had collected allowed me to think across forms. Now I want to theorize slowly in a form that best suits my thinking. So here I am, decades later, making connections between the work of Virginia Woolf and Mexican American fathers in the borderlands.

In her work, Stengers reaches back to *Three Guineas* for the transformational strategies it proposes for systems, institutions, and sites of male power. The parallels between her work and Woolf's are readily apparent in their critiques of patriarchal institutions and the questions they raise about "civilized" environments. Woolf proposed that if women's colleges were to continue to exist (and, again, she thought they should), they needed to be rethought from the ground up: the ideal would be "an experimental college, an adventurous college" and preferably poor so as to be immune to the influence of wealthy donors (33). She promoted the value of learning beyond the competition that drove male students and scholars. The emphasis on antagonism discourages collaborative or integrative approaches to education that enrich both mind and body. Like Woolf, Stengers voices concerns about the "gender of science," the perception that the discipline and its practitioners are exclusively male. "The reality of the situation," Stengers points out, "would be that science is neutral as far as gender goes" (*Another Science* 24). Still, ideas and attitudes about gender persist, more specifically about who constitutes a "real researcher," a designation used to patrol the borders of science. For instance, women who take on family obligations alongside their work as researchers are seen as not having the same dedication as their male colleagues.[6] Stengers argues, however, that the ungendering of the sciences would create disciplinary anxiety: without the deeply entrenched ideas about the gender of their discipline, the sciences might be seen as lacking rigor or relevance. Stengers sees these same attitudes as part of the violence that patriarchal institutions engender, as Woolf argues throughout *Three Guineas*, to protect themselves and their power.

Another key intersection between Woolf's and Stengers's appraisals involves the role civilization has in transforming environments. Given the genocidal practices associated with the promotion of civilization in colonial history, the emphasis on this idea should give us pause. After all, for countless people like Zitkála-Šá, civilization has been a great machine grinding up everything in its path to clear a way for itself and its proponents. But neither Woolf nor Stengers offers an umbrella endorsement of civilization. Instead, Woolf openly questions both its organization and its practices. She urges that we "never cease from thinking—what is this 'civilization' in which we find ourselves? What are these ceremonies and why should we take part in them?" (63). Woolf advocates that we never fail to question the structures and sources of civilization and whom they serve or exclude by design. Stengers, alternately, promotes her own conception of "civilisation." Her idea is related to the need for "civilised engagement" with other scholars, which she envisions as the cornerstone of a slow science: "So slowing down the sciences means civilising scientists, civilisation being equated here with the ability of members of a particular collective to present themselves in a non-insulting way to members of other collectives, that is, in a way that enables the process of relation-making," which can break down isolating barriers (*Another Science* 100–101). Both Woolf and Stengers encourage us to look at the invisible structures from which authority is derived or to which we give over power without critical thought—those aspects of academic work designed to separate us. Relationality encourages us to look beyond ourselves to find the connections among and between people, thoughts, and ideas as one explicit method of scholarly transformation.

Yet Stengers, like Woolf before her, does not address class privilege or engage meaningfully with race or ethnicity when calling for slow changes to the sciences; they both miss an opportunity to generate the kinds of connections for which Stengers advocates.[7] However, she does allow an opening for such considerations: "Slowing down means becoming capable of learning again, becoming acquainted with things again, reweaving the bounds of *interdependency*. It means thinking and imagining, and in the process *creating relationships* with others that are not those of *capture*" (*Another Science* 81–82; emphasis added). The relationality that Stengers envisions, through reweaving, assumes an equitable exchange that happens once we slow down, and it does not involve the use of force or depend on the seizing of resources or ideas. Ideal, to be sure. However, as the Great Lakes Feminist Geography Collective, too, reminds us, slow scholarship encompasses many things, but it is also a means for addressing "structures of power and inequality" (1238). Yet which groups and individuals have access to power and where that power comes from, as well as how they experience inequality, is as relational as it is individuated by race, ethnicity, class, and gender.

Sociocultural analyses are not new, especially not to women's, queer, or ethnic studies. Yet a slow approach offers an important additional critical dimension. "Strands of this emergent field" ask us to look again at familiar ideas, texts, objects, or fields "slowly and deliberately" (GLFGC 1238). This means revisiting, for example, well-known texts and key conversations, in our respective fields, on which disciplinary knowledge formations are based. It also means that we do so purposefully, slowly, and with intentionality. The objective is to become reacquainted with and reflect on these established sites to identify, create, or strengthen other types of connections (commingling) through our own "thought-style" (Stengers, *Another Science* 100). For me, that means, in the following section, reassessing the films *A Walk in the Clouds* (1995), *Real Women Have Curves* (2002), and *Quinceañera* (2006); the impact of the film *The Empire Strikes Back* on my knowledge formation; and Luis Alberto Urrea's lesser-known first novel, *In Search of Snow* (1996), set in the borderlands of the American Southwest. Each analysis focuses on what happens to and among Brown men in established sites of patriarchal power. Whether reinforcing localized male authority or refusing the legacies of paternalism, all the men in these texts attempt to navigate and exert their own forms of control. Some thrive; others rebel; and another, as Woolf once proposed, burns it all down.

FILM

ANCIANOS NOT ABUELOS
Making Space and Mediating Male Power

The first memory I have of the Big Grandpa (figure 3), so named for his height, is of him sitting on the steps of the goldenrod-colored house he shared with the Big Grandma at 1674 Kiam Avenue, the one with the squat pomegranate tree out front. This is not the shotgun house down the street, where my brother and I watched on a small black-and-white television Mil Mascaras and Andre the Giant battle it out on Houston Wrestling. *I do not remember him at the rectangular residence. "El house," so named for its L-shaped floorplan, is where we would sit outside, him with his coffee and me with my Kool-Aid. Sometimes when there was fruit, I would stand in front of the tree, pointing at various candidates and waiting for the Big Grandpa to nod in approval before waving me over. I loved scooping a handful of seeds into my mouth and then biting down lightly to release their tart sweetness. Separating the seeds from the membrane was easy for my small hands, but I had not yet mastered how to tear open the tough outer peel. From one of his many pockets, he would produce a small knife to cut off the tiny crown of the fruit before scoring around the outside to make it easier to break open. Together we would share our snack in silence.*

This chapter, sans the part about the Big Grandpa, started as a prospective journal article almost fifteen years ago about Mexican American families in film, though it was always about older Mexican American patriarchs. I sent it out for review and received a recommendation to "revise and resubmit." The thoughtful and generous feedback that accompanied the journal editor's reply would have made revising the piece a straightforward matter. For whatever reason, I never did. Attempts to reengage

FIGURE 3. *The Big Grandpa, Houston, Texas. 1971.*

with these ideas always ended in failure. More specifically, the various iterations of this project have died—repeatedly—with drafts of the materials in this chapter. The underlying causes for my Sisyphean struggle with it range from chronic health issues and hospitalization to professional setbacks and family deaths, including those of my beloved mother and great aunt. These were only some of my difficulties with developing the chapter draft. Reflecting on the conditions in which I originally wrote the piece, I realized that I felt rushed to publish a "down payment" on a future project as I prepared my case for tenure.[1] Only days before sending my case to the college promotion and tenure committee, I had received a physical copy of my first book, and already I was being asked by the institution to repeat that process all over again without a moment in between to catch my breath.

I understand that this is the job. However, I had also served on a total of twenty-three dissertation, master's report, and honors thesis committees, all during my probationary period. Still, as Maggie Berg and Barbara K. Seeber recognize in *The Slow Professor: Challenging the Culture of Speed in the Academy* (2016), we, as academics, have a number of incredible privileges "not enjoyed by the majority of the workforce: job security provided by the tenure system; flexibility of hours and the changing rhythms of the academic year; and the opportunity to think, create, and pass on our enthusiasms to others" (3). For these reasons, and others, many of us choose to do the work that we do. Rarely do we discuss what it costs us. I was exhausted and already burned out as a junior professor. So, naturally, the semester after receiving tenure, I moved into an administrative position, which I occupied in some form for about seven years. Although slow approaches to scholarship encourage us to see "the benefits of unexpected 'disruptions' in the research and writing process," what I saw instead was that the conditions in which I attempted to produce the intellectual labor central to my job were neither clean nor fair (GLFGC 1238). As a result, each return to these materials meant revisiting a site of wounding.

As I set out again to begin work on drafting the chapter, a familiar feeling came over me. I thought, "Here we go again; this is where all my progress will be laid to rest." This time, however, I was not alone. Recognizing that, as Berg and Seeber state, "[a]cademic training includes induction into a culture of scholarly individualism" and that "to admit to struggle undermines our professorial identity," I shared my fears anyway (2). My writing buddy was facing her own problems with a section of her book that refused completion. Talking about the difficulties helped, though it was how we talked about them that really made the difference. It was not the content with which we were struggling but the feelings around the content, explicitly those involving trauma and loss. We listened and witnessed for each other in community (our own clan of two), which propelled us to write our way through and past the obstacles. We did so not because of institutional expectations or demands placed on us. Rather, we *chose* to maintain meaningful connections to and through our work. Slow theories and practices call attention to power and agency, but as Luke Martell observes, "[T]he bigger issue is autonomy" (par. 41). More and more, as academics, we lack autonomy over our time, knowledge formation, and intellectual production. So here I am, again, by choice, asserting my limited power in a patriarchal, corporatized system to disrupt it by making a space for different forms of knowledge production and to trouble what "counts" as scholarship. Understanding my own work in this way has shown me what I have been trying to say through the analysis in this chapter on Mexican and Mexican American patriarchs and patriarchal power in film.

Physical presence and representational space have not been afforded Latinx or diasporic Mexican characters in film.[2] In conventional Hollywood films, historically, Charles Ramírez Berg observes, the narrative emphasis on a "white, handsome, middle-aged, upper-middle-class, heterosexual, Protestant, Anglo-Saxon male" who seeks to protect the status quo necessarily relegates BIPOC characters to the roles of "villains, sidekicks, temptresses"—subordinates who challenge or serve the white hero (*Latino Images* 67).[3] The characters and characterizations of Latinxs in these secondary parts fall into recognizable types identified and analyzed independently by, in addition to Ramírez Berg, Chon A. Noriega, Gary D. Keller, and Christine List.[4] In the overall history of Latinxs in US cinema, Ramírez Berg sees six prevailing stereotypes: "*el bandido*, the harlot, the male buffoon, the female clown, the Latin lover, and the dark lady" (*Latino Images* 66). However, Ramírez Berg qualifies his assertion, noting that "there have also been exceptions to this rule" (66).[5] The *anciano* represents an exception to the conventionally limited and limiting representations of Latinxs in film. None of these older men represent conventional stereotypes of Latinos, for they are not bandidos, buffoons, or Latin lovers, and their roles are not secondary to Anglos'. While the cinematic *anciano* resembles a familiar dramatic type, akin to the indulgent, permissive grandparent figure, the ethno-racial, cultural, and socioeconomic contexts in which filmmakers place the *anciano* make him a figure deserving of critical attention. This scrutiny becomes especially important when the emphasis in films shifts from the white world to other ethno-racial communities, where Anglos are absent or in the cultural minority. Rather than a consideration of stereotypes or representations of Brown subjects, this chapter instead analyzes cinematic *ancianos* to determine how, and whether, these older male subjects create alliances across genders, generations, and sexualities to make social, cultural, and emotional space for those whose actions challenge the integrity of and male-domination over *la familia*.

The image of a super-sized Mexican American family overseen by an overbearing, albeit benevolent, patriarch is now a familiar trope in mainstream popular culture, but the image of a cohesive Brown family is a fairly recent one. In the late-nineteenth- and early-twentieth-century American popular imagination, Mexicans, as depicted on the US stage, in film, and in literature, were a contemptible and inferior race whose members distinguished themselves through their subservience to Anglos or through their sexual or revolutionary exploits. With their guns, sombreros, *bigotes*, bad accents, and even badder attitudes, male Mexican characters, primarily greasers and bandidos, have been mainstays in American cinema since its inception.[6] Correspondingly, Mexican women in early American film were depicted as sassy, spicy, or super sexy señoritas, sometimes all three at once. These enduring types do not lend themselves to either complex characterization or depictions of quotidian life, so Mexican characters in this early period rarely emerged as heroes, had families, or served as productive members of a community.

In the mid-twentieth century, however, a limited number of films— *The Ring* (1952), *Salt of the Earth* (1954), and *Giant* (1956)—did include functional families of the Mexican diaspora that did not rely on stereotypes. Nevertheless, on the whole, Brown families have been represented as largely "fragmented and dysfunctional," often due to the death or unnarrated absence of either parent (Ramírez Berg, "Bordertown" 43). These negative depictions of Mexicans serve as a means of narrating Anglo superiority in film. As Ramírez Berg asserts, "[T]he lack of an organizing paternal sensibility makes for an abnormal, structurally unstable family unit, subtly establishing the psycho-social reasons why ethnics are different from—and inferior to—the mainstream" (43). The lack of reliable men leads women to devote themselves to motherhood, struggling under economic, emotional, and social burdens, as in films ranging from *Bordertown* (1935) and *La Bamba* (1987) to the more recent *East Side Sushi* (2014) and *The Curse of La Llorona* (2019). When Mexican or Chicano fathers actually do appear in films, too often they are confined to a scene or subplot that also extols the virtues of Anglos, as in *Giant*, *Lone Star* (1996), or *McFarland, USA* (2015).[7] Alternately, *Walkout* (2006), *Machete* (2010), *A Better Life* (2011), *Instructions not Included* (2013), and *Spare Parts* (2015), among others, depict fathers of the Mexican diaspora as ineffectual and incapable of maintaining family integrity. *Fools Rush In* (1997), *Selena* (1997), *Price of Glory* (2000), the first three installments in the *Spy Kids* series (2001; 2002; 2003), *Our Family Wedding* (2010), and *Coco* (2017) break from this convention by focusing on Mexican and Mexican American patriarchs as members of unified families, an institution venerated by director Gregory Nava in his romantic 1995 classic *My Family/Mi familia*.

The following list represents the films that served as my entry point into the study of Latinx characters in film:

> *Flying Down to Rio* (1933)
> *Bordertown* (1935)
> *Down Argentine Way* (1940)
> *Mexican Spitfire Series* (1940–1943)
> *Treasure of the Sierra Madre* (1948)
> *High Noon* (1952)
> *¡Viva Zapata!* (1952)

Giant (1956)
The Searchers (1956)
Touch of Evil (1958)
The Wild Bunch (1969)
The Three Amigos (1986)
Born in East L.A. (1987)
The Milagro Beanfield War (1988)
Stand and Deliver (1988)
Mambo Kings (1992)
El Norte (1993)
Mi Vida Loca (1993)
Blood In, Blood Out (1993)
I Like It Like That (1994)
Desperado (1995)

MY FAMILY?

> I hope that, as the society develops and more films like *My Family* get made, they will continue to be successful and we will be able to see more images up on the screen that are . . . not stereotypic but that are positive, that place us in the society and with our communities, put family in the center of our culture, which it is.
> Gregory Nava, "Filming the Chicano Family Saga"

José walking from his Mexican village to *el norte*; Maria, cradling her infant son, struggling to cross a raging river; Chucho shot by a police officer beneath a bridge; Jimmy and Isabel dancing in the street, moving across time and cultures. A quarter of a century has passed since the release of *My Family* (1995), a movie about four generations of the Sanchez family, who reside in East Los Angeles.[8] The film was a stark turn from Edward James Olmos's dark neorealist film *American Me* (1992) and Taylor Hackford's *Blood In, Blood Out* (1993), in both of which gang life and incarceration figure prominently. Though lighthearted at times, Nava's film does not shy away from border crossing, migration, deportation, social injustice, assimilation, or incarceration. The members of the Sanchez clan have these experiences to differing degrees as the film delves into the complexities of multigenerational family life.

My Family's focus on an intact barrio family, not to mention the film's wide cast of characters, represented a departure from previous depictions of Mexican American families. In spite of the pressures to "make white people major characters . . . and to cast non-Latinos" in exchange for a larger production budget, Nava insisted on having Latinxs at the center of his story in order to "take the audience into a Chicano household" (Britt).[9] He gave viewers a Chicanx family that included restaurant owners, a college graduate, an activist, and an aspiring writer, narrating the story of this family across four generations, all played by Latinx actors. The film also gave audiences a healthy dose of toxic masculinity and violence. With its Chicano director, predominantly Latinx cast, and relative box office success, the film, and particularly its focus on a unified Latinx family, marked an important historical moment for Mexican Americans in film.[10]

When I first saw the film at a local theatre in Lincoln, Nebraska, where I was attending graduate school, I remember wanting desperately to love it. I had never seen a movie quite like the one promised on the poster and in the title. I was tired of seeing bandidos and brownface, or white-presenting actors made up to look like Mexicans. I was equally weary of the sounding of race through mariachi horn blasts, the ominous strains of stringed instruments, or a clacking of castanets on soundtracks announcing the presence of Latinx characters on-screen. I wanted something that represented a more contemporary perspective. In a film that purported to span generations, the odds were in my favor. Familiar Latinx actors loomed large over a sizable Mexican American family wedding party on the colorful movie poster. As someone with over twenty-five first cousins, the image of the large family was immediately familiar to me. Once the film started, I realized it was not about my family or any other I knew.

The film resonated with audiences, who appreciated that it felt like a departure from previous stories about Latinxs. Conceptually, however, Nava's visual offering of the Chicanx family reads more like a pastiche of Latinx types bound within heteronormative ideas of the nuclear family than an offering of anything new. Perhaps that is by design: Nava merges race and the family-drama genre, which handily fit into other pre-existing patriarchal narratives. The family in Hollywood films, according to Sarah Harwood in *Family Fictions: Representations of the Family in 1980s Hollywood Cinema* (1997), is "simultaneously represented as a 'natural,' universal and inevitable form while also being constructed as a fragile, threatened entity requiring support for its survival" (5). Family dramas entwine patriarchal authority, heterosexuality, and whiteness. Centering on family life, relationships, and conflicts, the narrative valence of the genre ranges from interpersonal and generational to cultural and political, but the racial makeup of families at the center of these films, historically, has remained static. As a result, whiteness and the American family in film became intertwined, one fortifying the other. The repeated and almost exclusive emphasis on the white family reinforced ideas about its importance as a complex social unit worthy of narrative attention. As Francis Ford Coppola did with Italians in *The Godfather* (1972), Nava, by focusing on a Chicanx family, disrupts racial scripts about who constitutes family in America and illustrates how systems of power exclude particular racial and ethnic groups.[11] This idea is in keeping with Nava's desire "to offer mainstream audiences," as Rosa Linda Fregoso notes, "an understanding of the 'concept of the Latino family'" (*meXicana Encounters* 75). Nevertheless, the Chicanx family at the heart of *My Family* exists as a myopic reversal of its previous depictions as fractured or inferior to its white counterparts.[12]

In 1977, Mexican-born sociologist Alfredo Mirandé published a comparative analysis of extant and emerging views on Chicano families in US culture and was one of the first to talk about "*la familia*" and its depiction as an "idealized and romanticized image" ("Chicano Family" 748). The study involved reexamining previous sociological studies that pathologized Mexican Americans and then comparing these views to sympathetic perspectives generated by "Chicano writers."[13] Mirandé notes that although "Chicano perspectives on *la familia* have served as a badly needed corrective for the negative and stultifying social science view, they have not been without their own pitfalls" (747–748). Reductive and often racist ideas about ethnic groups appear across disciplines and are replicated uncritically. Acknowledging both the motivating impulse and the necessity to countermand deprecatory views of *la familia*, Mirandé, nevertheless, criticizes the effect of these efforts:

> Although the more positive view of the Chicano family emerged as a response to stereotypical characterizations, it too has demonstrated a strong tendency to make sweeping generalizations about the family that neglect or minimize its internal diversity. In their quest to negate pejorative depictions, defenders of the family have substituted a series of positive and idealized stereotypes, which, ironically, incorporate many of the same beliefs they sought to supplant. Thus, negative stereotypes have been discarded in favor of positive and romanticized characterizations that result in polar caricatures of the Chicano family. (751)

Mirandé cautions that in addition to their failure to depict diversity, these idealized images of the family do not correspond to real life.[14] He therefore urges "a more balanced and objective view" that conveys "the reality of Chicano family life without exaggerating or distorting that reality" (751). Although Mirandé attempted to present an impartial view of the Chicano family, he was not immune from the kind of romanticizing he cautioned against.[15] The treatment of Mexican American families in film follows a trajectory, not unlike the ones found in sociological and other scholarly studies, moving from negative to positive portrayals but also literally from absence to presence.

The centralization of a *unified* Mexican American family notwithstanding, Nava's film also represents a masculinized narrative about men, narrated by a man with express concerns regarding the futurity of the men in his family.[16] *My Family* uncritically replicates the necessity of a present father for familial integrity and the successful continuation of a male-dominated household. It also positively conveys, as Richard T. Rodríguez states, "that Chicano and Latino families are inherently ruled by patriarchy" (75). Alternately praised in the mainstream media at the time for being "ambitious" and criticized for being "wildly uneven," *My Family* today holds an important place in Chicanx studies (James).[17] The film has been the subject of considerable negative criticism, in particular for its deep commitment to paternalism, as well as for its trafficking in familiar types, such as the migrant, the pachuco, the gardener, and the criminal. While some critics see the film as simply offering a "sappier, passive perception of family," others see it as unabashedly reinforcing heteropatriarchy at the expense of other or actually diverse kinship formations (Nieves and Algarin 222).[18] The substantive work of several scholars calls attention to the masculinist and patriarchal organization of *la familia* that the film celebrates. These include Fregoso in *meXicana Encounters: The Making of Social Identities on the Borderlands* (2003), Carmen Huaco-Nuzum in *"Orale* Patriarchy: *Hasta Cuando Corazón* Will You Remain *el Gallo Macho* of *Mi Familia?"* (2006), Rodríguez in *Next of Kin: The Family in Chicano/a Cultural Politics* (2009), and Daniel Enrique Pérez in *Rethinking Chicana/o and Latina/o Popular Culture* (2009), among others.

My Family epitomizes what Mexican American studies scholars refer to as *la familia* romance. This genre distinguishes itself from the mainstream family drama by positioning the Brown heterosexual nuclear family writ large on-screen and in the cultural imagination as an ideal, uniform institution. However, while serving as a celebration of a cultural institution, the representation of Mexican American families in recent films poses a different set of problems in terms of their portrayals. Fregoso analyzes *A Walk in the Clouds*, *My Family*, *Selena*, and other Chicanx film productions that promote *la familia* in ways that are "uncritical of heterosexism and repression of queer sexualities" and fail to reflect the diversity and complexity of actual Chicanx families, a criticism she shares with Mirandé (Fregoso, *meXicana Encounters* 86). In other words, although the recent narrative emphasis on Mexican American families signals a marked change from their previous representations, cinematic constructions of *la familia* serve to entrench ideas about absolute heterosexual male authority.

The purpose of this analysis, however, is not to defend paternalism nor to recuperate *familia* romances; instead, it is to consider the ways in which three family-centered films that followed Nava's landmark feature trouble heteropatriarchal authoritarianism through the figure of the *anciano*, whose site of power is *la familia*. The films are *A Walk in the Clouds* (1995), *Real Women Have Curves* (2002), and *Quinceañera* (2006). Rather than relying on Anglo defenders or assuming subservient roles to white heroes, mature Brown patriarchs, within the structure of *la familia*, such as El Californio (Léon Singer) and José Sanchez (Eduardo López Rojas) in *My Family* and Grandfather (Ricardo Montalban) in the *Spy Kids* movies, care for and help to save their own loved ones.[19] These older men exist in extended families, but as Montalban's character's moniker indicates, they are *viejitos* or *abuelos* rather than *ancianos*, as I use the term.[20] In other words, although they may watch over their families, they do not openly advocate for individual members whose place in the family is threatened.

SENIOR PATRIARCHS, BEYOND BANDIDOS AND BUFFOONS

The designation *anciano*, a familiar term to Spanish speakers for a male of advanced age, has not been used previously as a way to identify Latinos in film. In this analysis, the term refers to a type of cinematic Mexican or Mexican American man, one from an older generation who is part of an extended, multigenerational family or cultural community. Translated literally, the term, as a noun, means "an elderly man"; this definition, though, fails to capture the different registers of its use, particularly the way it conveys specific information about the age and rank of men in a paternal hierarchy. For the purposes of this chapter, the cinematic *anciano* tells us about the place and roles of Mexican and Mexican

American patriarchs within the familial structure. The *anciano* has a respected authority and wisdom that is often conveyed through storytelling, aphorisms, and lore—characteristics that are frequently assigned to a church, community, tribal, or village elder. More than simply an *abuelo* ensconced unproblematically within the familial structure, or a *viejito*, who though perhaps revered or even beloved is ineffectual, *anciano*, as a relational term, refers to a maturing patriarch who maintains his status and influence in family governance while acknowledging and making a space for a new formal patriarch in the hierarchy of men.

Contemporary depictions of older Mexican and Mexican American male characters represent alternative male subject positions beyond impotent or stereotypical representations of Latinos in film. The *ancianos* under consideration here—Don Pedro Aragon in *A Walk in the Clouds*, by Alfonso Arau; Abuelo in *Real Women Have Curves*, by Patricia Cardoso; and Tío Tomas Alvarez in *Quinceañera*, by Richard Glatzer and Wash Westmoreland—all live in California but represent vastly different depictions, in terms of class and environment, of the same figure. Spanning more than fifty years narratively, these family dramas represent but also idealize the heterosexual, nuclear Mexican American family, one that is threatened by social forces from both within and outside of the cultural community. Don Pedro Aragon (Anthony Quinn), whose name calls to mind the Spanish monarchs who financed Columbus's expeditions, in *A Walk in the Clouds* is the aging patriarch of a Napa Valley family vineyard run by his volatile son. Amid California pastoral splendor in the mid to late 1940s, Don Pedro dwells in relative bliss with his extended family and the well-cared-for house servants and vineyard workers. In contrast, Abuelo (Felipe de Alba) in *Real Women Have Curves* lives modestly and quietly with his son's family in East Los Angeles, filling his days with telenovelas and clandestine excursions out of the house accompanied by his granddaughter Ana, who longs to break free from her family to attend college. Whereas Abuelo resides within the family home, in *Quinceañera*, Tío Tomas (Chalo González), a lifelong bachelor who also lives in East Los Angeles, sells *champurrado* to neighborhood residents and rents a bungalow with a garden he has turned into an Edenic oasis, a refuge in the middle of a barrio being gentrified by white outsiders.

In the films under consideration here, the *anciano* is rooted within family and community and has the power to protect, in a limited way, his *own* people. The *anciano* serves to uphold patriarchal control of unified Mexican and/or Mexican American families in the face of cultural and social change. The archetype illustrates the necessity of patriarchs' accommodating as well as sanctioning certain perceived transgressions to maintain families and male authority over them. Therefore, the *anciano* ensures the survival of the existing patriarchal structure of the Mexican American family through a monitoring and modeling of the methods men in power use to ensure their continued authority. The duty undertaken by the *anciano* may lead some to conclude prematurely that the place where the Anglo hero and Brown patriarch can come together is not in the interstices of culture or class, but in the shared idea of male power regardless of race or ethnicity. However, the *anciano*'s job is more than simply to uphold male power. In addition to sanctioning and overseeing the transfer of male authority to the next generation, he must negotiate with—as well as resist—dominant cultural and socioeconomic forces against which Mexicans, Mexican Americans, and Chicanxs struggle, such as changing gender roles or technological advancements. From their positions in the cultural and geographic borderlands, these *ancianos* reinvigorate the need for a dynamic father or father figure in the face of unplanned pregnancy, children breaking free from familial dictates, or queerness.

Two of the films at the center of this chapter are more than a decade old, and *A Walk in the Clouds* premiered more than twenty-five years ago, following a string of Latinx-themed films focusing primarily on men.[21] Revisiting *A Walk in the Clouds*, *Real Women Have Curves*, and *Quinceañera* to "look again," as slow scholarship encourages us to do, elucidates how films subsequent to *My Family* diversified aspects of the titular social institution by featuring a wealthy proto-Chicanx family with ties to Spain and the Aztecs; a family of independent business owners; and a family whose spiritual practices are rooted in strip-mall evangelicalism. These films also critique heterosexual masculinist forms of authority, not to dismantle but to reinforce paternalism in the family as a primary locus of power. In the hierarchy of male power in these films, *ancianos*, men from an older generation, advocate and make space for women and queer folk, demonstrating for young patriarchs, culturally and politically, that no one in the family is expendable.

A Walk in the Clouds, *Real Women Have Curves*, and *Quinceañera* all feature female protagonists, Victoria Aragon (Aitana Sánchez-Gijón), Ana Garcia (America Ferrera), and Magdalena (Emily Rios), respectively, who act in ways that threaten the patriarchal integrity of the family and that also imagine other possibilities for it, both of which undermine the authority of the father. Victoria in *A Walk in the Clouds* and Magdalena in *Quinceañera* each engage in premarital intimacies that result in pregnancy. The *anciano* figures in these films, Don Pedro and Tío

Tomas, have conceded, on the surface, their authority as patriarchs to a younger generation of men, who authorize the condemnation of Victoria and Magdalena. In defiance of the new patriarchs, Don Pedro and Tío Tomas demonstrate their true power as elders by making a space within (or adjacent to) the family and demonstrating compassion for these young women and their perceived transgressions, a move that ultimately will reinforce male power within the family instead of diminishing it. Similarly, Ana, the protagonist of *Real Women Have Curves*, challenges the dictates of her father and overbearing mother by having protected sex with her Anglo boyfriend and applying to a college across the country without her family's knowledge. While her *anciano* has fewer resources at his disposal, which constrains his ability to advocate for his granddaughter, he does help to facilitate Ana's cultural and sexual transgressions that empower her to pursue her dream. In each film, the benevolent *anciano* serves as a nurturer and advocate for female characters, yet women are not the sole benefactors of his protective influence. In *Quinceañera*, the family of Carlos (Jesse Garcia), a man who purportedly has a criminal past, ostracizes him. The cause of his exclusion, however, does not stem from his supposed unlawful behavior but rather from his queerness. Instead of turning his back on Carlos, Tío Tomas provides him shelter and prepares his nephew to assume his future role as a patriarch who will have the power to further transform, over time, his family. While the actions of the *ancianos* appear inclusive and desirable, they are still done in the service of shoring up patriarchal power and authority over *la familia*.

The diverse national and ethnic backgrounds of the filmmakers included in this analysis (Mexican, Colombian, British, and Anglo American) defy attempts to draw a correlation between how the *anciano* figure is put to use in a film and the cultural, ethnic, or national identities of the filmmakers. *A Walk in the Clouds*, by Mexican-born Arau, features an *anciano* who, in his ostensibly selfless attention to an Anglo, brings to mind the familiar subservient cinematic person of color, a figure that director Spike Lee calls "the magical Negro."[22] Lee defines these figures as ones "who appear out of nowhere and have these great powers but who can't use them to help themselves or their own people but only for the benefit of the white stars of the movies" (5). Although the designation "Negro" suggests otherwise, the term can apply widely to any BIPOC person who occupies a self-abnegating role in relation to white authority—for example, as suggested by Lee's interviewers, Tonto in his service to the Lone Ranger.[23] The *ancianos* in this study resemble, in part, the magical Negro and the wise sachem, particularly in their closeness to the earth.

This type of characterization suggests that their power is derived from nature. Don Pedro in *A Walk in the Clouds* lives in a fecund, unspoiled environment. In *Real Women Have Curves*, when relating his folktale and imparting his wisdom to Ana, Abuelo in *Real Women Have Curves* is framed by a lemon tree heavy with fruit. Tío Tomas's lush garden outside of his home in *Quinceañera* signifies a pristine haven, untouched by the changing environment and demographics of the barrio. Conceptualizing American Indians and other marginalized groups categorically as Negroes emphasizes the ways in which filmmakers return to the same conventional ethnic types to reaffirm the mainstream cultural value of whiteness. The *ancianos*' ability to protect and preserve their own families and cultural communities, an ability neither the magical Negro nor the wise sachem is afforded in film, distinguishes these older men from other racialized characterizations.

Conversely, in *Quinceañera*, Tío Tomas, a character believed to be based on the uncle of British director Westmoreland, appears to be the most progressive offering of an *anciano*, for he devotes himself to the cultivation of his queer Brown family. A critical analysis of Tío Tomas and of the film must also take into account the fact that the directors were consciously aware of their outsider status in the predominantly Mexican American neighborhood where they resided and where they set the film. They had limited knowledge about the subject of their own film, so Westmoreland and Glatzer encouraged the cast and crew to play active roles in its making. In a number of newspaper articles, including those in the *New York Times*, the *Boston Globe*, and the *Chicago Sun-Times*, Glatzer and Westmoreland repeatedly emphasize the collaborative nature of the film (Rochlin; Gorov; Emerick). Paralleling Allison Anders's approach to her girl-gang-in-the-barrio film *Mi Vida Loca* (1993), the directors drew on the expertise and experiences of the barrio community they called home, from casting local Echo Park residents to requesting that actors select items from their own closets for their costumes to handing over the English-to-Spanish dialogue translation to the actors. Rather than initiate a conversation about the appropriation of Mexican and Mexican American culture in film, given the limited number of films about Brown patriarchs included in this analysis, my work concerns itself with how three *ancianos* take up the role of mediator and the spaces they make for others in their families. To paraphrase a point made by bell hooks, it is not so much the color of the person who makes the images that matters but "the perspective, the standpoint, and the politics" (*Reel to Real* 7). Indeed, an analysis of the *anciano* figure reveals a complex negotiation between patriarchs and social power as figured in ethno-racial terms.

"EVERY MAN HAS TO FIND HIS OWN WAY" AMONG *LAS NUBES*

Of the *ancianos* discussed in this analysis, Don Pedro Aragon represents an exemplar of the figure through his devotion to securing male authority and protecting his family from internal and external forces that threaten to tear it apart. He invests in the former to ensure the continuation of his power in the heterosexual nuclear family, as well as his place in the family vineyard, the source and seat of Aragon male power. *A Walk in the Clouds* represents a truly fantastical offering of the *familia* romance. The Aragon vineyard, Las Nubes, serves as the film's primary setting and looks like a Maxfield Parrish painting come to life. The vineyard is presented as an ideal place, as the title suggests, an ethereal home where Brown people live and labor in a paradise untouched by or outside of the post–World War II social politics of its time. Viewers quickly learn though that Las Nubes exists as a fraught utopia, one overseen by an overbearing father, Alberto (Giancarlo Giannini), who attempts to control every aspect of his family's life. Alberto's father, Don Pedro, is not that different from his son. The *anciano*'s approach comes across as kindly and accepting, attitudes characteristic of grandparents, traditionally, in Mexican American families. According to sociologist Mirandé, though Chicanx grandparents play an important part in the lives of children, they "are likely to be seen as warm and affectionate rather than as authority figures" ("Chicano Family" 752). Don Pedro is, thus, a more compassionate and benevolent patriarch than his son. Having relinquished control of the vineyard to Alberto, Don Pedro, as an *anciano*, nevertheless retains the capacity to exercise control over the family. He is capable, therefore, of offering more than his affection; he can defend those in need of protection, an ability that is tested after Victoria returns home, secretly pregnant and "married."

Long before Keanu Reeves was the internet's boyfriend, he played the white savior Paul Sutton, the already-married World War II veteran who protects Victoria from her dictatorial father and later rescues the Aragon family vineyard from permanent destruction. On her way back from college to Las Nubes via bus, Victoria discloses to Paul, whom she met only moments before, that she is pregnant from an affair with her college professor and is afraid to go home and face her father. Victoria describes Alberto as a domineering, potentially violent man who values family honor above all else. She explains to Paul about her father's unforgiving, fierce nature by quoting his oft-repeated threat "I will kill anyone who dishonors my family." When Paul interprets her father's sentiment as a "figure of speech," Victoria corrects him: "It's not. My father means what he says. He's very old-fashioned. I come home this way without a husband, he'll kill me. I know he will." Victoria's fear suggests, at the very least, verbal abuse and threatening behavior on the part of her father, or worse, a history of abuse within the family. She attempts to convey to Paul that her decision to exercise control over her own body will be perceived as a direct affront to her father's authority and his plans for her to marry a Mexican man of name and substance.[24] Because of his inexplicable desire to help a beautiful stranger, Paul concocts a plan for facing her father. The idea is that she will introduce Paul to the family as her husband; following a brief stay, he will then abandon her, and shortly thereafter, Victoria will "discover" she is pregnant. Despite the absurdity of the plot, the film wants audiences to root for the Victoria and Paul romance. After all, what is more patriarchal than to cheer for heterosexuality and a nuclear family, real or not? As the "couple" move forward with the ruse, they arrive at Las Nubes and encounter Alberto brandishing a shotgun in the vineyard, an ostensible confirmation of his potential for violence.

The couple's entrance at Las Nubes highlights the opposing approaches to authority put into practice by the two patriarchs, so that Alberto's volatile emotions contrast with Don Pedro's quiet benevolence. As Alberto enters the family home, he bellows for his wife. Hearing the ruckus, the *anciano* Don Pedro first appears, out of focus, behind the "newlyweds," who are framed in the foreground (figure 4). The audience soon learns that Alberto's objections to Paul are that he is a "gringo," that he is a working-class chocolate salesman, and that Victoria married him without the blessing of the Church or her family, institutions that reinforce heteronormativity and authoritative male power. Don Pedro walks silently into the hall looking dismayed. Father and son stand on opposite sides of the room, foreshadowing their opposing views, as the latter continues his tirade about why women should not be allowed to leave the home to go to college or to the city, presumably beyond the reach of his authority. Upon seeing her grandfather, Victoria immediately goes to him, embraces him, and pleads, "Grandpa, make him stop, please." He kisses her forehead and holds her in his arms, which Alberto reads as a sign of consent. In this scene, the safe space the *anciano* creates for Victoria is within his embrace. Together, they stand in defiance of Alberto's at-

FIGURE 4. *The "newlyweds" as they arrive at Las Nubes in* A Walk in the Clouds. *Don Pedro, like a guardian angel watching over the pair, appears over Paul's shoulder.*

tempt to exert his will. He responds, "That's right, that's right, coddle her, the whole bunch of you. But I tell you right now, this will not stand so long as I draw breath." Alberto turns to face Don Pedro and appeals to his father's authority: "You, you are the head of the family. Say something." The *anciano* approaches Paul and instead of reproaching his granddaughter's "husband," he introduces himself and welcomes Paul into the family. Despite the claim about Don Pedro's position as governing patriarch, Alberto is the one who is "in charge" of Las Nubes, though he has yet to find an effective means of rule.

Don Pedro's behavior poses a challenge to Alberto's familial authority. The *anciano* does not judge his granddaughter for returning home unannounced and married to an unknown man. As the film unfolds, Don Pedro highlights the need for Alberto to change, a necessity made evident through not only his relationship with his daughter but also that with his son, Pedro "Pete" Aragon, Jr., who returns from Stanford University with ideas about modernizing the family business, which Alberto at first refuses to consider. Don Pedro monitors his son's performance as acting patriarch and sees that Alberto's unreasonable behavior threatens family unity. In response, Don Pedro enacts clandestine measures to counteract Alberto's oppressive rule. He does not, however, choose to intervene in behalf of his grandson and namesake's cause; instead, he willingly supports Victoria by turning his attention to educating Paul and guiding him through the cultural terrain so that he may fit into the family.

In contrast, the emphasis on Mexican Americans and their communities alleviates the immediate need for the *ancianos* in *Real Women Have Curves* and *Quinceañera* to serve as teachers to Anglo outsiders. Although both do teach and nurture, they do so for members of their own families, whereas Don Pedro oversees Paul's familial and cultural education, teaching him the five-hundred-year Aragon family history, which includes taking him to a fenced area high on a hill in Las Nubes to see the originary grapevine brought over from Europe. Behind the plant stands a stone monument adorned on top with a cross, which marks the site as a source of spiritual, familial, economic, and geographic power. The trek into the clouds refers to a patriarchal authority greater than Don Pedro's, one that governs all of Las Nubes and its residents—God's. Journeying to the sacred site seemingly integrates Paul into a patriarchal line of succession, suggesting that the future of Las Nubes lies with the Anglo hero. Paul, like his apostolic namesake, undergoes a conversion: in the face of his obligations to his job and legal wife, who awaits him back on Earth, Paul, who is beginning to fall in love with Victoria and Las Nubes, longs to stay. Sensing Paul's inner struggle, Don Pedro tries to persuade him to remain with the Aragon family. Preternaturally aware of the truth about Paul and Victoria's relationship from the outset, Don Pedro has a regard for Paul as Victoria's husband and a member of the family that is unconditional, and his position remains unchanged throughout the film.

With few exceptions, Don Pedro actively and openly reinforces the authority of his son Alberto, as indeed he must in order to ensure male familial authority. The first night after Victoria and Paul's arrival, the residents of Las Nubes are roused from their beds by an alarm bell warning of an unexpected frost. As the Aragon family stands among the vines, Don Pedro defers to Alberto's expertise and awaits his son's pronouncement about the future of the crop. Once Alberto delivers his judgment, Don Pedro then follows without question his son's plan for saving the grapes. In this moment of absolute authority and controlled chaos, Alberto recognizes, as he watches Victoria and Paul interact, that the "newlyweds" are clearly in love, yet he also knows instinctively that they are not being entirely truthful with the family. So, while he, like his father, is incredibly perceptive, Alberto is unsure how to proceed, in the same way he is unsure about how to wield his nascent power. He clearly understands the change signaled by his daughter's marriage to an Anglo outsider; still, he is uncertain how to react to the circumvention of his authority, so he responds with anger and frustration. Later, as Paul and Don Pedro watch Alberto oversee the harvest, the *anciano* conveys unequivocally that assuming the mantle as patriarch, more specifically as the papa, is a process: "It's not easy being in charge. It was not easy for me; it's not easy for him; every man has to find his own way." Although Alberto has yet to find his way, Don Pedro confides in Paul, "I have faith in my son." He also takes this opportunity to tell Paul, "I have faith in you." The don attempts to position Alberto and Paul as allies, not rivals, in the preservation of the Aragon heteropatriarchy.

When Victoria later reveals the truth that she and Paul are not married, Alberto storms off. In spite of his previous threats to kill anyone who dishonors his family, he harms neither Paul nor Victoria for their deception. Once again, Don Pedro's response is to shelter Victoria in his embrace. Each time she turns to the *anciano* for comfort, she reinforces his authority and undermines her father's attempts to rule. After reluctantly leaving the vineyard to reunite with his legal wife, Paul later returns with news of his impending divorce, which frees him from his loveless marriage and paves the way for him to marry Victoria. Paul's reappearance at Las Nubes, however, prompts an inebriated Alberto to lash out at Paul for lying and humiliating the Aragon family. In his rage, Alberto knocks over a lantern, accidentally setting fire to the entire vineyard and almost killing his son, thus threatening the future of Brown male succession in the family. Alberto's mishandling of his authority results in the vineyard being burned to the ground. Following his destruction of Las Nubes, as Alberto sits weeping, he reveals to his family the cause of his violent behavior: "I was afraid. I was afraid of losing you. All of you. I didn't know any other way to love you. Can you teach me? Please? Can you teach me?" Alberto cites love and fear as motivation for his oppressive, unreasonable behavior. In this equation, threats of violence equal love. The fear of loss, presumably his children's movement away from the family home and business, is tied explicitly to Alberto's ability to exercise physical control over the lives of his family through proximity. After pleading with his family to help him find a new way of expressing his devotion (read: authority), Victoria kneels before her father and embraces him; the rest of the family follows suit, forming a circle around the defeated patriarch. Although Alberto's rage has threatened the future of the entire Aragon family, he remains at the center of everything. As the family mourns their losses, Paul ascends into the clouds, for he alone believes that the originary vine has survived the fire. Like Moses, he comes down from the mountain carrying the root, delivering the despairing winemakers from their misery. Las Nubes is reborn by the grace and intelligence of the decorated Anglo war hero, who responds to the tragedy with rea-

FIGURE 5. *The future of Las Nubes: Alberto, Don Pedro, and Paul with a piece of root from the originary vine, which survived the fire.*

son rather than emotion. So, while the *anciano* seems progressive and forward thinking about the changing world, he still needs Paul, whom he has groomed, to save his family.

The final scene of the film confirms Don Pedro's success in aiding Alberto's transformation and solidifies the patriarchal hierarchy. At the same time, it also provides visual proof of Don Pedro's larger plan for both Paul and the future of the family. As evidence of his commitment to change, Alberto welcomes Paul into the family, going so far as to hand him a piece of the surviving root to protect and cultivate with Victoria, forever binding him to the land and the family. Before Paul descends the slope to join Victoria, the three men are framed together in the foreground (figure 5). The arrangement appears to convey their current and future roles as patriarchs in the family hinted at in the earlier scene in the clouds at the family monument: Don Pedro is positioned on the rocky terrain above Paul, who as the hero is positioned slightly higher than Alberto. This alignment quickly shifts when Alberto ushers Paul down toward Victoria and the other women, so that the men are tiered as *anciano*, papa, and "son," with Paul set to inherit the mantle of familial patriarch. Upon closer inspection, a fourth male complicates this line of patriarchal succession. Surveying the scene from above, Pedro, Jr., watches his father, grandfather, and Paul create racial and generational alliances. In other words, the *anciano* teaches Pedro by example. Bespectacled, small in stature, an intellectual, and marked by delicate features, Pedro, Jr., seems an unlikely queer or nonnormative candidate to someday become head of the family, particularly in contrast to Paul, who during the fire had saved his life. But as the *anciano*'s namesake, Pedro, Jr., who returns from the outside world with a new name (Pete) and new ideas, has proven himself capable of adapting to difference, a quality he shares with his grandfather.[25] Don Pedro had the foresight to support diversifying the family, and his willingness to do so saves the family. Pete's plans for Las Nubes will diversify the family business and protect their economic livelihood from forces of nature such as frost and fire. Therefore, although Paul is the hero, he is not the future of Las Nubes; this responsibility belongs to Pete. Paul merely represents the outside cultural and social forces with which the family, and more specifically the patriarchs, must contend in order to survive and thrive. Through his wisdom and power, Don Pedro instrumentalizes whiteness to secure a queer future for the family. In doing so, he models for Pete a method for securing generational Brown male authority over the family.

The Big Grandpa wears a navy blue wool double-breasted blazer on this near one-hundred-degree day, khaki slacks, brown wing tips, and a white shirt pressed smooth beneath his jacket. His green jadeite coffee mug sits beside him. His right hand holds steady the polished handle of his cane. He pats the spot beside him on the shaded concrete steps, and I obey. The concrete is surprisingly cool on my bare legs. Once I am settled he begins to speak. I look up at him as he makes a sweeping motion with his arm, and I imagine he is telling me how the neighborhood, the cars, the people, all of this is different from when he grew up. I know this because of the look on his face, the look that tells me he is remembering something from long ago. I imitate his movement and say, "All of this?" He nods, "Sí."

THE *TESORO* OF BEING REAL

As in *A Walk in the Clouds*, the *anciano* in *Real Women Have Curves* plays an active yet clandestine role, for the most part, in reinforcing male power in the family. In another conventional offering of *la familia*, the film features Papa (Jorge Cervera, Jr.) as the primary breadwinner and figurehead, while Mama Doña Carmen (Lupe Ontiveros) oversees the lives of her daughters, Ana and Estela, whom she expects to find husbands and to sacrifice their aspirations for the economic livelihood of the Garcia family. Abuelo and two unnamed male cousins also reside with the family, and while the roles of the latter are minimal, in the absence of sons, the cousins serve as laborers for Mr. Garcia's lawn-maintenance business and represent the most immediate Garcia male heirs. Although Abuelo remains primarily in the background, as an *anciano* he sets in motion events that secure Ana's happiness, lead Papa to assert his authority over his family, and publicly unite the Garcia men in one cause.

Ana, a bright, self-possessed young woman, longs for self-determination. In this case, an overbearing patriarch does not hamper her dream, to attend college; instead, supportive men surround her: Papa, Abuelo, the cousins, and Ana's high school teacher Mr. Guzman. Doña Carmen, however, forecloses on her daughter's hopes, in part because she sees college as frivolous and incapable of teaching Ana the valuable skills necessary for winning and keeping a man—the most important "duty" for any daughter. Institutional, financial, and other familial considerations, such as the expectation that Ana will work full time after graduation at Estela's dressmaking business, further bar the protagonist from her educational goals. Mr. Guzman works at the institutional level to aid Ana in her plight, assisting her with college admission and financial aid applications. He also visits Ana's house to plead her case to Mr. and Mrs. Garcia, emphasizing Ana's extraordinary intellectual ability and aptitude for university studies. Carmen rejects Mr. Guzman's efforts, stating that Ana must work for the economic livelihood of the family. Although Papa would like Ana to attend school, he neither advocates for her nor mediates between his wife and daughter. Rather, he defers initially to Carmen's authority, which temporarily stops the argument, leaving Ana disappointed and frustrated.

Men operate behind the scenes, initially Mr. Guzman and later Abuelo, to help facilitate Ana's independence and self-determination while maintaining and sustaining heteropatriarchal authority. Although the two men never speak to each other, both work, on different fronts, to help Ana pursue her goal. At home, Abuelo helps to empower Ana by reinforcing her self-worth and imparting a lesson about the importance of seeking one's treasure in life. Although strong-willed and confident, Ana is also deeply insecure and unwilling to act on her desire to turn her back on or break free from her family, her mother especially. As the *anciano*, Abuelo conveys to Ana, with his ostensibly random tale about a *cueva de oro*, important messages about rebellion and the power of belief. The scene follows one involving Carmen complaining in the kitchen to a *comadre* about her unmarried daughters; outside, Ana sits eating and preparing fruit with Papa and Abuelo, two generations of men with whom she finds comfort and support. The settings and sequences are bridged

FIGURE 6. *Abuelo preparing to tell Ana about the* cueva de oro *in* Real Women Have Curves.

with a shot of two caged birds hanging on the back balcony of the house: in light of Mama's lament and Ana's feeling of captivity, the birds represent the mother's efforts to cage her daughters. Mama sees marriage and motherhood as the only life options that substantiate a woman's worth. In contrast, Abuelo as the *anciano* tells Ana she is a *tesoro*, a treasure whose value is independent of anyone. Abuelo uses the reference and occasion to tell Ana the story about the cave as a means of conveying indirectly his wisdom to his troubled granddaughter (figure 6). Papa comments that the story is *pura leyenda*, but Ana interrupts and asks, nevertheless, to hear the tale about a cave filled with gold hidden during the Mexican Revolution.

The material and historical circumstances of the *anciano*'s narrative in *Real Women Have Curves* are important for what they convey to Ana about value, adventure, and rebellion. Abuelo, who once longed to find the gold, tells Ana that he has found his true treasure in her and now wants her to find her own. The scene concludes with Ana contemplating his advice and then cuts to a shot of her aboard a city bus. Also seated on the bus are a mother and her small daughter. As the child begins to cry, her wails filling the bus, Ana puts on earphones to drown out the noise physically but also to silence symbolically that particular future for herself. Ana is caught between her mother's expectations and her longing for a life that is not defined exclusively by men. So, while it is clear that Ana understands the lessons of the story, she remains unsure how to act on the knowledge.

Abuelo also facilitates Ana's rebelliousness and provides her the space to explore her identity as an independent woman. In doing so, the *anciano* challenges his son's authority while at the same time empowering his granddaughter and paving the way for her romantic, and later sexual, relationship with Jimmy, an Anglo classmate. Ana and Abuelo conspire to orchestrate time for her to get away from the watchful eyes of their family. When Papa asks where Abuelo and Ana are going one evening as they prepare to leave the house, Abuelo looks his son in the eye and lies, telling him they are going to a movie and adding that no one should wait up for their return. Papa gives his blessing and tells the duo to have a good time, illustrating, perhaps, his own awareness of the oppressive ideas embedded in *la familia* or even his hidden desires to relinquish control over his loved ones. Having successfully escaped, the twosome part company once they reach the corner. As Ana ventures off in the night alone to meet Jimmy, Abuelo visits with friends, drinks, and listens to music at a neighborhood cantina. The ongoing ruse allows Ana to continue seeing Jimmy without her parents' knowledge for their sexual rendezvous, which contributes to Ana's growing confidence in her body and her ability to exercise control over her life.

Ana and Abuelo's relationship provides a source of freedom and empowerment for both. However, Carmen also uses the connection between the two to keep Ana in line, a point best illustrated during Mr. Guzman's second visit to the Garcia house. Mr. Guzman explains that he has used his Ivy League connections to gain Ana special consideration for admission to Columbia University. (This detail is less believable than a cave filled with gold.) She is not only accepted to Columbia but also awarded a full scholarship. Though Mr. Garcia is visibly hesitant about his daughter traveling across the country, he and Ana are nonetheless thrilled with the news—yet Mama, once again, quashes Ana's plans. This time, however, she uses Ana's relationship with her grandfather to emotionally manipulate her daughter, asking, "You don't want to abandon Abuelo, do you?" Seeing him as a pawn to emotionally blackmail her daughter into staying put, Mama plays upon the sentiments Ana has for her grandfather. What Mama does not see and Ana momentarily forgets is that her grandfather is not without some measure of power. So when Ana takes one look into Abuelo's face, she makes the decision to abandon her dream. Abuelo's hurt expression reflects his disappointment about being used to undermine his granddaughter's aspirations, not sadness at the thought of her leaving. Perhaps even more disappointing is that once again, Mr. Garcia stands by his wife's decision and sends away Mr. Guzman.

Papa and Abuelo eventually join forces to assert their power as patriarchs to help Ana. But first, with the institutional and economic issues resolved, the only remaining entrenched obstacle for Ana to overcome is her mother. After terminating her relationship with Jimmy and helping Estela save her factory, Ana finally finds the courage to act on the underlying significance of the *anciano*'s story about the lost treasure: she decides to act on her heartfelt desire to attend Columbia by approaching her father to enlist his support. Reading the expression on his daughter's face, Papa knows Ana's decision before she speaks a word and gives his blessing and consent for her to go to New York. As a condition of his support, he makes Ana responsible for telling her mother, which seems like empowerment *and* punishment, both of which reflect his authority as patriarch. Later, at dinner, Doña Carmen senses the tension. Papa tells her to "sientate, por favor" because "Ana tiene algo para decirte."[26] It is clear that everyone from the cousins to Estela has heard about Papa's decision except Carmen, who is the last to know.

Having previously undermined the authority of his son, Abuelo supports Papa's decision to "allow" Ana to attend college on the opposite coast, a move that aligns the men in the family against the matriarch, Carmen, who has made a concerted effort to deny her daughter a self-determined future. Before leaving for college, Ana asks for her mother's blessing. Carmen denies her daughter's request, choosing to stay locked in her room. The male cousins wish Ana well before she leaves for the airport with Papa and Abuelo. Papa's decision to overrule Mama results in the estrangement of mother and daughter, thus appearing to fracture the family, threaten familial integrity, and put the wisdom of patriarchal authority in question. However, the final image of the theatrical release can be read as reflecting the preservation of the home and cultural environment in the face of change: Ana confidently strides down the streets of Manhattan, which calls to mind her mother's earlier efforts to teach her daughter to "walk like a lady." On the other side of the country, far from her barrio home, Ana not only carries her mother's words and ideas with her but puts them into practice. The feel-good, girl-power ending has, in truth, been orchestrated by men. Without their intervention, her new life would not be possible, thus substantiating their authority, wisdom, and benevolence. The patriarchy maintains itself by supporting a vague, liberal feminism.

An alternate ending in the form of an epilogue that aired on HBO and that appears on the DVD version of the film confirms what the theatrical ending implies. One year later, Ana returns home to participate in her sister's fashion show and reconcile with her mother in front of Papa, the *anciano*, and the cousins who are in attendance. Her homecoming provides visual confirmation that the *anciano* and Papa have successfully kept the family intact. There is also some indication that in going away to college and becoming a more confident woman Ana has unexpectedly fulfilled her mother's desire to make herself more attractive in order to secure a husband—the gawking expression on Mr. Guzman's face as he watches Ana walk the runway indicates that he sees her very differently than before, possibly even as a love interest. The alternate ending does more to reaffirm patriarchal authority over the family and conventional women's roles, for in their wisdom and forethought, Papa and the *anciano* preserve the heterosexual nuclear family in a way that Mama and her overt marriage-and-motherhood agenda could not.

QUEER QUINCE

Quinceañera's narrative emphasis on a queer Chicano and an unmarried, pregnant, fourteen-year-old Chicana makes it the only film in this analysis that troubles the ideal image of *la familia* and its governing patriarchs. The film focuses initially on Magdalena, the daughter of an Evangelical minister who discovers in the months before her quinceañera that she is pregnant in spite of never having had intercourse. Refusing to believe his daughter's claim about her virginity being intact, Magdalena's father, Ernesto (Jesus Castanos), expels her from their home. Magdalena's narrative then merges with that of her cousin Carlos, who has been ostracized from the family by his father, Walter (Johnny Chavez), after Walter discovers that Carlos regularly cruises gay-porn websites. Tío Tomas, great-uncle to both Magdalena and Carlos, defies Ernesto's and Walter's commands by welcoming both outcasts into the space of his home. As the senior patriarch in the film, to whom the responsibility for overseeing the governance of the family has fallen, Tío Tomas, the family's *anciano*, opens a path for the papas to confront such issues as homophobia and their expectation that their daughters will dutifully fulfill prescribed, conservative roles for women to preserve family unity. Tío Tomas as an *anciano* advocates for the acceptance of Magdalena and Carlos while also safeguarding them in the hope that one day they will be welcomed back home (figure 7). In the end, the *anciano* brings the outliers back into the family, which is one of the duties associated with the figure.

The patriarchs in *Quinceañera* demonstrate that they are willing to use violence to assert their authority and to "safeguard" the family against

FIGURE 7. *Tío Tomas adding a picture of Magdalena next to the one of Carlos on his altar in* Quinceañera. *He works on multiple fronts, spiritual and familial, to advocate for the outcasts he has taken in.*

outside threats, which to them include homosexuality. Early on, well before Magdalena learns of her pregnancy, Carlos's outsider status is established after he arrives at his sister Eileen's quinceañera. While she is glad to see her brother, Eileen (Alicia Sixtos) looks around nervously and tells Carlos to leave before their father notices him. Walter does spot Carlos, and though the source of the conflict between father and son is unclear at this point, Walter yells at him, "I told you not to be around this family!" Having disowned his son, the drunken father accuses the young man of "trying to embarrass the family." He concludes his tirade by striking Carlos and telling him, "You disgust me." Other men close ranks around Walter and try to throw out Carlos, who refuses to leave. One of the men then punches Carlos and tosses him onto the sidewalk outside of the reception hall. As Carlos tries to fight his way back into the party, Tío Tomas intervenes and tells his nephew to go home. The move is a protective gesture on Tío Tomas's part to save his nephew from the violence of the men acting on Walter's orders. These men literally deny Carlos a physical place in the family by discarding him on the street.

Tío Tomas distinguishes his actions from the behavior of other men in *Quinceañera* in several other ways. Until Magdalena arrives, Tío Tomas is the only person in the family who will have contact with Carlos. He shelters his nephew in a liminal space, still with family but outside of his immediate family, and provides him a place to live, as well as understanding. Equally important is the space Tío Tomas makes for Carlos to assert his queer identity. Whether or not Walter has shared the explicit reason for Carlos's expulsion from the family, it is apparent that Tío Tomas, after living for some time with his nephew, *knows* about his sexuality even before Carlos begins an affair with James and Gary, the new Anglo landlords of Tomas's home. One night as Carlos prepares to meet Gary, with whom he has begun to have sex exclusively, Tío Tomas, with his back turned to Carlos and the audience, tells his nephew that he is pleased Carlos has someone in his life. Tomas shields Carlos from possible embarrassment by allowing him privacy as he figures his response. Carlos pauses and attempts to read his great-uncle's body language clearly, looking for any trace of judgment in his words, but finding none. The expression on Carlos's face suggests that he interprets Tomas's comment as a genuine sentiment.

Tío Tomas's approval of Carlos's "friends" demonstrates the *anciano*'s ability to accommodate and adapt to change to preserve and perhaps begin the reconfiguring of his family. However, Tío Tomas's willingness to take in Carlos and Magdalena without question could also be the result of his identification with their outsider status and his desire to effect familial change in his lifetime. In other words, Tío Tomas may well in fact be gay, along with being queer. His lifelong bachelorhood and knowledge of Carlos's relationship with Gary and James, alone, are not enough to determine his sexuality. Yet these facts, when coupled with the story of Tomas's suicide attempt when he was nine, suggest that the *anciano*'s awareness of his nephew's queerness is not the result of simple observation. One evening during dinner, Carlos has Tío Tomas recount to Magdalena the story of his failed suicide. Tomas explains that at the time he wanted to be a different person with a different life. Although he never discloses what led him to try to kill himself, we can imagine the difficulties he might have faced as a queer boy in a large Mexican family—with twenty-one siblings—in the late 1920s and early 1930s. He goes on to state that when he woke up alive in the hospital, he believed he had been given the new life for which he had longed. The "new life" that Tomas awakens to can be read as heterosexuality or, rather, the knowledge of how to perform it in order to conceal his queerness. At one point in his past, he had almost married a "very nice" girl; the courtship had been interrupted when he was forced to return home to care for his sick mother. Tío Tomas attempts to safeguard Carlos and Magdalena so that they may live their lives out in the open and not be compelled to make desperate or fatal choices.

Prior to Carlos's taking up residence at the *anciano*'s house, his life is defined by a series of bad choices: he vacillates between the familiar bandido and Latin lover stereotypes. But during his time with Tío Tomas, Carlos transforms from an angry petty thief to a responsible, thoughtful, caring nephew and cousin. He contributes to the household income and helps Tío Tomas around the house, at one point even offering to assist his tío in the making of *champurrado* to sell. After Magdalena arrives, Carlos eventually helps her, too. With the exception of Tío Tomas, Carlos is the only one who believes in Magdalena's virgin pregnancy; he takes her to the library and teaches her how to look up information about her unusual circumstance on the internet. When Magdalena's clothes no longer fit and she has no money to buy maternity clothes, Carlos gives her his new shirt to wear. He facilitates her integration into life at Tío Tomas's house and encourages the patriarch to tell her the family stories and history, presumably to take her mind off her estrangement from her parents. Carlos also accepts the queerness of his uncle's home. Floral patterns are scattered throughout his home, and delicate decorative plates adorn the walls. Similarly, his outdoor garden is lined with hanging beads and other conventionally feminine embellishments such as cherubs and colored-crystal picture frames. Though none of these make him gay, they do make him queer within a family where men perform hypermasculinity through violence and domination. Tío Tomas nurtures and cares for Carlos and Magdalena, and, equally importantly, they let him. Over time, the three solidify the bonds of their own outcast family and adjust to their new lives.

Eventually external forces encroach on this haven, leaving the future of this family of exiles uncertain. The cultural and social space within the home collapses after Tío Tomas's eviction by Gary's partner, James, who has discovered his lover's affair with Carlos. In the midst of this upheaval, Carlos attempts to assume responsibility for the future of his surrogate family after he is fired from his job at the car wash for vandalizing James's vehicle in retaliation for turning the family out of their home. As Magdalena tends to the wounds Carlos has received while fleeing the car wash, Tío Tomas overhears a conversation between the two cousins. Carlos offers to serve as a father to Magdalena's child and divulges his plan to find a well-paying job so she can continue to go to school and the three can stay together. While pleased with his nephew's pledge, the thought of leaving his beloved home proves too much for Tío Tomas, and he dies of a broken heart. Tío Tomas, though, dies knowing that Carlos and Magdalena will continue to care for and protect one another.

Tío Tomas's death, while tragic, sets the stage for the surviving patriarchs' critical self-reflection and the cousins' reentry into the family. At the funeral, Carlos steps forward to fill the void left by the *anciano*, a responsibility for which he has been prepared. Carlos and Magdalena have been schooled in the family history, and they alone carry the legacy of Tío Tomas's life, stories, and love. Eulogizing Tío Tomas at his graveside, Carlos refers to the *anciano* as a saint who "loved everyone and judged no one," a pronouncement that shames both papas and further exposes their bigotry and intolerance. While Tomas's death and Carlos's loving memorial help bring the family together, it is the doctor's confirmation that Magdalena has conceived without intercourse that ultimately forces Ernesto to reexamine his own faith and his decision to ostracize his daughter. After the funeral, Ernesto asks for Magdalena's forgiveness, which she immediately grants. Calling to mind the safe space Don Pedro creates for Victoria, with his daughter safely locked in his embrace, Papa promises the young virgin mother-to-be, "Aqui adelante todo sera diferente."[27] Tío Tomas, as an *anciano*, and Carlos, as the figurative son, have transformed Ernesto, the father, and secured his place, for the time being, as the spiritual and familial patriarch.

In the end, *both* Magdalena and Carlos are welcomed back into the family through a formal religious ceremony presided over by Ernesto (figure 8). Carlos, serving as Magdalena's quinceañera escort, and Magdalena, dressed in white and draped in a blue shawl with crystals on it that calls to mind the mantle of the Virgin Mary, stand before a male trinity—Ernesto, a picture of Tío Tomas, and God—to receive the sanction of the patriarchs and the community gathered in celebration of Magdalena's passage into womanhood. Carlos and Magdalena, together, in terms of their positioning and the ritual's emphasis, represent the future of the family. As an emerging queer papa, Carlos will have the power, as did Tío Tomas before him, not only to shelter but also to advocate for those who challenge established cultural and social mores, thus replacing one particular kind of patriarch with another. While his ability to serve in this capacity seems hopeful, Magdalena's future appears bleak. She is redeemed from her status as a whore only when her virginity is confirmed. Ultimately, then, her impregnation without intercourse solidifies the virgin/whore dichotomy for at least another generation of women.

What appears to be the most progressive offering of *la familia* is in fact the most conservative, reinforcing Anglo superiority and domination. The gentrification and changing demographics of the neighborhood mean that before long, Ernesto and his family will be priced out of their home and their cultural community displaced. Not coincidentally, Mexi-

FIGURE 8. *Magdalena and Carlos walk down the aisle at her quinceañera, signaling their return to the family.*

can and Mexican American men are imbued with a small measure of authority at the exact moment they are to be rendered powerless, ineffective, and erased from the landscape. Ernesto's promise, therefore, is a lie. *Nada sera diferente*,[28] not for Magdalena, and certainly not for the representation of Brown men in film. *Quinceañera*, like its historical predecessors, reaffirms the mainstream value of whiteness at the expense of Brown families.

Over the past two and a half decades, as Nava anticipated, a number of films representing different iterations of Chicanx families have appeared, including, in addition to the three just discussed, *Fools Rush In* (1997), *Price of Glory* (2000), *Tortilla Soup* (2001), *La Mission* (2009), *Machete* (2010), *Our Family Wedding* (2010), *From Prada to Nada* (2011), and more recently *Coco* (2017). This current crop of films demonstrates some diversity in the construction of Mexican American families vis-à-vis, for example, familial integrity, class, and kinship: the mother is absent in *La Mission*; the titular hero of *Machete* loses his wife and daughter; the Ramírez family of *Our Family Wedding* is comfortably upper middle class; and the orphaned Dominguez sisters, raised in lavish wealth, experience a drastic lifestyle change after taking up residence with their working-class aunt in *From Prada to Nada*. While each of these films privileges heteropatriarchy, most move away from romantic ideas about the heterosexual nuclear family. Although cinematic constructions of

Latinxs are as much a fantasy as other unenlightened racial tropes, such as the magical Negro or the wise sachem, the *anciano* represents an important, albeit problematic, means for rethinking the roles and authority of Mexican and Mexican American men both socially and culturally. At the same time, the future of these families remains precarious.

The Big Grandpa gently touches my shoulder, which tells me I should pay attention. I hear the word "Saltillo" and a name I recognize from school, Pancho Villa, the man with the guns and big hat. With certainty, I know Big Grandpa is telling me about his days with Villa. How they rode together, shooting bad men and singing songs. I try to picture my grandfather young, in a white shirt, black cowboy boots, and a big hat, astride a horse. He is telling me that they were friends, but that he had to leave Villa and his men to make a life for himself in this neighborhood, in this house on Kiam Avenue, so that we might sit together and he could gift me with stories.

PERSONAL NARRATIVE

"NO, I AM YOUR FATHER"

Located at 2922 South Shepherd Drive in Houston, Texas, the Alabama Theatre demonstrated the appropriate amount of architectural restraint for a late-Depression–era building, distinct but not overly ornamental. Built in 1939, the 739-seat suburban movie house, a landmark set between two of the city's most well-known communities—the well-heeled River Oaks and Rice University neighborhoods—was a mix of Art Deco and Streamline Moderne styles: its smooth-edged geometric stucco exterior made striking by curved panels on the façade arranged in an ombre pattern above the marquee, inlaid terrazzo-designed yellow spirals at the entrance, and murals depicting scenes reminiscent of Dionysus and the maenads framing the proscenium. The Alabama opened on 2 November 1939 with *Man About Town*, a musical comedy directed by Mark Sandrich and starring Jack Benny, Dorothy Lamour, and Edward Arnold.[1] A featured venue for roadshow pictures, over the next forty-four years the theatre would weave its way into the fabric of the city, enjoying popularity among affluent moviegoers until its decline in the late 1970s.[2] *Mortuary*, a low-budget slasher-meets-would-be-detective film featuring Mary Beth McDonough (best known for her role as Erin on the television show *The Waltons*) and beloved Texas native Bill Paxton, was the last film shown at the Alabama before it closed in 1983.[3] But the week before Memorial Day in 1980, people excitedly trading theories about plot points and characters waited in line, sometimes sitting on the sidewalk all day, cordoned off behind low-slung fiber rope, for a chance to see the much-anticipated sequel to George Lucas's *Star Wars* (1977) (figure 9).

By mid-August, the crowd no longer snaked around the building. Only a handful of people turned up for each showing of *The Empire Strikes*

FIGURE 9. *Fans waiting in line outside the Alabama Theatre to see the film* The Empire Strikes Back. *1980. Photo: Ben DeSoto, © Houston Chronicle / Houston Post files.*

Back (1980), which had been the talk of the summer since its premiere on 21 May. On one Saturday morning when my father and I arrived, the parking lot was practically empty. He had chosen the theatre—situated more than thirty minutes from our home—carefully, for its single-screen offering presented the greatest chance of succeeding in the day's objective. Between us on the bench seat of my father's yellow-and-white 1972 Chevrolet Cheyenne truck was a metal cooler filled with sodas, cotto salami sandwiches, and other snacks meant to sustain us for what we hoped would be a movie marathon. Our plan to watch the film three or four times hinged on receiving permission to enter and exit throughout the day so we could stretch our legs and grab a bite to eat in between showings. Studying my father's demeanor as we pulled into the lot and parked, I tried to match mine to his, focused and deliberate. As he strode toward the theatre, I caught a glimpse of the US Marine Corps sergeant he had been, his stride twice the length of mine. I struggled to keep up.

Stepping onto the curb, my father extended his arm out by his waist, the thick fingers on his hand spread wide, telling me to stop, that he would proceed to the box office alone. The glass-enclosed space housed a teenager casually flipping through a magazine. My father approached and stooped slightly to speak into a slotted brass disc that looked like a shower drain. While he spoke to the theatre employee, I stared at my feet, stuck in place. I did not want to watch my father plead our case to a blond male teen. Then the worry took hold. If we were not allowed to enter and exit without having to pay each time, something I knew we could not afford, then I would have to soak up every possible detail. There was no way of knowing when and if I would see the movie again. If he said yes, it meant that at two-hour-and-seven-minute intervals, I would live inside the *Star Wars* universe, where the Force and lightsabers are real, where farm boys become heroes, and where princesses wield blasters. After what felt like an eternity, I looked up just as the young man glanced in my direction. His shrug and my father's over-the-shoulder smile told me we were there for the day.

Inside the cool and quiet lobby, I stood reverently trying to take in the velvet, brass, and marble. I did not see the creep of shabbiness, only the grandeur. I eyed the stairs to the balcony. A sign perched on the landing told me it was closed. Before disappointment took root, my father approached holding out his hand and together we passed through a set of double doors into the darkness of the grand theatre. The low ceiling of the overhead balcony pressed down on us until we emerged into the open auditorium. We made our way down the aisle judging our distance from the screen in an effort to find the perfect seats. We settled on two directly beneath the illuminated central ceiling medallion. From our spot approximately halfway back from the screen, we saw that the theatre held us and a few others.

Three years earlier, after we had waited six hours for seats at the Galleria cinema for the midnight showing of *Star Wars* (1977), the theatre had been so crowded that my family, including my parents and brother, was lucky to find two pairs of open spots one row apart. I had sat next to my mother, who slept her way through intergalactic battles delivered in Dolby stereo sound that rattled my ribs. Throughout the film, I had turned around in my seat, hoping to catch my father's eye to confirm the magnificence of the spectacle before us. What I saw instead was a man transformed into what could only be described as a younger version of himself, one given over to the power of Lucas's magic. We were the only ones in our family to be caught in the movie's spell. Filmmaker Alex Rivera describes seeing "*Star Wars* at a drive-in as a kid in upstate New York" as a "near religious experience" (Miranda). For me, it was that and more. The film was a manifestation of Obi-Wan's description of the Force: "It surrounds us, penetrates us, and binds the galaxy together" (*Star Wars: Episode IV*). *Star Wars* also fortified the already strong relationship between my father and me. And now we had spent the last months, weeks, hours in anticipation of the sequel.

At our first viewing of *The Empire Strikes Back*, as the lights dimmed seconds before the John Williams score filled the theatre and the iconic narrative crawl stretched its way toward the horizon, I saw my father remove something from his breast pocket and carefully balance it on his knee. Then the symphony of sound crashed into the theatre and I was immediately lost in ice, tauntauns, and the landscapes of Hoth. Yoda's lessons on Dagobah, Lando's betrayal, Han Solo's swagger before being frozen in carbonite, and of course Darth Vader's vicious attempt to corrupt Luke swirled around in my head as I struggled to take it all in, especially Vader's lie. He could not be Luke's father. Too soon, the movie ended and the house lights brightened as the closing credits scrolled before us. Without exchanging a word, we headed toward the doors. Blinking into the sunlight as we exited the theatre, I turned to face my father: "Vader's lying, right? He just has to be." The last part sounded desperate, pleading.

My father's face softened: "Let's talk about it when we get to the truck." Uncertain what would change in the seventy-five steps across the parking lot, I nevertheless complied. The Alabama Theatre sign reached high into the sky like a radio tower, and we sat in its shadow. Despite the sliver of shade, sweat pooled instantaneously on the vinyl beneath me. My father rested his hands on the steering wheel, and I looked at him with anticipation, waiting for him to confirm or at the very least explain how and why Vader lied. Instead, he said, "I don't know."

"It doesn't make any sense," I complained. "He was trying to turn Luke, to get him to doubt his friends, right?"

My father looked at me sympathetically before reaching into his pocket and pulling out a small tape recorder. Holding it up for me to see, he offered, "Let's listen to it again." I recognized the device but did not quite comprehend where it came from and how it had come into his possession. Sensing my puzzlement, he explained that he had borrowed it from work to record the movie in case we were not allowed to stay for the day and that the recorder had to be returned on Monday. He began pushing buttons on the sleek silver machine. The reels on the cassette squealed in protest as he rewound, stopped, and pressed Play several times, searching for the scene in question. With only the musical score and dialogue for clues, when we heard "Impressive, most impressive," he knew we were close. We identified the moment that Vader cut off Luke's hand and held our breath as we listened to the film's biggest reveal, Vader's oft-misquoted line "No. I am your father."[4] The strains of "Darth Vader's Theme" followed this pronouncement. I concentrated so hard on hearing what we were searching for that I did not stop to think about the forethought it took for my father to sign out what was then the extravagantly expensive piece of technology, and the willing financial risk he assumed if anything were to happen to the delicate machine. All of this my father did to allow us to hold on to a tangible piece of the film, if only for an extra day.

Over snacks and Shastas for the next thirty minutes, we listened to lightsabers clash and the music swell. As my father rolled back the tape again and again, I wanted to believe that Vader was lying to Luke. I wanted to believe that he was a pawn of the Emperor being used to gain control of Luke as he grew into his power. I refused to believe Vader's words. My father and I tried to recall other moments in the film: Luke's battle with Vader in the cave; Luke striking off Vader's head, his iconic mask rolling on the floor and exploding to reveal Luke's face beneath. Surely that meant something, but what? The sounds and the music provided hints, though we were unsure how the pieces fit together. As we prepared to return to the theatre, we formulated a plan. We would be detectives, searching for clues, scouring scenes and taking note of any dialogue, gesture, or plot point that might provide insight or bring us closer to the real meaning behind Vader's words and his plan.

We repeated the exercise in the parking lot three more times before finally heading home for the day. At thirteen, I had become a student of film. Motivated by a desire to disprove the villain's lie, I saw film differently, recognizing both its parts and the whole and the relationship between the two. Filtering through the film and matching it with scenes from *Star Wars: Episode IV—A New Hope*, I began to understand the nuance of dialogue and the slippage of meaning, though I could not have put it into words. After the fourth screening, I knew Vader was telling the truth. What Yoda described as Luke's "failure in the cave" was not an error because Luke had activated his lightsaber first, becoming an aggressor to Vader. He failed because he did not understand the meaning of facing himself. I was sure I knew. We packed up the cooler and, with the windows down, headed into the muggy Houston night, but not before my father pressed Play on the recorder so we could listen one more time to the sounds of a galaxy far, far away.

Forty years later, I still cannot watch *The Empire Strikes Back* without thinking about the details of that day. The specific parts—the Alabama, our movie marathon, the audio recording, my nascent film analysis, and my dad—have all become intertwined into a whole experience. When I recount the story to others, they seem amazed and inevitably say something along the lines of "You must have had the best father in the world." They are correct. I did, though my brother had a more severe variation of the same man. My version of our father was always in the bleachers at volleyball or softball games. He taught me to fish, handle firearms, work on cars, and troubleshoot and perform home repairs. He took pride in my academic accomplishments and always encouraged me to pursue my intellectual interests, even when he did not agree with them.[5] At times, he could be demanding and distant, but these qualities were not enough to dissuade me from the belief that he was absolutely the greatest. The love we had for movies, which was ours alone, only strengthened my conviction.

In all our cinematic adventures of the 1980s, from *E.T. the Extra-Terrestrial* (1982) and *Blade Runner* (1982) to *Ghostbusters* (1984) and *Dune* (1984), we never felt alienated from the characters or the stories—or rather, I did not. I knew I liked science fiction, fantasy, and action films, and I never thought about the people and places that were and were not depicted in these genres. Movies were about great stories, not about representation. Only years later would I recognize the racial and cultural politics of American cinema history, most especially the whitewashing of my beloved intergalactic space opera. My thinking around the original film has changed over time. With its diagonal, horizontal, and barn-door wipes, to name a few devices used, the film draws from classical Hollywood films. From the initial musical overture to the structure of the film to the walk-out music, *Star Wars* saga movies have all the elements of a roadshow picture. Whereas Alex Rivera has "come to see the story of Luke Skywalker as the story of a migrant," I see the film as an absent-father story (and the tale of a young man's desire to know or reconcile with the same) wrapped in a frontier narrative (Miranda). Drawing on familiar visual and narrative conventions, including dusty outposts, cantina ruffians, and bounty hunters, *Star Wars* plays out like a space western. The would-be hero comes from a family of farmers on a planet populated by nomadic indigenous groups—the Jawas, who trade with the settlers, and the Tusken Raiders, who pose a violent threat to the farming population—both clearly stand-ins for American Indians. The film's emphasis on Luke's rugged individualism, particularly in his pursuit and realization of his status as a champion of the rebellion, is in the service of what Charles Ramírez Berg identifies as the cinematic status quo. And while Oscar Isaac (Guatemalan-Cuban) as Poe Dameron and Lupita Nyong'o (Kenyan-Mexican) as Maz Kanata in *Star Wars* episodes VII, VIII, and IX (2015; 2017; 2019) and Diego Luna (Mexican) as Captain Cassian Andor in *Rogue One: A Star Wars Story* (2016) represent recent notable Latinx acting additions to the Star Wars universe, Jimmy Smits, playing

Bail Organa, was the first Latinx actor in the Skywalker saga. His role as the adoptive father of Princess Leia Organa (Carrie Fisher), Luke's twin from whom he was separated at birth, makes Bail one of the most significant fathers in the nonology, responsible, in part, for raising a strong, independent, Force-inclined daughter who eventually, after serving as a diplomat and a fighter, becomes a general of the rebel fleet.

During our peak movie-going years (1977–1986), never once did my father and I see a family on-screen that looked like ours, one that was precariously middle class-ish, much less one that was at the center of a summer blockbuster or mainstream film. I try to imagine what it would have been like as a child to have known that Leia's father was a Brown man. I am not sure that it would have impacted how I felt about film or strengthened the bond with my own father. I do know that a new generation of children is growing up with Miles Morales in *Spider-Man: Into the Spider-Verse* (2018), Lin-Manuel Miranda in *Mary Poppins Returns* (2018), and Michael Peña in everything from *Ant-Man* (2015) and *Ant-Man and the Wasp* (2018) to *A Wrinkle in Time* (2018) and *Dora and the Lost City of Gold* (2019), the last film based on the animated television series featuring a dark-skinned Latinx little-girl adventurer in the lead, which ran for fourteen years (2000–2014). They will know a cinematic world in which they are not only visibly present but also more than comical sidekicks or ominous props in the mise-en-scène.

Sitting in the darkness of the theatre moments before a movie begins, I remember the little girl that I was, filled with anticipation and wonder, excited to look for clues that might unlock a mystery. I am not her; too much has happened since. Still, the seeds of what she discovered that summer day have taken root. Having learned the language of film, the conventions of genre, and familiar plots, I am rarely surprised by a movie character's actions or a narrative outcome. When I share this with students, they often lament, "Doesn't that ruin it—the whole experience?" They insist that the purpose of movies is to lose oneself in the visual stories. I tell them nothing has been spoiled as a result of my knowledge, and not everyone's enjoyment is derived from the ceding of self. Instead, movies are where I find myself over and again, reminding me of where it all started.

LITERATURE

FATHERS AND RACIALIZED MASCULINITIES IN LUIS ALBERTO URREA'S *IN SEARCH OF SNOW*

Pre-script: The chapter that follows represents another beginning for this book. It started as a conference paper more than twenty years ago. After my presentation, a conference organizer, who also happened to be an editor, asked me to submit the work to her peer-reviewed journal. But I did not have confidence in the sparse critical frame I had given the analysis, so the paper sat on a disc and then in a file waiting for me to revisit it. I always liked In Search of Snow *and my close reading of it and fully intended to develop it into a chapter or an article. The years rolled by, and then, in 2019, I saw a call for a journal special issue that looked like it had been written exactly for me and my analysis of racialized masculinities in Urrea's novel. Sometimes slow works that way. Given the article word limit, some of what I wanted to say about the work and its characters did not make it into the final piece. The opportunities to revisit and expand my ideas were too great to resist. So I gave in, enthusiastically.*

> A man to be a man is to live a lie, I'm told. The lie of
> manhood, the mask, the caricature. A man to be a man
> must live the truth of man-being, the power of it. Beyond
> the madness, into the manness.
> Luis J. Rodríguez, "On Macho"

While cleaning the men's room toilets of a broken down, nearly forgotten Texaco gas station in the middle of the Arizona desert, the protagonist of Luis Alberto Urrea's first novel, *In Search of Snow* (1994), Mike McGurk, scrawls on a stall door, "BEING A MAN MAKES ME FEEL ABOUT 100% FOOLISH" (16). The proclamation represents both a confession and a critique of masculine performance and expression, especially when placed alongside other graffiti, including boasts, propositions, and insults—all dealing with sex or sexuality—and drawings of male and female anatomy. Set against the backdrop of post–World War II America in the US Southwest, the narrative initially centers on Mike and his father, Wallace "Turk" McGurk, a white, middle-aged, bigoted, blue-collar gas station owner and monument to hypermasculinity and self-consciously performative masculinity.[1] Urrea uses this father-son relationship to question racialized masculinities derived from sources such as books, films, comics, and sports and the impact of these performances on the lives of these two men.

As an additional dimension, through his depiction of the entangled cultural and racial histories of the people in the US Southwest, Urrea draws attention to the differences among and between the Latinx men who reside there. At the intersection of literary, masculinity, Mexican American, and Indigenous studies, this chapter focuses on how each of the main male characters in the novel, Mike McGurk, Bobo García, and Ramses Castro, struggles with "being a man" to illustrate that the legacy of particular forms of masculinity oppresses, with equal force, a generation of racially diverse Latinx men, who, in this trio, self-identify as white, Mexican, and Apache. At the center of this triad lies another father-son relationship, between Ramses's grandfather, Delbert Sneezy (an Apache senior), and Turk, whose choices—and behaviors—bring the Latinx men into the same orbit and influence their racialized performances of masculinity.[2]

While much critical attention has been paid to Urrea's other works, such as *Across the Wire* (1993), *Nobody's Son* (1998), *The Devil's Highway* (2004), *The Hummingbird's Daughter* (2005), and *Into the Beautiful North* (2009), Markus Heide's "Learning from Fossils: Transcultural Space in Luis Alberto Urrea's *In Search of Snow*" (2002) and Lee Bebout's "Troubling White Benevolence: Four Takes on a Scene from *Giant*" (2011) represent some of the only criticism done on the author's first novel, in which fathers and sons figure prominently.[3] Although neither Heide nor Bebout focus directly on masculinities, the section in the latter's work concerning Mike's racialization serves as a critically important point in identifying the cultural and social influences that most impact Mike's performance of "white" masculinity.[4] But to speak of masculinity is to recognize it as both nebulous and highly specific, based on social, economic, and cultural factors, among others. As Jack Halberstam asserts,

> Masculinity in this society inevitably conjures up notions of power and legitimacy and privilege; it often symbolically refers to the power of the state and to uneven distribution of wealth. Masculinity seems to extend outward into patriarchy and inward into the family; masculinity represents the power of inheritance, the consequences of the traffic in women, and the promise of social privilege. (2)

All of these instantiations of male power are rooted in white heterosexuality. The farther one moves away from this idealized locus of power, the greater the disenfranchisement from privilege and the protections it offers.

In Search of Snow centers white masculinity to underscore the racial dynamics at the heart of the novel and, at the same time, to demonstrate and dismantle the myths fundamental to Turk's performance. The constructed-ness of masculinity, especially regarding white men, has been widely discussed and analyzed. Still, as Michael Kimmel asserts in *Manhood in America* (2012),

> Manhood means different things at different times to different people. Some cultures encourage a manly stoicism we might find familiar. Many men in many cultures seem preoccupied with demonstrating sexual prowess. But some cultures prescribe a more relaxed definition of masculinity, a more emotional and familial man. Nor are all American men alike. What it means to be a man in America depends heavily on one's class, race, ethnicity, age, sexuality, region of the country. To acknowledge these differences among men, we must speak of *masculinities*. (4)

The Latinx masculinities analyzed in this chapter involve working-class heterosexual men (two of whom are World War II veterans who served in different theatres) in their late twenties living in Arizona. On occasion, the masculinity enacted by each of these men is "emotional" or "familial," but it is rarely "relaxed." Rather, their masculinities are highly self-conscious and often fraught efforts informed by familial and cultural determinants. As Todd W. Reeser observes, "Gender and race are so often connected and dependent on each other that it is difficult to talk about one without talking about the other" (144). Following Turk's death, the attention shifts to the formulation of masculinities as expressed by Mike,

Bobo, and Ramses. All three men, albeit only two knowingly, are of Mexican descent, yet each opposes this ethno-racial category, particularly as it would inform aspects of his performance as a man. However, all three express their masculinity, reluctantly or with zeal, through violence, domination, heterosexuality, and negative emotions.

Over the past twenty-five years, a body of critical scholarship about Latinx masculinity focusing on many of the same issues has been produced in fields ranging from sociology and psychology to film and gender studies. This foundational work opened avenues for critical inquiry into Latinx manhood and masculinity that illustrate the cultural, generational, and sociological divisions in masculinist performances. In a necessary critical turn, however, a group of Latinx writers and scholars scrutinize the complex formulations of their *own* masculinities through the personal narratives and essays that appear in Ray Gonzalez's edited collection *Muy Macho: Latino Men Confront Their Manhood* (1996). "To have Latino men," as Gonzalez states, "write about their fathers, sexuality, and the cult of silence between men is a literary task taking place for the first time" (xiii). Notably, Urrea contributed a piece titled "Whores" to the collection. In it, he documents and reflects on the sexual violence against men and women embedded in Mexican masculinity. Openly discussing issues of race, class, gender expression, and sexual orientation, as many of the authors do in *Muy Macho*, Gonzalez argues, serves to "enlarge the dialogue and communicate a more accurate portrait of American masculinity" (xvi). At times, however, some of the contributors replicate the toxic aspects of masculinity that the collection is meant to critique. Put simply, not all express enlightened views. These authors reinforce rather than dismantle very narrow views of heterosexual Latinx masculinity. In his review of *Muy Macho*, "Confronting or Confounding Masculinities?" (1999), David Manuel Hernández recognizes the important work of the collection yet ultimately remains dissatisfied with the results, stating that Gonzalez "has pulled together a diverse set of contributions in terms of the backgrounds of the writers, but this diversity does not translate into the complexity of gender discourse" (210). The collection is much more of an explanation or reflection than the "confrontation" promised in the book's title. Still, the authors and critics notably initiate candid conversations about their experiences with and expressions of masculinity. These are the same issues—violence, sex, belonging, and relationships—that often appear in their work, including Urrea's *In Search of Snow*.

In addition to facing many of the problems that Latinx and Chicanx men have in their masculine performances, Indigenous men must also contend with colonial histories of genocide, relocation, removal, and termination. In American Indian, First Nations, and Indigenous studies, Sam McKegney's collection *Masculindians: Conversations about Indigenous Manhood* (2014) and Robert Alexander Innes and Kim Anderson's collection *Indigenous Men and Masculinities: Legacies, Identities, Regeneration* (2015) engage directly with the legacy of settler colonial violence on Indigenous men through popular culture forms, including film, television, and other media, as well as offering ways to rethink masculinities in Indigenous contexts. Too often, Indigenous men and their expressions of masculinity are caught between "performing colonial heteropatriarchy and resisting it" (Hokowhitu 83). An important aspect of the work done by the scholars in these collections includes analysis of how Indigenous men internalize and enact masculinities formed in the aftermath of colonization that "limit Indigenous men to heteropatriarchal, hypermasculine, stoical, staunch, and violent discursive formations[,] often channeling them into destructive behaviors" (Hokowhitu 94).[5] Ramses Castro, as discussed later in the chapter, embodies and performs the colonial forms of masculinity in acts of violence against himself (though he would not see it as such) and others. Still, if the image of the aggressive warrior, for example, was created to justify and motivate colonial violence against Indigenous people (and it most certainly was), then the enactment of this posture continues that violence at the expense of Native lives and lifeways:

> Indigenous men are more often viewed as victimizers, not as victims; as protectors rather than those who need protection; or as supporters, but not ones who need support. We see this resulting from the hegemonic masculinity that is perpetrated through white supremacist patriarchy. . . . These perceptions are so pervasive, it is next to impossible for Indigenous men not to be exposed to them. As a result of the colonization of their lands, minds, and bodies, many Indigenous men not only come to accept these perceptions but they also come to internalize them. (Innes and Anderson 9–10)

These views reinforce white heterosexual masculinity, which depends on opposition to sustain itself. As such, Native men become complicit in their own subjugation through the adoption of violent or aggressive masculinities.

The relational dynamics of the masculinities that form the basis for this chapter's analysis are predicated on the actions of Turk McGurk, who brings Mike McGurk, Bobo García, and Ramses Castro into proximity and establishes the connections among the three men. White, Latinx, and Indigenous masculinities, though distinct, when placed in what Reeser calls in *Masculinities in Theory* (2010) a "racialized triangle," exert social and cultural influence on each other (208). While Mike is the hub in this network of masculinities, Bobo takes on the role of mediator between him and Ramses, whose rivalry stretches back to the time they were children. Over time, Mike and Bobo align against Ramses, not out of racial hatred but in response to his emotional instability and the physical threat he poses to them and their freedom.

Turk resides at the center of the conflicts in the novel, or at the very least has a hand in all of them. From sandlot fights to combat in World War I to bare-knuckle brawling, Turk's entire life and death are characterized by violence. Whereas fighting was a means of self-defense when he was a child, following the Great War McGurk uses violence to fortify his masculinity, particularly in the wake of his wife's death, and as a form of capital in an effort to achieve economic prosperity by becoming a business owner.[6] "Wartime victories," as Kimmel asserts, "had allowed a generation of men to rescue a threatened sense of manhood, and the expanding peacetime economy augured well for economic success" (139). But when a rumored federal highway project that would have sent traffic in his direction and ensured his financial prosperity fails to materialize, Turk is left with a hefty mortgage for property in an isolated desert location. In the absence of economic success, he invests, or rather, reinvests, in an alternate endeavor, a masculinity rooted in racist, sexist, and homophobic rhetoric, in an effort to assert, or reclaim, his manhood. After all, he had success fulfilling this role during the war, and not much success anywhere else in his life. During the interwar period in the US, "[m]asculinity could be observed," according to Kimmel, "in specific traits and attitudes, specific behaviors and perspectives. If men expressed these attitudes, traits, and behaviors, they could be certain that they were 'real' men, regardless of their performance in the workplace" (150). Instead of deriving them from an internal source, Turk draws his attitudes about masculinity from comic books such as "Two-Fisted Tales" ("made by men for manly men"), *Three Mesquiteer* western films, canonical American and British fiction, stories of frontier heroes in the vein of James Fenimore Cooper's Natty Bumppo, and the extralegal sport of bare-knuckle fighting. These sources inform his efforts to recoup his manhood and perform it for his son, Mike.

Over time, Turk, the son of an alcoholic, becomes an exaggeration of heterosexual white masculinity, one that he pieced together from various sources and that breaks down over time. Elwood Watson and Marc E. Shaw assert that the nature of masculine performance is dynamic: "Masculinity is not a solid, immovable construction. An individual does not guard one definitive gender position: from moment to moment, forces redictate, replace, and reimagine its reconstructing" (1). Turk, however, does in fact guard one definitive position, so much so that his static performance crosses over into parody. This does not mean Turk is without self-awareness. He knows his performances are an insufferable sham, a point made evident when he tells Mike, "I *am* a royal pain in the ass!" (*In Search of Snow* 88). At this stage, the senior McGurk has devoted his life to this particular practice and it is, in his own view, too late to change. His anger and violence define him entirely.

Interactions with his father figure, Delbert Sneezy, provide Turk additional opportunities to perform his self-conscious brand of masculinity. In their relationship, Delbert, an Apache, and Turk each "play" the role of an adversary—Delbert's "Indian" to Turk's "cowboy." Each exudes a fair amount of apparent disdain for the other. Underpinning this performance is a surrogate familial bond that was put in place after Turk's father, Carroll, died and Delbert assumed responsibility for the young Turk for a short time.[7] Turk is unwilling to compromise his hypermasculine performance by showing his gratitude to and appreciation for Delbert; instead, he conveys his sentiments toward Delbert through insults and feigned conflict, using imitations of violence as an avenue to show affection. When Delbert arrives at Turk's station, the balding Turk tells him, "Look, Grandpa—there are no women here for you to carry off and molest. . . . And there are no children here for you to slaughter" (31). Rather than passively accept Turk's ignorant bigotry and outright racism, Delbert responds in kind: "Must've been some Sioux boys, yeah? . . . They come through here already, looks like. Scalped you pretty good. Took your hair up north to hang on the lodge pole" (31). Their relationship is not based on subjugation or unequal power relations. The irreverent performance they enact "had developed by unspoken mutual consent" (33). Instead of being assigned or written into this role by Turk, Delbert understands Turk's limitations and *chooses* to interact with him in this way. In spite of all their posturing, the real affinity and affection these two have and feel for each other is clearly evident, thus revealing their behaviors as self-aware performances of racialized masculinities.

Initially, Mike seems complicit in Turk's brand of hypermasculinity and at times even enables it. Raised by an aging bare-knuckled brawler and "self-proclaimed hero of trench warfare" who is foulmouthed and fond of fart wars, Mike became accustomed to Turk's "diatribes against every race and ethnic group that didn't have the good fortune to be a McGurk" (7, 11). Throughout Mike's life, Turk takes measures to ensure Mike's adoption of "manhood" rooted in whiteness, along with its attendant power and privileges. Mike sees his father's relentless efforts for what they are: "Mike had watched Wallace perform Turk continually, from year to year, adding to it as he had added rooms to the gas station" (23). Nevertheless, the elder McGurk constantly polices Mike's behavior because he is worried his son might be queer, or "airy-fairy," Turk's favorite term to disparage anyone who does not perform heterosexual masculinity according to his standards.[8] Turk's homophobia stems from his own anxiety about being an inadequate father who did not demonstrate for his son the proper attitudes and ideas associated with "real men." These concerns align with the sentiments of the time: "If a man failed to express these attitudes, traits, and behaviors, he was in danger of becoming a homosexual" (Kimmel 150). Since he felt inadequate as a masculine figure during Mike's childhood, Turk had attempted to instill a particular view of "manhood" by immersing his son in tales of adventure, settler colonialism, and rugged individualism, such as those found in *The Jungle Book* and *Tarzan* (*In Search of Snow* 26).

Books become a significant source for Turk's performances of masculinity, none more so than Mark Twain's *Life on the Mississippi* (1883). The memoir, which recounts Twain's training as a steamboat pilot prior to the Civil War, is filled with adventure and artifice. Turk allows himself to enjoy performing scenes from the novel as he reads to his son: "Turk couldn't help himself. Three or four sentences into the reading, a bizarre light came into his eyes, and he rose from the bed and began to act out the roles. The more scabrous and outrageous the scene, the more Turk emoted" (26). Of these readings and enactments, Turk and Mike revel in what they both identify as "the fight," which Turk performs "with one fist raised over his head" and a slight shuffle (26, 27). Their shared enjoyment of this ritualized performance represents one of the few connections Turk and Mike have to a source script and to each other. Over time, though, "Turk thought it improper for a man to read to his son anymore" (28). Turk allows his views of masculine behavior to break his bond with Mike. And when Turk replaces bedtime reading with "fart wars," he reconfigures their relationship as conflict and/or competition.

Their status as veterans becomes an additional way for Turk to affirm his, along with Mike's, masculinity. These efforts only further isolate Mike and belittle his wartime experience. For instance, when Mike returns from World War II tight-lipped and ashamed to tell his father he killed no one while stationed in North Africa, Turk muses openly about Mike's silence on the issue. In a feeble attempt to reestablish a connection with his son through some shared experience, Turk boasts about his own service in World War I, even going so far as to glorify mustard gas: "Now, *that* was *war*! Don't give *me* any of that Hemingway twaddle! . . . Mustard gas! What you should have seen was mustard gas. By Christ, it took a real man to face the hideous effects of that. . . . Don't tell *me* about pantywaist Nazis. I've seen what mustard gas will do to a man" (22). Turk appears to scorn the affective elements of or existential reflections on postwar life. Trenches and mustard gas, in Turk's estimation, constitute the only real components of a "manly war," and the rest are "twaddle." His constant emphasis of the word "me" establishes Turk as the singular authority on issues concerning "real men." Contrary to his warmongering posture, Turk primarily derives his view of combat from fictions. Rather than remain silent on this issue like Mike, Turk is content to "borrow" the feats and views of others and pass them off as his own. In short, Turk's performance of the "real" is a sham. However, his inundation of Mike with war stories and history, and his relationship to both, reveals to some extent the masculine "inheritance" he wishes to bequeath to Mike: "Turk had this way of offering up grisly blobs of trench warfare to Mike as some sort of male legacy" (22). Ultimately, the strains of Turk's masculinity reduce him to an absurd caricature whose behavior and performances expose the derivative constructedness of these ideals.

Father and son rely on similar source materials as inspirations for their masculine postures. In spite of Mike's attempts to resist Turk's influence, the junior McGurk acknowledges that, more and more, he sounds like his father. Still, movies and literature have a strong influence on Mike's own ideas about masculinity. For example, in anticipation of meeting for the first time his cousin Lily, who is on her way to college, he practices his best James Dean in an effort to impress her: "He hung his left elbow on the top of the first pump and affected a nonchalant droop, right thumb hooked in his pocket, feet loosely crossed at the ankle. He tried a cigarette but couldn't get it to hang just right off his lips" (42). Mike's choice to imitate James Dean is an interesting one considering the actor was best known for his roles as Cal Trask in *East of Eden* (1955) and Jim Stark in *Rebel without a Cause* (1955), characters with fathers who are never satisfied with their sons. Being isolated in the desert with his father has left Mike incredibly naïve, almost as if he is in a state of arrested development. Even though he is twenty-nine years old, he acts like a nervous teenager who is playing at being cool in order to seduce his cousin, who turns the tables and seduces him. Separated by class, geography, and a ten-year age difference, the two find common ground in their love of literature.

The McGurk family library includes works from authors such as the aforementioned Mark Twain, along with Herman Melville, Jane Austen, and Charles Dickens, though none has a greater influence on Mike than Hemingway. Father and son disagree on the merits of Hemingway, for in Turk's estimation his work conveys an inferior masculinity and experience of war. But something about Hemingway's work resonates for Mike, whether it is Nick Adams's rugged individualism, Jake Barnes's sense of loss, or Santiago's struggle against nature and the elements, or all of these combined. Mike, like so many other men of his time, sees Hemingway's work as an urtext for mid-century masculinity. Later in the novel, Mike and Bobo have a conversation about this concept. The exchange appears on the page as scripted dialogue akin to what one sees when reading a play:

> **BOBO.** I don't get Hemingway, vato.
> **MIKE.** I get Hemingway. How can you be a man and not get Hemingway?
> **BOBO.** All that bullshit. All them bull runs and drinkin' wine from bags. That war shit. (174)

Through the form and format of this conversation, Urrea calls attention to the cultural scripts that serve as inspirations and sources for the masculinities present in the novel.[9] Mike's emphatic statement that he, indeed, "gets" Hemingway reveals the potential power of these sources. For Mike, understanding Hemingway is the equivalent of being a man. "The mythical image of Hemingway as the embodiment of virility in his writing, his exploits, and his very physical presence," according to Richard Fantina, "asserts itself as quintessentially dominant and aggressive masculinity" (1). Despite Turk's protestations about Hemingway's twaddle, the two are alike in the masculinity they embody. Therefore, Mike understands Hemingway, and this knowledge is rooted in whiteness. "If a key morphology of masculinity is implicitly defined as white," as Reeser proposes, then "any hegemony or advantage assigned to that masculinity can be attributed to the category of whiteness, while non-white bodies are made into another masculinity" (145). Mike's question, therefore, has the effect of emasculating Bobo or placing him in another category of masculinity altogether, thereby leaving Mike as the only "real" man in the pairing.

The Chicano veteran rejects Hemingway's construction of masculinity as "bullshit" because, in Bobo's assessment, Hemingway constructs a model for white men based on bulls, alcohol, and war. Instead, Bobo is fond of John Steinbeck, which makes sense considering his "novels center around men made marginal by economic hardship" (Kimmel 157). Race can compound issues of poverty and also impact the types of marginalization experienced by men of color, as Urrea's novel makes evident through Mr. García, Bobo's father, who is permanently disabled from working in the copper mines. Bobo claims to have read the "*Tortilla*" and "Okie" books without indicating what about them he likes (*In Search of Snow* 174). While one might conclude that the depictions of Mexicans are what appeal to Bobo, both Steinbeck and Hemingway, as Cecil Robinson maintains, were most fond of Mexicans and Spaniards "when they could be shown as primitive, elemental, close to the earth" (12). The connection to the land in the two Steinbeck novels Bobo mentions is, in all likelihood, what appeals to him because it reminds him of home. As a veteran and a former wrestler, both of which required him to travel at home and abroad, Bobo spends considerable time away from his hometown of McQueen, Arizona, to financially support his parents and siblings. The economic situation of Bobo's family is compounded by race in a way that Mike does not "get" because of his whiteness.

Mike may not recognize the power and privilege of white masculinity, but he exercises both on more than one occasion, thus illustrating that he has internalized some of what Turk has taught him about race and gender. He displays these attitudes most explicitly in his first encounter with Bobo. Spotting Bobo across the room, Mike sees nothing more than a "Mexican," an "apparition," and a "phantom" (*In Search of Snow* 67). The references to noncorporeality have the effect of denying Bobo a body and, by extension, subjectivity and personhood. It is also a way for Mike to safeguard his own masculinity by neutralizing Mexican manhood, for, as Reeser notes, "Masculine anxieties are projected onto gendered others, but race can be a key factor in how those projections get played out" (144). Mike's white privilege leads him to cast the Mexicans as antagonists, without having to acknowledge how his presence unsettles the patrons in the bar who are ethno-racially different from himself. So while Mike may not be aware of his whiteness, it certainly registers for the Mexican and Indian customers. As Bebout maintains, whiteness is "entrenched in a legacy of terror and violence, often hypervisible only to its potential targets" (*Whiteness* 8). Yet Mike is the one who feels threatened, by the Mexicans: "They were dangerous, hopped up with new style—greasy ducktail hairdos and cavernous draped jackets that dropped past their knees." The diasporic Mexican men and their sartorial style intimidate Mike. In an effort to assert his dominance, he responds to feelings of vulnerability by "slowly thunking his boot heels on the boards, circling the room, slyly watching these weirdo zoot-suit greaser pachucos" (*In Search of Snow* 67).[10] Mike relies on his "cowboy" persona, via the "thunking" of his boots, to sonically and culturally claim power in this situation as an extension of his whiteness.

At the same time, his racialization of the Mexicans, coupled with his pejorative view of them, supports Bebout's assertion that the "Mexican Other, real and more often imaginary, has played a significant role in the fashioning of white identity . . ." (*Whiteness* 2). Thus Mike's whiteness is affirmed through his negative appraisal of the Mexicans in the bar. Not only are they strange but also their postures are perceived as potentially aggressive. Scanning the room, Mike takes note of "a Mexican, slouched against the wall, right hand inserted in his pocket like a knife" (*In Search of Snow* 67). He conceives of the as-yet-unidentified Bobo as a "knife-wielding" menace based solely on his ethnicity and appearance:

> Mike took in his double-soled black shoes, baggy pants cuffed in tight at the ankles, gold watch chain looping under pocketed hand, waistband up to his navel. The Mexican wore a sleeveless undershirt. A small cross glowed on his chest. He wore a razor-brim hat pulled low across the bridge of his nose. All his face was in shadow—the only part visible was his mouth. (67)

The words "razor" and "shadow" reinforce Bobo's construction as dangerous, attesting to the idea that "black and brown bodies of men of colour incite an overwhelming fear for onlookers . . . who interpret their *minority masculinity* as threatening and deviant" (Beydoun). Mike sees no other possibility in this "greaser" other than that of menace. When he feels intimidated, Mike does not hesitate to rely on the skills Turk taught him.

Bobo deftly manipulates Mike's racist assumptions about Mexicans to alter the power dynamic of the situation. The confrontation reveals the effectiveness of the pachuco persona, which through hairstyle and clothing "flaunted conventional norms of all social classes" as a means of antagonizing white masculinity (Mirandé, *Hombres* 136).[11] Playing upon

Mike's fear, Bobo says, "Watch it, amigo. . . . We dangerous" (*In Search of Snow* 67). Bobo, whose name means "stupid, foolish, or simple" in Spanish, is none of these things, for he immediately reads Mike's intentions and prejudices to become the vicious Mexican of Mike's imagination.[12] The decision to enact this role, on Bobo's part, serves as both a confirmation and a critique of Mike's posturing. "One strategy to destabilize or to resist" racialized masculinities, in Reeser's view, "is to overdetermine them, as a way to bring them out in the open" (160). Bobo then heightens this performance by declaring, "These here Messkins, they carry *knives*, baby!" (*In Search of Snow* 67). To further destabilize the situation, Bobo shifts his dialect and register from Chicano to Anglo. He tells Mike, "A Messkin . . . why, he'd just as soon stab you as look at you. It's true. Read your history books! . . . And keep them white women away from us! Watch your womminfolk, pard! Keep them brown-backed vermin offen your womminfolk!" (68; first ellipsis in original). In a manner reminiscent of Turk's, Bobo cites an historicized Anglo masculinity as an authoritative source regarding the delinquency of Mexicans and the threat they pose to white women. Bobo moves seamlessly from one racialized performance to another, illustrative of Reeser's observation that "while a man performs a racialized style of masculinity, he may also perform another style of masculinity than that assigned to his body" (159). Furthermore, by imitating rough, frontier dialect, he evokes the prejudices of European American pioneers against racialized or ethnic men, which often reduce diasporic Mexican men and Indians to sexual predators and pests. Mike's response is "to flee to white territory," while on the other side of the room "[t]he Mexicans were laughing uproariously, slapping the phantom on the back" (*In Search of Snow* 68). Bobo capitalizes on Mike's racist assumptions about Mexicans to alter the power dynamic of the situation. In doing so, he demonstrates Guillermo Gomez-Peña's assertion that "[d]ominance is contextual. . . . at different times and in different contexts, [we] enjoy some privileges over other people and perform the ever-changing roles of victim and victimizer, exploited and exploiter, colonizer and colonized" (13–14). Gaining the upper hand in this encounter with Mike, Bobo wins the approval of his fellow Chicanos.

Although Bobo accomplishes his goal of making Mike feel like an interloper at the bar, at times, among his own group, Bobo feels like the outsider, restricted by the roles Mexican men and Chicanos are allowed and allow themselves to perform. A conscious refusal to act out these one-dimensional roles may serve to isolate Bobo from the men in his own ethnic group. After his service in the war and his stint as a professional wrestler, Bobo settled in Arizona amidst a community of Chicanos, who respect him, for the most part, because of his former occupation as a wrestler. His authority and reputation in this group are wholly derived from his ability to conduct himself as a fighter. This position offers him some measure of power but also makes him vulnerable to attack by any man who "wouldn't have minded trying to beat him up" (*In Search of Snow* 147). Bobo knows this group has certain expectations concerning male behavior, so he plays at fulfilling them in the same way he had enacted a series of masculine gestures in the staged performances of professional wrestling. In the company of his companion Rigoberto "Mula" Archuleta, Bobo "pretends" to have fun while "drinking the cheapest beer they could find, living off the pickings of three stolen cars sold to the cops in Agua Prieta" (146–147). Bobo, in truth, loathes this way of life, but he performs approval to belong: "Bobo sat there and laughed with them, rutted with their aromatic women, whistled at their various pathetic guns, knives, chains, scars, tattoos. And he hated them all" (147).[13] His loathing is not self-directed or even racially motivated. Instead, his disgust is directed at and comments upon their "tough guy" performances. Having served in the war and witnessed the atrocities of Buchenwald, Bobo perceives their behaviors as nothing more than masculine posturing. Therefore, his desire to distance himself from the behavior of these men and other culturally prescribed masculinities, explains, in part, his decision to accept Turk's offer of employment.

Turk hires Bobo to work at the McGurk Texaco station as a mechanic. Given Turk's previous behaviors, this decision is a curious one. However, his choice makes sense considering Mike's mixed-race identity. While Mike's Mexican identity is never stated explicitly, there is ample evidence to suggest that he is Anglo-Mexican. Bebout cites a key scene in the book to support this idea. "Mike's racial lineage," as Bebout asserts, "is also troubled by the image of Mike's long-deceased mother. In a scene that evokes an archeological dig, Mike looks through pictures of his mother" ("Troubling White Benevolence" 32). The final photo in the stack shows Connie "in a Mexican dress, about thirteen, in front of wooden birdcages, hair in a thick braid falling to her left shoulder" (*In Search of Snow* 173). Bebout points out that "[w]hile she is not racially classified, the Mexican dress at the young age reinforces the possibility of Mexican ancestry" (32). There is yet another compelling part of the scene that further substantiates her identity as a Mexican: "Mike slid his finger under the flap of old paper and pulled out a *brown*, half-torn photo. His mother stood in the sun, one hand shielding her eyes and another lightly touching her chest" (*In Search of Snow* 172; emphasis added). As Mike leafs through the photos, "[t]heir curling brown surfaces" stick to his fingers (172). The brownness of the photos, the sun casting a spotlight on his mother, and her gesture, as if to say "This is me," taken along with other evidence, such as Turk's near reverence for "'Rencor' [b]y Dueto Hermanos Esteves . . . on the Mexican Columbia label" and the transfer of brownness from the photos onto Mike's skin, provide a strong indication of Mike's and his mother's Mexican ancestry (85). Later, while visiting Bobo's family, Mike exclaims, "I want to be a Mexican" (208). Although Mike has been schooled in postures of white masculinity, he has no idea how to be a Mexican man, even though he likely is one. His search for his mother and her final resting place may provide an opportunity for Mike to discover this aspect of his identity. Until then, his relationship with Bobo and his "adoption" of the little girl Umbelinda expose him to a different set of cultural concerns and racial prejudices experienced by Mexicans. Yet these alone cannot teach him what it means to be a white-presenting Mexican man, an issue with which Urrea is personally familiar and has written about extensively throughout his work.[14]

After Turk's death, Bobo moves from a position of antagonist to ally vis-à-vis Mike. The familiar camaraderie that develops between Bobo and Mike demonstrates how "the relation between . . . two men may begin as antagonistic or seem impossible and then move beyond impossibility, imitating a cultural interdiction against interracialism that is overcome through male bonding" (Reeser 205). This outcome is made possible by Turk's hiring of Bobo. Bobo and Mike's pairing mirrors other interracial duos found in popular television shows at the time of the novel's setting, such as *The Lone Ranger* (1949–1957) and *The Adventures of Kit Carson* (1951–1955), though if Mike is Mexican, the relationship is more akin to that in *The Cisco Kid* (1950–1956), which featured a Mexican *caballero* and his faithful Mexican companion, Pancho.[15] Regardless, the power dynamics of Mike and Bobo's relationship, overall, are more evenly balanced than the ones in these shows. Consequently, not only does Bobo come to Mike's rescue on more than one occasion, Mike also helps Bobo and his family physically and financially. The duo often make joint decisions about where to go and what to do, and more importantly, they choose to remain together. Regardless of their apparent racial and cultural differences, Mike and Bobo find common ground. Their status as war veterans helps to explain their homosocial commitment to each other. According to Susan Faludi, such men "were eager to embrace a masculine ideal that revolved around providing rather than dominating.

Their most important experiences centered on the support and comfort they had given one another in the war, and it was this that they wished to preserve" (23). Mike and Bobo prioritize providing for the families. To be sure, Mike stays with Turk for reasons he does not understand. What he does know is that "without him there, his father wouldn't have survived a week" (*In Search of Snow* 24). Staying with his aging father, as caregiver and audience for his macho dramas, is Mike's way of asserting a masculinity distinct from Turk's. Similarly, Bobo provides financial support for his parents and numerous siblings, a number of whom are orphans cared for by the Garcías. Bobo and Mike's friendship represents a different expression of masculinity, one that has the potential to be transformative for both men, though especially for Mike. Through his relationship with Bobo, Mike observes a model for a father-son relationship different from the one he has known.

The visit to the García family home in McQueen, Arizona, initiates Mike's transculturation process put in motion by Turk's decision to hire Bobo. Mike's feelings and ideas about masculinity (and whiteness) change after witnessing alternate expressions of manhood demonstrated by Bobo and his father, particularly through their interactions. Mike's reaction to Mexicans changes from one of fear to a cultural longing that borders on white fantasy. When Mike first arrives at the García household, his prejudices are still firmly in place. His panic rises up, causing him to want to flee: "He wanted to get out of there before the rest of the Garcías came out—he imagined a whole household of pachuco gardeners, all of them with evil little goatees and switchblades, everybody so . . . *Mexican*" (188–189; ellipsis in original). Because Mike has a singular view, he cannot picture Mexicans outside of danger and violence. Watching from a distance, he sees the extended García clan come out to greet Bobo. The excitement and affection they display for each other is completely foreign to Mike. He is both in awe and envious of this family. When Mr. García approaches Bobo and the two embrace, Mike looks on in amazement. Raised "in a family with no word for *love*," Mike sees a father-son relationship rooted in tenderness and respect (24). Bobo and his father's interaction remind Mike of all that he has never had. When father and son embrace, and Mr. García plants a kiss on Bobo's cheek, Mike is undone; he is reduced to tears, crying out for both his mother and Turk. The Garcías respond to his outburst with "Operation Comfort Mike" (191). They fulfill a longing he has always had: to have a family to welcome and care for him. Mike not only decides he wants to be a Mexican but also begins to imagine a life with the Garcías, whose home he considers a "magic kingdom, utterly separate from the earth" (213). His perspective brings to mind the theme park Disneyland, then also referred to as the Magic Kingdom, which reflects Mike's view of the Garcías' home as an idealized place where he would like to take up permanent residence far away from the real world. Bobo endeavors to disabuse Mike of this fantasy by sharing the truth about his family's hardships and the racial discrimination they face daily. More than anything else, the arrival of Ramses Castro in Bobo's hometown forecloses on Mike's dream.

Casa García exists as a complete reversal of Mike's life and home at a gas station in the desert. Whereas Mike grew up alone with Turk, Mr. and Mrs. García oversee a household filled with a large family, including children whose parents were killed in mining accidents. Like the *ancianos* Don Pedro Aragon, Abuelo, and Tío Tomas, Mr. García exhibits a closeness to the earth. He cultivates an oasis in the middle of the desert teeming with various plants, fruits, and vegetables. His family defers to and treats him with respect, for example addressing him in Spanish using the more formal *usted* verb form. Rather than demanding such reverence, Mr. García "accepted the honor as a given" (193). He demonstrates a quiet humility that starkly contrasts with the performative nature of Turk's brand of masculinity. Mr. García also strongly eschews violence. In fact, Bobo disappoints his father by fighting with the white men in town—that is, until Mr. García learns that they spoke "indelicately" about one of his daughters (234). Mr. García's attitude quickly changes then and he tells his son, "In that case, Bonifacio, I hope you taught them respect" (234). The besmirching of family honor, particularly as related to women, warrants a physical response, and violence can be used to teach, in this case respect, though it must not be used indiscriminately. So later, when Bobo wants to kill the man who impregnated and then abandoned his sister Almita, Mr. García says explicitly, "No you won't" (234). Mr. García acts not as an *anciano* or mediating figure but as the family patriarch, authorizing or forbidding certain types of behavior. Bobo hangs his head in shame, knowing he wanted to act outside of his father's moral code. However, the most distinct difference between the McGurk and García households involves the power Mrs. García wields over the family, in comparison to the absence of Mrs. McGurk. In response to Almita's pregnancy, Mrs. García announces, "[Almita] is pregnant, and I don't want to hear any comments about it. Say nothing critical to her. I expect us to have love in this house" (235). Mr. García and Bobo exchange knowing smiles before both reply in the affirmative. They have built their father-son relationship on love, respect, and shared values. Through Bobo's interactions with his father, the reader sees how he vacillates between private and multiple public performances of masculinity.

Of all the characters in the novel, Ramses believes most in his racialized performance of masculinity, so much so that he gives himself and his freedom over to these ideas. Raised without a father, Ramses has not been subjected to hypermasculine performances such as the ones Mike endured. Unencumbered by hegemonic masculinist scripts, Ramses created his own expression of "being a man," which is both liberating and dangerous. Thus, despite their racial and generational differences, Ramses most resembles Turk, who becomes a symbolic father for the self-styled warrior. Delbert also bears some culpability in Ramses's weaponizing of masculinity to a lethal degree. Ramses first appears in the novel seated in his grandfather's truck, "a huge and sullen boy, so chubby he had breasts pushing at his tight T-shirt" (33). Delbert introduces Ramses as his "Mexican grandson" (33). Ramses, who is initially feminized, immediately rejects his grandfather's assertion of his identity by stating, "I'm Apache. . . . I am a warrior" (33). In his first spoken lines in the text, Ramses claims an American Indian tribal identity and self-defines as a "warrior," a performance that wholly defines his role in the narrative. However, more than simply claiming an Indian identity, he villainizes his Mexican heritage, telling Mike, "Mexicans are the enemy of the Apache. . . . After the white man" (33). Ramses's pronouncement speaks to the violence Mexico committed against the Apaches, through, for example, incessant attacks on their homelands and the hiring of foreign mercenaries who were paid "bounties for Apache scalps," including those of children (Hutton 15). Mexican aggression against the Apaches also gave rise to the tribe's most famous warrior, Geronimo, whose family was murdered by a Mexican militia. Having no way of knowing that Mike is both white and Mexican, Ramses nevertheless casts himself in the role of young McGurk's adversary and wastes no time in enacting the part.

From a young age, Ramses invests in performances of dominance that usually include violence. His is a "masculinity by opposition," one that "attempts to delineate two forms of racialized masculinity in a discrete way and to ignore shades of gray in favor of binarism" (Reeser 153). This view explains Ramses's desire to cast Mike in an opposing role. For instance, Ramses invites Mike to play cowboys and Indians—with himself as the Indian and Mike as the cowboy—and then immediately overpowers the young McGurk and stakes him to the ground. Completely helpless, Mike lashes out at Ramses, relying on what Turk has taught him—threats and masculine posturing. Immobilized in a spread-eagle position, Mike screams, "I'll find your house and burn it down with you in it! . . . I'll wear your teeth for a necklace" (*In Search of Snow* 34–35). Mike responds with threats that echo settler colonial violence against Native people, confirming his position as Ramses's racial and cultural opponent. His willingness to fully inhabit the role to which he has been assigned inspires in Ramses a modicum of affinity for the young cowboy. In response to Mike's promise of violence, Ramses responds in kind: "We used to cut open your guts and pull stuff out, twirl it around a big stick and let our dogs eat it" (35). Mike does not succumb to defeat, proving himself a worthy adversary for the aspiring warrior. When Ramses eventually cuts the branches, releasing his captive, Mike lunges at his former captor, diving "straight into his gut head-first. They slugged it out for five minutes, snot and tears and nose blood all over them" (35). Easily provoked, Mike performs the part of cowboy to Ramses's Indian. In contrast to Delbert and Turk, this conflict does demonstrate a power differential. The two older men are playing at conflict, but Ramses draws Mike into a row with the explicit purpose of dominating him. Following their encounter, Mike has a strange feeling: "Something seemed torn in the world, and Mike couldn't get a hold of the edges of it. They maintained such a perfect distance from each other that even their shadows did not touch" (35). Ramses initiates Mike into the violence of settler colonial history and the racial (racist) and gender scripts it creates, and Mike performs his part well, perhaps too well. The conflict tears down Mike's very insulated view of life in the Arizona desert. The gulf that exists between the two young men remains intact and defines their relationship throughout their lives.

Ramses disappears from the novel only to re-emerge later as an adversary, this time to the elder McGurk. The meeting of Turk's cowboy and Ramses's Indian represents a battle of equals, not in terms of ability or strength but in a commitment to a singular performance of masculinity, which each embodies. In an attempt to recapture his youth, Turk agrees to fight Ramses, who has become a bare-knuckled fighter like himself. Turk attempts to minimize his opponent as a threat by calling him names, alternating between "beener" and "Apache." Far from a term of respect, the latter is meant to deride Castro as a familiar and conquerable foe and to reinscribe him into an historic narrative of conquest, one that Turk relies on and feels will ensure his victory. Furthermore, as Taiaiake Alfred points out in "Reimagining Warriorhood," the idea of the violent warrior was created to justify the violence of conquest; as such it represents an image "to be slain by the white conqueror" (79). Turk's bravado about the impending bout worries Mike, who tells him,

"Father. I've heard bad things about Ramses Castro is all. Shoot, the guy staked me out in the desert once" (*In Search of Snow* 61). Turk ignores his son's concerns, choosing instead to focus on Mike's defeat in his contest with Ramses. Motivated by the perceived "wrong" done to his son, Turk chooses to go forward with the fight, refusing to recognize that he and Ramses are unevenly matched physically. Although the two opponents share some of the same qualities, the elder McGurk's fatal mistake is that he believes he can outdo Ramses in terms of performing the role of a soldier or warrior. Turk believes he can triumph over Ramses; for Ramses, defeating all that Turk represents is more important than winning the fight. The different approaches of the two men demonstrate the ideological differences between winning the battle and winning the war. For Ramses, the only central character to have never served in an armed conflict, the fight with Turk is a war.

Whereas Mike and Bobo both make efforts to evolve their masculine performances, Ramses does not deviate from his warrior persona, exemplifying what McKegney identifies as a "masculindian." The neologism, "[b]uilt from a collision between the floating signifiers 'masculine' and 'Indian,'" according to McKegney, "draws attention to the settler North American appetite for depictions of Indigenous men that rehearse hypermasculine stereotypes of the noble savage and the bloodthirsty warrior" (1). But as Ramses demonstrates, white people are not the only ones internalizing these depictions of Native men. Ramses formulates his masculine persona from other American Indian men, heroes and fighters. For Ramses, Geronimo and Crazy Horse, men he describes as his "presidents," "popes," and "heroes," are source scripts for his masculine performance (*In Search of Snow* 138). He relishes his warrior role, which he sees as an avenue to power and respect. Ramses desires to win and to assert his dominance at any cost, which makes him lethal. On the evening of the fight, "Ramses Castro stood like a monolith at the far end of the hall. Red-eyed and gleaming with sweat, he wore a red bandanna tied around his head and a long braid hanging down his back. He had with him an entourage of zoot-suiters, Indians, and farmworkers" (66). The racialized image of Ramses, sweaty, red-eyed, with braids, evokes cinematic images of ominous Indians, at least from Mike's perspective. For the zoot-suiters, Indians, and farmworkers present, however, Ramses is their champion. His acting out of sanctioned aggression against settler colonial oppression, of which Turk is merely a convenient site, is enviable. More than simply achieving a symbolic victory, Ramses also scores a literal victory. With a single blow, he brings down Turk and all he represents. In this moment, the self-professed warrior does not savor his triumph by announcing himself as the winner. He chooses instead to focus on his opponent's defeat by telling Turk, "You lose, asshole" (70). With Turk vanquished, Ramses shifts his focus to Mike, recasting him in his former role as "enemy" so that Ramses can continue to act out his warrior performance.

Ramses's masculinity of opposition necessitates placing Mike in this adversarial position. And just as Turk's performance of masculinity remains unchanging over time, so does Ramses's, even though Indigenous masculinity, as Daniel Heath Justice asserts, "isn't a static thing; it's dynamic, ever in motion" (150). Ramses, in spite of looking to figures such as Geronimo and Crazy Horse as sources of inspiration, derives his identity from narrowly defined versions of history and warfare, as Turk does. Furthering this connection, Ramses informs Mike that his "old man . . . knew what he was doin'. It's the way of the warrior" (*In Search of Snow* 138). Ramses understands Turk because adhering to these ideals enables one to clearly define one's enemies, and Ramses needs Mike to see this point, going so far as to tell him, "You know . . . it's good to have an enemy. I think you need an enemy" (139). By creating a foe, Ramses fortifies and ensures the continuation of his role as a fighter. And in a move that expresses Ramses's desire for Mike to adopt this point of view, Ramses "ambushes" Mike in the bathroom. After pinning Mike down in a stall, which is reminiscent of his earlier staking, and wrestling away his knife, Ramses stands over him and calmly proclaims, "I win" (142). Once again, Ramses does not celebrate his triumph; however, this time, rather than proclaim his enemy's defeat, he declares victory over Mike. Although Bobo, as mediator in this triangle, saves Mike from certain death, Ramses later informs Mike that the two men "ain't finished" (154). In fact, Ramses will never be finished with Mike because his identity as a warrior is dependent on the junior McGurk. Through Ramses's adherence to a singular performance of Indian masculinity, he writes himself into a script that requires the endless commission of acts of violence. Brendan Hokowhitu stresses the importance of acknowledging the historical and cultural ways that Indigenous people often become complicit in these behaviors: "[T]he challenge Indigenous peoples face is to realize that the strategic function of traditionalized Indigenous masculinity and sexuality have now become an encumbrance, and that often we are left holding on to false traditions that only serve to exclude and limit Indigenous men" (94). Therefore, Ramses's chosen performance is contingent on Mike's racialization, either as white or Mexican, and most importantly, on his presence. Ramses sacrifices everything, including his relationship with his grandfather and his community, to maintain his oppositional masculinity through proximity to Mike.

Beneath it all, Ramses's performance of masculinity stems from his longing for a father, a fact made evident as he listens to one song ad nauseam on the jukebox. After Turk's death, Mike wanders drunk into the "Chikisin," an Indian bar. The name Chikisin, a word that Mike knows to mean "brother" in Apache, reflects the brotherhood and community inside the bar, to which he clearly does not belong. Still, he stumbles in without a second thought. His presence immediately registers for the patrons: "There was an audible dip in the noise level" (*In Search of Snow* 135). Someone yells in Spanish from the back of the room, "This vato thinks he's el mero chingón!"; the woman behind the bar "regard[s] him with angry-looking eyes"; and another patron says "something in Apache" (136). None of this registers for Mike, though he does notice Ramses's presence: the "improbably large Indian [shuffled] in front of the Wurlitzer, singing along" to "Roly-Poly" (1946), by Bob Wills and His Texas Playboys (136), which was popular in honky-tonks at the time. Ramses listens to the song about Roly-Poly, a dutiful little boy with an insatiable appetite, "ten times in a row" (137). Ramses's affinity for the song may have to do with his own experiences as an overweight child. The boy in the song has an idealized existence, including a "daddy" who watches over him and affectionately refers to him as "his little fatty." Roly-Poly eats, grows strong, and does "chores" around the house. Under his father's supervision, the singer "bets," Roly-Poly is "gonna be a man someday." Roly-Poly's appetite is not merely for food but also for his father's attention. All his behaviors are in an effort to gain his father's approval. The song speaks to the futurity of the boy's manhood, a kind of speculative masculinity, which the father has the power to confer. Although we are not given an indication as to the whereabouts of Ramses's father, his absence means that Ramses has no one to serve in this capacity. Arguably, Delbert could do this for Ramses, but he expresses greater affinity for Mike and Turk, and later Bobo, than he does for Ramses. For this reason, Ramses's performance of Indian masculinity could be motivated in large part by a desire to win his grandfather's attention and affection. Mirroring Turk's desires, Ramses wants both an audience and approval for his particular expression of masculinity. The song, therefore, becomes Ramses's own affirmation of himself as a boy and a man.

While Ramses forfeits his relationship with his grandfather, Delbert repeatedly contributes to its demise, which reflects his always-shifting position in the novel. As stated, Delbert's feelings appear to lie not only with Turk and Mike, but also against Ramses. Delbert chooses kinship over blood. In Delbert's history, he worked alongside Turk's father, Carroll, in the San Carlos Apache Police: "Delbert was his chief officer, and they rode their horses together in and out of canyons after Tom Horn had moved on" (*In Search of Snow* 32). The reference to Tom Horn provides insight into Delbert's position in relationship to the McGurks and to other Apaches. Horn, who worked as a translator and a civilian scout for the US Cavalry, was present at Geronimo's final surrender, after which the Apache leader spent the remaining portion of his life imprisoned, first at Ft. Marion in Florida and later at Ft. Sill in Oklahoma, where he died.[16] And Carroll "had once policed the Apache" in Horn's company (9). A large group of San Carlos Apaches sided with the US government against Geronimo and the Chiricahua Apaches. As a member of a policing unit descended from the San Carlos Apaches, Delbert became complicit in one side of a history of internecine violence that aligned itself with the settler colonial army against Native people. His participation in this legacy lends some insight into why he opposes his grandson Ramses. Delbert also alienates Ramses emotionally and beats him up physically on at least one occasion.[17] Conversely, Delbert tries to look after Turk, especially after he agrees to fight Ramses, offering advice and a spiritual blessing, both of which Turk refuses. Aware of how dangerous his grandson truly is, Delbert urges Turk not to fight Ramses and warns him, "Don't be a hero, Turk" (65). Turk believes he can beat Ramses; even if he cannot, he is willing to die to reclaim his status as a warrior. When Turk refuses to listen to reason, Delbert offers sage to smudge and purify him, but Turk dismisses the overture as "Indian bullshit" before walking away (65). Turk turns his back on Delbert's protective efforts, including the practical and the spiritual. Fully aware that pride is a major issue in the bout, Delbert leaves Turk to his fate. Before departing, though, he tells Mike, "Put money on the Indian" (66). More than believing in his grandson's ability as a boxer, Delbert believes in Ramses's investment in his role as a warrior and knows Ramses will outperform Turk in this capacity.

Ultimately, Delbert shares responsibility for what Ramses has become. His relationship with Turk and devotion to Mike isolate Ramses, for instead of validating and supporting Ramses as an Apache man, he disparages him: "Ramses thinks he's Geronimo's right-hand man. Listen to me, Mike.... Geronimo would have took one look at that boy and walked the other way. My grandson's crazy. Period" (159). The narrative does not offer any specific insights into Ramses's mental instability, though we do see an escalation of violence over the course of the novel ranging from binding and staking Mike to the ground as a child and becoming a bare-knuckle fighter to threatening Mike's life and destroying property. Repeatedly, Delbert negates the central part of Ramses's identity as a man and advocates for violence against him. He even goes so far as to tell Mike, "Get a big gun and shoot the hell out of Castro while you got the chance" (159). To compound this betrayal, Delbert bestows the title of "warrior" on Mike and declares him a "man" as they prepare to depart, on their westward adventure at the end of the novel, for Los Angeles.

Before leaving Arizona, Mike and Bobo make a concerted effort to break free from the past by blowing up Turk's gas station that has been foreclosed on by the bank. But Mike retrieves his father's grandfather clock first: "It sounded its bell in the seat beside him twelve times in a row, and it seemed to take all night to finish" (258). The line calls to mind both John Donne's *Devotions upon Emergent Occasions, and Several Steps in My Sickness* (1624) and Hemingway's *For Whom the Bell Tolls* (1940), which address the themes of death and the interconnectedness of humanity, and death and war, respectively. The chiming of the clock symbolizes funerary rites marking Turk's passing and Mike's release from his influence. However, the bells also suggest, particularly in relation to *For Whom the Bell Tolls*, that Turk, like Hemingway's hero Robert Jordan, may have sacrificed himself so that Mike could be free. Wounded after blowing up a bridge, Jordan, whose injuries are fatal, stays behind so that the rebels, including the woman he loves, can escape to fight another day. Bobo and Mike's decision to blow up the gas station furthers the parallel between the novels. With his newfound freedom, Mike must decide what kind of man he wants to be. Bobo and Ramses have already decided. The novel does not settle this issue for Mike or offer solutions for the three to resolve the uneasy relationships they have with their ethno-racial masculinities. In fact, the novel ends with Mike, Bobo, and Delbert, who are now fugitives, in transit on their way to Disneyland as Ramses, following at a distance, sings along to Bob Wills.[18]

Ramses's destructive actions in McQueen prevent Mike from staying and being a father to Umbelinda and Bobo from seeing his family in the foreseeable future. The trek west defers the futurity of Mike's obligations as a father to Umbelinda, which is unfortunate because by all indications he would be a good father. Of the six little girls in the Garcías' care, Umbelinda is the only one to forge a connection with Mike, first as a translator for Mr. García and then through their interactions over the course of Mike and Bobo's visit. When the duo are forced to flee after they vandalize a store and Ramses destroys the local sheriff's truck by sending it through the store's window, a devastated Umbelinda begs Mike not to go. She cycles through a range of emotions and behaviors, from pleading and crying to being angry and hitting. With no experience whatsoever in dealing with little girls or having a kind and loving parent, Mike responds instinctively with tenderness and affection. When he tells her he loves her, Umbelinda asks him to be her father. He agrees and promises to return for her. She confers the status of father on Mike and calls him Papa. His desire to distinguish himself from Turk and his longing for a family meet through the promise he makes to his Mexican daughter as he becomes obligated to family in a completely different way. Before heading west, Delbert tells Mike, "You've got a child now. . . . You've got to shape up," reminding him of his obligation (251). Still, none of Mike's choices, from blowing up the gas station to escaping to Disneyland, suggest that he is ready to take on such a responsibility. So he will remain as physically absent from his daughter's life as Turk was emotionally from his.

The triangulation of these Latinx men reveals how their performances of masculinity act on and influence each member of the group. Cultural expectations concerning Mike's, Bobo's, and Ramses's masculinities affect all three men in marked ways that emerge in their various performances as cowboy, pachuco, and warrior, respectively. Similarly, each exhibits distinct attitudes about Mexicans, and to a certain degree, Mexican-ness: Mike longs to be Mexican; Bobo hates and loves being Mexican; and Ramses completely rejects his Mexican ancestry. Mike's and Bobo's attitudes represent change over time, while Ramses holds steadfast in his self-negating stance. In any case, these attitudes inform their conceptions and performances of masculinity. As Kimmel emphasizes, "Manhood does not bubble up to consciousness from our biological constitution; it is created in our culture" (4). Through his cast of characters, Urrea illustrates how the interrelatedness of race and gender complicates these designs for generations of fathers and sons.

Postscript: At the same conference where I delivered the earliest version of what would become this chapter, I attended a panel featuring two senior scholars, one assistant professor, and one graduate student—all men. The two senior scholars prattled on for thirty minutes each. As they talked and talked and talked, I watched the assistant professor take a pen to his paper and furiously cross out entire sections. When it was his turn to present, he spoke for fifteen minutes. Even though he had shaved off five minutes from his allotted twenty, it left only five minutes for the graduate student's paper and the Q&A. Rather than try to speed through his paper within the small window of time, the graduate student stood up and sum-

marized his argument in less than a minute as he wrote key terms from his analysis on the chalkboard. Then he sat down. It was the best presentation of the four. When no one asked questions, the panel was over. So much was wrong about what happened in that panel that I think about it often. The moderator failed that student by not enforcing time limits; the audience failed the student by not advocating for him. I also failed the student, but as the sole woman of color in that room, who was only a junior professor at the time, I honestly did not know what to do. Only the senior professors succeeded. They did so by taking up as much time and space as they wanted without regard for anyone else, and we let them. They also demonstrated with absolute clarity and precision the power differential, even among men. No one on the panel acknowledged or apologized for what happened. Everyone walked out and moved on. To this day, every time I sit down to moderate a panel, I think about the experience of that student. As a result, I have become fiercely protective of each individual's allotted time, even more so if they are BIPOC or queer folx. Slow approaches to scholarship and knowledge production are not simply about what we can do for ourselves; they are also about what we can do for others. And our own failures can move us forward.

PART II
Instrumentalizing Indigeneity

SLOWNESS, FATHERHOOD, AND THE INSTRUMENTALIZATION of Indigeneity meet in Ridley Scott's dystopian sci-fi neo-noir *Blade Runner* (1982). Atop a building, Replicant Roy Batty (Rutger Hauer), with rain washing down over him, delivers a heart-wrenching affirmation of his humanity to Rick Deckard (Harrison Ford).[1] As a Blade Runner, a special type of police officer, charged with hunting down Batty and his white companions Pris, Leon, and Zhora, who have returned illegally to Earth, Deckard sits and watches as Roy's life slips away. Replicants are bio-enhanced humans, genetically created with "superior strength, speed, agility, resilience, and intelligence," who are made to do the jobs humans either do not want to do or find too dangerous ("Replicant"). Valued only for their labor, Replicants are not seen as human.[2] In an effort to better control these genetic creations, human engineers programmed them with a four-year life span to prevent them from developing empathy.[3] What the Replicants in *Blade Runner* want, what they are willing to fight for, is more life (i.e., longer lives). They risk returning to Earth to see their "father" and creator Eldon Tyrell to plead for more time. The Replicants attempt to alter their future by taking control of the present.

In academe, people regularly say, "[Fill in a person's name] is a machine." Individuals perceived as highly successful or productive are on the receiving end of such an assessment, one meant, almost exclusively, as a compliment. But machines are tools.[4] To be a machine means setting aside free will; it means being instrumentalized to meet objectives determined by others. For example, "[c]omputers may be thought to act rationally, in the sense of acting logically, but they do not act to any purpose of their own, only to the purposes of others" (Gwaltney 35). To maintain their worth, these individuals must continue to produce at the same or, preferably, increased levels. Failure to do so can result in loss of status, devaluation, and/or replacement. For human workers, success can also mean taking us further away from ourselves. We are more than we produce. Aspects of who we are combine in different and unexpected ways that can inspire, frustrate, innovate, and enliven our knowledge production. As Barbara Seeber states, "Scholarly 'findings' depend on who is searching; and the searcher in turn is constituted by what she finds" (Berg and Seeber 59). The interdependency of this relationship gets lost if we take a "solely instrumentalist approach to thinking" (59). When this happens, in Seeber's view, we "become machine-like," and if we become like machines, then we become neoliberal subjects (59). Resisting mechanization is paramount to slowing down and creating meaningful connections to ourselves, our lives, and others.

Slow research involves critical self-reflection. Looking inward and determining what motivates us or excites us about our scholarship is not simply a feel-good exercise. But even if it were, so what? We should be capable of finding joy in our work, though doing so is certainly not required. At the very least, we should be able to locate some aspect of ourselves in what consumes so much of our lives. Many of us have lost touch with what initially inspired us as teachers and researchers. Students have said to me, "I want to be a teacher [or professor]." Maybe they were motivated by family members, beloved instructors, or an emotional or intellectual connection to certain subjects or texts. These feelings propelled them down a path of knowledge production and self-discovery. What I discovered is that teaching makes up a big part of who I am, in and outside of the classroom. The same is true of research. I love the feeling of discovery, of being in the library stacks and finding a random book that takes my work in an unexpected direction, experiencing what Julio Alves called "unintentional knowledge."[5]

Our relationships to knowledge production can change over time. Sometimes it happens so quickly that we fail to notice. However it happens, systematically our affinity for and curiosity in scholarship, which are extensions and expressions of the self, too often get replaced or are overshadowed by other priorities, such as program assessment, development (fundraising), or administration. So much of what we are expected to do as academics has very little to do with teaching or research. Regardless, the public perception that "all we do is teach" persists. I still cringe when people say, "It must be nice to have summers off" or "If you only teach [X number] classes, what do you do with the rest of your time?"

When my mom was alive, she would immediately disabuse people of their misconceptions. Living with two full-time academics, she saw the ever-increasing creep of work into our home lives—evenings, weekends, holidays, and all year round. As demands on our time and labor increase, our ability to choose when and where to place our efforts dwindles, except for the most privileged among us.[6]

Re-centering the self in our work can help us to identify what allows us to thrive and what sucks the life out of us. However, as the Great Lakes Feminist Geography Collective notes in "For Slow Scholarship," "[S]low scholarship cannot just be about making individual lives better, but must also be about re-making the university" (1238). As a result, in the GLFGC's view, slow scholarship involves "cultivating caring academic cultures and processes" (1238). Caring for ourselves and others represents a radical act of refusal in an academic corporate environment that focuses more and more on the bottom line than on the people—students, faculty, and staff—on whom it relies for its very existence.

Knowing how or where to begin such a large-scale transformation can feel overwhelming. To add, such efforts present a number of challenges, especially in a system that exacerbates (creates?) inequality. But slow scholarship is about generative possibilities, not single solutions. For example, the GLFGC turns toward a feminist praxis as a means of addressing uneven power relations to "cultivate an explicitly *feminist* and collective model of slow scholarship" (1238). The organization does so in its article through the balancing of collective and individual stories about the embodied effects, such as mental and physical stress, that result from working at neoliberal universities. Additionally, the group offers strategies for actively resisting the culture of speed and counting. For Berg and Seeber, "Slowing down is about asserting the importance of contemplation, connectedness, fruition, and complexity" (57). We no longer have the benefit of looking at something for an extended period of time to cultivate nuance or intricacy of thought. Taking too long to produce certain kinds of work, especially in the humanities, comes with consequences: negative performance reviews, increased teaching or service loads, exclusion from merit raises, or demands to narrate the "gaps" in our scholarly trajectory, meaning we have to explain what we have done with our time in the absence of visible or quantifiable output.

We have naturalized busy-ness, talking about and performing it, into who we are as academics. Worse, we mirror the busy-ness of others, real or not, to escape having judgment passed against us, and for what? To avoid the perception that we are doing something other than work? We lose connectedness with colleagues, students, and ourselves, not to mention friends and family. Going slow, as Berg and Seeber emphasize,

> gives meaning to letting research take the time it needs to ripen and makes it easier to resist the pressure to be faster. It gives meaning to thinking about scholarship as a community, not a competition. It gives meaning to periods of rest, an understanding that research does not run like a mechanism; there are rhythms, which include pauses and periods that may seem unproductive. (57)

Too often we compete for limited resources that would allow for rest and recharging (sabbaticals, research leaves, or course releases). After all, we are not machines or Replicants, at least not yet. But even Replicants realized eventually that they were more than their work and wanted to do something more with their time than work. To go slow is not only about time but also about what we do with and in those intervals of time when we stop or decelerate the pace of our lives.

There is no one way to go slow. In fact, there are times when speed can invigorate or enliven our scholarship. Yet if institutional or cultural transformation is the objective of slow, and it is, then we must also turn a critical eye toward our disciplines and ourselves as practitioners and knowledge producers. "Understanding and being capable of reflecting on one's own research practices is important," as Galina Kallio and Eeva Houtbeckers maintain, because "academic practice . . . may be part of the problem when research reproduces the underlying paradigms that have led to the ongoing ecological, economical and societal crises," to name but a few (2). We must practice self-reflection, and when doing so, we need to consider whether our disciplinary practices or processes of knowledge production create or exacerbate disparities. To make these determinations, we have to reflect periodically on who we are as knowledge producers and what we value.

> People can't do something themselves, they wanna tell you you can't do it. If you want something, go get it. Period.
> Chris Gardner, *The Pursuit of Happyness*

If someone wants me to remember something, they should tell me a story. Better still, augmenting that story with images increases the probability that I will store it in my long-term memory.⁷ I am a visual and aural learner. Together, oral stories and images create the co-constitutive relationship at the heart of my knowledge production. The appeal of literature and film in conversation makes sense to me because the layering of different narrative forms makes a story all the more powerful in my mind. However, as stated in the introduction, different sources of knowledge do not carry the same value in the academy. In *The Courage to Teach: Exploring the Inner Landscape of a Teacher's Life* (2017), educational activist Parker J. Palmer argues, "In [academic] culture the self is not a source to be tapped but a danger to be suppressed, not a potential to be fulfilled but an obstacle to be overcome" (18). So, for example, storytelling is seen as subjective, too personal and embodied to be an objective source of knowledge. As academics, we are taught, encouraged, to suppress the self in our work and rewarded for doing so. "This 'self-protective' split of personhood from practice," as Palmer reasons, "is encouraged by an academic culture that distrusts personal truth. Though the academy claims to value multiple modes of knowing, it honors only one—an 'objective' way of knowing that takes us into the 'real' world by taking us 'out of ourselves'" (18). So what happens if we re-center the self in our knowledge production as researchers and teachers, as a way to reconnect with what excites us about what we do as knowledge producers?

For me that means re-centering stories and their importance to my intellectual life. Every story represents a chance to find order and to make meaning. We can become as we imagine ourselves to be in the stories we read, hear, or tell. We can propagate or erase histories. And we can make visible what once was. Sometimes we are the tellers. Other times, we are being told. As Canadian author of Cherokee descent Thomas King reminds us, "The truth about stories is that that's all we are" (*Truth* 2).

The social and political movement to instill cultural pride known as Chicanismo, as both a story and an epistemology, had a significant impact on my knowledge formation as a scholar. I was initially drawn to Chicanx studies by its emphasis on Mexican Americans and the familiarity of the people, places, and languages at the center of it all. Chicanismo helped me to feel seen and served as a source of pride for me. It gave me a rarely found confidence. It provided a structure to reconcile conflicting accounts of family history that includes both Spanish and Indigenous ancestors. In other words, it did everything it was imagined to do regarding community building and its demands for self-determination. Over time, along with other issues, Chicanismo's instrumentalizing of Indigeneity through the signifier Indian (read: Aztec) became more difficult for me to reconcile with the embodied realities of living tribal communities on both sides of the US-Mexico border.

Historically, Chicanxs and Indians have been allies in their respective sociopolitical movements but have moved along separate intellectual and political fronts. Relations between the two groups are not always harmonious. The ideological and cultural desire to claim Indigenous ancestry or to identify as Indian can place Chicanxs at odds with Native groups and scholars who question the motives, as well as the potential cultural impact, of Chicanxs' adopting, for example, Native social and/or spiritual practices.[8] A difference exists, however, between a claim of Native identity or tribal affiliation and Indigenous ancestry itself. D'Arcy McNickle (Confederated Salish and Kootenai) contends that "Indians remain Indians not by refusing to accept change or to adapt to a changing environment, but by selecting out of available choices those alternatives that do not impose a substitute identity" (10). Chicanx represents one such substitute identity, placing Aztecs and Aztlán (the mythological homeland) in the center of an imagined nation, representing not so much a failure of the imagination as a narrow conception of Indigenous. Cherríe Moraga offers her own complicated views outside of the two narratives central to Chicanx claims to Indigenous identity, El Plan Espiritual de Aztlán and Rodolfo "Corky" Gonzales's epic poem *I Am Joaquín/Yo soy Joaquín* (both discussed in my chapter "Fatherhood, Chicanismo, and the Cultural Politics of Healing in *La Mission*"):

> Most Chicanos can claim, through physical traits alone, that we are of Native blood (we often joke that Chicanos are usually the most Indian-looking people in a room full of "skins"). The majority of us, however, has been denied direct information regarding our tribal affiliations. Since our origins are usually in the Southwest and México, Chicanos' Indian roots encompass a range of nations including Apache, Yaqui, Papago, Navajo, and Tarahumara from the border regions, as well as dozens of Native tribes throughout México. (*Last Generation* 165–166)

Moraga demonstrates that Chicanismo should always have been recognized as multinational at its core. Chicanismo created an opportunity for Nations and tribes to speak together, to accommodate the many who reside or take geographical, ideological, or political refuge within its space—a nation of Nations.

I'm an Apache. I'm not a Mexican.
Ramses Castro, in Luis Alberto Urrea, *In Search of Snow*

Blade Runner instrumentalizes Indigeneity to both elevate whiteness and announce its absence in the Los Angeles of 2019, when the film is set. Most of the white people healthy enough to travel off world have gone, leaving behind a racialized world in ruins. The mise-en-scène conveys the futuristic dystopia through perpetual rain, buildings abandoned and deteriorating, and the proliferation of ethno-racial populations, most visibly coded as Japanese, Turkish, Latinx, and multiethnic, as represented by the Blade Runner Gaff (Edward James Olmos).[9] Towering above the flying vehicles (spinners), acid rain, and fire-belching smokestacks sit two buildings that resemble the Mesoamerican Pyramids of the Sun and the Moon located in Teotihuacán, Mexico.[10] The name Teotihuacán, translated from Nahuatl, the language of the Aztecs, means "the place where men become gods." The twin pyramids emitting beacons of light serve as the headquarters of the Tyrell Corporation, which makes Replicants, and the residence of its founder, Eldon Tyrell. The pyramids symbolically represent the ethno-racial populations in Los Angeles—the people indigenous to Earth.[11] Tyrell's home, personal and corporate, in these structures reflects not only his social and economic positions of power, but also his godlike ability to create Replicants. Tyrell behaved like a god by creating life, and deities often die at the hands of their children, as Roy Batty demonstrates when he kills his father/creator.

If, as Gretchen M. Bataille posits in the introduction to *Native American Representations* (2001), "Indian images reflected the creators of those images more than the people themselves," then an analysis of these figures should tell us about the motives and objectives for instrumentalizations of Indigeneity (4).[12] For example, Chicanxs have used Indigeneity in their project of nation building to achieve cultural, social, and political objectives. María Josefina Saldaña-Portillo, in *Indian Given: Racial Geographies across Mexico and the United States* (2016), asserts, "The racial unconscious of Chicana/o identity is located at the juncture of Mexican and U.S. racial geographies. . . . [I]t was produced through an engagement with lost indigenous identity rather than through an engagement with contemporary indigenous peoples" (232).[13] Loss represents one motivating factor for instrumentalizing Indigeneity. Leveraging it for political or public gain (e.g., as Elizabeth Warren and Johnny Depp have done), or for the possibility of laying claim to resources allocated to Native people in the US, is another. The character Ramses Castro in Luis Alberto

Urrea's *In Search of Snow* instrumentalizes Indigeneity to create a sense of belonging he does not feel in his own family and to position himself against the whiteness his grandfather seems to love.

The fathers and patriarchs who narrate stories about and around Indigeneity included here in the three chapters of part 2 do so with specific goals in mind—belonging, healing, and mobilization—that, ultimately, exacerbate racial, cultural, sexual, and social divisions. My aim is not to defend instrumentalizing Indigeneity. In fact, I want to be clear that Native identity is about people, culture, kinship, place, and sovereignty—it is not a tool. I have witnessed firsthand the damage that treating Indigeneity as an object can cause—the pain, anger, and resentment. And I have also seen what happens when people have nowhere to put their knowledge of or their feelings about Indigenous ancestors. Because of these and other factors, this section of the book has been the most difficult to write. Critical introspection and disciplinary reflection meet in the chapters included in "Instrumentalizing Indigeneity," taking me to places in my life that I do not necessarily want to go.

PERSONAL NARRATIVE

NOBODY EVER SAID WE WERE AZTECS

On the highest tier of the Tejano monument in Austin, Texas, stands a conquistador, outfitted in a cuirass atop iconic ballooned breeches, sword slung at his waist.[1] With hand raised to brow, he surveys the land and legacy of Spain, vaqueros and their families, the settlers of Tejas. The monument "acknowledges and pays tribute to the contributions by Tejanos as permanent testimony of the Spanish-Mexican heritage that has influenced and is inherent in present-day Texas culture" (Gutiérrez). Positioned on the south lawn of the Texas Capitol grounds, the monument was unveiled on 29 March 2012 and celebrated over a three-day period with mariachis, speechifying, and panel talks about the history of Mexicans in Texas. Little to no mention was made of the Caddos, Karankawas, Coahuiltecans, or Lipans, revealing the fraught relationship between people of Spanish ancestry and the Indigenous populations in the US. Indians are either subsumed under the larger category of Mexican, erased in the furthering of ongoing settler colonialism, or idealized and made central to the ideological formations of colonialism, especially as princesses and other settler colonial fictions.

Nobody ever said we were Aztecs. I had heard definitely Spanish, maybe Mayan, and something about Comanche, but never Aztec. What I did know unequivocally was that in my family being of Indian heritage was complicated, and the darker skinned you were, the more complicated things became.

One summer evening, I received a call from a classmate inviting me to go swimming at her grandparents' country club in Livingston, Texas, which was about seventy-five miles north of Houston. Though I had no idea what a country club was, still my excitement was not easily contained. I begged my parents to give me permission to go with Buffy Covington and her family on the all-day outing. After speaking at length with her folks and locating the exact destination on a map, my parents reluctantly consented, but not before sitting me down and giving me the longest safety lecture in the history of history, and for good measure, they also threw in a lesson on race relations in Tejas. "Never go anywhere alone." "Make sure to cover up when you're not in the pool." "Stay with the Covingtons." "Find a phone in case you need to call us." "We didn't hang out with the Anglo kids, except some of the poor ones." "Our parents would have never allowed us to go away for the day with people we barely knew." "We couldn't even swim on the same day as the people we went to school with." I lost track of everything they were telling me because all I could think about was that I had been invited by a classmate to a place where we could swim all day and, according to Buffy, eat whatever we wanted without having to pay for it.

The day was one of the happiest of my childhood. Like beloved sisters, we swam, ate, braided each other's hair, and slept in the sun, for almost ten hours. And as unbelievable as it seemed, Buffy was right. Through a walk-up window, an outstretched arm passed us hamburgers, fries, chips, sodas, and ice cream. All we had to do was sign her grandma's name. On the car ride home that evening, bronzed, burned, and sated, we dozed, heads together, bodies slouched into the back seat like sagging question marks. As Buffy's mom pulled into our driveway, we were greeted by my father's silhouette filling the doorframe. Not wanting the day to end, I waited until my father approached the car, which afforded the opportunity to linger a moment longer with my new best friend. I gave Buffy a hug and exacted an absolute promise that she would call the next day. I left my father in his white T-shirt and knit pants standing in the warm night air to wave good-bye to the Covingtons as they backed down the steep driveway. Buoyed by the joy of my exotic excursion and the intimacy of a solidified friendship, I bounded into the living room, anxious to recount my adventure. Before I could speak, my grandmother took one look at my deeply tanned skin and *trenzas* and pronounced, "Pareces como una india."[2] Despite being a monolingual child, I knew this was not a compliment.

ME. Mami, where was your family from?
MAMI. Spain.

ME. And then where were they from after that?
MAMI. Spain.

She was, of course, an Indian princess, one who was kidnapped by a Mexican outlaw named Rangel Padron. *My father swore he never told me this story.* He was on the run for stealing and rebranding horses that he would then sell back to their owners or neighbors. His extralegal status prevented him from remaining in any one place for too long. Her band of Comanches were in hiding, as well, and her people did not need the attention of the federales who were seeking the fugitive Padron. They fell in love, or so I was told. Her family did not approve. The tribe threatened to kill him if he did not leave. He promised to depart before sunrise. The young woman, uncertain about leaving her tribe to accompany a man who was being hunted, had her mind made up for her when Padron rode out of the encampment that night. Refusing to abandon her, he chose instead to kidnap her. As they made their way into South Texas, crossing into what was then Northern Mexico, she faced the painful realization that even if she could escape and return, she would be an outcast. She would never again see her people. Once a safe distance away, allegedly around present-day Goliad, Padron and the princess settled on a small piece of land, under the name Perez rather than the highly sought-after Padron. As a child, I believed, unquestionably, the truth of this tale. I saw her, like so many Indians of the imagination, in buckskin and beads, riding across rocky terrain crowded with nopal and mesquite reaching out with thorns and tangled arms to greet her.

Spanish, Hispanic, Hispanic not of African descent (because of anti-Blackness), Mexican, Indian, Pueblo, Navajo, Ojibway, Native Hawaiʻian, Italian, Sardinian, Black, Middle Eastern, Jewish, and a few others I am forgetting. Regardless, I am aware of how I am perceived in this world, with or without my consent.

Downtown Lincoln, Nebraska. It was evening. I was sitting with a group of fellow graduate students in the smoky darkness of a bar favored by locals. Too many of us were wedged into a booth, some spilling onto chairs that formed a lazy half-circle at the opening. As the evening wore on and the crowd ebbed, I noticed for the first time a group of Indians gathered around a table in the far back corner: two men, two women. One of the men wore a dark blue and white checkered shirt with chipped pearl snaps that resembled jagged-tooth smiles. A black beaver Stetson sat forward on his head shadowing his eyes, which I could feel on me from time to time. Slowly, I became more aware of the table of Indians than I was of the people sitting right in front of me. From the corner of my eye, I could see that the man in the black hat had repositioned his chair so that he was exactly forty-five degrees to the left of me, which meant even when I was looking forward, he was always on the periphery of my vision. His location allowed me to watch him without ever looking directly at him, so I saw him clearly when he lifted his beer mug as if to toast me, a gesture punctuated by the laughter of his companions. Later, when the server brought me a beer that I did not order and I expressed my confusion, once again the sound of laughter spilled out of the corner, telling me who had sent it over. The bar suddenly became too loud, too stifling, too small. I quickly offered something in the way of a goodbye to my associates and attempted to untangle my coat and scarf from the back of the chair, knocking it over in the process. With a growing urgency, I made my way to the door.

The exit from the oppressive heat of the bar felt like an escape despite the swirling wind throwing snow in every direction, slicing at my face and arms. I began to bundle myself against the elements. From behind me, I heard someone call out, "Cousin." I did not turn for I knew with absolute certainty that I was not the one being called. Again I heard "Cousin," only this time louder. With some effort, I circled round into an icy gust, eyes squinted and shoulders drawn, a feeble attempt to keep warm. In front of me stood the Indian cowboy from the bar. He stood without a jacket, back to the wind, hands stuffed in his front pants pockets.

He tilted his head back and pointed at me with his chin before asking, "What tribe?"

"Tribe?" I echoed.

While my word hung in the frigid air, he asked another question, and his expression grew grave. "Why didn't you come sit with the other Indians?" As he spoke, he narrowed his eyes, looking past me at a point somewhere over my right shoulder. The effect made me feel as though he were expecting someone or something to come up from behind me. Feet planted facing forward, I twisted my upper body back to follow his gaze. Seeing no one, I turned forward again to face him and saw the corner of his mouth pull up into a half smile.

From far away I heard myself say, "I was with friends."

His countenance did not change. "Them people in there." It was neither a question nor a reply.

"Chicana," I responded rather belatedly. "I am Chicana." It was as if we were speaking across time and continents, words heavy with accusation and uncertainty, traveling great distances. Snowflakes dusted his hat as he looked out from under the brim.

"What tribe?" he asked again.

On a snowy, windswept sidewalk in the high plains, Aztlán seemed so very far away, elusive. As I cycled through possible responses, I was unsure what to say. What answer would satisfy his question? And why was he singling me out? With all of these and countless other thoughts racing through my mind, I chose to tell the truth: "I don't know, Mexican Indian, maybe Coahuiltecan, my grandfather was from Saltillo, but there are family stories about being Comanche. We don't know for sure." My explanation turned confession surprised even me, for I had offered information to a complete stranger that I had not shared with my closest friends, though I did not tell him about the alleged kidnapping of the chief's daughter or the flight with her captor across the border. Something about him and the persistence of his question demanded a particular kind of response, one that closed the distance between us.

Our position in the human thoroughfare forced the flow of bodies to either side of where we stood. The snow began to collect at our feet. People scurrying out of bars and restaurants gave us a wide berth. In between their passing, I caught glimpses inside the bar, where my companions remained as they were. No one craned her neck in the direction of the door. No one climbed over seated patrons to make his way toward me. No one. I was not missed. I was not worried about. The disappointment must have registered on my face. With a hint of satisfaction, he intoned, "So you *are* an Indian."

"I guess," I countered, "though not in any way that people would recognize, and besides, I'm not sure."

"What people? 'Cause I'm sure *I* recognized it." Before I could respond, he continued, "You are what you are. Maybe you think you're better than us because you go to the college. When you didn't come over, we thought fer sure you had forgotten who you are. But seems you haven't figured it out." He paused for a moment, cocked his head sideways, then added, "Best you figure out who and what you are or they'll decide for you," which he delivered with a nod, a gesture that gave the appearance of his agreeing with his own pronouncement. "Tókša akhé," he said, and with that farewell, he turned and strode down the sidewalk, the snow crunching under his heavy leather soles. He stopped for a moment, as if he had forgotten something or was about to return. Instead, he threw one last line over his shoulder, "You may be better than them, but you ain't better than me . . . *Indian*." The last word was punctuated with a bark of laughter. I followed him with my eyes as he weaved in and out of the drunken crowds, until I lost sight of him and his white hat.

Indian Boy, that was what my father's coworkers called him. In Houston during the 1980s, a grown man's knowledge of engineering, skill as a draftsman, and acumen as a patented inventor still did not matter as much as the color of his skin. Or maybe they mattered too much.

Chris Verdi, who sat behind me in social studies and art, had been pulling on my low pigtails all morning long. His doing so was unusual but not completely unexpected. As a redhead regularly bullied for his shellacked hair and husky Toughskins jeans (the ones with the reinforced knees) from Sears, Chris had grown frustrated at being victimized. So he had started to try his hand at being the tormentor. He focused his physical and verbal abuse on girls and the smallest boys in the class. On this particular day, my pigtails, which swung at my back only inches away from the front of his desk, were an easy target. At regular intervals, he would yank on my hair, alternating between left and right, though sometimes both pigtails at once. I told him to stop. I tried to ignore him. I told the teacher, who reminded me that "no one likes a tattletale." And then, in the same breath, she had even suggested that maybe Chris liked me, which was definitely worse than his pulling my hair. All I wanted was for him to stop. So I was grateful when art class started. I hoped he would focus on the assignment, which involved cutting out felt patterns for a project we would assemble in the coming weeks. Between collecting our supplies from the stations around the classroom and listening to the art teacher go over the instructions, he was distracted, which put an end to things, or so I thought. I worked intently on cutting out my paper shapes first. And then, once completed, I held a paper pattern in place with one hand and used the pointed, not the blunt-tipped, blade of the scissors grasped firmly in my other hand to guide my cuts along the edges. Before too long, once again, I felt a familiar tug on my right pigtail. My head bobbed once, twice to the side, accompanied by the unmistakable sound of scissors slicing through hair. With two quick snips, my hair tumbled down onto the floor. As I watched one of the double-knotted grosgrain bows my mother had tied in my hair that morning flutter to the ground, something inside me came roaring to the surface. I spun around in my chair, opened my scissors, and, reaching high over my head, brought the blade down with the full force of my rage. Verdi screamed in anticipation of the metal plunging deep into the top of his thigh. My scissors were barely sharp enough to cut felt, and not even the pointed tip could penetrate the Dacron Type 59 polyester, DuPont 420 nylon, and cotton of his Toughskins jeans. But my intention was clear enough. He left me alone from that day forward. At home, as my mother tried to fix my shingled hair, she told me what I had done was wrong. When my father came in to tell me good night, he ran his hand over my bobbed hair and kissed my forehead without saying a word.

When the light-skinned Eugenia, daughter of land-owning Mexicans in south central Texas, married the poor and dark-skinned Eduardo, her parents disowned her. She lived out the rest of her brief life in a one-room shack next to a cotton field with her husband and seven children. They buried her in a corner of the Mexican cemetery away from others.

In the late 1970s, films such as *Smokey and the Bandit* (1977) and *Convoy* (1978) helped to inspire the citizen's band (CB) radio craze. Vehicles traveling down interstate highways would reach out to strangers over the radio to communicate about traffic or weather conditions and to issue warnings about speed traps set up by police or simply to pass the time conversing on long trips. Almost as important as the type of radio equipment one purchased was the handle, a nickname that was analogous to contemporary usernames, the name by which the CB user would identify and be identified by others. When selecting a handle, users drew inspiration from their personalities, communication styles, hobbies, goals for using the CB, or how they wanted to be perceived by others. My father chose Winterhawk, the titular protagonist's name in the 1975 western about a Blackfoot chief trying to save his people from smallpox.

    ME. This is the most difficult part to write.
    PB. Whatever part you are working on is always the most difficult.
    ME. Not like this.

Perhaps as much as 68 percent, though conservative estimates place the figure closer to around 43 percent: the numbers correlate with whispers and pieces of stories I heard growing up. Through genetic testing, I have learned that as recently as the 1800s, at least one of my ancestors was 100 percent Native American. Yet these percentages tell me absolutely nothing about the tribe, band, clan, or Nation from which I am descended. What they tell me is that in the not-so-distant past my ancestors were part of an Indigenous kinship group. The exact name and memory of both are now lost. In a relatively short amount of time, the great civilizing machine chewed up all that history and knowledge and spat out my family with great efficiency, or maybe we crawled into the apparatus by choice or through coercion. Regardless, the result was the same.

The results of DNA tests tell us a story about where we come from. Like all stories, they are not definitive or necessarily true. Kim Tallbear identifies, in her comprehensive critique *Native American DNA: Tribal Belonging and the False Promise of Genetic Science* (2013), the interrelated problems involving Native American DNA analysis and testing: dishonest sample collections; the monetizing of Indigenous biological materials; the creation of genetic pathways for challenging tribal sovereignty; and the instrumentalizing of Native DNA to lay claim to resources such as casino revenues or to gain an advantage in college admissions. In the last ten years, I have paid for two different genealogy tests as part of the process of developing an understanding of my own family history. The decision was motivated not by the anticipation of *finding* Indigenous ancestors, but instead by a desire to understand why these relations were purposely obscured.

Colonization, racism, nationalism, and immigration constitute some of the factors that complicate family genealogies. Yet in my case, I also come from a family of liars and storytellers. The tales of the two commingled with such great frequency that lies became family truths, and truths slipped into history. This means that when repeating a family story, one never knows its veracity, so telling such a story with conviction becomes crucial. My mother, who, with her green eyes and fair skin, could pass for white, always said her family originated in Spain. I did not believe her, especially after I met my grandfather, a short, dark-skinned man.[3] My father, tall, brown, with dark hair and dark eyes, whose parents were from Saltillo, Mexico, and Lockhart, Texas, began over time to identify as an Indian. I did not believe him, especially as I watched him stitch this new identity together from pieces of stories, books, films, and other popular representations.

When I received my most recent DNA results, a few days before writing the introduction to this part of my book, I was humbled by the results. My parents had been telling the truth, or rather, they had been living their specific versions of the truth. Based on the visual story of the chromosomal pairs, one parent was of predominantly European ancestry that included Spanish, North African, and Sephardic ancestors, with some Native heritage; the other was principally Native and most likely originated from Nuevo León, Mexico, which is near Saltillo in the bordering state of Coahuila. Reading the results caused my perspective on "truth" to shift. Not because they alone provided definitive facts but because they correlated with family stories. This knowledge speaks to my detribalization, that I am of Native ancestry without a known community of origin.

FILM

FATHERHOOD, CHICANISMO, AND THE CULTURAL POLITICS OF HEALING IN *LA MISSION*

On Friday, 14 May 2010, at the Cinemark Theater in Austin, some of the cast and crew of *La Mission* appeared at a screening of the film to promote it and speak with audience members. I invited my mom to the event, hoping she might have the chance to see some of the stars in person, though really just Benjamin Bratt, whom she adored. During the Q&A, Bratt emphasized the importance of supporting an independent film about Chicanos: "Buying a ticket to see this movie is an act of radicalism. You're telling Hollywood you don't want to see *Iron Man 46*. You want to see movies with corazón. You want to see raza."[1] The crowd filed out of the theatre when the event concluded, and brothers Peter Bratt and Benjamin Bratt, along with Jesse Borrego, offered to stay around and take pictures with fans. After waiting in line for about twenty minutes, my mom was ecstatic about the opportunity to pose with Benjamin, which is evident in her ear-to-ear smile in a photo I took of her (figure 10). She was disappointed with the result, though: she had forgotten to put on lipstick.

Independent, activist filmmaker Peter Bratt's first film, *Follow Me Home* (1996), featuring Alfre Woodard and Salma Hayek, debuted as an Official Selection at the Sundance Film Festival. The cross-country roadtrip film about a group of Black, Native American, and Chicanx street artists traveling from Los Angeles to Washington, DC, to cover the White House in their art won critical acclaim. It garnered both the Best Director Award at the American Indian Film Festival and the Audience Award for the Best Feature Film at the San Francisco International Film Festival in 1996. Bratt followed up his freshman film with a second feature, *La Mission* (2009), focusing on the lives of a Chicano father and son who live in the San Francisco Mission District: protagonist and self-identified

FIGURE 10. *My mother with actor Benjamin Bratt at a screening of the film* La Mission. *2010.*

Mexica Che Rivera (played by Benjamin Bratt) and his teenage son, Jesse (Jeremy Ray Valdez). One reviewer called the film, made with longtime Mission community residents, "[t]he most important Chicano film made since Patricia Cardoso's 2002 *Real Women Have Curves*" (Foster 249). Peter Bratt's film shares themes with Cardoso's: both address social issues such as education, familial relationships, and the need for strong community ties.

La Mission focuses on a father-son bond tested by violence and a family secret. When talking about the film, Peter Bratt speaks fondly of the Mission District's diversity and strong sense of community, while emphasizing that "the Latino family is at the heart and soul of the neighborhood." While the film depicts aspects of Latino family life positively, it also offers a pointed critique of violent, patriarchal, heteronormative Chicano masculinity and its effect on families and communities. Leandra H. Hernández describes the film thusly: "Rooted within Catholicism, homophobia, and the rigid patriarchal Mexican structure of the family, Che becomes a violent, aggressive, and insufferable father and community member as he spends the entire movie coming to terms with his son's sexuality and verbally and nonverbally abusing family and friends throughout the process" (263). A single parent, MUNI bus driver, recovering alcoholic, ex-convict, and artist, Che frequently responds to conflict with physical force. For example, after learning his son, Jesse, is gay, during an argument, Che drags his son out of the house and throws him down on the sidewalk. The issue of homosexuality, according to Peter Bratt, is "still a huge taboo subject within the community" (P. Bratt and B. Bratt).[2] Che's ire is greater than his affection for his son, who is a bright student bound for UCLA. Bratt has stated that *La Mission* represents "an exploration of violence and different ideas of power, and how that informs our masculinity—not just within the Latino culture but the culture at large" (B. Bratt et al.). The loss of that power and the dissolution of his family pushes Che into freefall. Faced also with the loss of his son and his sobriety, Che confronts his own legacy of self-destruction to discover he is a man who is in desperate need of a healing. Although *La Mission* never makes clear why Che deserves redemption, it gives it to him nevertheless. Che turns to Indigeneity for it: he finds curative power in various aspects of Native identity—both real and imagined—enacted through witnessing, singing, praying, and dancing.

To date, much of the critical analysis of the film focuses not on Indigeneity but on toxic masculinity or queer identity within the context of Mexican American and Latinx culture. Richard Reitsma's "Quo Vadis, Queer Vato? Queer and Loathing in Latino Cinema" (2012); M. Cristina Alcalde's "What It Means to Be a Man? Violence and Homophobia in Latino Masculinities On and Off Screen" (2014); Leandra H. Hernández's "Paternidad, Masculinidad, and Machismo: Evolving Representations of Mexican American Fathers in Film" (2016); and Gabriel S. Estrada's "Two-Spirit Mexica Youth and Transgender Mixtec/Muxe Media: *La Mission* (2009), *Two Spirit: Injunuity* (2013), and *Libertad* (2015)" (2017) all represent critical work at the intersection of gender, Latinx, and queer studies. However, given the prominence of Indians and Indian iconography in *La Mission*, very little has been written about this aspect of the film. As Estrada observes, the film is deserving of a "more Indigenous-focused film analysis," particularly in light of the fact that Che self-identifies as Mexica (3). The instrumentalization of Indigeneity throughout the film sets the stage for the resolution of Che's conflict with himself, which involves not only coming to terms with his beliefs about cultural identity and masculinity but also understanding how they isolate him from the people he professes to care about.

This chapter focuses on the father-son relationships in *La Mission*, offering a comparative study between the two pairs, Che and Jesse, and Rene (Che's brother-in-law) and his son, Rene, Jr. The two fathers not only have vastly different parenting styles but also offer two versions of Chicanismo, one best described as old school, movement era and the other as more modern. I include in my analysis movement-era sources from the late 1960s and early 1970s (anthologies and lesser-known works) to contextualize Che's particular brand of historical Chicanismo and its centralization of Native identity.[3] The narrative instrumentalizes Indigeneity as a means of personal healing for Che and as an avenue for repairing his fractured relationship with Jesse, and it reflects both the ethno-racial diversity and the history of the Mission, a place the director and his siblings called home.

INDIANS OF ALL TRIBES, NEW TRIBALISM, AND THE PAN-*HUMANO*

La Mission represents the fulfillment of a longtime dream for Peter and his brother Benjamin to tell a story set in the neighborhood that played such a central role in their early lives. When they were growing up, "the city's Mission District," Reed Johnson remarks, "was the soul of [their] compact universe." The multiethnic community served as home for Peter, Benjamin, and their three siblings and became the site of their activist education. "In the 1970s," as Cary Cordova reflects, "the Mission became an important site for American Indian community organizing, offering important meeting places" (139). Their mother, Eldy Banda (Quechua), a nurse and community organizer, took her children to participate with the group Indians of All Tribes (IAT) in the takeover of Alcatraz Island (1969–1971), traveling to and from the island several times a week in the effort to return control of the island to Native people.[4] At the time, Wallace "Mad Bear" Anderson (Tuscorora), one of the leaders of the occupation, expressed an explicit solidarity between American Indians and Chicanos, identifying the two as "[t]he only people who have a right to live on Alcatraz" (de la Garza et al. 4). American Indians and Chicanxs worked together for this shared cause. Back on the mainland, Banda's involvement as an organizer made the family's "home a nerve center of sorts during the occupation of Alcatraz," with Native people from all over coming, going, and camping in their front yard (Gerhard). Peter Bratt remembers the event as a response to the culmination of years of Native oppression, when "native people across the country began standing up for their rights as human beings, and as members of sovereign nations" (P. Bratt).

Alcatraz was not so much about the sovereignty of any one Nation as it was an expression of Pan-Indianism, tribes coming together to advocate for Native people and a shared set of causes.

Although the events at Alcatraz lasted only eighteen months, Banda's commitment to American Indian activism has been lifelong and has had a direct impact on her children. Peter Bratt's "awareness of place," as Susan Gerhard notes in a review, "saturates every frame of *La Mission*." The writer/director's experiences in the Mission reflect the cultural exchange and collaborations of American Indian activists from around the country along with neighborhood racial and ethnic groups that reside in the area located on the land of the Ohlone People, whom early Spanish colonists called Costanoan. Thus, the Mission District represents historical and ongoing racial and cultural geographies informed by the legacies of Spanish colonization in California, the Indian Relocation Act of 1956, and more recently, gentrification, to name a few.[5] American Indian, Mesoamerican, and South American Indian iconography and spirituality permeate *La Mission* from the opening sequence to the final scene, reflecting the diversity of Indigenous cultural productions and practices found in the titular district. Bratt fills the mise-en-scène with Indigenous iconography. It is everywhere: on storefronts, lowriders, bodies, posters, postcards, and T-shirts, in homes, books, and especially on the streets, in towering wall paintings. Cordova explains that the "muralists invoked their diverse indigenous heritages to align themselves with the concerns of American Indians and the larger Third World Community" (139). In other words, Bratt leveraged visual representations demonstrating a broad understanding of Indigeneity as a means of creating political solidarity with other colonized groups and to convey ideas reinforced through his early life in the Mission.

The iconography in *La Mission* marks the neighborhood as an Indigenous space, one derived from "a matrix of Aztec, Mayan, and Mesoamerican iconography, mythohistory, and symbology," described in the following chapter as an Aztext (Perez, "New Tribalism" 491).[6] But it also pulls from Comanche, Mohawk, and other Pacific Northwest–inspired Native traditions.[7] Peter Bratt intercuts Che's opening stroll through the neighborhood with painted images of an Indigenous woman with a child on her back and a jaguar priest with the animal's skin draped over his body. The images are from the large mural *500 Years of Resistance* (1992), located at the corner of 24th and Florida in the Mission District, an artwork that "[tells] the story of conquest from the perspective of the Indigenous" (Khoury). The mural also includes scenes of Mexican and/or Mexican American laborers and Spanish conquistadors mixed with World War II soldiers. In the upper-right-hand corner of the left wall appear figures such as Father Miguel Hidalgo, whose famed Grito de Dolores, on 16 September 1810, launched Mexico's battle for independence, and Kateri Tekakwitha (1656–1680), an "Algonquin-Mohawk" and the first American Indian woman canonized by the Catholic Church.[8] El Salvadoran artist Isaias Mata, who painted the mural and then restored it in 2013, made changes to the image during his renovation to show "more resistance" by Indigenous people to European conquest. Mata goes on to explain that he wanted to show "a cosmological vision of Indigenous peoples worldwide" while at the same time illustrating shared beliefs through, for instance, the image of the jaguar, which holds importance as a god for "the Aztecs, Mayans," and other Indigenous people of Mesoamerica and South America (Jung). Also featured in the mural are images of an Olmec head and a feathered warrior being crucified. The images in the film's opening sequence place in tension colonial invaders and Indigenous people and show them engaged in combat and syncretism.

Through these and other images, as well as cultural practices, Peter Bratt creates a visual pastiche of Native identities and influences lacking in tribal specificity. This does not mean that Native people are not present or represented in the film. Rather, *La Mission* lacks any evidence of a distinct tribal community. Stated another way, the film is devoid of what Gerald Vizenor (White Earth Ojibwe) calls "the tribal real" (4). So while *La Mission* relies on simulations of Native presence to redeem its protagonist, it does so through their absence, all but ignoring the Indigenous history of and in the Mission. Seen in this way, the film participates in the problematic visual history of representing Indians in American cinema, the subject of which is addressed in such works as the documentary *Reel Injun* (2009), codirected by Neil Diamond, Catherine Bainbridge, and Jeremiah Hayes, and the books *Reservation Reelism: Redfacing, Visual Sovereignty, and Representations of Native Americans in Film* (2011), by Michelle H. Raheja, and *Native Recognition: Indigenous Cinema and the Western* (2012), by Joanna Hearne, among countless others, stretching back decades. However, recognizing the lack of tribal specificity for the Native people featured in the film and the failure to indicate a tribal territory, outside of broad ideological or political imaginings, does not lend insight into how and why the film instrumentalizes Indigeneity.

Understanding what the film does formally and politically with Indigenous identity is crucial, particularly in light of Benjamin Bratt's claim that *La Mission* is "really heavy in the Chicanismo. It's an earnest attempt to portray the heart and soul that exists in this kind of community. But even though it's that culturally and geographically specific, it's something that is not only pan-Latino but it's pan-*humano*" (B. Bratt et al.). An emphasis on the local (in this case, the Mission—a community in a geographically specific place) as a means of connecting people more broadly (panhuman, which also resembles pan-Indian formulations), in the way Bratt describes, parallels the relationship between Gloria E. Anzaldúa's borderlands and her theory of new tribalism, discussed in the next chapter. One informs and builds on the other. The pan-humanism depicted in *La Mission* shares qualities with Anzaldúa's new tribalism, namely, in the way that it represents the neighborhood as a place where Black, Native, Mexican, and Asian American, as well as Pacific Islander, community members and cultural practices commingle through entwined racial histories and/or by choice. Within this framework, Peter Bratt visually situates Indigeneity as integral both to the film and to Chicanx culture through Aztec dancing and artwork, including murals, framed paintings, religious iconography, and lowriders.

FATHERHOOD, LOW AND SLOW

For Che, lowriders function as a form of cultural currency, circulating ideas about community pride, Chicanismo, heterosexuality, and most especially, masculinity. Che is an aggressive, violence-prone, confrontational homophobe who believes that strong, opinionated feminist women are "confused." Lowrider culture is also at the center of Che's male friendship group and his relationship with Jesse. In addition to an activity in which the father and son participate, lowrider culture, Richard Reitsma argues, represents one of the ways that Che "fights to keep his son tied to Latino cultural traditions as manifested in San Francisco's Mission district" (235). For Rene, however, lowrider culture represents a part but not all of who he is as a man and father. Kind, accepting, and more in tune with cultural and political changes than his contemporaries, Rene is not so much the opposite of Che as an individual who has done the slow work of questioning his values and altering his worldviews and behaviors in response.

The film reveals early on Che's status as a father in a scene involving the making of a lowrider, thereby entwining fatherhood and the neighborhood's car culture. Che enters the garage calling out, "Yo, yo can we dance with yo dates?"[9] From inside a primer-covered 1964 Chevrolet Im-

FIGURE 11. *Rene* (right) *reading Che's paternal pride about his son's accomplishments in* La Mission.

pala, Rene responds, "Only if I can have her sister." The masculinist exchange confers heterosexuality on both men, though not the nature of their kinship. Che's dialogue then reveals both his objective at the garage and his pride as a father. Brothers-in-law Che and Rene have joined forces to collaborate on a lowrider for Jesse as a graduation gift, and Che has designed a special dedication that characterizes the closeness of their father-son bond. He wants painted in "Aztec gold" on the trunk of the car "The best friend I got." Framed in a medium close-up, Rene registers Che's pride and happiness (figure 11). The shot also places the men in conversation visually and invites comparisons between the two. Che's initial response to Rene's reaction ("What?") demonstrates his defensive posture and instinct for confrontation. But Rene, who has a gentler nature, merely wants to express his admiration for the father-son relationship, telling Che, "I think it's cool the way you back him up." Che's attitude notably shifts: "Tsht. It's all right. Did I tell you [Jesse] made the honor roll again?" His son's academic accomplishments represent a source of pride for Che, yet they too are tied to his perception of heterosexual masculinity, one in which Jesse's success reflects directly on Che's success as a father. The car Jesse will receive as a gift represents both his academic success with graduation and the continuation of his connection to lowrider culture, the Mission, and his father, so Jesse's upcoming turn away from lowrider culture represents a rejection of heterosexual Latino masculinity and by association his father's brand of Chicano heterosexual masculinity, one characterized by anger and hostility.

Che's propensity for aggressive confrontation comes to the fore early in the film when he threatens two young men on his bus for playing their music too loud. Unbeknownst to him, his behaviors set in motion a circle of violence that later envelops Jesse. Although Che's anger always simmers just below the surface, he boils over with rage when confronting Jesse about his sexuality. Che repeatedly slaps his son and physically throws him out of the house. While hurling homophobic epithets, Che publicly beats Jesse on the sidewalk. In front of family, including Jesse's American Indian grandfather, Virgil Ten Bears, friends, and neighbors alike, father and son exchange blows on the sidewalk.[10] When Che's lowrider friends try to step in and stop the fight, the irate father threatens them with violence as well. As the two are pulled apart, Che yells at Jesse, "You're dead to me!" Che's public display is both to condemn and to distance himself from Jesse. "With an alpha-male like Benjamin's character," as Peter Bratt explains, "he is this masculine, powerful figure who has really earned his stripes as this badass dude who can get down if he has to. And . . . the ultimate threat to that identity is having a gay son." Bratt adds, "It completely thwarts and challenges who he is, especially if this is his only child. Often times, most men see our sons as reflections of ourselves . . ." (B. Bratt et al.). Therefore, according to Bratt's point of view, Che sees Jesse's homosexuality as a personal failure and worries that he too might be perceived as gay. Like Turk McGurk in *In Search of Snow*, Che knows his entire identity is wrapped up in a particular performance of racialized masculinity that his son threatens. Tellingly, Che abandons the lowrider project for Jesse because the compulsory heterosexuality associated with it cannot coexist with his son's queerness.

Rene's relationship with his son intersects with that of Che and Jesse. After the fight, Rene and his wife, Ana (Talisa Soto Bratt), take in Jesse. After Ana tends to her nephew's physical wounds, the scene cuts to Jesse reading aloud to Rene, Jr., who is seated next to him. The boys are positioned in the same frame, much like their fathers in the earlier garage scene in a medium shot. Through the mise-en-scène, Peter Bratt creates a complex conversation about the sacred place of women, sociocultural belonging, and the relationality of Mexican and US Indigeneities. Ana, positioned behind the boys and flanked by candles on either side, represents the watchful, venerated mother, a prominent theme in *La Mission*.[11] On the right side of the frame, in front of a white door, sits a green oxygen tank with a red handle. Rene, Jr., wears a nasal cannula, connecting him physically to the oxygen tank and symbolically to Mexico, as represented through the red, white, and green colors of the Mexican flag present in the scene. Seen another way, Mexico is oxygen; it is the air he breathes. Although the film gives viewers no indication as to the boy's specific condition, the two sons, one disabled and the other queer, share the same space, creating a visual equivalency between Rene, Jr., and Jesse. Around them square shapes fill the frame, reminiscent of both boxes and bricks, the former symbolizing containment or the way the boys will be categorized in wider social environments, the latter resembling the stones used in Mesoamerican structures, including temples. Jesse reads Rene, Jr., the book *Storm Boy*, by Paul Owen Lewis, about a Native boy in the Pacific Northwest who is separated from his family and longs to return home. The story mirrors Jesse's alienation from his father, and in turn his yearning for home enlivens *Storm Boy*'s narrative. On the other side of the room, next to his daughter, Rene sits and listens as he quietly works on his computer. In the Mexican and Indigenous coded space of Rene and Ana's home, children, regardless of gender, sexuality, or ability, are watched over and protected by caring parents. *La Mission*, consequently, offers *la familia*, the heterosexual nuclear Brown family, as a site capable of accommodating sanctioned forms of difference, even without the mediating influence of an *anciano*.

As opposed to Che, Rene represents a version of fatherhood not dependent on domination or intimidation. Furthermore, he accepts his children as they are and not as he would like them to be, though this was not always the case. While staying with his *tía* and *tío*, Jesse watches Rene lovingly interact with both his son and his daughter (figure 12). But Jesse does not know the transformation Rene underwent to become more devoted to and accepting of his children or how his previous failures as a father almost ruined his marriage, as discussed later. Jesse can only see the result. In other words, Jesse sees who his *tío* has become, not who he was. Rene's transformation matters because it suggests that if he can change, then perhaps Che can too.

Rene does, however, share his story of transformation with Che, leveraging it to advocate for Jesse. The two men once again are framed within the same space, underscoring their connection, though this time in a kitchen instead of a garage, with Rene in the foreground, emphasizing his authority in this scenario despite the fact that he sits and Che stands throughout the entire scene. In spite of himself, Che asks about Jesse. Rene responds, "He's a great kid, I'm thinking of adopting him."

FIGURE 12. *An over-the-shoulder shot of Jesse watching his* tío *Rene display physical affection for his children. The reverse angle conveys Jesse's longing for such a supportive relationship.*

The scene represents one of the few instances in the film in which Che demonstrates emotional vulnerability. He wonders whether Jesse's homosexuality is a punishment from God. Rene admits to similar thoughts after the birth of his son: "Watcha, when Rene, Jr., was born and the doctors told us about his condition, I was thinking exactly what you are right now. God's punishing me for all my sins, for all the shit I did or didn't do, why else would he give me a defective son, right?" Rene's refusal to accept or even hold his son almost broke apart his marriage to Ana. The possibility of the boy's death inspired Rene to change. After his son stopped breathing one night, Rene prayed for him to live. He tells Che, "I mean, I got down on my knees and begged, homey, not for his heart to be normal or for him to even breathe on his own. Chale. I just wanted him to live. I wanted him to live so I could pick him up and love him. That's it. Just let him live and I'll be happy." The message is clear: both of their sons are alive, and as fathers they should be content with that fact, regardless of their physical condition or sexuality. Rene's confession proves powerful enough to convince Che to invite Jesse back home, but their fragile relationship is made even more tenuous by Che's prohibition of any mention of Jesse's sexuality or of his white boyfriend, Jordan.

Che closely resembles Turk McGurk, with lowriding standing in for bare-knuckle boxing, although Che regularly works the heavy bag in the alley behind his house. The two men are so devoted to a singular version and performance of masculinity that they risk their relationships with their sons, at least for a short time in Rene's case, to preserve it. Che faces the same fear of losing a son that Rene had experienced when Smoke, the young man Che threatened earlier on the bus, shoots and nearly kills Jesse in an anti-gay hate crime. Following this attack, Che delivers an ultimatum to his recovering son, forcing the young man to choose between his father and his boyfriend. Jesse decides on the latter. His son's decision leads Che to forsake his sobriety and then take a wrench to the hood of the lowrider he and Rene have completed during Jesse's recuperation. He repeatedly strikes the hood, damaging the paint and the body, though whether he is lashing out at lowrider culture, heterosexual masculinity, Jesse, or all three at once remains unclear. Regardless, Che falls into a downward, isolating spiral until he hits rock bottom. Once he is there, Chicano Indigeneity helps him find his way back so he can try to mend his relationship with his son.

"MEXICA LIKE YOU": CHICANO INDIGENEITY

> To make alliances with other nationalist struggles taking place throughout the country in the late sixties, there was no room for Chicano ambivalence about being Indians, for it was our Indian blood and history of resistance against both Spanish and Anglo invaders that made us rightful inheritors of Aztlán. After centuries of discrimination against our Indian-ness, which forced mestizos into denial, many Mexican-Americans found the sudden affirmation of our indigenismo difficult to accept. And yet the Chicano Indigenous movement was not without historical precedence.
> Cherríe Moraga, *The Last Generation*

The place of Indigeneity in the Chicanx imaginary is often fraught. From the outset, *La Mission* works to visually construct Chicano Indigeneity without ever problematizing it, though ultimately, as Gabriel S. Estrada offers, the film does critique "Mexica cis-heteropatriarchal violence against male-bodied femininity, homosexuality, and women" (2). Visual representations of Native life and lore have a profound impact on the story and on Che's characterization. Rather than take up the position of the mestizo, or mixed-blood, Che sees himself as Indigenous. He takes great pride in Native cultural productions and his Native identity. Both are reflected on the walls of his home, the streets of his barrio, and the bodies of the lowriders he loves.¹² For Che, as in the early days of the Chicano movement, "many Indian symbols in Mexican and Mexican American culture are interpreted as Chicano. Some are the Aztec figures on Chicano magazine covers; the Aztec eagle on the *Huelga* banners of César Chávez and the United Farm workers. . . . These and other unconscious symbols affirm a new trend among Mexican Americans to accept the Indianness in their heritage" (Lux and Vigil 101). Notably, these images, and more, appear in the film. Lourdes Alberto explains that "indigenist aesthetics . . . permeated every aspect of Chicana/o political life and culture and [remain] a vibrant component of contemporary Chicana/o identity" (108). And as Alberto further explains, Chicano "indigenism" manifested "with no central organizing machinery" (107, 108).¹³ In other words, while Native identity was quickly centralized and celebrated, who or what constituted Indigeneity was simply presented as the Aztec Empire writ large.

As an artist, Che is also a cultural producer who incorporates Aztec themes and myths in his work, at times reproducing or altering famous scenes by Mexican artist Jesús Helguera, whose classic images were circulated via calendars and notably include *Amor indio* (1965) and *La leyenda de los volcanes* (1940).¹⁴ The latter figures prominently at the film's conclusion. Stylized versions of these popular images appear on cars and on the walls of Che's garage in various forms—in poster prints and on a clock, a tapestry, and a calendar. Catrióna Rueda Esquibél asserts that Helguera's dramatic scenes of Mexican Indian myth and lore establish "a visual link between modern Mexicanos (and by extension Chicanas/os) and the Aztec heroes of a bygone era" (296). They also help to centralize Aztecs in the cultural imaginary of Chicanismo, Chicanos' cultural nationalism, while at the same time creating a visual relationship between the past and the present.

Che takes this relationship a step further, marking himself as an Indian subject through his body art. The tattoos on his chest, back, and arms form a visually complex web of images that tell part of the story of who and what Che is, conveying ideas about gender, heteronormativity, place, and Chicano nationalism. His right pectoral bears the image of two buxom women and his left an adorned cross or gravestone that reads "Mi querida madre" in memory of his mother. "MISSION" is tattooed in Chicano gothic, a font used for all his tattoos, across his upper abdomen. The Golden Gate Bridge appears on his left deltoid, with the word "BROWN" beside it; correspondingly, on his right arm another buxom woman in a sombrero perches provocatively next to "PRIDE," which would mean something entirely different in the Castro District of San Francisco (fig-

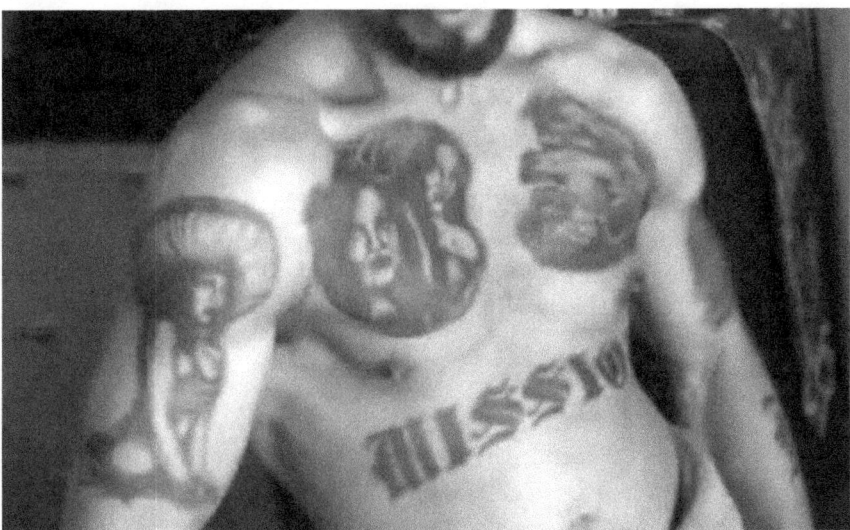

FIGURE 13. *Tattoos of three hypersexualized women form counterpoints to Che's memorial to his mother on his left pectoral.*

ure 13). Across his shoulder blades spans "MEXICA" over a stylized image of la Virgen in San Francisco. Finally, on his forearms are the letters "S" and "F." Che's tattoos mark his already racially marked body in a narrative of his own making. These signs and symbols are fully revealed, not publicly, but in private, secluded moments, when he is working the heavy bag shirtless in the alley beside his house; as he irons his pants, wrapped only in a towel knotted at the waist, in preparation for a Friday-night cruise; or when he is having sex with his neighbor Lena. Che is an old-school *vato*, as revealed through his dialogue and sartorial style. "Tattoo," as Marc Blanchard states, "is about revealing, being revealed and gazing upon the revealing" (295). The film attempts to present Che as more than a cinematic homeboy, the contemporary iteration of the bandido; he is a "MEXICA" filled with "BROWN PRIDE," a man of the "MISSION, SF," who loves his mother and hypersexualized women.

"MEXICA" on Che's back speaks to an unspecified Indigenous past; however, the interpolation of the Virgen against the Golden Gate Bridge suggests that Che is a modern Mexica of California. The truth is, he is lost somewhere in the middle. In their essay "Return to Aztlán: The Chicano Rediscovers His Indian Past," Guillermo Lux and Maurilio E. Vigil explain that "Chicano derives from a tribe of the Aztecs known as *Mexicas*," who spoke Nahuatl, a language belonging to the Uto-Aztecan family (98). Pete Silva Sloss further elucidates the connection between the Mexica and the word "Chicano": "Etymologists would probably say ['Chicano'] has its roots in the Nahuatl 'Ch' sound that the Spanish tongue doesn't carry, thus the original Mexicas, the Mexicanos, were Mechicas and Mechicanos" and eventually Chicanos (172). Repeatedly, Che demonstrates cultural knowledge of this ancestry, displaying and disseminating it in his home and to the community.[15] His decision to identify as Mexica represents a particular iteration of Chicano cultural nationalism steeped in Indigenous pride that Benjamin Bratt explains is still very present in the Mission:

> It was by choice for Peter to create a character who was in a very obvious way proud of his cultural heritage, and in particular of his indigenous background. Within the label of Chicano is a political consciousness[—]an understanding [that] by calling yourself that you're a mix of a lot of different cultural influences. You're embracing the Spanish heritage on some level, but more importantly you're acknowledging the Indian heritage in your bloodstream. That's something that's alive and well and thriving, thank God, in the Mission district today. It's depicted in the murals, it's in the literature, the art, the Aztec dance groups. (P. Bratt and B. Bratt)

According to Bratt, for Chicanos, Indian identity thrives and is acknowledged through cultural production and expression. Although the actor mentions a "mix" of cultural influences, they are reduced in *La Mission* primarily to Spanish and Indigenous, with the latter dominating, despite the fact that the Catholic mission system in California was used as a means of subjugating Native people and ended up decimating them with the civilizing machine that included cultural genocide and the introduction of novel diseases. Che's claiming of the Mission as an Indigenous place can be seen as counterhegemonic, his mere existence a defiance of that history, but the film does not engage with the issue in any substantive way. Locating "Indian heritage" in the blood seemingly aligns with the governmental qualifying and quantifying of Native identity with "a Chicano political consciousness." Eva Marie Garroutte notes, "Most federal legal definitions of Indian identity specify a minimum blood quantum—frequently one-quarter but sometimes one-half—but others do not. Some require or accept tribal citizenship as a criterion of federal identification, and others do not" (16). Garroutte outlines the various means and methods by which some Indians are counted and others are not. The factuality of Che's claims of Native identity is a foregone conclusion, evinced through tattoos and lowrider art. Furthermore, he mediates Chicano-inflected Indigeneity for audiences, educating them alongside Mission neighborhood teens about an important source of cultural identity.

Che's body markings tell audiences he is Mexica, an Indian of the San Francisco Mission District, which is within the territory of Aztlán. On a local radio station, as Che and fellow lowriding enthusiasts cruise the streets, the DJ calls out, "It's the midnight hour, and you're cruising to Radio del Barrio Aztlán. This dedication is going out to all the homies out there in the San Fran Mission." Rene proudly wears a shirt that reads "Aztlán." These and other references make Aztlán the political and geographic setting for the film, a locale central to Chicano identity: "The Indian name 'Aztlán' has a universal meaning that connotes a spiritual union, the beginning of Chicano cultural nationalism. Aztlán was the mythological homeland of the Aztecs, the Nahua[tl]-speaking people before their migration southward to Yucatan" (Lux and Vigil 100). Claiming Aztlán as a literal Chicano homeland puts Indigenous identity at the center of the nation. The ideological, political, and spiritual importance given to Aztlán in the late 1960s helped to establish an Aztec hegemony in Chicanismo that endures to this day and accounts for the preponderance of Aztec iconography and symbols found in Chicano art, such as in Sara Estrella's poem "Soy Chicana de Aztlán," where the speaker proudly declares, "I am an Indian" and "I Am a Chicana of Aztlán" (320). Though scholars situate Aztlán geographically in the American Southwest, the site works primarily as a political and cultural territory that generates and sustains Chicano identity.[16]

As an originary place, for the *raza*, Aztlán was an articulated claim to "Native" land and liberation. Ideologically, Michael Pina argues, Aztlán "is a spiritual homeland whose realization lay within the grasp of a determined nationalist program" (38). In March 1969, at the first National Chicano Youth Liberation Conference, held in Denver, the attendees drafted and adopted El Plan Espiritual de Aztlán, which "presented for the first time a clear statement of the growing nationalist consciousness of the Chicano people. It raised the concept of Aztlán, a Chicano nation, and the need for Chicano control of the Chicano community" (El Plan). The place name spoke to an Indigenous history and the reclaiming of that history from conquest and colonization by the Spanish. According to Rudolfo A. Anaya and Francisco Lomelí in *Aztlán: Essays on the Chicano Homeland* (1989), "The legend of Aztlán never died; it was only dormant in the collective unconscious. For people of Mexican descent, Aztlán exists at the level of symbol and archetype. It is a symbol which speaks of origins and ancestors, and it is a symbol of what we imagine ourselves to be" (iii). Aztlán was both a physical and an ideological site, where the people could organize, mobilize, and be empowered. The preamble to El Plan, written by the poet Alurista, proclaims, "[W]e, the Chicano inhabitants and civilizers of the northern land of Aztlán from whence came our forefathers, reclaiming the land of their birth and consecrating the determination of our people of the sun, declare that the call of our blood is our power, our responsibility, and our inevitable destiny" (1). But as Saldaña-Portillo poses, "Why does the southern border of Aztlán always end at the U.S.-Mexico border? Why must it appropriate the territory of thousands of Native Americans in its mapping?" (*Indian Given* 197). For Chicanos, Aztlán was a biological imperative, rooted in bone and blood. Those political imaginings are at the heart of the nation, the visual representations of which appear throughout *La Mission*.

The call for self-determination organized under the banner of Aztlán overshadowed the diversity of the tribes and nations that encompassed, or resisted and in some cases even rejected, the Mexica Empire.[17] The authors of El Plan laid claim to Indigeneity through skin color: "We are a bronze people with a bronze culture. Before the world, before all of North America, before all our brothers in the bronze continent, we are a nation, we are a union of free pueblos, we are Aztlán" (1). This emphasis on color casts the Aztlán nation and its citizens as particular kinds of racialized subjects (mestizos) and was adopted by poets Apolinar Melero and Nephtalí De León, who refer to "Bronze-skinned warriors" and bronze "sacrifices," respectively, to delineate empowerment or persecution.[18] Color became a means of identifying citizen subjects of the nation of Aztlán. Che places a similar emphasis on Brownness to reinforce familial bonds. When arriving at home, he playfully shouts out to his son, "Where the Brown people at?" He also uses Brownness as a means of creating solidarity across racial and ethnic lines, telling his Black friends and coworkers, "Stay Brown," to which they respond, "Can't do nothing but." His friends also issue the call "Stay Brown," and Che responds accordingly.

Indian-ness is more than simply a color; it signifies the cultural and demographic revolution to come, or, as Che calls it, the "re-Browning of America," alluding to a literal and symbolic return of control of the "bronze continent" to its original inhabitants—Chicanos. Che makes this assertion in an impromptu lecture on the Virgen de Guadalupe, the patron saint of Mexico, who Catholics believe appeared to Juan Diego and asked the Indian convert to Catholicism to deliver a message to local religious authorities. Sitting in his man cave/garage, Che sketches an image of the Virgen on paper as two local teens, including one named Little Man, watch and ask about the drawing:

> LITTLE MAN. What's Tee-pee-yac, anyway?
> CHE. Tepeyac. It's the mountain where the Virgen first appeared to Juan Diego.
> LITTLE MAN. How come you're makin' her all dark like that?
> CHE. Because her original name, her Indian name, was Tonantzín. She only became La Virgen after the conquerors forced their language and religion on everybody, you know?
> LITTLE MAN. For real? So is she, like, is like Aztec or somethin'?
> CHE. She's Mexica like you and your homey here.

Here, Brownness, Chicano nationalism, and Indigeneity form the key components of Che's identity. Lux and Vigil explain that "the brown Virgen de Guadalupe, the patron saint of the Mexican campesino," is "the Christian counterpart of the gentle Indian goddess Tonantzín. Tonantzín was worshipped at the place where the Basilica of the Virgen de Guadalupe now stands in the Valley of Mexico" (100–101).[19] A banner of the Virgen often appeared alongside the Aztec eagle at Chicano marches and *huelgas*.[20] The mise-en-scène reinforces the political message behind the lesson. Memorabilia (or rather, Chicanoabilia) fills the space: photos of farmworkers and Chicano civil rights activists, a Cesar Chavez street sign, Helguera reproductions, and car-club trophies appear alongside posters of icons Clint Eastwood in the film *A Fistful of Dollars* (1964) and Marlon Brando as Don Vito Corleone in *The Godfather* (1972). The decor locates the garage at the intersection of Mexican and American popular and political cultural influences, where ethno-racial politics and characters that embody violent forms of masculinity meet. Against this backdrop, Che delivers his lesson straight out of the nationalist script. When Lena overhears the conversation, she asks Che if he is "preparing for the revolution." His position as a Chicano nationalist is irrefutable, yet his status as a radical is unclear.

Che Rivera, whose name calls out to the Marxist revolutionary Che Guevara as well as the Marxist painter Diego Rivera, is both subject to and a symbol of Chicanismo. He is a father figure for an iteration of the nation that existed in the early 1970s, in which "a masculine, cultural nationalist configuration of indigeneity predominated," and that some still cling to even today (Alberto 108). As Rafael Pérez-Torres rightly points out, "[T]he term 'Chicano nationalism' is often bandied about as shorthand for a position within Chicano thought for a rigid (and often essentialist) notion of identity and claims for national sovereignty," but this is not the case in *La Mission* (*Mestizaje* 15). Che's brand of Chicanismo stands in opposition to a more progressive iteration of the nation and its citizen subjects. In other words, Chicano nationalism is at odds with other, more dynamic versions of itself.

Whereas Rene has adapted to meet the challenges of managing his blood sugar (signifying he is either prediabetic or diabetic), providing care for a child with chronic health problems, and reworking lowriders to run on more environmentally friendly fuel, Che is stuck in the past.[21] The license plate on his lowrider reads "PREWWII," marking it and Che as belonging to an earlier era. Che repeatedly demonstrates an inability to adapt to contemporary life. As Peter Bratt explains, "On purpose, Che is a symbol of the patriarchal culture around him, and like that culture, is at the threshold of great change. He can either maintain old habits and attitudes, or he can adapt, grow and mature. Either way, he is bound for pain" (P. Bratt). Not only the wider world is changing but also his own family and barrio. In one scene, Che struts by some neighborhood teen girls sitting on a stoop listening to rap, and they laugh at the sight of him. Little Man, who is sitting with them, defends Che, telling the girls he is an "O.G." (original gangster) who is cool and deserving of respect. The girls, however, continue to laugh, seeing him as absurd or at the very least anachronistic, representative of a time and an idea that have long passed. Even among his friends, Che is a bit behind the times. His core group of friends, who are American Indian, Black, and Chicano, are knowledgeable about current trends in low-calorie cooking—which he is not—and also about cruising "low and slow." However, they too possess conservative ideas about gender roles. As they sit around Che's man cave complaining about how women cause child-custody issues, pursue educational opportunities, and read too many self-help books, Gary Ten Bears says that maybe Che is right, "women are confused." Rene, who has not participated in the conversation, interjects, "Maybe they're finally calling you on your bullshit." Rene does not buy into the same performances of masculinity as the other men in the lowrider group, though at times he laughs at their crude jests. For Che, however, his cisgender, heterosexual masculinity is no joke.

Rene consistently demonstrates an embodiment of Chicanismo that is not essentialist. Whereas Che tends too easily and readily toward physical violence, Rene offers compassion and counsels for reconciliation. In his own home, he reinforces solidarity with other Indians living in and outside of Aztlán through the books he makes available to his children, such as *Storm Boy*. Rene does not appear to have a problem with his nephew's queer identity, and his understanding of the nation is one that accounts for and includes queer-identified citizen subjects like Jesse. In the kitchen scene, Rene tells Che that Jesse's sexuality is not a big deal among their lowrider friendship group. Che believes this is only because "it ain't their son." Rene tries to defuse the situation and support his nephew, responding, "Maybe, but then again maybe it ain't such a big deal." Che pushes back hard against Rene's assessment, telling his brother-in-law, "You believe that shit, homey, you been livin' in this fucking town too long." The implication is that living in a gay mecca such as San Francisco has made Rene more accepting of homosexuality, which is not a good thing in Che's mind. Che's refusal to change eventually alienates him from friends and family, which leads him to abandon his sobriety. Che's house, his life, and even his appearance fall into disarray. The film suggests that Che and his construction of Chicano nationalism need remaking for the dynamic present and future. He is in need of transformation and healing, which he finds in the Indigenous cultural heritage he promotes.

EMBODYING A HEALING

> We are and have always been the natives of this land.
> Nephtalí De León, *Chicanos:*
> *Our Background and Our Pride*

As his strong connection to Chicanismo would predict, Che cares deeply for and respects Indigenous healing practices and those who engage in them. For example, during the fight between Che and Jesse, Virgil Ten Bears is the only one able to de-escalate the situation by gently saying to Che, "Nephew, that's enough," because Che admires him as his senior and a healer. Virgil is an elder in the neighborhood who is clearly a Native but whose tribal affiliation (Ho-Chunk) is not identified and whose Native language, represented in song and prayer, goes untranslated on-screen and in the subtitles. Additionally, when Jesse is shot and his recovery is uncertain, Che calls upon Ten Bears to perform a bedside healing ceremony in Jesse's hospital room. Western medicine coexists alongside

Native healing practices, inclusive of prayer and smudging (the burning of incense or other plants, herbs, or resin, such as copal, which is believed to have healing or curative properties). These forms of medicine work together to contribute to Jesse's recovery. Che believes strongly in the effectiveness of these rituals and practices, so it is fitting that they also serve as a means of his own restoration and healing.

Embedded in the narrative structure of the film is a healing ceremony that is initiated as soon as the opening credits appear in red against a black background, although the nature of the ceremony does not become clear until toward the movie's end. These colors hold particular significance for Anzaldúa, who regularly drew from Aztec thought and myth for some of her most influential theories, such as the Coatlicue state and the Coyolxauhqui imperative, both of which can be transitional and/or transformative states of being.[22] In "*Tlilli, Tlapalli*: The Path of the Red and Black Ink," Anzaldúa theorizes through her writing process, within the context of Aztec belief, and reflects on the responsibilities she bears as a "singer," or poet: "For the ancient Aztecs, *tlilli, tlapalli, la tinta negra y roja de sus códices* (the black and red ink painted on codices) were the colors symbolizing *escritura y sabiduría* (writing and wisdom)" (*Borderlands* 69; translations in original). For different tribal groups, the colors red and black hold different meanings, ranging from earth and fire to spiritual life and aggression, among a number of others. The red and black in the opening of *La Mission* evoke the visual tapestry of Aztec Indigeneity in the film and the wisdom Che must seek from it.

The appearance of the Bratt brothers' 5 Stick Films Inc. logo, a red and black handprint, on-screen is accompanied by extradiegetic drumming followed by the sound of a single set of hurried footsteps, as if someone were running. The percussive rhythm calls to mind an accelerated heartbeat that one would expect in a person in pursuit of or in flight from another. The audience is left to puzzle out the meaning of the indeterminate sprint because a character, or even a place, has yet to appear. The film then cuts from the opening credits to an establishing long shot and then to a medium long shot of the Mission District, after which, from sky level, the camera cranes down the deteriorated Mission Theater sign, which is ragged and has panels missing in its marquee. Walking beneath the sign is Che. His placement there draws attention to him as a protagonist and associates the sign's qualities with his character. "La Mission," in Chicano gothic font, the same one used for Che's tattoos, then appears on-screen, locating the character within a particular place and time (the present). Viewers still do not know whether the character on-screen is walking to or away from the sound of the drums, but the title sequence hints at some relationship between the two. And again later, during the fight with Jesse, the sound of drumming plays over the action.

From the first moment audiences see Che, he is already unknowingly on a downward path. His association with drumming and the vintage theatre sign, the latter conveying age and abandonment, help prepare the stage for Che's ceremony, which is initiated by an image on a mural he passes of a woman in broken chains blowing on a conch shell. The sounding of the conch marks the beginning of a ritual, in this case a performance of *danza azteca*, a cultural and spiritual practice of dancing that can take the form of *"un rezo encarnado* (embodied prayer)," though it can serve many other purposes as well (E. Huerta 5; translation in original). In *La Mission*, *danza azteca* appears in three key scenes. First, as Che strolls through the Mission District on the way to work in the opening scene, a crowd has gathered to watch a group of Aztec dancers, including a man, a boy, and three women. The *danzantes* are in motion and copal is burning inside a *sahumador*, "a clay vessel in which incense is burned," beside a conch shell in the middle of their performance circle (E. Huerta 4). Che looks, yet he does not stop. In the second instance, as Rene drives Jesse away from home after he has been disowned by his father, the boy, with his face bloody and battered, sees the Aztec dancers from the window of his uncle's truck. These *danzantes*, all women, are standing in repose, praying, burning copal, and blowing the conch shell, signaling the beginning or end of another ceremony, but also symbolically calling out to Jesse for a healing and/or prayer. And after Che bottoms out physically and emotionally, the final and most substantive inclusion of *danza azteca* occurs. Performances of *danza* appear in the narrative when the necessity of Che's embodiment of Indigeneity is most crucial.

Indigeneity in *La Mission* is embodied through cultural practice, nowhere more powerfully than through *danza azteca*. The art form is a means of enacting community strength and healing rooted in an Indigeneity that has ties to early Chicano nationalism: "The indigenous identities manifested through *danza azteca* are linked to the larger move by Chicanos to reconnect with their indigenous cultures, which began in the 1960s and 1970s" (Ceseña 81). The medium and method of Che's spiritual awakening matter, though he has yet to internalize the lessons *danza azteca* conveys in order to heal. "As with other expressive forms such as theater, poetry, and music," according to Elisa Diana Huerta, "*danza azteca* allows Chicanas/os to articulate cultural knowledge and indigenous legacies. Additionally, it allows for an *embodiment* of indigeneity" (12).

Although Che does not participate in the physical *danza*, he does participate in the ceremony. In doing so, he gains access to the means of repairing himself and his family.

The restoration sequence in many ways mirrors the film's opening. It begins after Jesse has left for UCLA. Che is again dressed in brown, as he was when the audience first saw him, but at this point, he is disheveled, un-groomed. Gone are the strut and confidence; he takes no pride in his appearance. Upon his entering a liquor store to buy tequila, drums begin to beat, this time accompanied by the sounds of a flute and a rattle. From inside the liquor store, the scene cuts outside to an image of the Virgen being held by a *danza capitán*, the leader of the group. As the drumming continues, an altar on the street comes into view, in front of which a seated woman holds a sign that reads "No Violencia." At intervals throughout this sequence, Peter Bratt positions the camera as if we, the audience, are standing or dancing among the *danzantes*, making us both witnesses to and participants in the ceremony. Smoke from the fire inside the *sahumador*, "the sacred fire, burning during the ceremony," rises up and washes over the dancers and the people, dressed in black, who have gathered (E. Huerta 4). The camera cuts away from this scene to Che continuing his walk through the neighborhood, and viewers see familiar images. Che passes the same mural with the Indigenous woman and child. This time the audience sees a different part of it that includes the hummingbird that is reminiscent of the geoglyph on the plains of Nazca, Peru, but also is representative of the Aztec god Huitzilopochtli, who was often depicted as the colorful, diminutive bird.

The camera then once again holds on the image of the mother and child, which serves as an emotional prelude to the events that follow. Che's reverse route creates a visual symmetry that suggests either a return or the closing of a circle. The action conveyed by the initial mural image of the woman blowing on the conch shell comes to life as a conch sounds in the distance. This time Che looks up and over toward the source. Instead of passing by, he walks over to the dancing, stopping to watch the *danzantes*, who "understand themselves as the carriers of the legacy of Azteca-Mexica cultural, political, and social practices" (E. Huerta 15). As the scene progresses, the full impact of that legacy unfolds. The dancers are there to provide, through the ritual of *danza*, solace and healing for a community being torn apart by violence. Che's role as witness makes him a part of the ceremony because, as Anzaldúa states in a different context, "the 'witness' is a participant in the enactment of the work in a ritual" (*Borderlands* 68). Finally, Che realizes what is happening—this is a public mourning in support of the family of Smoke, Jesse's assailant, who has been killed. The understanding allows him to confront the devastating and isolating effects of violence, in which he has played a significant part. It helps Che to see that his bullying of Smoke on the bus for playing his music too loud motivated the teenager to seek revenge against him by targeting Jesse.

Danza azteca serves as an epistemological bridge between what Che has been and the man he might become. The ritual helps him to see exactly who he is, what he stands for, and how his commitment to a particular masculine nationalist identity has driven away his son. David William Foster similarly observes that dancers play "a determining role in Che's crucial anagnorisis at the end of the film" (250). Whether or not the *danza* serves as a cleansing, or *"limpia,"* as Foster calls it, for Che is unclear. Certainly, though, his participation as a witness in the ceremony is revelatory. The film intercuts flashes of Che's previous acts of intimidation and abuse with the *danzantes'* movements, illustrating that he "slowly begins to recognize that the violence he has learned as a tool for survival in a tough neighborhood has come to define him and prevent him from connecting with individuals for whom he cares deeply" (Alcalde 547). Che recognizes his role as an agent of violence. Through the pounding of the drum, Smoke's death and the suffering it is causing both Smoke's family and the community are collapsed so that Che sees his own behaviors as part of a larger problem of internecine violence. Gabriel S. Estrada offers a similar conclusion: "As a result of the ceremony, Che begins to dis-identify with the cis-heteropatriarchal cycle of violence that motived Smoke to nearly kill Jes" (9). Once Che understands the effects of his behaviors, at home and in the community at large, it starts to rain. Che turns his face upward as the sky opens up, pouring down on him, symbolizing his baptism into the knowledge that his Indigenous identity is a spiritual one that must be embodied and practiced, not only written or represented. The conch shell sounds two more times, as if in confirmation of his newly acquired knowledge. Slowly, the *danzantes* fade one by one from the scene until only Che and the drummer are left. Sounding out the final note, she dissolves, leaving Che alone in front of the altar. He kneels before it and gives the tequila he purchased as an offering to Smoke's memory.

Back at home, Che prepares for the completion of the ritual by cutting his facial hair and readying himself for an uncertain future, when he hopes to reunite with his son. As he stands in front of the mirror shirtless, with the camera positioned behind him, we see "MEXICA," but in this instance we see his face, too, so that the equivalence between the two is clear. "MEXICA" is not simply a tattoo he wears on his body; it is who he is, and as the film implies, he is transformed. This transformation is made evident through Che's decision to drive the lowrider intended for Jesse to Los Angeles. The vehicle and its driver head south, mirroring the migration of the Mexica to a new home. It is also a road trip that Che hopes will end in a father-son reunion and reconciliation. The mended lowrider represents syncretism and transformation: with its 1964 Impala body and 1967 Mustang steering column and front end, the car mixes years and car parts from Detroit automotive competitors Chevrolet and Ford; it runs on biofuel (vegetable oil, specifically); and it features a reconfigured image of the painting *Leyenda de los volcanes* on the trunk. Gone is the sexualized dead princess in repose. Prince Popocatépetl is still positioned with his head bowed and clenching "a rock to steady himself" (Esquibél 299), but now he is bent not in mourning but in devotion. In the distance, Tonantzín hovers with her arms stretched wide, watching over and appearing ready to embrace the solitary, humble Indian prince. Che replaces the sexualized object of desire in the painting, the dead Princess Ixtaccíhuatl, with the caring, protective mother, reframing the emphasis of the myth and disrupting the heterosexual longing conveyed in the original scene. Beneath the image painted on the car appears his affective display for Jesse ("The best friend I got"), a dedication that makes visible the father's devotion and affection for his son, regardless of his sexuality.

Che's imagined identity, through the wholesale adoption of Chicano Indigeneity, allows him to replace one imagining with another. The car that Che is driving to deliver as a surprise gift to Jesse represents an updated vision of the nation and of the father: it honors the past while attempting to connect with the present and the future. It also represents the symbolic reunification, through the driver and the image on the car, of the heteronormative family: father, mother, and son. Through a revision of the Indian at the center of his identity, Che is able to reunite, at least symbolically, with his family. But a car alone will not easily fix what Che has broken with his son. Che will need to talk about the "feelings" that he forbade Jesse to discuss, and he will also need to listen. In whatever way the father and son choose to reconcile, they will most likely do so low and slow.

ALL MY RELATIONS

The film puts tremendous pressure on the Indigenous narrative to intervene in or "fix" the mess Che has made of his life, and ultimately, it does.

As the credits roll, the audience is made to feel optimistic about Che's chance for reconciliation with his son, though the film does not end there. Beyond the production credits, Peter Bratt gives audiences a final message that reads "To All My Relations." The expression bookends the extradiegetic sounds in the film's opening, thus bringing the ceremony/film to a close. Cherokee author Thomas King explains the meaning behind the saying: "'All my relations' is the English equivalent of a phrase familiar to most Native peoples in North America. It may begin or end a prayer or a speech or a story, and, while each tribe has its own way of expressing this sentiment in its own language, the meaning is the same." King adds that the phrase "is an encouragement for us to accept the responsibilities we have within this universal family by living our lives in a harmonious and moral manner" (*All My Relations* ix). Whether as an enactment of new tribalism or of a pan-*humano* community, Che finally sees the interconnectedness of all his life with that of his son and other Mission residents, as well as the part he played in Smoke's death. He sees all too clearly that Smoke's hatred of Jesse stemmed from a profound homophobia that rivaled Che's own, and he is awakened to the possibility of resisting the impulse toward violence. The post-credit scene is a tight close-up of Lena's eyes as she opens them, suggesting that she, not Che, is the source of the feet in flight. Through her work at a women's shelter and in her own life, based on the thick scars that mark her body, revealed in an earlier scene, she is very familiar with the violence perpetrated by men like Che. His openness to change and understanding of his role in the perpetuation of violence will have a ripple effect, with implications not only for himself, Chicanxs, or Jesse but also for the larger, multiracial, multiethnic community in which he lives and for all his relations.

LITERATURE

NEW TRIBALISM AND CHICANA/O INDIGENEITY IN THE WORK OF GLORIA ANZALDÚA

> *Tengo miedo que* in pushing for mestizaje and a new tribalism, I will detribalize [Indians]. Yet I also feel it's imperative we participate in this dialogue no matter how risky.
>
> Gloria Anzaldúa, "Speaking across the Divide"

One of the most influential cultural theorists of the late twentieth century, Gloria E. Anzaldúa contributed significantly to women's, gender, queer, Chicana/o, and transnational studies. Born and raised in the Rio Grande Valley of Texas, on the border between Mexico and the US, Anzaldúa used this borderland as a central idea in her work, a literal and metaphorical space that shaped her life and the lives of others like her who inhabited multiple positions in the physical, cultural, sexual, and political landscape. Rather than see this in-between space as disadvantageous, Anzaldúa envisioned it as a potential site of power, a place of seclusion where border dwellers could grow strong. In her multi-generic text *The Borderlands/La Frontera: The New Mestiza* (1987), she claims and expresses the various facets of her identity: as a Mexicana, Tejana, Chicana, and mestiza, which she defines as a woman with "mixed Indian and Spanish blood" (5). For many, *Borderlands* is revelatory for the way it affirms a self that is often erased or pushed, sometimes violently, into the margins of dominative or competing heteropatriarchal cultures, whether Anglo or Chicanx. Anzaldúa addresses these and additional issues in her theory of the borderlands, a physical and intellectual locale where she is an agent of change for herself and others. Her cultural theory, especially her conceptualization of *mestizaje* and the new mestiza, have resonated not only with US feminists and women of color but also with readers worldwide, based on the inquiries I continue to receive from students and scholars interested in her archives housed at the Nettie Lee Benson Latin American Collection at the University of Texas at Austin. Her place in Indigenous studies, however, is more vexed. Indeed, Anzaldúa struggled to account for what she understood as the Indigenous part of Chicanx identity. Whether she was theorizing *mestizaje*, or "new tribalism" (an extension of her previous ideology), and in the process inspiring and empowering many people, this struggle remained incomplete and ultimately unsatisfying.

Following Anzaldúa's death on 15 May 2004, from diabetes-related complications, the *PMLA* honored her intellectual legacy in the Theories and Methodologies section of its 6 January 2006 issue. Contributors Tey Diana Rebolledo, Debra A. Castillo, Maria Herrera-Sobek, and Linda Martín Alcoff reflected on Anzaldúa's work, particularly her impact on border and transnational studies. Of specific relevance to my work here is Alcoff's article "The Unassimilated Theorist," in which she reflects on the fact that Anzaldúa and her work, though "often cited," remain "undertheorized" (256). The impact of Anzaldúa's work is indisputable. It serves as inspiration for scholars and activists around the world, including those in Russia, Taiwan, Israel, and Saudi Arabia, among others, who in personal correspondence convey the explicit connections between the state of marginalized people in their home countries and life in the borderlands. Collections such as *EntreMundos/AmongWorlds: New Perspectives on Gloria Anzaldúa* (2008), edited by AnaLouise Keating; *Bridging: How Gloria Anzaldúa's Life and Work Transformed Our Own* (2011), edited by AnaLouise Keating and Gloria González-López; and *Teaching Gloria E. Anzaldúa: Pedagogy and Practice for Our Classrooms and Communities* (2020), edited by Margaret Cantú-Sánchez, Candace de León-Zepeda, and Norma Elia Cantú document her impact on the scholarly, spiritual, and pedagogical lives of her readers and plot new directions of critical inquiry across disciplines.

Not long after Anzaldúa's death, however, Alcoff maintained that in the areas of women's and gender studies, Latino studies, postcolonial theory, and particularly feminist theory, Anzaldúa "is rarely critiqued as a serious thinker should be" (256). Alcoff argued that Anzaldúa's work needed to be tried and applied to understand fully its lasting philosophical and theoretical impact. Numerous critical analyses of the type Alcoff called for exist or have emerged, including *Unspeakable Violence: Remapping U.S. and Mexican National Imaginaries* (2011), by Nicole Guidotti-Hernández; "Who's the Indian in Aztlán?" (2001), by María Josefina Saldaña-Portillo; and *A Xicana Codex of Changing Consciousness* (2011), by Anzaldúa's former coeditor, Cherríe Moraga. At the time, Alcoff responded to this lack with her own critical reflection on how Anzaldúa's borderlands theory of *mestizaje* is brought into contemporary conversations about hybridity, a theory of identity rejected by many prominent

American Indian scholars, such as Craig Womack in *Red on Red: Native American Literary Separatism* (1999).

In theorizing *mestizaje*, Anzaldúa foregrounded the idea that one's subject position, especially in the borderlands, is constantly in flux, but the goal of the border dweller is to work toward coherence and not fragmentation. For this reason, as Alcoff points out, "Anzaldúa's description and analysis of mestiza consciousness is not at all in line with the postmodernist celebration of hybridity; the fact that she is used as support for this indicates that her work is not read carefully or critically enough" (257). Alcoff highlights an important distinction between using Anzaldúa's work as a means of critical engagement with material and cultural production and political activism in the borderlands, for example, and critically engaging with her theories. Anzaldúa's philosophical and theoretical assertions, in Alcoff's view, need to be thoroughly scrutinized and tested. Alcoff concludes her own critical assessment of *mestizaje* and hybridity by stressing, "For Anzaldúa, the positive articulation of mestiza identity is a project to be undertaken, rather than something that already exists" (257). *Mestizaje* is a dynamic process, constantly changing, constantly evolving, and it serves as a precursor to Anzaldúa's emerging theory of new tribalism.

More than fifteen years have passed since Alcoff issued the call to engage Anzaldúa as a serious thinker. The goal was not to criticize Anzaldúa but to apply rigor and due diligence to her intellectual legacy as a theorist. Alcoff argued that

> despite a significant volume of work now in print and despite her wide renown in some spheres, Anzaldúa's effect remains to be developed. Too few have read more than *Borderlands/La Frontera* or *This Bridge Called My Back*. Too few have done a sustained critical analysis. It remains for those of us who believe there is a wealth of potential in Anzaldúa's work to bring it into current debates. (256)

This chapter represents a sustained critical analysis that plots new tribalism as an evolving theory and analyzes its potential application and impact, while paying particular attention to whether or not it entrenches further the imaginary Indian at the center of Chicanx identity.

Tribe. The word calls to mind family, kinship, peoplehood, community. In the contemporary popular imaginary, the CBS reality game show Survivor (2000–present) is responsible in large part for the cultural currency of the terms "tribe" and "tribal."[1] *Rather than the ties of a kinship* group determined by blood or a shared worldview, the tribal affiliations the TV producers assign to their participants are based on which combination of personalities will be the most combustible and provide the most drama, that is, conflict, backstabbing, sexual hookups, and so forth, in order to draw the most viewers, which translate into ratings and ad revenue. In the 2006, season 13, installment of the series, set in the Cook Islands, the "tribes" were initially divided by race (identified as African Americans, whites, Hispanics, and Asians), which momentarily wed the term "tribe" to actual ethno-racial groups.[2] After the third week, the tribes were integrated, but it should be noted that old racial alliances were, for the most part, maintained. This, however, afforded very little protection for the participants of color, who for the first six weeks of the season were the only ones voted off the show, reinforcing Anglo dominance within Survivor's manufactured notion of "tribe."[3]

Anzaldúa's thinking about Indigeneity has roots in the Chicano civil rights movement. Mixed-bloodedness, Spanish and Indigenous Mexican, primarily, is pivotal to the identity of revolutionary subjects called Chicanos and is the central theme of Corky Gonzales's epic poem *I Am Joaquín/Yo soy Joaquín*, written in 1967 and named for the famous California "bandit" Joaquín Murieta, the subject of the first American Indian novel, *The Life and Adventures of Joaquín Murieta: The Celebrated California Bandit* (1854), by Cherokee author John Rollin Ridge. Chicano *mestizaje*, as Rafael Pérez-Torres clarifies, exists as an ideological and cultural, rather than a biological, condition, one distinct from the postrevolutionary national project of Mexico (*Mestizaje* 6–8). While recounting and wending his way through cultural history, Gonzales invokes the Indigenous through "the eagle and serpent," a reference to the foundational mythology that led to the establishment of Tenochtitlán, the capital city of the Aztec Empire (16). Gonzales's vision of Joaquín is inclusive of diverse strata of Indigenous people, "the mountain Indian[s]," the "Yaqui/Tarahumara/Chamula," and the "Zapotec" (39). He places particular emphasis on Indigenous empire and male nobility through such figures as Moctezuma, Cuauhtémoc, "Nezahualcóyotl, / great leader of the Chichimecas," and Mayan princes, creating a patriarchal legacy of male leadership and power (16). Women are relegated to the roles of virgin (La Virgen de Guadalupe), goddess (Tonantzín), and "black-shawled" mourners (42). With only one of these as a realistic possibility, women had limited options in the project of nation building and in the Chicano political imaginary.

As one of the stories at the center of the Chicano movement and in the foundational work of Chicano literature, *I Am Joaquín* locates the rights and responsibilities of power squarely on the shoulders of men, as does Che in *La Mission*. At the same time, it extends Aztec hegemony into that particular historical moment, the late 1960s, but replaces it with what is best described as an "Aztext," a matrix of Aztec, Mayan, and Mesoamerican iconography, mythohistory, and symbology. The absence of a specific tribal history, oral and/or written, allows for the Aztext to serve as an ever-evolving, romantic, fictional placeholder for an Indigenous past, a palimpsest that writes over and further obscures the individual tribes subsumed by and outside of the Aztec Empire.

In addition to its distribution in mimeograph form at student rallies and conferences, *I Am Joaquín* was performed in the fields for migrant laborers by El Teatro Campesino and, in 1969, adapted into a film by Luis Valdez, the troupe's cofounder. Valdez called upon pre-Columbian spiritual practices and philosophies to create a Chicano dramatic form, one that did not simply mirror or mimic *gabacho* theatre. El Teatro Campesino began in 1965 beside the fields where workers were picketing Delano grape growers. The participants in the Delano grape strike, which lasted five years and helped raise awareness across the country about the unfair treatment of farm workers, became some of the first actors in Chicano theatre. Tony Curiel asserts in his introduction to the collection of Valdez's early works, "El Teatro was born to express the verisimilitude of the striking campesinos' reality" (3). Rather than performing elaborate scripted or formalized plays, this early theatre relied on what came to be known as *actos*, meaning acts, deeds, or even ceremonies presented in full-length single acts.

Sacrifice and suffering often characterized the lives of the campesinos. Valdez drew from these experiences to call attention to the staging of ceremonies or dramas that involved the entire community. For Valdez, these ceremonies hearken back to the Aztecs: "In Mexico, before the coming of the white man, the greatest examples of total theatre were, of course, the human sacrifices" (7). Early Chicano theatre empowered workers because they were the ones who "produced, acted, directed, designed and improvised" the parts (Curiel 3). Workers performing in the *actos* could not only portray their daily struggles but also articulate their grievances and openly criticize their oppressors. Through the *actos*, a field worker could take on the role of a *patrón* and satirize his racist treatment of the campesinos. Alongside the *actos*, Valdez devised a complementary form known as *mito* that sought out and cultivated connections between Chicanos' and pre-Columbian art and thought. According to Jorge Huerta, "The Valdezian *mito* is a very personal inquiry into Aztec,

Maya, and Native American philosophy that the author has maintained to this day" (36). Together, *actos* and *mitos* represent Valdez's effort to create a distinctly Chicano theatre, one rooted in Indigenous thought and practice.[4]

Indigeneity and the claiming of Aztlán as a mythic homeland were central to early Chicano nationalism and were guiding principles of the Chicano civil rights movement, *el movimiento*. Chicano identity politics recognized and embraced an Indigenous past and cultural heritage while simultaneously asserting that conflict and contact with European invaders gave birth to the Chicano people. Ongoing social and political struggles represent the legacy of a colonial project that plays itself out on the body, mind, and spirit of Chicanos. El Plan Espiritual de Aztlán, adopted in March 1969 at the first National Chicano Youth Liberation Conference, held in Denver and convened by Corky Gonzales, was a declaration of self-determination for Chicanos and a claiming of the nation of Aztlán as a homeland. The assertion of Indian-ness in El Plan is made through the language of "bronze culture," the habitation and civilization "of the northern land of Aztlán," the origin of Chicanos' forebears, and "reclaiming the land of their birth and consecrating the determination of our people of the sun" (El Plan). The proclamation does not specifically identify the history of any one particular Indigenous group, choosing instead to declare "the independence of our mestizo nation" (El Plan). Inclusive of Native and native claims, the explicit definition of "mestizo" is not offered or outlined clearly in the plan.

Indigeneity, as an epistemology, has been fundamental to Chicano nationalism. Chicana feminists, such as Cherríe Moraga and Gloria Anzaldúa, in turn, have used Chicano nationalism to critique the masculinism and heterosexism at the heart of the Chicano Nation. As Moraga asserts,

> What was right about Chicano Nationalism was its commitment to preserving the integrity of the Chicano people. A generation ago, there were cultural, economic, and political programs to develop Chicano consciousness, autonomy, and self-determination. What was wrong about Chicano Nationalism was its institutionalized heterosexism, its inbred machismo, and its lack of a cohesive national political strategy. (*Last Generation* 148–149)

Documented in collections such as *Chicana Feminist Thought: The Basic Historical Writings* (1997), edited by Alma M. García, which includes personal essays, poems, and speeches, among other forms, and more recently *Chicana Movidas: New Narratives of Activism and Feminism in the Movement Era* (2018), edited by Dionne Espinoza, María Eugenia Cotera, and Maylei Blackwell, the Chicano civil rights movement saw the entrenchment of prescribed gender roles. Even with prominent sexist narratives to the contrary, women were active agents in the social change and political action of the movement. Men nevertheless positioned themselves as historical agents descended from cultural and ethno-racial forefathers, as in Gonzales's poem. These same men sought to relegate women to the margins of a movement by a marginalized people, without a hint of irony. As a result, women were perceived simultaneously as in and outside of the project of nation building, but for men, this meant only populating the nation and giving birth to its future inhabitants, thus limiting Chicanas to reproductive functions.

In *Borderlands/La Frontera*, Anzaldúa's "mestiza consciousness" attempts to account for the in between-ness of those outside of the nation(s), those who are "prohibited and forbidden" because of their sexuality, gender, race, or ethnicity (77, 3). Anzaldúa offers Indigenous figures and beliefs associated with the Aztecs/Mexica as strategies of spiritual and psychic integration and transformation for the new mestiza and for male-centered conceptions of the nation. Saldaña-Portillo sees Anzaldúa's doing so as "a refreshing contradistinction to earlier Chicano deployments of mestizaje," adding that "Anzaldúa draws from the female deities in the Aztec pantheon," an approach that is not without its problems, "to explain a variety of Chicana-mestiza customs, to explain patriarchy in Chicano culture, to explain Chicana sexuality" ("Who's the Indian" 415). Anzaldúa turns to Native thought and religion to address the problems with Chicano civil-rights-era tribalism and its complete devotion to the heterosexual family and kinship group at the expense of its distinct members: "Much of what the culture condemns focuses on kinship relationships. The welfare of the family, the community, and the tribe is more important than the welfare of the individual" (*Borderlands* 18). This turn toward the individual creates avenues for exposing the Chicanx tribe as a closed system in which domestic and social issues such as familial violence, sexual abuse, and homophobia exist openly in the nation. New tribalism, then, becomes her challenge to the old Chicanx tribalism in the nation of Aztlán.

The conceptualizing of popular, commercial tribes appears to be the realization, and extension, of Michel Maffesoli's ideas found in The Time of the Tribes *(1996). Maffesoli sees the organization of people into tribes as a postmodern condition, "heterogeneous fragments, the remainders of mass consumption society" (Shields x). As opposed to tribes as rooted in ethnic nationalism, Maffesoli argues that as the cultures and mechanisms of modernism decline, people will begin to seek alternate organizational strategies based, for example, on taste, sentiment, or fashion, in an effort to validate individual consumption with other like-minded consumers, also now identified by marketers as microcultures of consumption.⁵ Maffesoli characterizes this new social dynamic as neo-tribalism, consisting of what he sees as "the constant interplay between the growing massification and the development of micro-groups," or tribes (6).⁶ The constant movement of people from one tribe to another makes these groups, in Maffesoli's view, transitory and therefore highly unstable. Maffesoli's definition of the tribe is best understood as an attempt to theorize the disintegration of mass culture: "As for the metaphor of the tribe, it allows us to account for the process of disindividuation, the saturation of the inherent function of the individual and the emphasis on the role that each person (persona) is called upon to play within the tribe" (6). Furthermore, he adds, "It is of course understood that, just as the masses are in a state of perpetual swarm, the tribes that crystallize from these masses are unstable, since the persons of which these tribes are constituted are free to move from one to the other" (6). Yet this instability does not undermine a tribe's shared rituals or its powers of inclusion, exclusion, or governance, both formal and informal.*

A mere five years after the publication of *Borderlands*, Anzaldúa began speaking about a new tribalism. The term itself and how Anzaldúa began to conceive of it were the result of disparaging critical engagement with her work. In the winter of 1991, cultural theorist David Rieff published an article in *New Perspectives Quarterly* on the "Latination of America" entitled "Professional Aztecs and Popular Culture" in which he accuses Valdez and Anzaldúa of being "professional Aztecs" (46). Rieff's primary criticism of the work of these artists and activists is that in their total devotion to race and culture, they fail to consider the issue of class. He saw their efforts as a kind of "utopianism" that involved giving the world a "good rewrite" (44). Rieff, whose mother was Susan Sontag, also observed, "What is remarkable about the new tribalism is the way in which it is so completely *self-absorbed*" (44; emphasis added). The same year, in February at a UCLA conference, someone passed the article on to Anzaldúa, and from that point on, she "borrowed this term from Rieff," though she admits to being uncertain as to whether he originated the idea (Anzaldúa, "Now Let Us Shift" 578n17). So what Rieff saw as a point to critique, the emphasis on the individual, Anzaldúa saw as a strategy for remaking Chicanx tribalism so that it could begin to address some of the problems within the nation, for example, abuse and long-standing exclusionary practices.

Through the unraveling and weaving of the many layers of her identity, Anzaldúa embraced her complexity while at the same time remaining completely aware of the complications that can (and did) arise in making claims on one's cultural inheritance. It is important to note that she did not identify as an *india*. She did, however, claim Indian ancestry through *mestizaje*, a distinction that was important to her, and she cultivated many of her personal and philosophical principals from an Aztec/Mexica worldview. Anzaldúa did not ignore "the biological mixtures of Basque, Spanish, Berber Arab and the cultural mix of various cultures of color and various white cultures" that are a part of Chicano ethnic and racial history (Anzaldúa and Ortiz 9). Her reliance on female figures from the Aztec pantheon, most notably the goddess at the center of what she calls the "*Coatlicue* state," demonstrates a privileging of Indigenous thought over other cultural forms and her own contributions to an Aztext (*Borderlands* 42). The modeling of beliefs based on any cultural or racial group requires a critical examination of the social underpinning of the culture and its people, along with the motivation and reasoning behind such "borrowing" or instrumentalizing. Anzaldúa, unfortunately, does not engage with the fact that the Aztec Empire was an oppressive entity that forced conquered tribes to pay tribute and/or submit to its power. Saldaña-Portillo sees Anzaldúa's particular emphasis on Aztec female figures as replicating initiatives in Mexico, namely, the Institutional Revolutionary Party's state-sponsored promotions in the twentieth century of "mestizaje and indigenismo" at the expense of living tribal communities ("Who's the Indian" 416): the advocating of Indigenous thought and history replicates a narrative of a unified Indigenous nation under the name Aztec, one that expunges smaller existing tribes in the US and Mexico from cultural and political memory. Nicole Guidotti-Hernández makes a similar assessment:

> The common reading of Anzaldúa as taking up the mantle of mestizaje as a theory of Chicana/o liberation in some ways denies the violence, both physical and epistemic, that occurs when the essentialized Indian—who cannot pass for mestizo or cannot celebrate a mestiza/o cultural heritage and is in fact Indian

in the eyes of the U.S. and Mexican nations—is eliminated from the conversation. (19)

Anzaldúa's conception of *mestizaje* is meant to be a category of inclusion that accounts for Indigenous ancestry; its connection to Aztec/Mexica antiquity, namely, female figures in its pantheon, confines the source of Chicanx Indigeneity to the past rather than in living tribal traditions in the present. This confinement in history commits the kind of violence through elimination that concerns Guidotti-Hernández.

Despite acknowledging how Anzaldúa, through her specific use of Aztec goddesses, breaks with previous deployments of *mestizaje*, Saldaña-Portillo finds problems with this alternate configuration, one that also contributes to erasure. She warns, "When [Anzaldúa] resuscitates this particular representation of indigenous subjectivity to be incorporated into contemporary mestiza consciousness, she too does so to the exclusion and, indeed, erasure of contemporary indigenous subjectivity and practices on both sides of the border" ("Who's the Indian" 416). The criticism is a familiar one lodged against Anzaldúa, who expressed the same concern about how her work might be read: "I'm afraid that what I say may unwittingly contribute to the misappropriation of Native cultures, that I (and other Chicanas) will inadvertently contribute to the cultural erasure, silencing, invisibility, racial stereotyping, and disenfranchisement of people who live in real Indian bodies" (Anzaldúa and Ortiz 12). When she became aware of Saldaña-Portillo's criticisms, Anzaldúa responded by saying, "I appreciate her critique but my sense is that she's misread or has not read enough of my work" (14). Yet Saldaña-Portillo is not the only critic to see appropriation in Anzaldúa's work.

A careful reading of Anzaldúa's new tribalism reveals that it is not tied explicitly to antiquity; however, there are other equally problematic aspects. Her emerging ideas on the principle represent the theorist's efforts to open up the category of *mestizaje* to account for "what happens when our sense of tribe and identity changes, when it expands" (Anzaldúa, "Quincentennial" 185). Native kinship formations are at the heart of this new tribalism, as is the place of the individual within the group. As Anzaldúa explained to Irene Lara in an interview,

> New tribalism is a kind of mestizaje. Instead of somebody making you a hybrid without your control, you can choose. You can choose a little Buddhism, a little assertiveness, individuality,

> some Mexican views of the spirit world, something from blacks [sic], something from Asians. I use the image of an orange tree, like an árbol de la vida, to illustrate. Some kinds have a very strong root and trunk system but don't put out as much of the fruit, so you graft them together to get a variety with better oranges. (Anzaldúa, "Daughter" 42)

The central metaphor, based on the image of her *tío*'s dying orange tree described in an essay in *This Bridge We Call Home: Radical Visions for Transformation* (2000), a tree "still possessed of a strong root system and trunk," creates a mixed message about new tribalism as both theory and praxis ("Now Let Us Shift" 560). Fundamental to new tribalism is agency, which allows for personal subject formation. But its design depends heavily on cultural taking. Although Anzaldúa indicates that she uses new tribalism "to formulate a more inclusive identity, one that's based on many features and not solely on race," what those features are, outside of certain behaviors or character traits, remains unclear (Anzaldúa and Ortiz 9). She further states, "In order to maintain its privileges the dominant culture has imposed identities through racial and ethnic classification. The new tribalism disrupts this imposition by challenging these categories" (9). Yet in naming racial groups, she ostensibly replicates the same classifications as the dominant culture she critiques. Without further guidance, new tribalism is at once superficial, an à la carte culture, personality, and spiritualism (either inclusive of or independent of organized religious practices), and biological, like the creation of a hearty orange tree, its strength and the quality of its yield attained by crossbreeding.

Anzaldúa was searching for a way to transcend race and biology, but new tribalism's central metaphor—the orange tree made strong through grafting—on genetic inheritance calls to mind the Mexican philosopher José Vasconcelos's theoretical imagining of a *raza cósmica*. Minister of education under President Eulalio Gutiérrez Ortiz, Vasconcelos imagined a cosmic race, one made strong through genetic selection of desired racial characteristics, with the loss of the Indigenous and the emergence of the mestizo as the end result. Although Anzaldúa envisioned new tribalism as "a social identity that could motivate subordinated communities to work together in coalition," there is a biological determinism embedded in its definition (Anzaldúa and Ortiz 9). The metaphor of the tree does not quite capture the kind of transformation Anzaldúa talks about because the changes are imposed on a living entity: in other words, the tree did not choose to have its strength or productivity altered.

What manufactured, neo-, urban, and modern tribalism share, in addition to an almost complete emphasis on consumption, is an abandonment of ethnic and racial designations. These tribes, regardless of their organizing principles, become a response to a perceived material or social lack. Moreover, they attempt to order through affiliation. In other words, the tribe is a post-facto designation, a destination, rather than a shared history.

Regarding Anzaldúa's evolving theoretical considerations, 1991 proved to be a watershed year, for in it, she also sat down for a conversation with Inés Hernández-Ávila and began to theorize through *mestizaje* toward new tribalism, stating, "Nos/otras and the New Tribalism describe the formation of personal and collective identity" (Anzaldúa, "Quincentennial" 178). At this time, she expressed specific interest in finding out "what happens when our sense of tribe and identity changes, when it expands to include a new kind of tribalism" (185). Without fully understanding Anzaldúa's definition of "old tribalism," it is difficult to ascertain what aspects are being "remade" or discarded. Still, in the early phase of her thinking, Anzaldúa defines new tribalism as "a kind of mestizaje that allows for connecting with other ethnic groups and interacting with other cultures and ideas" (185). While Rieff may have served as the inspiration for the term, Anzaldúa, like an alchemist, transmuted his ad hominem attack into her theoretical basis for bringing people together.

New tribalism allowed Anzaldúa to account for the world outside of the borderlands but was theorized from the US side of the *frontera*. New tribalism emerges from the original theoretical concept of *mestizaje*, and while remaining very much a part of it, attempts to address the effects of globalization on individuals and communities. Anzaldúa explained to Hernández-Ávila: "Now we live in a global village; we live in each other's pockets and not in isolated ethnic plots. We depend on exchange of goods, ideas, and information. Modern life goes on and we can never go back, we can never completely isolate each group from other groups" (Anzaldúa, "Quincentennial" 186). Dynamic and evolving theories, *mestizaje* and new tribalism reflected Anzaldúa's desire to be even more inclusive, building bridges across borders, oceans, and continents. And it is this point that Alcoff does not take into account when she states, "Whether Anzaldúa's analysis of the particularities of Chicana hybridity is applicable to hybrid identities generally or to hybrid identities specifically now, in the current climate of globalization, needs reflective analysis" (257). On some level, Anzaldúa must have sensed this about her own work, and she began to theorize in a way to account for and accommodate a global perspective.

An interview with Debbie Blake and Carmen Abrego in 1994 demonstrates that Anzaldúa had begun the slow process of refining her thoughts on new tribalism, revealing that it emerges in part as a response to the rigidity of Chicano nationalism: "My tribe has always been the Chicano Nation, but for me, unlike the majority of Mexican Americans, the indigenous lineage is a major part of being Chicana" (Anzaldúa, "Doing Gigs" 215). "Tribe," therefore, is synonymous with the Chicano nation, and Anzaldúa takes this opportunity to make a distinction between Chicano and Mexican American, with the former centralizing Indigenous heritage, though it is unclear how exactly. Anzaldúa continues, "Nationalism was a good thing to seek in the '60s, but in the '70s it was problematic and in the '80s and '90s it doesn't work. I had to, for myself, figure out some other term that would describe a more porous nationalism, opened up to other categories of identity" (215). What did not "work" for Anzaldúa was the movement's failure to "address the oppression of women" and the overemphasis on "trying to secure the *male* part of the culture, male ideology" (214). Therefore, new tribalism, along with "nos/otras," served as a means of "disrupting categories," a move necessary in Anzaldúa's view because "[c]ategories contain, imprison, limit, and keep us from growing. We have to disrupt those categories and invent new ones" (215). Yet what effect does this disruption and invention have on ideological, historical, and political conceptions of tribes and tribal people? And if Indigenous lineage plays "a major part" in being Chicana, how does it manifest or get enacted?

Both interviews appear in AnaLouise Keating's edited collection *Interviews/Entrevistas/Gloria Anzaldúa* (2000), where in the introduction Keating restates Anzaldúa's definition of new tribalism, and adds that it represents "a disruptive category that redefines previous ethnocentric forms of nationalism" (5). New tribalism, with its "vague and undetermined" characteristics, represents another borderland. It also symbolizes a turn away from nationalism, where kinship is no longer defined exclusively by blood, geography, or any bureaucratic entity. Anzaldúa reflects on this point in the preface to *This Bridge We Call Home*: "Many of us identify with groups and social positions not limited to our ethnic, racial, religious, class, gender, or national classifications. Though most people self-define by what they exclude, we define who we are by what we include—what I call the new tribalism" ("(Un)natural Bridges" 3). Yet by this time, though never simply a rhetoric of inclusion, new tribalism had become intertwined with a larger and equally dynamic spiritual belief system involving *nepantleras* ("women of the border") and *naguales* (spiritual and literal "shape-shifters"), which together have the capacity to transform people and the way we think about global culture.

Anzaldúa remained insistent that we need to regularly revisit categories and groupings of people. New tribalism represents her concerted effort to do so, as an ongoing process of self-reflection and social formation:

> We need a new tribalism. We need a different way of shuffling the categories. As long as we rely on language, we'll have categories even though they're very limiting and imprisoning. Every few years we should blur the boundaries, make them porous. If we reshuffle all the categories, can we come up with new identity markers, new ways of composing members of different groups, into new groups? I've come up with "new tribalism" y allí estoy. I'm stuck. [laughter] Every so many years I add a little bit, extend the categories, pero I don't think the problem will ever be solved because life transforms all the time, so of course categories only work for so long. (Anzaldúa, "Daughter" 42)

For historical, social, cultural, and political reasons, among others, it is unlikely that sovereign Indigenous Nations would share her point of view. Indigenous scholars might be wary of blurring the boundaries, ignoring distinct tribal histories, or constantly making and remaking Indigenous definitions of identity, not to mention the instrumentalizing of Indigeneity for individualistic purposes. The desire to think of terminology and theory as dynamic is important but does not address why people need to or choose to turn to cultures outside of their own when the shelf life of intellectual and ideological projects is constantly expiring. It does not promote the interrogation of the inherent subject position assumed by members of dominative groups, nor does it problematize the idea of various cultures' serving as cultural, social, or spiritual resources. On the surface, it sanctions cultural tourism and the fetishizing of difference and does not address the power relationship in this kind of taking, a situation dramatized in Sherman Alexie's novel *Reservation Blues* (1995).

In *Reservation Blues*, two New Age white women, Betty and Veronica, who initially appear as groupies for the Indian band Coyote Springs at the center of the novel, long to be Indian, admiring Indians' supposed harmony with nature and other stereotypical characteristics. Betty and Veronica, whose names call to mind the classic comic book duo from the *Archie Comics* series, achieve their dream when Cavalry Records signs them to record for their label as "Indian" artists. The lyrics to one of their songs about eagles crying, connecting with the land, and Mother Earth and Father Sky include the women affirming, despite their white skin and blond hair, that they are "Indian in their bones" (Alexie 295). They also authorize people who share a similar racialized longing to identify in the same way:

> And it don't matter who you are
> You can be Indian in your bones
> Don't listen to what they say
> You can be Indian in your bones. (295–296)

For the Anglo duo in redface, Indian-ness is at once biological, buried in the spongy marrow of the bones, and a choice, something accessible to anyone who makes a claim; it is a choice even when the claim is a sincere one, for sincerity often provides the most privileged root of entitlement. It answers to no one and does not reside in contemporary lived experience or historical relationships with "land, culture, and community" that are fundamental to Indian identity, according to Acoma Pueblo poet Simon J. Ortiz (Anzaldúa and Ortiz 21). Instead, it is something always present and realized through skin bronzer, feathers, and beads. It is divorced of tribal histories and legacies. It is transformative without consideration of how the parent culture is being transformed in the taking.

As Coco Fusco points out in *English Is Broken Here: Notes on Cultural Fusion in the Americas* (1995), "[A]bsorption and mimicry of Native American, Mexican, and African American cultural forms and philosophies have been absolutely central to the formation and transformation of white Americanness" (68). Those undertaking this kind of appropriation, nevertheless, rarely take into account "the conditions of colonized societies and other contexts where national autonomy, national culture, and/or subaltern identity are fragile, imperiled, or symbolically effaced by external forces" (70). After hearing the recording by Betty and Veronica, the book's protagonist, Thomas Builds-the-Fire (Spokane), destroys the tape and then quickly runs around his house gathering those things precious to him in fear that "somebody was going to steal them next" (296). Alexie illustrates, therefore, that "playing Indian" supplants actual Native people, history, culture, and identity. Playing Indian also silences Native people symbolically and sometimes quite literally from speaking about their own communities. Regardless of their claims to Indigenous ancestry, Chicanxs are not immune from this kind of taking from Natives. Anzaldúa herself stated, "Chicana/os are not critical enough about how we borrow from lo indio. Some Indian Americans think all Chicanas/os plunder native culture as mercilessly as whites" (Anzaldúa and Ortiz 14–15). This plundering or theft is detrimental to Indian peoples and no less violent than previous and/or ongoing colonial projects.

Neo-tribalism shares similarities with "urban tribalism"—social or familial groups governed by an understood and often unstated set of rules concerning membership and behavior. Urban tribes formed in metropolitan environments, initially through underground movements such as the Punk scene and tattooing or piercing clubs—that is, until these movements and practices entered the mainstream. Members of contemporary "urban tribes" balance their participation in the group with their modern lives, often relying upon technology, especially social media, as a means of "connecting" with other like-minded individuals or expanding their tribe.[7] *These groups are distinct also from "modern primitives," as Victoria Pitts notes in her study* In the Flesh: The Cultural Politics of Body Modification *(2003): individuals who identify in this way "simulate the practices of a number of indigenous or tribal cultures and represent those cultures on the Western body" (125). Therefore, modern primitives actively seek out non-Western tribal cultures and practices.*[8] *Thus urban tribes are about organization; modern primitives are about embodiment.*

While the issue of cultural appropriation, especially in terms of Native artifacts, rituals, and kinship formations, is a serious concern in the face of detribalization, how does one acknowledge or even begin to claim or account for Indigenous heritage without erasing or disenfranchising living tribal communities? Anzaldúa's untimely death left these and other central and ongoing questions unanswered. "Now Let Us Shift . . . the Path of Conocimiento . . . Inner Work, Public Acts," the final selection in *This Bridge We Call Home*, offers Anzaldúa's definitive thinking on new tribalism as an alternative to assimilation and separatism. It is a method for imagining a unified whole. New tribalism, as she writes in the preface, allows not simply for the transgression of borders but also for the internalization of those conflicts as a means of healing: "Imagination, a function of the soul, has the capacity to extend us beyond the confines of our skin, situation, and condition so we can choose our responses. It enables us to reimagine our lives, rewrite the self, and create guiding myths for our times" ("(Un)natural Bridges" 5). Ultimately, new tribalism juxtaposes novelty with history, while at the same time focusing on an individualistic process rather than a relational one. It also proposes to remake tribalism or make tribalism anew, while failing to recognize that many tribal communities are happy with current and ongoing guiding ideas or organizing principles. Besides issues of inclusion and difference, what about tribalism is being "remade," and what impact does that have on other tribal communities?

To be tribal or tribalized is to partake in the civic and communal life of a group that is made up of families or people who share a common ancestry and often kinship or ceremonial relations. In the US, "tribe" is most often associated in the cultural imagination with the more than five hundred nations of American Indians, federal recognition, issues of sovereignty, casinos, or reservations. To be tribal can, indeed, mean maintaining one's ancestral lands, language, and community; access to resources and the continuation or termination of a people's lifeways; crushing economic adversity for some and profound prosperity for others. Stated more explicitly, there is no singular way of being tribal.

For Anzaldúa, new tribalism was a metaphor for a lived experience, a way for groups to work together in coalition and an organizational structure for bridging humanity. But Chicanxs cannot live solely through metaphors and mythology. To be Chicanx or Mexican American is to make language compromises; it is the longing for a homeland; it is the exaltation of imagined origins; it is the expression and feeling of loss; or it is some or none of these. What we have lost is not singular nor necessarily shared. We need to define with specificity who we are and where we come from. We need to acknowledge the effects of internalized colonialism that simultaneously classed and racialized a nation of detribalized mixed-bloods and mestizos. We need to examine the ways that Chicanx ideology historically has privileged particular kinds of Indigenous bodies and Indigeneity over others. Finally, we need to trouble narratives of poverty and the compulsory working-class status of Chicanxs or Mexican Americans to account for who we are in the present.

Modern tribalism often involves the participation in some shared ritual, as in Victor Turner's idea of communitas. *Rather than establishing equilibrium within a liminal group, raising some members up while lowering others, ritual in modern tribalism, whose members most often belong to the cultural majority, involves little more than the creation and consumption of alterity to satisfy individual cravings for cultural experiences not their own, a practice that calls to mind bell hooks's idea of "eating the Other."*[9] *The rituals of modern tribalism signify romantic re-*

turns to imagined colonial fantasies. The consumption of an imagined primitive is the modern tribe's response to the failure to find satisfaction in or fulfillment from consumer culture, an idea that hearkens back to Maffesoli. Therefore, the consumption and enactments of tribalism, or their version of them through mimicking ethno-racial or non-Western tribal practices, provide cohesion and connection within modern tribes.

Anzaldúa's new tribalism is as flawed as it is beautiful, an incomplete strategy for connecting people socially and globally, independently of race or nation. In their imagining of a nation, Chicanxs have not always confronted their deeply conflicted history with Native peoples in Mexico and the US. We may see ourselves as indigenous, but are we Indigenous? A 2012 brief by the US Census Bureau indicates that of the thirty-three million individuals who identified as Mexican in the 2010 Census (Mexican, Mexican American, or Chicano), 175,494 also self-identified racially as American Indian (United States Census Bureau 17). The number makes Mexican American Indians the fourth largest tribal group in the US after Cherokees, Navajos, and Choctaws. But what are the tribes within the larger category of Mexican American Indians? Where is the nation and does it exist outside of the imaginary? How do we participate in the civic and/or cultural life of the nation? What is our investment in Indigeneity? Is Chicanx solidarity with Native people merely a symbolic one? Chicanxs want the right to claim our history as ethnic Mexicans, though we must take care in how we make that determination. According to Moraga, "As displaced Xicanas and Xicanos, there can be no new tribe without the reparation of the home tribe" ("The Salt" 124). But where is the home tribe? What is its constitution? And where is home? How is it determined? And how can it be restored when its origins are elusive, having been erased through genocide or other colonial projects? Moraga urges us to return to our home sites, "our own 'tribes'—our home cultures—and make progressive change there, specific to our historical cultural conditions" (126). For those of us whose family histories are elusive, the determination of those historical and cultural conditions is ours to make. Yet how can we do this in a meaningful way without simply replicating the problems with new tribalism, or even the pan-humanism, under a different name?

Regardless of Anzaldúa's assertions that *mestizaje* and new tribalism are reflections of her desire not to "inadvertently contribute to the cultural erasure, silencing, invisibility, racial stereotyping, and disenfranchisement of people who live in real Indian bodies," the possibility of these concepts' doing so is high (Anzaldúa and Ortiz 12). Moraga echoes this concern along with others about appropriation: "From the perspective of living tribal communities, the idea of a new, ethnically inclusive tribalism may resonate as yet another neocolonial attempt to dehistoricize and weaken the cultural integrity of aboriginal nations. This, of course, was not Gloria's intention, but the danger of such appropriation is not to be minimized" ("The Salt" 124–125). Anzaldúa's advocating for a boutique and special tribalism comprising a little bit of this and a little bit of that should give us pause, for on its surface, it seems to invite cultural tourism and appropriation at the expense of actual tribal nations. Although Anzaldúa's understanding of the issue would evolve, her use of the term "tribalism" was an attempt to underscore the dynamic—and shifting—cultural, social, political, and personal relationships among different kinship groups. In other words, it was a philosophical imagining of a transcultural or polycultural group, one meant to be inclusive, a further act of coalition building, another bridge. As an evolving idea, new tribalism left more questions than answers for thinking about global communities. But "what if," as Galina Kallio and Eeva Houtbeckers pose, "instead of producing more certainty through more knowledge, we need research to reveal more uncertainty through more sensitive and situated ways of knowing?" (11). Anzaldúa's new tribalism represents one such effort.

We do not need to "solve" the problem of new tribalism. We can recognize, however, that Anzaldúa sought to expand her idea of the borderlands to make it even more inclusive, to move beyond dualism, and to emphasize individual agency in an effort to make a better world. In many ways, it reflects her idea that "by changing ourselves we change the world" (Moraga and Anzaldúa 208). This is the work. Anzaldúa did not offer suggestions on the practical implementation or even the methods for realizing such a social philosophy. New tribalism, like so many of her theories, was never meant to be prescriptive. Nevertheless, embracing alterity, as Moraga also notes, without a critical examination of one's own racial, cultural, economic, or gendered privilege can look a lot like appropriation, cultural tourism, or worse. Such an examination requires the slow work of looking inward to question our motivations or, like Che in *La Mission*, taking ownership of the ways we participate in the marginalization or subjugation of others through the privileges we do have, however limited. Through "sensitive and situated ways of knowing" we can choose how to respond. Anzaldúa reminds us, "The struggle has always been inner, and is played out in the outer terrains. Awareness of our situation must come before inner changes, which in turn come before changes in society. Nothing happens in the 'real' world unless it first happens in the images in our heads" (*Borderlands* 87). Perhaps, then, the greatest realization of new tribalism is that, in the spirit of migration, Anzaldúa first imagined and then moved intellectually, politically, and spiritually to a new locale of her own making.

As far back as *Borderlands/La Frontera* and *This Bridge Called My Back* and up to *This Bridge We Call Home* and other, unpublished works, Anzaldúa theorized ways to bring people together. Throughout, however, like La Llorona calling out to all those who are lost, she never wandered far from the figurative and geographic borderlands that were so instrumental to the formulation of her theories and who she was as a person. She sought refuge in and drew inspiration from the borderlands, as well as from the ghosts that reside there. Others, as part 3 demonstrates, are still haunted by them.

PART III
Fantasmas and *Fronteras*

> Some of us may pursue speed and activity to avoid dwelling on things, insecurities or problems we want to avoid. Stopping or slowing makes it more difficult to avoid our demons.
>
> Luke Martell, "The Slow University: Inequality, Power, and Alternatives"

AND GHOSTS. Stopping or slowing makes it more difficult to avoid our *ghosts*.

As a consequence of my sheltering in place for over a year during the COVID-19 pandemic, time, for me as for so many others, started to blur in the absence of embedded routines, at home and at work, or transitional activities delineating one part of a day from the next. Many of us felt temporally unmoored. A quick Google search reveals a number of articles from that period related to the question "Why does time feel so weird right now?"[1] For me the strangeness of time meant that what was once far way in thought or memory was now more immediate but also wildly unpredictable. So I was almost always unprepared when a recollection came crashing through with a disquieting clarity. One such instance occurred on a family trip, the first time in sixty-two weeks we had left as a household to go stay someplace other than our home. The rental, approximately 2½ hours from our home in Austin, sat back from the shore of Lake Whitney, a reservoir located on the main stem of the Brazos River. We purchased licenses and brought along fishing poles to try our luck. Without live bait and no knowledge about what kinds of fish were in the lake, we threw our jigs in and hoped for the best, happy to be outside mask-free with no one else around. Casting from shore is always tricky: a line can get caught on the bottom or hung up on the weeds along the water's edge. In relatively short order, we negotiated the obstacles and set into a rhythm of casting and reeling. A few fish jumped here and there, which felt like both an invitation and a taunt. I cast in the direction of a splash, though my jig landed a little further out than I intended. As I began to reel in slowly, I could see the line floating on the water, and that is when

I heard my father, as if he were standing right behind me, say, "Don't let your line lay in the water. Reel a little faster." Instinctively, I obeyed, and in an instant he and I were on a boat, baiting our hooks with crickets, and casting into a lake, and he was telling me not to let my line sit on top of the water. For a moment, we were together in the before, sunshine on my skin, the scent of Coppertone mingling with lake water. And then a fish struck the line hard. I set the hook and began the fight to reel it in, and the weight on the line and in my chest was almost too much to bear.

For hours afterward, I felt haunted by a lingering feeling of disquiet. "Haunting," as Avery Gordon explains, "raises specters and it alters the experience of being in time, the way we separate the past, present, and the future" (xvi). The feeling was one, not of being taken out of, but instead, of being plunged deep within the self—where memories break free and grab hold. I have been making trips back and forth to the past, believing I can, at will, open and shut the door tightly behind me so nothing unwanted can slip through. But when one makes such visits, however slowly, to see and reclaim objects or experiences, the items we bring back with us are never clean. Something always comes with them. Gordon explains how "specters or ghosts appear when the trouble they represent and symptomize is no longer being contained or repressed or blocked from view," and when they appear, ghosts demand their due and our attention (xvi). *Fantasmas* do their best work in front of an audience. They are sometimes divas like that. Mostly they stay in their place, though they can also follow us home; just ask La Llorona.

I know quite a bit about ghosts. My first book is all about one. Whereas Gordon in *Ghostly Matters: Haunting and the Sociological Imagination* (2008) uses haunting as both "the language and experiential modality" for understanding the ways that "abusive systems of power make themselves known and their impacts felt in everyday life" (xvi), for example, the legacy of slavery or Indian removal, my book *There Was a Woman: La Llorona from Folklore to Popular Culture* (2008) focuses on the figure doing the haunting: La Llorona (the weeping or wailing woman). As a woman subjected to abusive systems of power, La Llorona was haunted by abuse and also by what she herself had done (i.e., murdered her children). My book analyzes how La Llorona has, in essence, been instrumentalized by those in and outside of her parent culture for a variety of purposes that range from entertainment to political activism. She can be a scary bedtime story or a behavioral deterrent, or she can help smash the patriarchy. Gordon's idea of containing ghosts, or rather, the failure to do so, has particular resonance for the conversation that takes place in part 3. It also made me think back to Isabelle Stengers and Virginia Woolf, both of whom urged us to seek out those elusive or invisible structures that exert authority over us, be they social, cultural, political, institutional, or personal. Sometimes, they are clearly identifiable, while in other instances, they are shadowy or hidden. Either way, such ghosts make their presence known.

> Mexican ghosts do not say boo. They weep.
> Myriam Gurba, "How Controversy over
> 'American Dirt' Inspired a Movement for Change"

In the introduction to *Slow Scholarship: Medieval Research and the Neoliberal University*, editor Catherine E. Karkov talks about the "joy of scholarship," of finding, exploring, returning to, or reflecting on what brought the collection's contributors to "scholarly research and careers in the first place" (9). The idea gave me pause when I came across it recently because I had not felt that particular emotion in regard to my own work in a while. It also made me think back to January 2020, when the controversy around Jeanine Cummins's novel *American Dirt* (2019) started to boil over, and how, at times, my scholarly production is devoid of any joy. But I can also see now how that novel, and the backlash it sparked, is clearly representative of a haunting. Gordon distinguishes between hauntings and trauma, noting that the former are "distinctive for producing a something-to-be-done" (xvi). *American Dirt*, which was widely endorsed by such literary luminaries as Sandra Cisneros, John Grisham, and Stephen King, demanded the attention of scholars, taking our attention away from other authors and works more worthy of it. The novel demanded of us a "something-to-be-done."

Balance is essential to any slow approach. As stated previously, slow is about agency and the ability to choose. Yet the choices of narratives Brown folx are given to consume, especially by mainstream books and films, are almost always in some way tied to suffering—either we dole it out or we are on the receiving end. I am not saying that stories about struggle and hardship do not matter, but any healthy diet depends on variety. However, mainstream books and films do not make the same investment in our joy or other affective registers that they do in our suffering. Mainstream publishers and studios create and feed a public appetite for Brown pain.

American Dirt represents an exemplar of such a product, one that instrumentalizes diasporic Mexican tragedy for profit. The book focuses on Lydia Pérez, most of whose family, including her husband, is slaughtered by men from a drug cartel while attending a quinceañera in Acapulco, Mexico. Lydia and her son, who escape the massacre, are forced to flee north to safety. Myriam Gurba's viral review "Pendeja, You Ain't Steinbeck: My Bronca with Fake-Ass Social Justice Literature" (2019) conveys in detail the cultivation of a white appetite for Brown pain through trauma porn peddled in works such as *American Dirt*. Trauma as entertainment minimizes or erases, especially for white readers, the historical, cultural, social, and/or political circumstances responsible for the hauntings that give rise to anguish or distress. However, Cummins states in her author's note that she wanted to bring awareness, through her work, to why Mexicans make the dangerous trip north. She also reveals cognizance of the fact "that the people coming to our southern border are not one faceless brown mass but singular individuals, with stories and backgrounds and reasons for coming that are unique," and she knows this because, as Betty and Veronica feel they are Indian in their bones in *Reservation Blues*, she feels "this awareness in [her] spine, in [her] DNA" (382). But in truth, Cummins is not the problem; she is merely a symptom of larger issues in mainstream publishing.

Publishers gravitate toward the familiar, often something they have a hand in creating, such as particular instantiations of race and/or ethnicities, those things that make difference legible and that preferably do not disrupt the status quo. That means publishers are only interested in particular types of stories about the Mexican diaspora and Latinxs, more broadly, drawn in particular ways. For example, they should have big families, live in colorful houses, love food, speak in broken English, demonstrate an oppressive devotion to religion, and, preferably, be poor. I know authors who have tried to write contemporary Chicanx or Latinx fiction without relying on these tropes and have had editors/publishers tell them to "add more spice" or "include some magical realism." *American Dirt* engages in a kind of racialized excess, particularly against the backdrop of the predominantly white publishing industry. Christopher González, in his seven-part series on the novel, "The Problem with *American Dirt*," the most comprehensive assessment of it to date, includes an analysis of the slow violence it enacts. Rob Nixon, in *Slow Violence and the Environmentalism of the Poor* (2013), describes this particular kind of aggression as "a violence that occurs gradually and out of sight, a violence of delayed destruction that is dispersed across time and space, an attritional violence that is typically not viewed as violence at all" (2). González extrapolates from Nixon's critical frame and sees the publishers' "efforts to raise the profile of this novel and its author [as], in effect, a slow violence on migrants and refugees in Mexico (directly) and Latinx people (generally)" ("The Problem"). The violence of *American Dirt* has also been wrought through the barbed-wire floral centerpieces used as decorations at the book's release party, the author's specious claims to a never-before-revealed Latinidad, and the plagiarism of events from Luis Alberto Urrea's nonfiction book *By the Lake of Sleeping Children* (1996), not to mention the seven-figure advance Cummins received for the novel.[2] The resources devoted to Cummins and her novel illustrate how publishers invest deeply in particular kinds of stories that reinforce the superiority of the status quo. Slow violence, therefore, produces its own kinds of hauntings.

The slow violence of the mainstream publishing industry, represented through the production and distribution of *American Dirt*, feeds public desire to consume particular kinds of palatable ethnicity, in this case a story about Mexicans with the right amount of spice and color. Cummins's novel fits the bill by including narcos, machetes, Día de Muertos, violence, and suffering (lots of suffering). Furthermore, the book's theme is timely and does nothing to threaten the status quo. People can feel sad or outraged, though not haunted, about border violence but do not actually have to do anything about those feelings. Still an additional layer of violence exists in the very publication of the book, which eclipses the work of writers such as the authors included throughout this study, whose lives and art have been informed directly by their relationship with and proximity to the border.

An important aspect of Gordon's theory of haunting involves the instigation of the "something-to-be-done," some action that clearly needs to be taken in response to the ghosts (xvi). As a haunting, the book requires such action. My colleagues and I spoke out through editorials, social media posts, and other popular formats. We gave interviews to news media in the US and abroad in which we made recommendations about the hundreds of other books people should be reading instead of *American Dirt*. And we received threats, via social media, as well as a good email scolding from a well-known white male author about censorship, thereby compounding the hauntings created by Cummins's work. Additionally, Gurba and other Latinx authors protested at the offices of the book's publisher. This group also established Dignidad Literaria, an organization that advocates for greater diversity in publishing, both in staff members and in the works they produce.³ I worked with other entities attached to a celebrity book club in an attempt to increase and promote diversity in publishing, only to have my ideas stolen and my phone calls go unanswered. *American Dirt* still went on to sell over half a million copies, and it still became a best seller (Shapiro). As González rightly observes, "The damage this novel has wreaked is only just beginning" ("The Problem"). We will be haunted by this work for years to come, until another replaces it, and the cycle of exploitation, profit, apology, and blame-shifting begins again. And there is no joy in knowing what will come.

> I am trying to think of time as an unfolding of who I am as a thinking being. Broadly speaking, I am trying to shift the focus from the product (the book, the article, the presentation) to the process of developing my understanding.
>
> Barbara K. Seeber, in Maggie Berg and Seeber, *The Slow Professor*

"Unpack," as in "unpack these ideas," is understood to mean looking at the individual components of a thing more closely. In scholarly writing, we occasionally include ideas or quotations as part of unpacking, though the import, to us, is usually clear. This kind of unpacking allows transparency and greater accessibility for the reader to the unfolding or development of an author's idea(s). The term can also mean taking items out of a valise, suitcase, duffle, backpack, grocery sack, or some other kind of container to store them away or put them to use. And, additionally, "unpack" can mean to unburden, to reveal items previously hidden away or carried. Unpacking makes me think about what I do when traveling away from or returning home, in which case, packing is about utility; unpacking is about assessment. Stated another way, what are the things we *think* we need, and what do we actually need?

So many times I felt an urgency—a need—to complete this book, any version of it, because as I was often reminded, "The clock is ticking." Every minute, hour, day, year that went by without my having completed it evinced my failure. I was writing and publishing articles, book chapters, reviews, and short stories, as well as collaborating on edited collections, alongside a substantial administrative obligation, but the inability to finish a monograph filled me with anxiety and more than a little shame that I most definitely needed to unpack. When I tried to talk with colleagues about these feelings, I was told to "just do it," as if a corporate slogan for athletic wear was the solution that I had needed all along. I was also advised to "sit down and knock it out" or "get it over with." The suggestions all advocated that I approach writing as "an instrumental skill rather than an epistemological experience" (GLFGC 1241). The emphasis was on the end result and not the process itself.

Writing is slow work that requires attention at all times to the micro (words, punctuation) and the macro (overarching analysis or argument). The process brings up any number of emotions, anxiety and exhilaration, frustration and pride—and it can also haunt us. Mary Lindemann, president of the American Historical Association, in her 2021 address titled "Slow History" alludes to the spectral-like qualities of writing: "The sensitivity to selecting words and shaping sentences that effectively convey our thoughts is not inborn but something painstakingly acquired. Yet it remains imperfect, always becoming, never quite *there*" (17). Writing simultaneously involves capture and letting go. Sometimes we know exactly what we want to say in the exact way we want to say it. And other times, the thought unfolds on the page, revealing itself to us. Still, there is always something we did not say, a perfect quotation we could not find, or a fully formed idea that arrived in the night that we promised ourselves was too good to forget but that slipped away with the sunrise. These instances leave behind them an indistinguishable trace and leave us wanting. Lindemann also reminds us that "good prose takes an awful lot of time; we write, we rewrite, we organize, we reorganize, and then we do it all again. Words are fantastic, protean creatures, often elusive and certainly frequently dangerous" (17). Writing makes us vulnerable, and it comes at a cost that usually feels worth the effort, but at other times, not at all.

Reflecting on the development of my knowledge production helped me to see that the version of this book I had planned to write over the years would not satisfy who I am today. Upon completion, the book would have met an objective, it would have been functional, and there was a time when that would have been all right. Not anymore. As the Great Lakes Feminist Geography Collective reminds us, "We learn by living" (1247), and I have. The unfolding of my thoughts through the process of writing has been an epistemological experience, revealing and highlighting sources of knowledge both that I have drawn from over the years and that are more recent formulations. And it has reminded me that we live in a land of specters. Some are of our own making. Others we have inherited. And still others were here long before we arrived.

> One need not be a chamber to be haunted,
> One need not be a house;
> The brain has corridors surpassing
> Material place.
> Emily Dickinson, "One need not be
a chamber to be haunted"

The individuals and characters discussed in this section of the book either haunt or are haunted, though sometimes they experience both at once. Toxic masculinity, racialized violence, restrictive cultural ideals, immigration status, homophobia, or ablism and other normative constructs manifest through and in characters' lives. And all require some form of action or response. "Haunting and the appearance of specters or ghosts," according to Gordon, serve as a notification that "what's been concealed is very much alive and present, interfering precisely with those always incomplete forms of containment and repression ceaselessly directed toward us" (xvi). What has been hidden or obscured often reveals itself with devastating effects. Whether tangible or abstract, these ghosts—the legacies of abusive power that reside in the literal or metaphoric borderlands—demand a reckoning. Often that involves death, as illustrated in the majority of the works analyzed in this section. Some do live to perpetuate the oppression they experienced and others give up their ghosts in an effort to create new futures for themselves and their children. Each discovers, in his own way, that the past does not stay put.

LITERATURE

FATHERS, SONS, AND OTHER (SHORT) FICTIONS

My father and brother once got into a fight. My mother stepped between them to stop it. I ran to my room and hid in the closet. My hands pressed over my ears were not enough to block out her screams.

Historically, authors of the Mexican diaspora in the US have made limited efforts to reflect on and trouble Mexican American and Chicanx masculinity in order to distinguish machismo as separate from misogyny, create alliances across genders and sexualities, and imagine other nonnormative masculine expressions that are traditionally marginalized, erased, or violently attacked. At the same time, however, within some of these same authors' works, we see veneration or condemnation, and sometimes both, of Mexican American and Chicanx male authority, most often that attached to or assumed by fathers or father figures. María Amparo Ruiz de Burton in *The Squatter and the Don* (1885), Arturo Islas in *The Rain God* (1984), Américo Paredes in *George Washington Gómez: A Mexicotexan Novel* (1990, written circa 1930), Luis Alberto Urrea in *In Search of Snow* (1994), and Jovita González and Eve Raleigh in *Caballero* (1996, written during the 1930s and 1940s) are but a few authors who have reflected on the cultural and social institutions that reinforce heterosexual male power, often to detrimental effect.[1] Though overwhelmingly heteronormative, these works represent a diverse set of histories, experiences, and cultural geographies: landowners, first-generation Mexican Americans, Californios, Tejanxs, Arizonans, war vets, and man-children, to name a few. With the exception of Urrea's novel (an analysis of which is included in part 1), a significant body of scholarship about the aforementioned works exists.

Early in this century, Ray Gonzalez in *The Ghost of John Wayne and*

Other Stories (2001) and Oscar Cásares in *Brownsville* (2003) probed the ongoing effects of paternal authority through their short fictions. The father and son characters in these collections attempt to define masculinity on their own terms and often face the painful realization that there is no viable space in which to carve out or maintain new expressions of manhood. By focusing on father-son relationships, Gonzalez and Cásares, both of whom are understudied border authors, examine a critical site and source of masculinity and male power. The sons in these stories see both their place in the patriarchal hierarchy and their relationship to it, which requires some action(s) on their part. They are moved to act in particular ways that Chicanx men in literature have historically not been inclined to do.

In the introduction to *The Chicano: From Caricature to Self-Portrait* (1971), editor Edward Simmen traces the evolution of Mexican and Mexican American representation from demeaning caricatures authored by Anglos to empowering self-representations written by Chicanos in selected short fiction from the mid-nineteenth century to 1970. Simmen ultimately argues that the work of Chicano authors such as Mario Suárez, Américo Paredes, and Genero González signaled a shift in both practice and criticism of Mexican and Mexican American representation in literature. All six of the Chicano authors featured in *The Chicano* are men. Therefore, the anthology presents the self-representation of Mexicans and Mexican Americans as the cultural work of men. Prior to and during the political activism of the 1960s and 1970s, Chicano authors largely reinforced the view of men as the primary agents of cultural and social change, especially in their efforts to make visible and authorize Brown male subject positions in literature. Works such as José Antonio Villarreal's *Pocho* (1959), Richard Vasquez's *Chicano* (1970), Tómas Rivera's *And the Earth Did Not Devour Him* (1971), Rudolfo Anaya's *Bless Me, Ultima* (1972), and Rolando Hinojosa's *The Valley* (1973), for example, centralize Mexican and Mexican American male subjects. Although these and other authors concern themselves primarily with emergent Mexican American and Chicano male subject positions in American literature, they also initiate a process of, albeit limited, critical interrogation of diasporic Mexican masculinity by identifying the cultural, social, or political forces that authorize male power during this period.

For instance, in Villarreal's *Pocho*, the protagonist, Richard Rubio, experiences a revelation concerning his mother, Consuelo, and the particular abuses she endures as a woman. The novel focuses on the members of the Rubio family, who emigrate to the US following the Mexican Revolution (1910–1920). Richard, American-born and the only son, attempts to span the gulf between his Mexican and American identities. The father, Juan, resides firmly in the center of his young son's life. Eventually Richard begins to see the pain his mother endures as a result of Juan's behaviors, more so in the wake of his father's infidelity:

> Then suddenly, clearly, he saw that she, too, was locked up, and the full horror of her situation struck him. He thought of his sisters and saw their future, and, now crying, he thought of himself, and starkly, without knowledge of the words that would describe it, he saw the demands of tradition, of culture, of the social structure on an individual. Not comprehending, he was again aware of the dark, mysterious force, and was resolved that he would rise above it. (95)

Although the dark, mysterious force is not named, Richard understands clearly that he is witness to the effects of male power and authority on the lives of women. Despite vowing to "never use the right he had as a male to tell his mother that she was wrong," he uses that same authority afforded to him, even as a boy, to humiliate Zelda, a local tomboy, into having sex with all the neighborhood boys as a way to diminish her power as the biggest and toughest kid in their "gang" (95). Zelda, Consuelo, and Luz, Richard's sister whom he spots in a car with a boy and drags from the vehicle, all discover that he is capable of "great cruelty" (143).[2] Too soon, he forgets what he saw so clearly as a child and instead uses his masculinity as a means of controlling, with a few notable exceptions, the women around him.[3] In these early critical reflections on masculinity, identifying social and familial injustice or oppression does not require immediate redress, translate into a call to action, or necessitate a yielding of power on the part of men. It is simply recognized and then forgotten.

Over the years, a body of critical scholarship about Latinx masculinity has been produced in fields ranging from sociology and psychology to film and gender studies, including work by Maxine Baca Zinn, Miguel Montiel, Alfredo Mirandé, Rosa Linda Fregoso, Carmen Huaco-Nuzum, Daniel Enrique Pérez, and Richard T. Rodríguez, some of which is discussed earlier. Foundational work by these scholars, along with Aída Hurtado and Mrinal Sinha in *Beyond Machismo: Intersectional Latino Masculinities* (2016), opened avenues for critical inquiry into Latinx manhood and masculinity that illustrate the cultural, generational, and sociological divisions in masculinist performances. In Mexican American and Chicanx literary studies, however, key works stand out, the scope of which stretches back almost 175 years. Alberto Varon in *Before Chicano: Citizenship and the Making of Mexican American Manhood, 1848–1959* (2018), for example, focuses on *pre*-1960 depictions of manhood through print culture and analyzes how these texts informed ideas about men and national belonging. Frederick Luis Aldama in *Brown on Brown: Chicano/a Representations of Gender, Sexuality, and Ethnicity* (2005) situates his work at the intersection of Chicanx, queer, and literary (and film) studies to consider a variety of storytelling genres that radically expand "the Chicano/a and American literary and filmic narrative landscape" (19). Together these scholars analyze the cultural, social, racial, and textual scripts that inform diasporic Mexican masculinity.

Through their borderlands short story collections Gonzalez and Cásares participate in the criticism of social and cultural institutions of male power. Characters are plunged into border landscapes that are haunted by ghosts, their fathers, and even themselves. There they face the legacies of paternalisms rooted in violence, toxicity, and other self-destructive behaviors. While some men choose to replicate, uncritically, the masculinities handed down to them by their fathers, others reject these outright. Instead, these men choose to pursue alternative expressions of masculinity that are not dependent upon force or subjugation. And still others are made to face the limitations of their own performance as patriarchs. In the process, the characters reject, critique, or complicate, sometimes too late, the behaviors derived from their fathers and from popular or cultural fictions.

THE KING

> Men, even more than women, are fettered to gender roles.
> Gloria Anzaldúa, *The Borderlands/La Frontera*

> RENE: [Jesse's] comin' tonight, right?
> CHE: Most definitely. In fact, I might even ride shotgun, let him drive.
> RENE: Orale, the king's finally gonna give up the throne.
> CHE: Chale, man, I said drive, not wear the crown.
> *La Mission*

In April 2012, Robert Rodriguez, director, producer, and editor of such notable films as *El Mariachi*, *Spy Kids*, and *Machete*, gave the talk "The Future of Latino Images in Film and Media" at the University of Texas at

Austin. He shared his experiences as a "Latin" filmmaker and his vision for the future of Latino images in film and media.[4] Rodriguez also announced his plan to launch a Latino-themed cable channel, El Rey Network.[5] The network would target English-speaking Latino audiences and, as a general entertainment channel, planned to include "reality [programming], scripted and animated series, movies, documentaries, news, music, comedy and sports programming" (Bouma).[6] The focus of the network captures the tension between targeting Latinos directly and providing a more broad-based, in other words mainstream, appeal.[7] El Rey Network launched in December 2013.

Rodriguez, who has always identified as an American filmmaker, had historically downplayed his Latinidad, so the decision to name his network El Rey, which means "The King" in Spanish, and to feature as the network's logo a gold crown, is a curious if not contradictory turn for the film rebel. The network name, as Rodriguez has explained, is "like the song" of the same name in that both are about "Latin pride" ("Chingon").[8] El Rey takes its name from a popular ballad written by Mexican songwriter and singer José Alfredo Jiménez in 1971 but performed most popularly by Vicente Fernández, known as "El Rey de Mariachi."[9] The lyrics detail a man's response after being thrown out by his lover as he attempts to convey his regal authority and predicts her inevitable regret for no longer having him in her life. Its refrain is perhaps better known to Mexicans and Mexican Americans than any national paean: "Con dinero y sin dinero hago siempre lo que quiero y mi palabra es la ley."[10] Fernández's soulful performance made "El Rey" an anthem and authorizing source for Mexican masculinity.

The cultural currency of the song and its message is such that Rodriguez's move to leverage the multigenerational, transnational capital attached to the ballad is savvy (and perhaps a bit cynical) for a man who has maintained a distance from identity politics. The name El Rey has immediate resonance among diasporic Mexicans, a population that represents 62 percent of all Latinos in the US.[11] The song draws upon a transnational cultural imaginary, one generated by the Mexican state and enacted by the nation for a particular kind of gendered performance—the charro.[12] Sergio de la Mora in *Cinemachismo: Masculinities and Sexuality in Mexican Film* (2006) sees the figure intertwined with a number of social and national forces:

> Machismo is intimately linked to State power and to the highly contested gendered social contract extended to Mexican citizens in the post-revolutionary period. Indeed, the machismo

attributed to Mexican men (the *charro*, popularized through *mariachi* music and the *comedia ranchera* film genre, or combatants who fought in the Revolution) is among Mexico's most internationally recognized symbols. (de la Mora 6)[13]

Mexico promoted and celebrated the figures of the charro and the revolutionary during the Golden Age of Mexican cinema (roughly 1936–1956).[14] These images were internalized and enacted by national subjects on both sides of the US-Mexico border. Rodriguez's use of "El Rey" captures and conveys an incredibly self-conscious form of masculinity, one that is far-reaching and deeply ingrained, for generations of Mexican and Mexican American men.[15]

The song also inspired the title of Domingo Martinez's 2012 memoir, *The Boy Kings of Texas*, a National Book Award finalist that documents Martinez's experiences growing up in Brownsville, Texas, on the border between the US and Mexico. Much of the book reflects on the impact on Martinez and his siblings of growing up with a violent father and a domineering grandmother.[16] In the prologue, Martinez, whose nickname, Yunior, is shortened to June, offers a cultural analysis of the song "El Rey" that includes his realization about the messages embedded in it pertaining to masculinity: "Right in front of me . . . was the lyrical genome for machismo. José Alfredo Jiménez had mapped the emotional DNA of the border male, had illustrated clearly what had so viciously plagued my father, and, well, his mother, who was as butch as they come" (x). Martinez demonstrates how the attitudes and ideas contained in the lyrics permeated the entire lives of his family, influencing men and women equally.

Martinez's grandmother, Gramma, enacts a "female masculinity" that both replicates and serves as a source for the heteropatriarchal violence that surrounds the family. The front matter of the book features an image of Gramma with a caption indicating that the photograph was taken in Matamoros, Mexico, in the late 1950s. Posed in the open door on the driver's side of an agricultural truck, she looks directly into the camera, one arm cocked on her hip and resting against the handle of her holstered gun. A thin leather strap high on the leg closest to the truck indicates she is carrying not one but two pistols—one on each hip. One leg of her work pants is tucked haphazardly inside her cowboy boot. Atop a crown of black curls sits a cowboy hat. This is an image of a beautiful, strong, hardworking Mexican woman. Armed with the dual pistols, she does not immediately convey masculinity, feminine or otherwise, but as Jack Halberstam asserts, "Masculinity . . . becomes legible as masculinity where and when it leaves the white male middle-class body" (2). Widowed, after her husband was murdered in a cantina, and a single mother at the age of seventeen, Martinez's grandmother worked as an agricultural laborer. While performing field work picking tomatoes, she learned to defend herself: "She was the very definition of butch. . . . She was competitive and mean, and would proudly get into fistfights with the young bucks who'd be surprised at how hard she could hit, hit like a man" (51). Her penchant for fighting with, and regularly defeating, younger men therefore put her in a position of dominance over them and rooted her feminine masculinity in violence. From the time he was a boy, Martinez's father, Mingo, watched his single mother perform a masculinity that would become a model for his own.

The nonnormativity of her behavior became apparent when Gramma married an American citizen. In the US, she was expected to enact the role of wife and mother in a manner befitting her newly elevated class and status as American citizen.[17] Nevertheless, years later, when she was widowed a second time, she became a gun-toting barrio loan shark, who, allegedly, may have killed her husband by withholding his insulin after he returned from a three-day bender with his mistress. The deaths of her husbands, along with her difficult childhood circumstances, honed her survival—by any means possible—instincts. When Gramma was a child, during the Great Depression, her parents passed her around to various family members until she eventually landed with an uncle. The man expected her to look after his five boys: "a mean, wild-boy tribe of haranguers . . . who would torture and assault her every chance they had, would keep her subjugated, inferior, reduced, and reminded of why she was there" (42). In exchange, she received half a tortilla a day. Gramma replicated the cruelty she had experienced at the hands of male family members as a survival strategy and passed the abuse on to the next generations.

In the memoir, Martinez repeatedly documents the destructive power of Mingo's masculine performance. In one notable instance, he responds to loss and emotional vulnerability with violence. After the family's beloved family pet Chihuahua is mauled by pit bulls that freely roam the neighborhood, Mingo and his wife and children are devastated, and this constitutes the only time Martinez ever saw his father cry. The relationship between the aggressive pit bulls and the vulnerable Chihuahua is an apt metaphor for competing forms of masculinity in the book. "Dogs become participants in symbolic exchanges," according to Michael Ramirez in his study on dog ownership and gender display, "offering animated affirmation of interpretations put forth by their human owners"

(388). The attack on the tiny Chihuahua, therefore, becomes an attack on Mingo's masculinity, which, according to his masculinist script, demands a rejoinder. Immediately following the family burial of the beloved pet, Mingo grabs his gun and drives off to kill all the dogs involved in the attack. Martinez's mother, Velva Jean, calls her son outside to watch the scene: "[M]y father slows his truck with menacing purpose and leans out the driver's side window with a .22-caliber revolver. I hear him shoot repeatedly, shoot every single dog as close to the head as he can. And . . . they all lay there dying, gray and brown lumps in the dusty early morning road . . ." The horrific scene prompts Martinez to confess, "I don't ever remember feeling so proud of my father again" (9). However, throughout the early period of their lives, Martinez and his brother are plagued by their father's sexual vulgarity, violence, and alcoholism, all of which demand a specific kind of masculine performance that is psychologically and emotionally exhausting for June and Denny.[18] At one point, Martinez, who sees no other way out from a cycle of toxic masculinity, naïvely prays to escape his father's influence.

Being king has a cost, one that is incurred by both men and women and that directly impacts families. June has no interest in becoming like his father and cannot get far enough away from him. As an adult, Martinez sees his family through the lyrics of "El Rey":

> Here was the source code for everything I was trying to escape: the generational compulsions and impulses of alienation, narcissism, self-destruction, emotional blackmail, and a profound conviction that everyone else in the world is wrong—*wrong!*—wrapped in a deep, all-consuming appeal to be accepted, protected by an ever-ready defensive, fighting posture, perfectly captured in a song. (x)

What Martinez and his five siblings learned from their Mexican father and grandmother is clearly a damaging performance of masculinity but one from which they cannot escape. In his essay "'I Am the King': The Macho Image," which also takes its name from the song's lyrics, Rudolfo Anaya attests, "Being macho is essentially a learned behavior; as such it is a conditioned behavior. We males learn to act 'manly' from other males around us. . . . Many cultural forces (from literature and religion to the latest musical fad, movies, MTV, or car styles) play a role in promoting the behavior of the macho" (59). The song "El Rey" provides a script for a form of Mexican masculinity that is translocal, transnational, and transgenerational. Rodriguez's, Martinez's, and Anaya's engagement with the song represents but one dialogue about one cultural source for a lasting and potentially destructive kind of masculinity that has influenced Mexican and Mexican American men on both sides of the border.

GHOSTS OF THE PAST AND PRESENT

> *The year is 1992. At an apartment in San Marcos, Texas, the sound of a tangle of keys turning in the lock can be heard. The apartment smells of cinnamon Glade air freshener. On the worn blue-gray carpet in the living room sits a Tejana in her twenties with a mass of raven hair knotted haphazardly in a scrunchie. She looks over at the door.*
> DP. You got it?
> AT, *from the other side of the door.* Yeah, I'm good.
> *Inside steps a tall, fair-skinned copy of the young woman seated on the floor. Where a dining table should be there are two desks. After making her entrance, the light almost-twin walks in and drops her bags on the desk facing the kitchen before plopping down next to the Tejana. They sit shoulder to shoulder. The almost-twin has returned from the first meeting of her creative writing class.*
> DP. So, how'd it gooooooooo?
> AT. It was good. The professor is great. The other students seem good. (*Pauses.*) Oh, and we even have a famous writer in the class.
> DP. A famous writer?
> AT. Yeah, he's an editor for a poetry journal *and* published some books of poetry. His stuff is really good. Maybe you've heard of him?
> DP. I doubt it. The only poetry I read is yours. What's his name?
> AT. Ray. Ray Gonzalez?
> DP. Never heard of him.

Although Gonzalez and I overlapped in graduate school at what was then Southwest Texas State University, we met only once, and I never had the opportunity to ask him about his work. Thirty years have passed since I first heard his name. During that time, Professor Gonzalez has become an award-winning, multi-genre author of over thirty books (fourteen single-author books of poetry; two short story collections; three essay collections; fourteen edited collections and anthologies) and has continued to serve as the poetry editor of the *Bloomsbury Review*, a position he has held since 1981. I have taught from his anthologies *Mirrors beneath the Earth: Chicano Short Fiction* (1992) and *Currents from the Dancing River: Contemporary Latino Literature* (1994) and from his edited collection *Muy Macho: Latino Men Confront Their Manhood* (1996), which influenced some of my initial thoughts about fathers, sons, and borderlands fictions. Over the years, Gonzalez has helped to disseminate and widely circulate Latinx and Chicanx literature, as well as shaped a generation or more of authors and poets. Despite numerous awards and his contributions to the fields of Mexican American and Latinx literature, a negligible amount of scholarship has been done on his work. An MLA search of his name and the titles of his books produces only a handful of interviews, reviews, and articles. Slow research urges us to look at those individuals whose works are understudied or overlooked and bring them, and their transformative potential, into existing conversations, in this case about fathers and sons.

Born in El Paso, Texas, in 1952, Gonzalez grew up in a world full of stories. In an interview with Alex Lemon, Gonzalez shares that his writing was influenced by a number of different sources: songs by the Beatles, Elvis, and the Supremes, Batman and Superman comic books, and illustrated classics such as *Robinson Crusoe*. Popular culture had a powerful impact on Gonzalez as a nascent storyteller, but so did his grandmother ("who had thousands of stories in her head") and the landscape of the Chihuahua desert he called home ("Interview" 122). However, he cites border culture as one of the biggest influences on his writing. From poetry to personal essays, the border, evoked through the senses, myths, legends, and people who reside there, permeates his writing. A whole body of scholarship could be done on any one genre of his work, much more than I could accomplish in any one chapter or book. Consequently, my specific interests in Gonzalez's work stem from his preoccupation with fathers and in particular the complicated father-son relationships depicted in *The Ghost of John Wayne and Other Stories*.[19]

Growing up, Gonzalez saw his father as an elusive figure in a home where his mother ruled with a heavy religious hand. "The result," as the author explains, "was a childhood shaped from a dominating mother and a distant, passive father who carried his secrets with him, intimate details of his own youth in a small border town in the middle of a vast desert" ("My Literary Fathers" 169). Gonzalez's fixation on his father is not so much about what the man did but what he did not do. Gonzalez struggles on the page to understand a man who was largely unknowable, and he admits to having written "at least one hundred poems about [his] father" (174). Scenes of his father in the pool hall and descriptions of the smell emanating from his feet after a long day as a used-car salesman, lines written about the silent ride to and from the movie theatre and the short, awkward phone conversations they shared later in life, these are things he knows about his father; the rest Gonzalez has tried to fill in through essays, poetry, and fiction.

Gonzalez's 1996 book of poetry *The Heat of Arrivals* includes a number of lyrical meditations on fathers, including one aptly entitled "Fathers." The poem appears in "The Energy of Clay," the third section of the book, which consists of "nothing but father poems" ("My Literary Fathers" 174). "Fathers" begins with an epigraph by Chilean poet Gonzalo Rojas that imagines paternal legacy as a rope that connects generations of men who are bound to and by that legacy. In spite of or perhaps because of these adversities, they still believe they will, as the narrator of Rojas's poem states, "conquer" or dominate to become, as the song "El Rey" imparts, kings. Yet the speaker in Gonzalez's poem offers a different perspective on the obligations of this particular birthright:

I look down and we are one,
suspended in the air, headed

toward the moment when we do
the same things, commit the same acts

to save ourselves from the hatred
and awful fear of our fathers . . . (*Heat of Arrivals* 77)

The rope creates a literal and metaphoric connection between generations of men, but it also ensnares them. To mitigate the fear and loathing of their fathers, the sons become like them, thereby extending the paternal tie.

The speaker sees the connections between past and present. He recognizes the details with such familiarity that he knows the exact moment when sons replicate the actions of their fathers, men characterized by "hard work and ignorance, / sin and betrayal, / escape and triumph" (77). Believing somehow that their lives will turn out differently and "better," they instead make the same mistakes and become tethered to a destructive legacy. These same men "hang" from their family tree "that bends in the wind" of shame "to hide / what [they] did from [their] wives and children," demonstrating that their behaviors directly impact their whole families and not just the men (77). The image brings to mind both a lynching and a hanging, acts that, as Monica Muñoz Martínez documents in *The Injustice Never Leaves You: Anti-Mexican Violence in Texas* (2018), along with other forms of violence, are woven into the history of the borderlands.[20] However, the men unmistakably have ensnared themselves by replicating a set of behaviors that the speaker sees as shameful. But he, too, is implicated in these acts. There seems little hope of disrupting this cycle as the men "hang and drift" (77). Gonzalez makes a similar observation about his own life: "We may not repeat every mistake our fathers made, but our inner turmoil, weaknesses, and strengths come from the same fibers of that code. Before we know it, we have our identity as men. It has been passed down from one generation to another. If we know this, how do we stop it or change it?" ("My Literary Fathers" 180). Though bound by their choices, the hanged men, who are incapable of saving themselves, await "the son born to climb the tree, cut the rope, / and watch the bodies fall" (*Heat of Arrivals* 77). The son's obligation is more than simply to stop the transmission of cultural knowledge about toxic masculinity or to release the man: the son must bear witness to the bodies plummeting to the ground; in other words, he must watch and then offer testimony about the disruption of reprehensible male behavior, thereby ending a generational practice.

The poem "Fathers" provides a useful avenue for both exploring and understanding the relationships between fathers and sons in Gonzalez's *Ghost of John Wayne*. Of the twenty-five short stories and flash fictions or micro-fictions included in the collection, only four focus explicitly on fathers and sons: "The Jalapeño Contest," "The Chinese Restaurant," "The Grandfather Horse," and "Fishing." In each, sons try to forge connections with their fathers, which proves difficult if not impossible. The diasporic Mexican fathers in these stories are characterized by violence, abandonment, and narcissism. Their behaviors elicit a response in their sons, who replicate, reject, or critique the actions of their fathers. Whether the sons in these stories confront or enact the personal fictions of their fathers' masculinity, all are haunted. Gonzalez presents these encounters in a landscape filled with ghosts. And in light of the book's title, none looms larger than Duke.

John Wayne, née Marion Robert Morrison, aka Duke, represents for a generation of Baby Boomer men and political conservatives the pinnacle of American masculinity. His tough-talking, side-shuffling swagger and drawling speech made him an icon for men in the US and around the world. Russell Meeuf, in *John Wayne's World: Transnational Masculinities in the Fifties* (2013), sees Wayne as "a crucial figure in articulating the boundaries and anxieties of a modern, capitalist, transnational masculinity in the 1950s, providing an important and resonant fantasy of male identity in a world being transformed by international social, economic, and political forces" (4). Wayne performed, perpetuated, and partook of the fantasy he helped to create, though behind the fantasy there often lurked a darkness, not unlike the one Richard Rubio saw as a child but sometimes one far worse. Arturo J. Aldama and Frederick Luis Aldama describe how their "Guatemalan–Irish American *mamá* tried to push her father's John Wayne–styled masculinity on [them]: guns, cowboy hats, burnt-yellow cigarette-stained fingers and lips, and shitkicker boots" (3). These qualities obscured the sexual abuse her father inflicted on his children and grandchildren. Many of the men who copied Wayne were as much of a sham as the man who performed him, including the character Turk McGurk in Luis Alberto Urrea's *In Search of Snow*, discussed in part 1.

Despite Turk's posturing, in an attempt to live up to his own internalized masculine ideals, in the end he fails. During Turk's final performance, his death, one punctuated by the statement "I'm ready for you, you sons of bitches," is pitiful, lacking even dignity (118). While spittle slides from a corner of Turk's mouth, John Wayne, Turk's ideal, flickers on the television screen behind him. Instead of dying in battle, Turk dies as the result of a massive head injury inflicted by the Apache Ramses Castro in a bare-knuckled bout meant to recapture Turk's former glory as a fighter. Turk's cowboy persona is defeated by an Indian.

In 1960, Wayne directed, produced, starred in, and sank most of his money into the film *The Alamo*. His passion project sought to highlight the valor of the Texians in the Alamo mission, who held off, for thirteen days, Mexican forces led by General Santa Anna in 1836. Though the Mexicans defeated the Texians, the Texians have been celebrated—in some circles still are—as heroes. Nancy Schoenberger in *Wayne and Ford: The Films, the Friendship, and the Forging of an American Hero* (2017) purports that *The Alamo*, filmed on a twenty-thousand-acre ranch near the Mexican border, "was a full-voiced celebration of [Wayne's] American patriotism" (152).[21] Wayne opposed the shifting political and cultural climates, which notably chipped away at white male power and authority, along with traditional American values, so the Battle of the Alamo, for Wayne, took on even more symbolic power. As Michael Kimmel observes, "The way Wayne saw it, the Alamo was a metaphor for America: Mexicans against us; black and white, simple" (182). Behind the scenes, the first-time director experienced a number of problems associated with the sheer scale of the epic. The film was considerably over budget, and by the end of filming, Wayne had acquired a hundred-cigarettes-a-day (or five packs) habit. Critics panned the film for its jingoism and saw the two-hour, forty-two-minute run time (not including the intermission) as excessive. Its failure nearly ruined Wayne, personally and financially. One might say he was haunted by *The Alamo*.

According to Gonzalez's collection's titular story, "The Ghost of John Wayne," Wayne's ghost purportedly roams the Alamo. His presence at the mission overshadows other ghosts, in particular the Mexican brothers said to reside there and the secrets they keep about the fateful battle. The caretakers of the Alamo are far more invested in the idea that Wayne's figure wanders the site than they are in possibly complicating the siege that inspired the cry "Remember the Alamo!" They prefer the whitewashed version of history that reinforces Anglo heroism and the status quo instead of the truth—that Mexico won. Wayne's presence affirms a singular view of patriotism and nationalism through the Alamo. But Duke's position within the cultural imaginary was far more complicated:

> Because of how Wayne came to symbolize hard-line conservative politics in the 1960s and 1970s, he became a political symbol deployed by those on both the right and the left: either he was a patriotic American hero, an always righteous man's man who nostalgically suggested a necessary but benevolent patriarchal and national authority, or he was a racist, sexist totalitarian who represented all of US culture's oppressive past . . . (Meeuf 3)

He was, in fact, what both sides believed him to be, and it is the specter of this racist, sexist, patriotic, patriarchal legacy that wanders through Gonzalez's collection. Men attempt to assert and live up to a masculinity that, as Stephen Metcalf purports, "is a by-product of nostalgia, a maudlin elegy for something that never existed—or worse, a masquerade that allows no man, not even John Wayne, to be comfortable in his own skin." Dukes, as well as kings, create an impossible fictional standard for any man, Brown, Anglo, father, or son. Few are in a position to inherit such a title, and those who do pay a steep price.

Gonzalez's "Jalapeño Contest" narrates the cost of claiming the crown of victory through the replication of a dangerous practice two men have learned from their father. The story centralizes the rivalry between two brothers, Freddy and Tesoro. They have not seen each other in five years but have reunited to sit down for the titular competition: "The contest is to see which *man* can eat more peppers. It's a ritual from their father . . ." (*Ghost of John Wayne* 31; emphasis added). According to the narrator, Freddy and Tesoro, who tried competing years earlier, stopped after consuming two peppers each. Both laughed off the incident then, but "[t]his time, things are different. They are older and have to prove a point" (31). Presumably bragging rights—manliness or the right to call oneself a man—lie at the heart of this contest. "The macho," according to Anaya, "learns many games while learning to be *número uno*. Drinking buddies who have a contest to see who can consume the most beer, or the most shots of tequila, are trying to prove their maleness. From the pissing contest to drinking, the wish to prove his manliness becomes antisocial, dangerous" ("I Am the King" 63). Freddy and Tesoro replicate the ritual of their father to determine who will be crowned king or champion. The table is ceremoniously prepared; a bowl filled with peppers sits between them, and each man has access to a salt shaker and beer.

The narrator provides very little information about either brother (except that Tesoro has long black hair and both brothers have "beer guts" [32]), so predicting a winner or deciphering the contest strategy of either, based on, for example, age, proves difficult and ultimately would be unsuccessful. Tesoro quickly outpaces Freddy's consumption of chilis two to one. As the competition progresses, each brother sees the suffering of the other, though neither quits or suggests they stop. By the time Tesoro, whose rate of breathing is visibly increasing, consumes his seventh pepper, both brothers begin to hallucinate, an actual reported side effect of eating large quantities of extremely hot chili peppers.[22] Freddy believes that Tesoro "is having a heart attack as he watches his brother fight for breath" (32). Still Freddy does not intervene. Their hallucinations continue and their suffering intensifies. Eventually, Freddy collapses on the floor in convulsions, and Tesoro projectile vomits "millions of jalapeño seeds all over the table" (32). Freddy sees his brother for the last time when Tesoro's body rises "above the table as an angel, dressed in green jalapeño robes, [and] floats into the room" (32). When Freddy awakens minutes later, he runs to the toilet, but not before shitting himself. Tesoro is nowhere to be found, but from the bathroom, Freddy looks back at the table and sees that jalapeño plants have grown out of the pile of seeds and produced fruit.

This is a competition that may have taken the lives of two brothers. Even if Tesoro is the victor (loser?) in the competition, as suggested by his ascendency, he takes his brother with him. They have endured self-inflicted suffering and soiled themselves in the process. As evinced through vomit and excrement, their bodies have reacted violently to the ingestion of their father's toxic and possibly deadly masculinity. Freddy and Tesoro have engaged in and internalized a practice that is painful, causes delusions, and degrades them. But it is also one that has borne fruit, based on Freddy's final vision. Whether or not the brothers survived the competition, the ritual has endured. No winner exists in this scenario, except perhaps the father. Regardless, both brothers lose.

The most hyperreal of the four stories about fathers and sons in Gonzalez's collection, "The Chinese Restaurant" offers both a critique of violence and a demonstration of how men naturalize it. Told through first-person narration, the story documents a reunion between a distant father and son eager to reconnect. The two men meet in a restaurant parking lot, where they "hug awkwardly," a more self-conscious than genuine effort to reconnect. The father's "thin and wrinkled" appearance registers immediately for the son, though later he also thinks about the limp his father has acquired, wondering whether it was through age or an accident (*Ghost of John Wayne* 35). Whatever picture of his father the narrator held onto over the years, the reality he finds does not match it. Although his father's appearance unsettles the narrator, witnessing the murder of the restaurant's cook shocks him more, as does his father's behavior immediately following the incident.

Despite not having seen him in eight years, the father wastes no time in asserting his authority over his adult son. When the waitress arrives at their table, the father, in an act of infantilization, orders both their meals without consulting his son. As the narrator starts to reflect on the lack of communication he has had with his father since his parents' divorce twenty years earlier, the cook suddenly bursts out of the kitchen pursued by his wife, whose rage is palpable as she slices through the air with a cleaver. Running from his wife as she chases him through the restaurant, the cook nevertheless pauses to shake the father's hand. Customer service and the polite rituals of men are not abandoned, not even when fleeing for one's life. The event barely registers for the father, who, as a restaurant regular, says he knows the couple, which suggests that perhaps this behavior is not out of the ordinary or worth acknowledging. When both husband and wife disappear into the kitchen, the father picks up the conversation by disclosing events from his life, including a heart attack four years prior.[23] The narrator barely has time to register his disappointment in or frustration with his father's lack of communication because the waitress runs out of the kitchen with their food, stopping only briefly to set their plates on the table before dashing out of the restaurant. Moments later, the cook stumbles out of the kitchen with the cleaver in his back and falls dead beside the father and son. When the narrator rises to leave, his father pushes him back down in his seat with a "cold hand" and motions for his son to eat (36). The father's response indicates a disregard for events that do not directly involve him or require his attention, which also means that he ignores the violence in front of him. His oblivion, or narcissism, may also provide an indication as to why his first marriage, to the narrator's mother, failed.

The son's clear-eyed observations of his father serve as a critique of his behaviors. In spite of the chaos happening all around him, the father focuses on why his son has not touched his meal. Not even when the cook's wife yanks the cleaver out of her dead husband's back before refilling their water glasses does the father acknowledge the horror of the scene. Once again, he motions for his son to eat. Like a deranged monarch, the father finds his son's untouched lunch more troubling than the dead man on the floor. At the same time, however, the narrator also sits and has lunch next to a dead man's body. His desire to please his father is greater than the moral imperative to call the police or at the very least leave the restaurant. The scene concludes with the father talking about his second wife as the narrator sits quietly, making him complicit both in the violence he has witnessed and in his father's attitude about it.

Of the four stories, "The Grandfather Horse" actually disrupts a patriarchal legacy and poses an alternate strategy for enacting masculinity, one that directly challenges the authority of the father. In the story, the relationship between a father, Antonio, and his young son Francisco changes after the reappearance of the legendary horse that has haunted the family. Years earlier, the horse's appearance had served as a portent of death: "Francisco's grandmother Lucha had died, and his brother Mario was drafted into the army" (*Ghost of John Wayne* 17). Though Mario returned safely from the war, he was killed not long after with two of his friends in a drunk-driving accident. Antonio corrals the wild horse, which ceases to buck after sensing Francisco's presence. This "ugliest" horse, marked by "old scars and wounds," and the "disturbing" sound of its neigh captivate the boy. For Francisco's parents, however, the horse, like the old wounds that mark its body, serves as a reminder of the loss of their son Mario (17). Each generation reads the same sign of the horse—dubbed the grandfather horse for its generational appearances—differently.

Antonio and Francisco's contrasting views affect how they interact with the horse and the history attached to it. Francisco wants to befriend the horse, while the father initially remains uncertain about its fate, a position that changes after he finds Francisco at the horse's pen feeding it an apple in the middle of the night. His son's tenderness toward the horse incenses the father, who sees the act as a threat and/or a sign of disregard for the family's history. When Antonio appears on the porch of the house brandishing a shotgun, the horse immediately begins to rear, and Francisco, who is only five, lunges at his father's waist to prevent him from killing the horse. The boy's protective instinct poses a direct challenge to his father's violent intent. Once again, the horse's appearance signals death, though this time a symbolic one. As the horse escapes "across the dark fields, its fiery neck" serves as "a torch lighting the way for something Francisco and his father lost that night" (18). The boy, who sought to establish a different relationship with the horse, one not characterized by fear or violence, alienates his father, and "for days afterward, father and son did not speak to each other" (18). The incident serves as a turning point for the young boy, who eventually grows up, leaves the family farm, goes to college, and becomes a successful agricultural businessman. Years later, when the horse's mummified remains are found on the family property, Francisco discovers, caught in the horse's teeth, a fresh apple stem.

In the patriarchal hierarchy that exists in the story (the grandfather horse, Antonio, and Francisco), the senior horse provokes a strong response from the father and from the son: violence and compassion, respectively. Ultimately, Francisco learns that his act of kindness to the horse that night produces the same result that his father sought with one major difference: while Antonio sought to violently eliminate the horse as a painful reminder of their past, Francisco tried to come to terms with it and in doing so not only vanquished that past but made the experience something fruitful, for as we learn in the last line of the story, "apple trees . . . grew abundantly on his land" (19). Therefore, his endeavor is lasting and productive. This particular kind of transformation illustrates a key idea in Anaya's essay "I Am the King," specifically that "[t]he essence of maleness doesn't have to die, it merely has to be understood and created anew" (73). Though maleness does not in fact have to endure, in the story it does. By rejecting his father's way of doing things, Francisco creates new future opportunities, for himself and his family, ones determined by a different kind of masculinity. Still, the actions come at a cost, and the reminder remains as fresh as the apple stem in the grandfather horse's mummified corpse.

Whereas in the three previous stories from Gonzalez's *Ghost of John Wayne*, sons replicate, critique, or reject the masculinities of their fathers, "Fishing" offers a glimpse of a more multifaceted masculinity, only to snatch it away at the end. Family histories, as well as how men carry the knowledge of them and what they do with it, form the backbone of the story. Two generations of fathers and sons exist in the narrative: Daniel and Roque, and Roque and Martin. The central conflict in the story arises when Roque takes his son fishing for the boy's birthday. Their fishing spot on the Rio Grande elicits a memory in Roque of a time when his own father brought him to a place not far up the river. The memory of this trip plagues Roque.

The father-and-son trip represents a shared experience for Roque and Martin, and it is also an opportunity for Roque to continue to teach Martin about fishing. But for Roque, his father, Daniel, is never far from his thoughts. Roque watches with pride as Martin remembers what he has been taught about casting and even imitates his father "by leaning over the railing" of the bridge (70). Later, when Roque begins to cry, his son worries that something has happened to ruin their special day. What the boy does not know is that from their place on the bridge above the river, his father can see the "Organ Mountains to the east," which brings to mind "his own father and how they used to fish in this area when Roque was a boy, long before the ugly bridge had been built" (70). The bridge represents a vantage point for Roque to see the past, although it also represents unwelcomed change. A wave of sentiment and vulnerability washes over Roque, which causes him to erupt in tears throughout the day but especially after Martin reels in a small catfish by himself. In his son's face, beaming with pride, Roque sees his own features.

Roque's seeming inability or unwillingness to communicate his emotions to his son threatens their close bond. Martin starts to believe his father did not want to go fishing. So when Roque grabs Martin in an embrace, the boy does not know what is happening or what to do: "Roque burst into loud sobbing, repeating over and over that he loved Martin. The boy pulled his face back from his father's heaving chest and took a breath. His father had never done this before" (72). Roque finally shares with Martin the story of Roque's uncle Tomas's death in the Rio Grande. Roque explains that Tomas had escaped Juárez police custody after being tortured by them for allegedly robbing and murdering two members of a wealthy family for whom Tomas worked. Daniel reluctantly agreed to help his brother, but Tomas drowned trying to reach his brother across the river. Although he tried to save his brother and almost succumbed himself, Daniel experienced overwhelming feelings of guilt that plagued him for the rest of his life. His brother's death caused Daniel to become obsessed with the river, even haunted by it: "He would . . . get drunk, and stumble up and down . . . calling Tomas's name" (73). Daniel ruined his marriage and subsequently "drank himself to death" (73). Roque interrupts his story when he notices a hit on his fishing line. The fact that Roque lands the biggest fish in recent memory from the river after telling the emotional family history to his son feels like more than a coincidence, it seems like validation of the father's affective display and his decision to share it openly with his son.

When two Mexican men appear and demand the fish on Roque's line, two contrasting forms of masculinity come into conflict: the threatening behavior of the Mexican men and the vulnerability of Roque and Martin. The three adults get into a skirmish and the fish falls off the line and back into the water. With his prize gone, Roque threatens the would-be thieves with violence: "Roque charged toward the stranger, fists clenched, but the younger man ran to the car. The driver gunned the engine with a thunderous roar as his partner jumped in. Roque picked up a couple of rocks and threw them at the fleeing car. One of them bounced off the side" (74–75). Everything he has spent the afternoon building with his son feels lost, especially later, when Roque decides to drive Martin to the spot where Tomas died—the source of Daniel's brotherly agony and Roque's emotional distress. Martin, who once again does not understand what is happening, watches his father get out of the car when they arrive at the fated spot. Still angry about losing the fish and the fact that his son does not comprehend the importance of the visit, Roque "grabbed his son roughly by the shoulder and pulled him out" (76). Although Roque's tenderness appears to have transformed into anger directed at his son, the father quickly "realized what he was doing and released his grip on Martin. He patted his son on the head and led him toward the water" (76). Roque stops short of taking his frustrations out on Martin. Instead, he reverts to teaching him about the history of the men in their family by showing the boy the "old tree where Daniel had tried to save Tomas" (76). Martin wonders how his father can be certain of the exact tree. This question prompts Roque to suddenly jump into the river, causing Martin to scream in horror.

Past and present meet in the river, where Roque finds himself not in water but knee deep in mud. As he tries to escape, he slips and falls, splashing mud and causing Martin to laugh. Held tight in the grasp of the river mud, Roque remembers his dying father saying, "Don't forget it is the river" (76). The river is the place where paternal and fraternal legacies are made and broken, for better and for worse. Following Roque's baptism in the river mud, he climbs toward his son and out of the muck, though he cannot escape without Martin's help. The pair fall back on the grass of the river bank, and Roque "grabbed Martin and held on tight as they laughed and laughed" (77). After a day filled with excitement, disappointment, and confusion, joy feels like a gift to Martin. Roque has also shared with his son guilt, pain, vulnerability, and tenderness and shown Martin a completely different way of being a man, one that embodies contradictions. The day's affective intricacies ultimately prove fleeting, as suggested in the final line: "They made Martin love and hate his father for the years to come" (77). The promise of a more nuanced masculinity haunts Martin because his father offers it to him and then takes it away. For Martin, the river represents a site where he found and lost his father, just as it does for Roque. The story "Fishing," which closes out part 2 of the three-part collection, illustrates a son's longing for a complex, deeper connection with his father.

Throughout *The Ghost of John Wayne*, Gonzalez demonstrates a dedication to men whose lives are both informed and overshadowed by the legacy of John Wayne's particular kind of masculinity. It is a fiction that touches everything, including the masculinities fathers perform and pass on to their sons. Martin and Francisco represent the only two sons who want to exorcise the ghosts of the past and plot a new path forward. We see this through Francisco's actions and Martin's regret. Francisco's radical empathy for the grandfather horse gives him the courage as a boy to stand up to his father and to break free from a cycle of violence. Martin, like the narrator of Gonzalez's poem "Fathers," wants to cut the rope to free both himself and his father but does not possess the means to do so. Perhaps worse, he *knows* that another form of masculinity exists. He has seen and felt it, which makes its disappearance all the more painful. The fathers and sons that populate Gonzalez's borderlands collection urge us to see the fictions that bind together generations of men so that we might imagine other possibilities for expressions of manhood outside of violence, narcissism, and deep-seated regret.

THE SOUTHERNMOST POINT IN TEXAS: BROWNSVILLE

> I write novels, stories, and essays about the border.
> Oscar Cásares, *Oscar Cásares*

> **STUDENT.** "Dr. Perez, are you and Professor Cásares related?"
> **DR. PEREZ.** "Related? What makes you think that?"
> **STUDENT.** "Well, it' just that you are both so, uh . . ."
> **DR. PEREZ.** "Yes? . . . We are both so what?"
> **STUDENT.** "It's just that you are both so tall."

Oscar Cásares likes to tell a story about the gibbon featured on the cover of his debut short story collection, *Brownsville*. No matter how many times I hear it, I still wince when he gets to the part about seeing a mock-up of the cover that featured the same lesser ape but with a pom-pom-edged sombrero atop his head—at least that is how I picture it, with pom-poms. Anyone who has read *Brownsville* knows that the image is a reference to the story "Chango" and that a sombrero appears nowhere in it, not even on the tiny primate's severed head. Nevertheless, the impulse to represent a short story collection that includes diasporic Mexicans through kitsch symbols such as tourist-fare hats is one not even a literary publisher can resist. The offense is made more egregious by the fact that Cásares's short stories offer nuanced depictions, outside of racial or racist tropes, of the social, economic, and generational diversity of the author's hometown of Brownsville, Texas.

Full disclosure, Cásares is a colleague in my department, and no, we are not related despite both being tall. I have heard him read from his novels *Amigoland* (2009) and *Where We Come From* (2019) and talk about his creative and public-facing work for over a decade. I have also invited him to my class to speak with students about storytelling and fiction writing. On one such occasion, I asked him about the father-son relationships in *Brownsville*. Specifically, I asked if he was offering some form of critique of paternalism or Mexican masculinity. He replied, "No. But if you think so, then maybe." What has always stood out for me about Cásares's writing is that his characters are neither romantic nor tragic. They are, above all, complexly human. Border journalist and Brownsville native Cecilia Ballí makes a similar observation, that Cásares "writes about the lives of characters who are mostly working-class and ethnic in a way that makes them neither victims nor heroes, that acknowledges their social difference only as background material and recreates their world from the inside out—so that the margins become the mainstream" (102). Like Gonzalez, Cásares focuses the reader's attention on individuals whose lives are overlooked or overshadowed but made remarkable through his storytelling.

In *Brownsville*, Cásares also offers meditations on men and masculinity, an objective established from the outset of the collection. The order and arrangement of the father-and-son stories in *Brownsville* create a dialogue about the nature of these relationships that progresses over two sections of the book. There are no father and/or son narratives in the third part. Additionally, the title of each section, including the third, "Don't Believe Anything He Tells You," originates from something a man says directly in an effort to assert his limited authority in or over a situation.[24] Broadly speaking, *Brownsville* is a meditation on men or at the very least on how their actions have consequences they often do not or cannot anticipate. The lead story, "Mr. Z," which appears in the first section, titled "I Thought You and Me Were Friends," features a boy caught between his father's ideas about respect and his boss's relentless abuse. The second section, "They Say He Was Lost," includes the story "Big Jesse, Little Jesse," about a father who is dissatisfied with his disabled, book-smart son and namesake. The story "Charro" immediately follows, depicting a small war between a father and a canine adversary. Shifting perspectives from son to father and, finally, to a man who reflects on his status as both, Cásares demonstrates how men of different generations attempt to negotiate with existing and emergent forms of masculinity.

"Mr. Z" focuses on a boy, Diego, who finds his father's ideas on work and responsibility difficult to uphold when faced with an adult bully. Following a visit to a local fireworks stand with his father, Diego is offered a job by the owner, Mr. Zamarripa, the titular Mr. Z. Diego's father grants his son permission to take the job, which makes the boy feel excited and proud. The job creates another point of connection, in addition to the love of fireworks, between Diego and his father. As a mechanic who often has to take on additional jobs to support his family, Diego's father believes work is important. His son's being recognized for his mathematical skill and polite demeanor by the stand owner serves as a source of pride for the father. The opportunity also represents the possibility for Diego to have a future outside of skilled labor, one that includes "college so that [he] can study to be a businessman" (18). The father, who wants this different life for Diego, sees the futurity of his son's financial well-being as dependent upon a successful performance at the fireworks stand but does not convey this directly. Instead, while driving the boy to his first day of work, the father tells Diego to pay attention to Mr. Z and be serious. They travel the rest of the way to the stand in silence: "These were the only words they exchanged . . . but Diego knew what [his father] meant. He wanted Diego to behave and not do anything to embarrass him in front of Mr. Z" (7). The boy recognizes the solemn tone of his father's voice as one that has historically preceded anger and his getting hit. His father's last words, "pay attention," are both an order and a threat.

Diego does not understand what is behind his father's words, though he does know that his behavior, good or bad, will reflect on his family. More specifically, it will reflect on his father, whom he does not want to disappoint. As he works alongside another boy, Ricky, Diego follows his father's advice by being serious and listening to Mr. Z. Diego quickly adapts to his new job selling fireworks at the cramped and busy stand. Toward the end of his first day, Diego thinks with pride about his new connection to his father through work: Diego "liked working hard. His father worked hard . . ." (11). However, Mr. Z's behavior on the job threatens Diego's ability to keep his word to his father. In between joking about defecation and scolding the boys for not pushing certain products, Mr. Z has his own ideas about work that he imposes on Diego and Ricky. He does not offer constructive advice when they make a mistake; he mocks them and makes veiled threats instead. His masculinity seems wholly dependent on his ability to dominate and control pre-teen boys. As he drives them home, Mr. Z offers Ricky and Diego a snort of whiskey in honor of their first day on the job and tells them, "Today you're working men, hombres trabajodores" (12). Regardless of his claim, eleven-year-old Diego and Ricky are *boys*, not men. The incident hints at Mr. Z's questionable ethics and sets up the central conflict for Diego, who feels trapped between two competing forms of masculinity—his father's and Mr. Z's.

Mr. Zamarripa pretends to be upstanding and respectable, but beneath the façade lies a man who makes lewd innuendoes about one boy's mother and harasses and torments the other child in his employ. The incidents intertwine, creating a shift in Diego's attitude about his job that makes obeying his father difficult. Mr. Z's performance of masculinity calls to mind Mingo's behaviors in *The Boy Kings of Texas*, especially after Ricky's young, attractive mom drops him off at work. Mr. Z is revealed as the source of the section title when he scolds Ricky for withholding the fact that his mother is attractive, telling the boy, "I thought you and me were friends" (14). Mr. Z evokes an unstated yet understood bond between men that includes promoting the availability of women. Bewildered by Mr. Z's comments about Ricky's mom, Diego thinks about how "you didn't talk about anybody's mother or sister" without causing a fight (14). Diego feels empathy for Ricky in the wake of Mr. Z's remarks, which motivates him to intervene in Ricky's behalf. As both a friendly and a protective gesture, Diego asks his father to give Ricky a ride to work from then on, which angers Mr. Z because it denies him access to the boy's mother and further opportunities to leer at her. Mr. Z responds by reasserting his authority and control over the children, targeting Diego in particular by making fun of his father, calling him a liar and a bullshitter. Understanding the performance and expectations of cultural and racialized forms of masculinity, Mr. Z capitalizes on this knowledge. He knows that Diego will not tell his father about the harassment and that Ricky has no father around to tell.

The two competing forms of masculinity cause Diego distress. He feels trapped by his father's insistence that he be respectful of Mr. Z and so cannot challenge Mr. Z's insults about his father. He cannot defend his father without disobeying him. Unwilling to tell his father about Mr. Z's behavior, Diego says he is tired after three days on the job as a way to signal his desire to quit. His father does not ask about his son's well-being or whether or not something troubles the boy. Instead, he tells Diego, in a serious tone, "You don't know what tired is" and reminds the boy he should be grateful for having a job (18). The reminder comes with the hint of a beating that will surely follow should the boy protest. Diego returns to work, but Mr. Z proves relentless in his attacks against his father. Driven to tears, the boy fantasizes about being older so he could "talk back to the old man," which would be a direct contradiction of his father's orders. Then, after he contemplates burning down the stand to get back at Mr. Z, Diego's thoughts turn more explicitly violent:

> If he were bigger, he would've fought him and knocked him to the ground. He'd hit the old man hard, maybe knock out a tooth. There would be tears in his eyes and blood dripping from his mouth. Diego would keep kicking him in the stomach until he begged him to stop. People passing by in cars would laugh. And he'd slap him with the back of his hand one more time, just to make sure the old man knew he had done wrong. (20)

Diego does not simply want to stop the abuse; he wants to beat, and humiliate, and emasculate (the back-handed slap) Mr. Z to make him suffer. Diego cannot even verbally defend his father without disobeying him at the same time.

Too small to fight Mr. Z and afraid of defying his father, Diego devises another plan that gives him the satisfaction of, without actual, violence. He defies his father's observation that "[s]ometimes you have to wait a little while for it to get better" by not waiting (24). He hits Mr. Z in the most vulnerable spot possible—the bottom line of his business. The boy starts giving away fireworks for free without Mr. Z's knowledge. The sensation gives Diego the feeling of "kicking the old man in the gut" (21). He relishes finding a way to strike back at Mr. Z while still keeping his word to his father. While the situation appears resolved for him in the short term, Diego must avoid getting caught, not only for giving away Mr. Z's merchandise for free but also for finding a solution that satisfies himself more than it would his father. At the age of eleven, Diego learns to rely on his intellect and creativity rather than his fists.

"Big Jesse, Little Jesse" and "Charro" both appear in the second section, "They Say He Was Lost," which takes its name from a man's description of the circumstances that led to his children's bringing home a stray dog.[25] However, as related to the content of the two stories, the statement refers to how *men* become lost or unsettled as a result of ineffective performances of masculinity. The protagonists attempt to replicate desired forms of masculinity that they then impose on others. These men, both fathers, face reckonings of their own making, for their shortcomings or failings.

Before launching into my analysis of the father-son relationship in "Big Jesse, Little Jesse" I want to take a moment to recognize something that happens to scholars with some frequency that we rarely speak about openly, except when commiserating. What happens when we find a book or article with a topic or analysis similar to our own? (Scream!) Fear and self-doubt can begin to creep in. Slowly, I have learned that we as scholars rarely say the exact same thing in the exact same way, unless theft or plagiarism is involved. Speaking from experience, I now see such instances as road signs telling me I am moving in a direction that will place my work in proximity to or in dialogue with scholars who have intellectual interests similar to my own. These are opportunities to listen, learn, and contribute, not roadblocks.[26]

In the evolving dialogue across the father-and-son stories in *Brownsville*, the narrative point of view shifts from son, Diego in "Mr. Z," to father, Jesse in "Big Jesse, Little Jesse," though both feature a third-person limited perspective. Because the narrative perspective so closely aligns with certain characters, boundaries or borders exist around what readers can and cannot know about characters' actions and other events in the story. This restricted point of view presents complications when it aligns with a self-centered character like Jesse, who struggles to accept his son and namesake, Little Jesse, a smart, sensitive six-year-old boy who has a physical disability, identifies more with his mother, Corina, and has no interest in sports or outdoor activities, which frustrates his father.[27] Jesse believes Corina babies Little Jesse; he also thinks Corina's family looks down on him as her ex-husband because he has limited financial resources. The point of view also reveals Jesse's attitude toward his son, who is not a diminutive copy of his father, as the title of the story suggests: "Because the story is narrated exclusively from Jesse's perspective, this dissonance between the story and its title reinforces a critique of the protagonist and his patriarchal perspective that positions his son as subordinate" (Minich, "Disabling" 41). A significant portion of Jesse's identity derives from his relationship and relationality to his son, with whom he shares little physical resemblance and no interests. Jesse's failure to see his own flaws, including his biases about nonnormativity, calls into question what else he may or may not perceive clearly.

The encounter with Rata and Rata, Jr., represents a secondary conflict in the narrative that exposes the primary one between Jesse and himself. Nevertheless, the clash between Jesse and Rata demonstrates how both fathers see their sons as extensions of themselves and their masculinities. When Jesse notices the father-and-son pair in front of him and Little Jesse as they wait in line to ride the bumper cars at a carnival, he dubs them Rata and Rata, Jr., in his mind because they both have a rat-tail hairstyle and imagines "the father and son sitting next to each other in barber chairs and telling the barber they want the same haircut" (Cásares, *Brownsville* 108). The thought makes Jesse laugh, but he also notices that "Rata Jr. looks like a perfect copy of his dad, only smaller and without the homemade tattoos and fresh love marks on his neck" (108). In relatively short order, Jesse racializes (with the name Rata instead of Rat), classes (the visible hickeys), and perhaps even criminalizes (based on the DIY tattoos) the father and, by extension, the son, who is a replica of his father. Because, as Minich states, "Jesse's fascination with Rata and Rata Jr. involves not only envy but also shame," Jesse mentally tears them down to neutralize the threat they pose to the view he has of himself and, by extension, of Little Jesse's disability ("Disabling" 47).

From Jesse's point of view, if father and son Rata are identical, beyond their shared physical attributes, then the behaviors of Rata, Jr., would be a reflection of his father's. The son, who is approximately the same age or perhaps slightly older than Little Jesse, is brazen, bold. He repeatedly snatches bits of cotton candy from Little Jesse without asking. Once in the bumper car, the boy targets Little Jesse, hitting his car repeatedly. Never once does Rata correct or redirect his son's actions. In fact, he defends his son's conduct and cheers him on, at one point shouting, "¡Chíngatelo!"[28]—suggesting a level of violence inappropriate to the situation (Cásares, *Brownsville* 110). Even when Little Jesse starts to cry in his car pinned against the rail, Rata, Jr., slams into him "one last time" (111). Only when Corina approaches to take her son out of the vehicle does Rata tell his son, "Ya déjalo, Junior. . . . He's a baby. He can't even reach the gas pedal with his leg" (111). For Jesse the comment about Little Jesse's leg is a breaking point, and he lashes out.

The incident in the bumper cars parallels a fight scene: Little Jesse and Rata, Jr., battling it out, albeit in bumper cars, while their fathers exhort them from the sidelines. Little Jesse does not understand the stakes of the conflict. His initial laughter turns to panic after Jesse yells, "Hit him back! . . . You can do it!" (110). Jesse's goading of his son causes Rata to do the same. The situation escalates because of the fathers' behaviors as they shout directions from the sidelines. Rata mocks Little Jesse, telling Jesse, "[Y]our boy can't drive for shit" (110). Jesse wants his son to fight back, and Rata wants his son to dominate in the conflict—to "fuck up" Little Jesse. The intensity of the situation boils over when Rata makes a comment about Little Jesse's disability. As if to confirm that the fight is between the fathers (from Jesse's perspective this is certainly the case), Jesse shoves Rata, not to protect his son but because he refuses to admit he is angry that Little Jesse cannot defend himself against Rata, Jr., whether in line, in the bumper cars, or in life. Jesse fixates on his son's perceived limitations so he does not have to focus on his own. But perhaps most of all, Jesse is angry that Rata and Rata, Jr., embody the fantasy he has for himself and Little Jesse. In other words, Jesse is disappointed and angry that Little Jesse is not his perfect copy, which is made all the worse by the fact that Little Jesse has no interest in being like his father.

The unreliability of the third-person limited perspective becomes evident immediately after the brief fight, which, as the narrator indicates, is "over almost as soon as it starts" (111). Apparently unable to perform their imagined masculine postures (Jesse wants to "kick [Rata's] ass" [111]; Rata wants to show Jesse what happens when people mess with him), the clash between the two men seems limited to some pushing and a few tough words. But after police come and arrest Jesse and walk him through the crowd, he "feels as though he doesn't exist anymore" (112). Only then do readers get a sense of what really happened during the fight: "His right cheek feels bruised and he can taste a little blood from the cut on his lip. His shirt is ripped open and his jeans have grass stains at the knees. His right shoe slipped off when he and Rata were on the ground" (112). So if the fight was, indeed, over before it actually got going, Jesse has had his ass handed to him in short order. Rata has obliterated Jesse's fragile masculinity and the sense he has of himself. As Jesse is led from the carnival grounds, onlookers point and laugh. Ultimately, as Minich stresses, "the story treats normative, able-bodied masculinity as the identity that must be explained. Jesse's misunderstanding of his son's disability is the problem to overcome, rather than disability itself" ("Disabling" 49). Jesse's embodiment and performance of masculinity deteriorates completely by the story's end, which suggests a potentially positive turn of events for the young father and his son.

Still, something has always bothered me about the conflict between Rata and Jesse, namely, how quickly their situation escalates. Toxic masculinity provides the most straightforward explanation for Rata's zero-to-five-hundred-mph acceleration of aggression. A reductive view of Rata would attempt to make a correlation between his homemade tattoos and some sort of gang affiliation, especially considering his advice that his son "fuck up" another child. Cásares, throughout the collection, avoids this kind of facile characterization. Rata and Rata, Jr., represent, unequivocally, an uncritical generational replication of a toxic Brown masculinity, but I am not convinced by the simplistic, not to mention racist, perspective that Rata is merely some violent homeboy, especially when the narrative offers another possibility. The father-and-son twinning in the story goes deeper than the third-person limited narration allows the reader to see because Jesse fails to see it as well.

Rata and Rata, Jr., as previously discussed, represent a doubling of the father-son relationship at the center of the story. Although Jesse generates his name for the duo based on their hairstyle, he underscores the relationality between the father-and-son pairs by replicating the subordinating position for Rata's son that exists between him and Little Jesse. Yet what Jesse fails to notice, or does not care to acknowledge, is that Rata's son, beyond the name Jesse assigns, actually has the same name as his father, who twice refers to the boy as Junior.[29] So both fathers have namesake sons. Another similarity between the two pairs has to do with the fathers' defensive postures. Standing in line "behind the other fathers and sons" at the carnival, when Jesse laughs at the thought of Rata and Rata,

Jr., at the barber, Rata "turns to look back at Jesse but doesn't say anything, just looks at him hard" (108). Jesse worries that the man thought he was laughing at him and is sizing him up. The fact is that Jesse *was* laughing. And the man *knows* it, evinced by the "hard" look he gives Jesse. Junior's father knows because, as the father of a disabled son, he too is on the lookout to defend his son against any attack. Never once in the story does Junior speak. Perhaps he is quiet and compliant, but he may also have a speech disability, which would explain why he takes Little Jesse's candy without asking and why his father comments that Jesse thinks his son is too good to share his cotton candy with Junior. The move is a diversionary tactic to take the emphasis off Junior and put it onto Jesse. Junior's father knows *exactly* what Jesse thinks of him and Junior, so he uses the boy to put Jesse in his place by sending him after Little Jesse. So that Junior will not be bullied, his father turns his boy into the aggressor. When he yells from behind the railing for Junior to go after Little Jesse, the boy complies. Junior, in contrast to Little Jesse, demonstrates a willingness to do exactly as his father directs. So Junior and his father are and are not the exact copies Jesse believes them to be.

Jesse and Rata both illustrate some of the most damaging ideas about masculinity that fathers pass on to their sons, or try to pass on. Each in his own way is toxic—Jesse for wanting his own small copy of himself in Little Jesse and alienating his son in the process, and Junior's father for teaching his son to problem solve with aggression or violence. As a result, both fathers are "lost," as the section title suggests. Although the story offers no strategy for moving forward, Minich believes it "hints at the work ahead for Jesse, the emotional and epistemic labor he must perform in order to create . . . a more honest and satisfying relationship with his son . . ." ("Disabling" 49). Indeed, through his own actions, Jesse creates the circumstance for himself to embody, however briefly, what terrifies him about his son and perhaps to leave behind a masculinity that stands between him and a meaningful connection with Little Jesse.

"Mr. Z" and "Big Jesse, Little Jesse" demonstrate how men, fathers in particular, perpetuate cycles of aggressive behavior. Of the three narratives that focus on fathers and sons, nowhere is this idea more clearly addressed than in "Charro," a story about Marcelo Torres, a man who tries to put a stop to his neighbor's dog's incessant barking, which keeps him up at night. There are a number of parallels between Marcelo, Diego's father, and Big Jesse. Marcelo has a son, Junior, who carries his father's name, as well as an infant boy. Although the story shows that Junior watches his father's behavior, particularly when he loses his temper with a teenage gas station attendant, their father-son relationship does not factor directly into the narrative. This does not mean that Marcelo lacks the capacity to influence his son's behavior. Rather, Marcelo, as demonstrated in the story, is far more influenced by his own father, who informs his actions against Charro, the barking dog. Like Diego's father, Marcelo values his work, but Marcelo has a middle-class job working as a USDA livestock inspector, which provides "a decent salary and medical benefits" for his wife, Olivia, and the boys (120), while Diego's father works as a mechanic who needs to do extra jobs to earn enough money. Marcelo, like Jesse, resents his wife's family, in this case Olivia's mother, for believing her daughter married beneath her station. The knowledge makes Marcelo defensive and somewhat indignant toward his mother-in-law, even after she is dead. However, what distinguishes Marcelo from these other characters is his willingness to examine the source of his masculine performance and then change his behavior.

Over the course of the narrative, Marcelo replicates and rejects his father's form of masculinity, until he ultimately expresses his own in ways not dependent on domination or violence, though not without consequence nonetheless. Marcelo's actions are precipitated by his neighbor's new chow mixed-breed dog, Charro, a name that invokes ideas about Mexico, men, and ideal masculinity. Underscoring this association, the charro, or "cattle rancher," according to de la Mora, represents "a quintessential virile image of the post-revolutionary Mexican nation" (2). Charro and his namesake explicitly connect to Marcelo's Mexican father, who "worked" with cattle, though it is unclear whether he was a cowhand and sometime rustler or the owner of El Rancho Capote along the Rio Bravo. He was, however, a man who believed unquestionably that "allowing his sons to be born Americans" was "his biggest mistake in life" (Cásares, *Brownsville* 136). The dog Charro, therefore, becomes a site of externalized conflict between Marcelo's and his father's forms of masculinity, American and Mexican.

Marcelo's father casts a long shadow on his son's life. In what he perceives as a pale imitation of his life growing up on the ranch, where his father "had taught him how to work," Marcelo spends his work days driving along the border inspecting animals (120). Because his father's ideals are never far from his thoughts, when the situation with Charro arises, Marcelo decides to confront the matter directly:

> Someone else might have settled the matter calmly . . . but Marcelo Torres wasn't a man who spoke with soft or tactful

words. He didn't speak this way on the ranch where he'd lived before he was married and moved to the city. He didn't speak this way at work as a livestock inspector for the USDA. And you can be sure he didn't speak this way when somebody's dog wouldn't stop barking outside his window in the middle of the night. (116)

Marcelo believes the dog's incessant barking demands a response and a timely solution. Not even when his neighbor, Sanchez, tries to explain that the dog belongs to his sons or that Charro serves as a guard dog in the wake a recent thefts does Marcelo back down. He insists that Sanchez "shut that animal up" (118). Marcelo's fury over the dog confuses even Sanchez. When the barking continues and threatens Marcelo's job because it makes him lose sleep, causing him to be tardy for work, he attempts other strategies to silence the menace.

The view that the dog's behavior threatens his livelihood and ability to care for his family motivates Marcelo's actions against the animal. The fight with the dog also conjures up memories of his father's own conflict with a neighbor, who accused, though we never learn the truth of the claim, the senior Mr. Torres of cattle rustling. While the issue was settled publicly between the two men, Mr. Torres later gathered his five sons together and armed each one with a pistol, telling them "the first one to see Norberto Valdez was to shoot him" (128). Besmirching the family name and honor is cause for Mr. Torres to advocate murder, and the family sees its successful accomplishment as fortunate. Marcelo recalls that "Benito, the oldest, was the lucky son. He spent ten years in the Reynosa jail. Nobody ever stopped to question whether it had been the right thing to do. All they knew was that their family had been threatened" (128). Murder and incarceration, as well as the loss of ten years of one man's life, are nothing compared to saving face. And while Marcelo acknowledges that the morality of an honor killing was never discussed among the men, in this moment he decides to take a series of actions against the dog that are smaller in scale than his father's but that all involve violence: they range from throwing his boot at Charro to luring him into his car and releasing him miles away from home. Marcelo even tries to poison the dog, but Charro proves *muy macho* and is not so easily defeated. The dog chews up the boot, finds his way back home, and survives the poisoning, making sure to throw up the contents of his stomach on Marcelo's front porch.

Marcelo cannot successfully attack, run from, remove, kill, or even defeat Charro or what he symbolizes. After he carries out a disturbing array of behaviors toward the animal in order to silence him, something inside Marcelo shifts and he changes tactics: he abandons his efforts and also vows not to "hurt the dog again" (132). Rather than assert his will through victimizing an animal, Marcelo changes his life and patterns of behavior. On the nights when Charro awakens him, instead of becoming incensed, he completes little tasks or chores he cannot find time for during the day. Eventually he learns to value this time, until Olivia unintentionally backs over Charro with her car, killing the dog. In the wake of Charro's death Marcelo mentally gathers the men in his family to witness both his failure to vanquish his adversary and his compassion for a creature that behaved according to his nature. A high-energy breed, Chow shepherds are known for making great watch dogs that if left "alone for long periods" have a tendency to "become bored and destructive" ("Chow Shepherds"). The dog, like Marcelo, acted in accordance with his nature and circumstances. Marcelo treats his one-time adversary with respect by making Charro a makeshift coffin and lining it with blankets. The act of burying the dog calls forth, once again in Marcelo, memories of his father: "[T]he last time he'd worked this hard was when his father had passed away and, in order to save some money, he and his brothers dug the grave themselves" (136). Thus the dog Charro and Marcelo's charro father become conflated through the act of re-membering, as Marcelo recalls: "[His father] wanted everyone to know he was puro mexicano and had no desire to change. . . . Marcelo had tried to live his father's life, but now it felt as if he were standing in the middle of a river trying to stretch his arms and touch both sides. No matter what he did, he'd never reach far enough" (136). Marcelo tries to span the gulf between Mexican and American masculinities and faces his own failure to do so successfully when, hours later, he has dug so deeply that he cannot get out of the grave without help. In essence, in thinking about his father and his legacy, while performing an act of compassion, Marcelo has dug his own grave.

The opposing views of masculinity present a situation for Marcelo that seems untenable. However, beyond the scope of the story, one presumes that to escape, Marcelo must call upon Olivia and Junior's help. Together, they can work to free him from the hole in which he finds himself, thereby bringing Cásares's dialogue on father-son relationships to a close. Marcelo's situation mirrors that of Roque in Gonzalez's "Fishing," where Roque needs his son Martin's help to escape the river and the past that keeps him trapped. The solution is but one that we might imagine in response to the legacy of El Rey, as a concept of masculinity, families working in concert to disentangle Mexican Americans and Chicanxs from a toxic paternalism. Though, as Martin's experience demonstrates, when change is but brief, resentment can flourish in its aftermath. So while some fathers and sons are willing to abandon the idea connected to El Rey and its attendant forms of power, the king will not be unseated so easily, unless he is challenged by an Aztec fire-god meta-human, and then all bets are off.

FILM

META AND MUTANT FATHERS

> The Western represents a basic story, which is never completely "told" but is reexamined and reworked in a variety of ways.
>
> Thomas Schatz, *Hollywood Genres: Formulas, Filmmaking, and the Studio System*

Since 2010, more than fifty major live-action narrative films, many of them sourced from comic books, have been about or featured superheroes. With notable exceptions, such as *Wonder Woman* (2017), *Black Panther* (2018), *Aquaman* (2018), and *Captain Marvel* (2019), these films focus primarily on white male heroes who defeat some form of evil to save cities, the world, or galaxies from menacing threats. Diverse characters often appear alongside or as members of a superhero team, for example, Storm (Halle Berry) in the *X-Men* franchise and Gamora (Zoe Saldana), Falcon (Anthony Mackie), and War Machine (Don Cheadle) in the Marvel Cinematic Universe (MCU), but in these instances, the films are not *about* them.[1] Rather, they are about how the actions of racialized, ethnic, and gendered characters impact the narratives of the groups' white males. In these conventional superhero films, white male heroes protect vulnerable populations, in all their multiplicity based on the racial and/or biological diversity of the crowds fleeing from or impacted by the impending doom de jour. Celebrated white super saviors, such as Superman, Batman, and Tony Stark, are willing to fight and, in some cases, die to save a diverse world.

The recent superhero films *Deadpool* (2016), *Deadpool 2* (2018), *Suicide Squad* (2016), and *Logan* (2017) diverge from this formula. All focus on genetically evolved individuals, meta-humans or mutants with extraordinary abilities, who abjure greater-good moral responsibility while still defending those in need.[2] The latter two movies explicitly offer sites for analysis of fathers and families in the borderlands. As "genetically evolved humans outcast by a bigoted and fearful humanity," meta-humans and mutants embody a borderlands positionality, in some cases being targeted directly for their differences (Fawaz 129). Global campaigns seeking state exploitation, regulation, or registration of their "prohibited and forbidden" bodies push these humans with astonishing abilities (e.g., teleportation, weapons mastery, shape-shifting, or element manipulation) into borderlands, where factions, unlawful, lawful, and in between, emerge (Anzaldúa, *Borderlands* 3). *Suicide Squad* endeavors to challenge race and gender conventions in superhero films through the positioning of women and racially diverse characters (Japanese, Mexican, Indigenous, and Black) in lead roles and the valorization of criminals turned heroes. In an ostensible reformulation of a white-savior story, *Logan*, on the other hand, makes an established fan-favorite hero the guardian of a diverse group of LatinX(-men) children while at the same time gesturing toward more substantial issues such as missing women along the US-Mexico border and the precarious status of Mexican-born children imprisoned at the border. This chapter focuses on two versions of superhuman fatherhood in films that are self-consciously stylized professional westerns. *Suicide Squad* fuses the bad Mexican, gangbanger, homeboy, and El Rey types in a character who accidentally kills his wife and two children. And *Logan* features an Anglo Canadian former hypermasculine icon ravaged by physical deterioration who discovers his DNA was used to father a Mexican girl. Both represent borderland fathers haunted by their past actions who try to make amends but find redemption only through death.

A world of cowboys and six-shooters is not far removed from one with aliens or genetically enhanced humans and superpowered weapons: these worlds cross over in films such as Joss Whedon's *Serenity* (2005), Jon Favreau's *Cowboys & Aliens* (2011), James Gunn's *Guardians of the Galaxy* (2014), and others.[3] Most famously, the *Star Wars* epic film series, *Episode IV—A New Hope* in particular, includes elements of the western: a farm boy on the frontier whose family is threatened by a hostile native population; a tale where the good guy wears off-white and the bad guy is clad in black. Within the ragtag group of freedom fighters working together to rid the galaxy of evil is Han Solo (Harrison Ford), who is initially dressed in black and white to demonstrate his moral ambiguity and who participates in the resistance, but as a hired gun. He eventually finds redemption through his moral alliance with the rebels. Solo is brought on as a smuggler not above killing. He possesses elite skills, not unlike superheroes, who have the power to do what others cannot or will not. The same idea is central to *Suicide Squad* and *Logan*, whose metas and mutants endeavor to safeguard the future of global and transnational populations.

Influenced by the prospect of individual gain, the protagonists in *Suicide Squad* and *Logan* serve as hired guns, similar to those found in professional westerns, who neutralize a population's scourge (evil Indigenous siblings and corporate goons, respectively), illustrating an instantiation of what John Shelton Lawrence and Robert Jewett call the "dominant American myth of the Western village cleansers" (107). This arrangement presents characters with opportunities for moral redemption and in the process reframes mainstream ideas about heroism and which communities are worth saving. Historically, this convention involved white gunslingers rescuing white people or towns. Through the race and ethnicity of central characters, one a Mexican American father, the other a white father to a Mexican child, *Suicide Squad* and *Logan* upend this formula. More specifically, the films tie race and ethnicity to the creation and destruction of families, either biological or made.

Both films adhere closely to the plot of contemporary professional westerns. Incarcerated at a secret maximum-security facility with no chance of parole, the members of the Suicide Squad, so named for the explosive pellets injected into their necks as a control measure, agree to "go somewhere very bad to do something that will get [them] killed," not because they are motivated to do the right thing but because they are forced to do so.[4] Only after completing their mission are they rewarded with reduced prison sentences. Gone is the local village or town facing a formidable threat and requiring protection. Instead, the Earth's entire population is in peril. As members of this unit, their job is to defeat one of their own—another meta-human—and in the process save the world. The titular hero Logan has more modest ambitions. As the unlikely caregiver to his former mentor, Professor Charles Xavier, founder of the famed X-Men, Logan, whose own health is fading, works as a limousine driver to earn enough money to buy a boat so together he and Charles can leave everything and everyone behind. After agreeing to drive a woman and her "daughter" north for a sizable payday, Logan, one of the last surviving mutants in the world, realizes the job involves more than simply transporting two people across multiple borders (geographic, national, and cultural, to name a few); it becomes about saving an entirely new generation of mutant children. The Suicide Squad members and Logan, therefore, find themselves in the position of having to use their abilities to fight someone else's enemy.

In *Sixguns and Society: A Structural Study of the Western* (1975),

Will Wright analyzes the structure of four different types of western film: classical, vengeance variation, transition theme, and professional plot.[5] The last type features heroes who are "professional fighters, men willing to defend society only as a job they accept for pay or for love of fighting, not from commitment to ideas of law and justice" (85). Such heroes are found in *Vera Cruz* (1954), *The Professionals* (1966), and *The Wild Bunch* (1969). The members of the Suicide Squad, who are pressed into state service, have no interest in rules or righteousness, but they, with one exception, do love fighting. Logan, who is not looking for a fight, accepts the job defending and transporting his client to finance a personal objective. Wright argues that in western films of the professional type, the focus "is on the conflict between the heroes and the villains," where "both are professional, and their fight becomes a contest of ability that is significant for its own sake" (86). In *Suicide Squad*, heroes and villains become entangled, making it difficult to tell one from the other. *Logan* furthers this idea by having the mutant and a cloned version of himself battle it out at the climax. Although a "concern with a fight between equal men of special ability is an aspect of all Westerns," Wright contends that "only in this particular version of the myth does the fight itself, divorced from all its social and ethical implications, become of such central importance" (86). Indeed, in the final battles of *Suicide Squad* and *Logan*, the protagonists fulfill their generic duty as protectors, which brings about narrative resolution.

The Magnificent Seven (1960), directed by John Sturges, with its eclectic group of gunslingers and opportunists who are hired to defend a Mexican village from the particularly ruthless bandit Calvera and his men, is an exemplar of the professional western, one from which *Suicide Squad* and *Logan* draw heavily. Persuaded by a meager amount of money and an opportunity to bolster their self-worth, seven men agree to fight in behalf of the village and, in the process, teach the residents how to defend themselves, not without complications. In this plot, Mexican lives and families in the borderlands are worth fighting and dying for. The classic film, which is not without its own problems, places two different kinds of fathering in dialogue, one malevolent and the other perceived as moral, though *both* rely on violence.

In a genre where Mexican and Mexican American men appear conventionally as villains, most often as bandidos entirely divorced from any family context, the western becomes an unlikely site for analyzing fatherhood. "The Western," as Stella Bruzzi notes, "has conventionally been viewed as a genre dominated by binary oppositions" (63). Within the logic of this oppositional frame, if Mexicans are the outlaws, then Anglos are necessarily the heroes. Fatherhood, however, complicates the position of the Anglo male in the western. For example, in *Shane* (1953), Joe Starrett, father to Joey and husband to Marian, is an impotent patriarch in the face of frontier violence. Morally and narratively, Joe cannot protect his family or the burgeoning community in the same way the titular hero can. Shane, who becomes the subject of Joey's adoration and Marian's attention, defends a community he can never be a part of by successfully eliminating the violent threat. As a consequence, he must then leave, in part so as not to supplant Joe's role as father and husband. Shane's lack of family ties liberates him to be the hero, but permanently locates him outside of the community.

Shane, in its considerations of violence and paternalism in relation to settler communities, illustrates how fatherhood, specifically, limits Anglo male power. When fatherhood in the western takes center stage, Bruzzi argues, a clear pattern emerges: "The archetypal schema adopted by the patriarchal Westerns of the 1950s is a powerful father (more often than not an irrational, despotic caricature) surrounded by a posse (commonly) of feuding sons" (62).[6] The father in these westerns has characteristics and narrative capabilities that are similar to those of the bandido, who is with some frequency irrational by nature because of his feeble intellect.[7] Charles Ramírez Berg argues that the bandido's narrative role as villain necessitates his elimination "in order to return the diegetic world to its tranquil, prethreat status quo" (*Latino Images* 40). Resolutions of the familial conflict, brought about by the "dissipation of the father's power," include the death of the father or the father's killing of his "worst" son (Bruzzi 63). The end result, Bruzzi argues, is that "these Westerns parody their own image of masculinity, the destructive symbiosis between autocracy (the father) and resentful acquiescence (the sons) acting as a parable for how masculinity should not be handed down through generations" (63). Similar dynamics, complicated by race, ethnicity, and gender, exist in both *Suicide Squad* and *Logan*. Fathers surrounded by literal and figurative posses grapple with how their legacies of violence have impacted or are impacting their children. The result, within the frame of the western, is that both fathers are eliminated and also redeemed in the process.

Even as *Suicide Squad* attempts to break with gender and racial conventions, the movie conveys an explicit anxiety about globalization, planetary border integrity, and infection. The containment and eventual elimination of the Mexican (and Indian) characters preserves and reinforces the national value of whiteness in the film in an era in which fear of immigrants and terrorist "outsiders" drives US politics in real life. Although *Logan* shares some of these concerns, namely, border integrity and containment, the film eschews the impulse to become another reformulation of a white-savior story. It does so, in large part, through the history of the X-Men, more specifically the social impetus for their creation as metaphors for racial difference during the civil rights era. Instead of being a white-savior story, *Logan* prioritizes the lives of a new generation of mutants, all born to Mexican mothers. The deaths of Charles, Caliban, and Logan mark an end to mutants serving as symbols for racial difference, giving way to a future where otherness will forever be intertwined with race and nation.

This chapter's analysis begins with *The Magnificent Seven* (1960) in order to demonstrate how *Suicide Squad* and *Logan* resemble, thematically and structurally, one of the most representative westerns of the professional variety. Demonstrating this exposes how the older film refuses certain racial scripts for Mexicans (and American Indians) that were meant to uphold the imagined superiority of white settler colonialism and frontier mythologies. Within this frame, Mexican or Mexican American characters, alongside Native people, were familiar antagonists and very rarely seen as worth fighting for, individually or as a group. Yet in both *Suicide Squad* and *Logan*, Mexican American and Mexican characters (fathers and children) figure prominently, as they do in *The Magnificent Seven*, so much so that their actions determine the outcomes of those films and in the process turn villains into heroes and heroes into legend.

INTO THE WEST(ERN)

With a powerful surge of percussion, strings, and horns, Elmer Bernstein's iconic theme for *The Magnificent Seven* communicates a level of action and intensity that builds excitement for the film but does not hint at the complicated social and cultural politics at play in it. Inspired by Akira Kurosawa's *Seven Samurai* (1954), *The Magnificent Seven*'s journey to the screen was as protracted as it was complex. The project faced lawsuits, including one by the Mexican-born actor Anthony Quinn (who would later in life play Don Aragon in *A Walk in the Clouds*), a pinched deadline to avoid a strike, and the intervention of Mexican officials.[8] As Brian Hannan observes, "Nobody expected *The Magnificent Seven* to turn out to be the pivotal film of the year, the western that would mark the end of one era (movies reliant on one or two main characters, moral codes, hymns to the American landscape) and the beginning of another (multiple characters, dubious morals, Mexico). It became the western's new border" (9). On one side of this new border were "tradition and myth, on the other irreverence and reality" (9). The oppositional position of *The Magnificent Seven*, one firmly rooted in irreverence and reality, anticipates the Baudrillardian hyperreality, "generations by models of a real without origin or reality," or the absence of the real, of both *Suicide Squad* and *Logan* and strengthens the connection among the films (1). The western of the cinematic imagination is nothing more than a stylization of a fictional west populated by racial, and racist, tropes that celebrate settler narratives of expansion and domination. *The Magnificent Seven* signaled a change in the western genre, reshaping its borders and concerns. Not surprisingly, social change, or rather the resistance to it, surfaces as a central theme in the film, as does paternalism and fatherhood.

At key moments, *The Magnificent Seven* offers social commentary about racial prejudice and the integrity of cultural communities.[9] Released in the middle of the civil rights era, the film gestures toward the importance of dignity and self-determination for Indigenous people and Mexicans, respectively, yet does so at the individual rather than the state or national level, reflecting a neoliberal ideology through both the actions and the attitudes of the seven. So while *The Magnificent Seven* celebrates the exceptionalism of these men as expressed in the title and the tag line ("they were only seven but they fought like seven hundred"), it also stresses their declining usefulness in the growing economic market of the US and the fact that their skills still have real value across the border in Mexico.

Although the film exhibits self-awareness in certain areas, it still relies on "brownface" for its lead roles: think Charlton Heston and his stilted Spanish in Orson Welles's *Touch of Evil* (1958). Eli Wallach (Polish/Jewish) plays the principal antagonist, Calvera, and Horst Buchholz (German), tinted a suitable shade of brown, is introduced as Chico, a young Mexican man and wannabe gunfighter, but the opening credits are also filled with Spanish surnames, such as Martinez de Hoyas, Monteros, Alaniz, and Lugero. Shot on location in "Cuernavaca and Estudios Churubusco, Mexico," the film credits intimate that Latinos, perhaps more specifically Mexicans, will play a significant role in the story and serve as more than local color or set decorations. "Critics have tended to view the presence of Mexico in Hollywood films," Stephanie Fuller observes, "either as an extraneous exotic backdrop or a space used to illustrate the expansion of US influence, without examining the complex relationship between these images of Mexico and American liberal politics"

(22). While the US may not have been inclined to think about this relationship, Mexico certainly was, particularly given its ever-changing relationship to (and place in) American film.

The egregiously offensive greaser films of the 1920s gave way to the more positive good neighbor productions of the 1940s in American cinema. By the 1950s "Mexico had [once again] become frustrated at the onscreen depiction of its countrymen, either as villains or as helpless" (Hannan 86). Incensed by the representation of its citizens in *Vera Cruz* (1954) and ahead of the release of *The Alamo* (1960), which turned a Mexican victory into a rallying cry for American patriotism, the head of the Mexican film bureau, Jorge Ferretis, blocked *The Magnificent Seven* from moving forward, "complain[ing] that 'the script places Mexicans in conditions of inferiority'" (Hannan 87). Ferretis, who "hated the central storyline," targeted specific areas for change, including having a Mexican gunfighter among the seven, keeping the villagers' clothes clean to avoid having them look "too poor," and "remov[ing] more of the clichés invented by Hollywood," among others (87, 88–89). Arguably, without the intervention of Ferretis, the film we know today would have been very different.

The opening scenes substantiate the centrality of Mexicans to the narrative's conflict. In the same way that westerns such as *The Searchers* (1956), *A Man Called Horse* (1970), *Dances with Wolves* (1990), and countless others distinguish good Indians from bad, *The Magnificent Seven* makes distinctions between good and bad Mexicans. The good Mexicans devote themselves to farming and caring for their families, while the bad Mexicans embrace a life of violent crime. Following the establishing long shot of the landscape, including the mountains in the distance and a fallow cornfield in the foreground dotted with white-clad figures, a group of riders emerge from the bottom right-hand side of the frame. The scene then cuts to three villagers shucking corn. Bass drums in a heartbeat rhythm and sharp strings, often associated sonically with cinematic Indians, accompany the arrival of men dressed as bandidos— wearing large sombreros and bandoliers—on horseback, denoting their role as the antagonists. As Calvera and his men ride into the village, the peons, who stand to watch, are given visual and moral authority in the frame through the upward-angle position of the camera. Calvera reveals himself as an extortionist who has stolen food and supplies from the village for years, leaving the residents with barely enough on which to live. Calvera complains that he must do so to keep his men fed, likening his obligation to that of a father to his children. Richard Slotkin describes Calvera as "a brutal and complex villain who acts like a bandit, but speaks the language of paternal authority—'I am a father to these men; they depend on me'—to justify his rape of the village" (77). Calvera represents the intersection of the father and the bandido in westerns. His violent paternalism is exploitative and destructive, illustrative of the "irrational, despotic caricature" of a father identified by Bruzzi (62). When one of the villagers, Rafael, charges at Calvera, calling him a "murderer" and a "thief," Calvera's men shoot him dead in the street. The scene confirms Calvera as a threat to the community of farmers and demonstrates the internecine violence that plagues the village.

In the moral universe of *The Magnificent Seven*, the villagers, depicted as childlike innocents, represent good borderlands Mexicans, who need vigilante protection. Conversely, the professional gunmen need employment; perhaps even more importantly, they need an opportunity to ply their skills. A group of men from the village travel to Tombstone, Arizona, to buy guns, despite their not knowing how to use the weapons, so that they can defend themselves and protect their limited resources.[10] The two groups cross paths during a key scene that takes place once the men from the village cross the border. "For the villagers," as Hannan observes, "the border town is a first stop while for the gunfighters it is the last" (164). From the crowd that has gathered to stare at an abandoned hearse, Chris (Yul Brynner) steps forward, offering to drive the vehicle containing the body of a dead Indian man named Sam, which no one else would deign to drive because of its occupant. Vin (Steve McQueen), another onlooker, joins him to ride shotgun, literally, to deliver the body to Boot Hill. Their willingness to drive Sam's body to the cemetery is motivated by a desire to use their skills as gunslingers rather than by any sense of righting a social injustice, but the Mexican farmers who watch the episode read Chris and Vin's actions as belonging to men of superior ability and high moral caliber who stand up for what is right. When the villagers approach Chris later to ask for help buying guns, he tells them, "Nowadays men are cheaper than guns." Although the exchange sets up the professional element of the western and initiates Chris's collection of men with extraordinary abilities, it also indicates that he knows the decline in value of men with his particular skills.

With few prospects and even fewer opportunities to use their expertise, the gunslingers are men out of time who wrestle with, long for, or are haunted by the past. "It is virtually impossible," as Jenni Calder maintains, "for the gunmen, already aware that they are fast becoming anachronistic, to do anything but try to carry on in the old way. They are casting themselves beyond the law, beyond the pale of a growing society whose progress inevitably brings materialism as well as stability" (191). Professionals thrive in situations of instability. Consequently, "stability is anathema" to them and their way of life (191). Their decreased economic value in the US is best illustrated when Chris and Vin initially seek out Bernardo O'Reilly (Charles Bronson) to join their effort. After being paid $600 for his participation in the Travis County War and $800 for his involvement in Salinas, Bernardo's willingness to put his life on the line for $20, along with the fact that he is shown chopping wood for his breakfast, demonstrates his severely diminished resources, though he is not alone in his economic circumstances.[11] Chris, Vin, Harry (Brad Dexter), and O'Reilly, are motived, in part, by money, Lee (Robert Vaughn) by the opportunity for redemption, Britt (James Coburn) by the challenge of the odds (thirty against seven), and Chico by his romantic longing to be a gunslinger.

Despite the fact that, as Calder suggests, "the film can be seen as the purest justification of the more dubious aspect of American foreign policy," for the most part the film avoids the white-savior fantasy (199). More than simply a group of "gallant Americans, the men with courage, the weapons and the skill, [who] ride over the border and defend a threatened Mexican village," the seven, constituted for a time of six apparently white men (Chris, Vin, O'Reilly, Harry, Britt, and Lee), empower the Mexican villagers, made up mostly of families, to take up arms and defend themselves (199). Before the force becomes a solidified seven, Chico, a young Mexican man, follows the six at a distance, hoping to join the group by showing his determination. Harry complains that the young man trailing them is an annoyance, to which Chris replies, "It's a free country." O'Reilly adds, "And it's his." Any pretense of US expansionism is quelled once the gunmen cross over into Mexico, where they acknowledge that they are interlopers in a country that does not belong to them. Nevertheless, in agreeing to kill in behalf of the Mexican villagers, the seven, working as Americans, represent a violent paternalism equal to that of Calvera.

O'Reilly's character, however, offers an alternative to violent paternalism, one that places emphasis back on Mexican families, and fathers in particular. His progressive geopolitical views align with his ethnic and cultural heritage, which the film reveals after audiences have had time to invest in the character. Overhearing a group of boys refer to O'Reilly as "Bernardo," Chris teases that the village has adopted the gunslinger, to which O'Reilly replies, "Bernardo O'Reilly, that's my real name. Mex-

FIGURE 14. *Bernardo with village boys after he has been mortally wounded in* The Magnificent Seven. *He tells the boys to look at their fathers and see the bravery in their willingness to fight for their families and their way of life.*

ican on one side, Irish on the other, and me in the middle." His identity as a person of mixed heritage reflects the actual mixing of cultures in the West, yet in the context of the film, it strongly aligns Bernardo with the Mexican villagers.[12] Of the seven, Bernardo, particularly through his interactions with the village's children, actively disrupts the veneration of the hired guns and performs a benevolent paternalism that contrasts with Calvera's malevolence. However, as was the case with Shane and Joey's father in the film *Shane*, Bernardo threatens to supplant the actual fathers in the village because the children idealize him. Slotkin argues, "Association with the tribal life of the village softens the gunfighters, specifically by evoking paternal feelings. The key figure here is Riley [sic], who becomes a father-figure to a group of children, and who will be killed at the end because of them" (81). More precisely, in an effort to protect a group of children who represent the future of the village, Bernardo sacrifices himself. As he dies, he redirects the children's admiration, and perhaps even the audience's, away from himself and toward the male Mexican villagers (figure 14).

Earlier, when the same group of boys call their fathers cowards for their unwillingness to stand up to Calvera and his men sooner, Bernardo pulls one child down across his lap and spanks him, at the same time admonishing the boys: "Don't you ever say that again about your fathers because they are not cowards." Bernardo tells them their fathers possess real courage because they are brave enough to farm, never knowing whether they will have enough to provide for their families. They possess a fearlessness he never had, he says. Later, when Bernardo pushes the boys to safety and is mortally wounded, he tells them, "You see. I told you. You see your fathers?" The camera cuts to the men armed with shovels and other makeshift weapons, successful in their efforts to rid the village of Calvera. "At the climax," as Hannan states, "freedom is not achieved by guns, but by villagers using ordinary farming implements" (167). Fighting alongside the seven, the village men have found the resolve to do what they must to protect themselves and their families.

As he nears death, Bernardo asks the boys, "What's my name?" and they repeat "Bernardo," to which he replies, "Damn right." The importance of the scene is threefold: it ensures that he will be remembered by the boys, who have promised to tend his grave; the multiracial man's claiming of his identity valorizes Mexican-ness; and the exchange represents racial solidarity between Bernardo and the boys, but also by extension their fathers and the village at large. Slotkin maintains that for O'Reilly, "acceptance of the children means accepting the part of himself that is Mexican, but he does this in a style that affirms his own higher paternalism—the paternalism of violence—even while he denies it" (81). O'Reilly's use of violence becomes an indictment of the same, so that when he redirects the boys' attention to their fathers, who are ordinary men and not gunfighters, he is pointing to the fact that they have the skills to "return to the real work of the fields and the living and loving forever out of reach of men for whom killing is their life" (Hannan 168). Chico's decision to stay in town and put down roots with Petra, a strong-willed local woman, demonstrates a level of bravery that Bernardo tells the boys he never had. At the same time, it signifies the return of a Mexican to his homeland, reestablishing community, national, and racial boundaries, while Chris and Vin, the only two other survivors, presumably, ride back to the US and an uncertain future.

Pushing against the boundaries of race and nation, while simultaneously relying on some of the worst impulses of Hollywood westerns in their treatment of Mexicans, Sturges's morally complicated film depicts Mexican families as having a value worth protecting and for which white men would die, a subtle but powerful message. The villagers, initially depicted as helpless children, rise up and kill the oppressive, murderous, despotic father Calvera. While the film unquestionably offers at times competing or complementary forms of paternalism, it upholds Mexican fatherhood as the ideal to which the children of the village should aspire. Chico's resolve to cast aside his gunslinger aspirations and start a family signals the continuation of the village and its way of life.

Antoine Fuqua's 2016 remake of *The Magnificent Seven*, which combines the professional western with the revenge plot, trades complex international relationships for multiracial diversity in the US. Land and gold are now at the heart of the conflict, the latter detail a nod to Harry and his fortune-seeking ways in the original. Anxiety about the changing world is no longer a prominent theme. The inclusion of Black, Mexican, American Indian, and Korean actors, as well as a woman, in lead roles does little to resolve the racial politics and problems of the original. In some instances it actually exacerbates them while also introducing new racial and gender complications. Gone are the village, Calvera, including his attendant paternalism, and Mexico, along with the value placed on a Mexican community. Instead, the focus is on the white town of Rose Creek, where farmers are being forced off their land by a ruthless Anglo capitalist.

The shift from a threatened Mexican village to the global community may not seem significant, but it is similar to the move from "Black Lives Matter" to "All Lives Matter." One calls attention to systemic violence and oppression that denies Black subjects their humanity and most basic civil rights, including the right to say their lives have value. The other flattens out all difference to place emphasis on human life without acknowledging the privileges that offer protections to some and not others, such as people of color, transgender individuals, and certainly not the children and families in the concentration camps along the US-Mexico border. *Suicide Squad* makes a move similar to that of *The Magnificent Seven* by shifting from a local to a more global focus. Though the locus of conflict is in Metropolis, New York, the stakes of the battle concern humans around the world. Within its global framework, *Suicide Squad* provides its bona fides as a western, or at the very least a colonial fantasy, through homicidal Mexicans and its instrumentalization of Indigenous-coded characters as villains. But the film also makes clear: there are bad Indians and then there are Aztec fire gods.

OF DADDIES, DIABLOS, AND THE DARKNESS

Against the backdrop of the setting sun, a woman, clad in leather with a red sash tied across her back and carrying a samurai sword, walks slowly toward the ramp of a Chinook helicopter. The scene then cuts to a reverse shot from inside the helo so that its open door frames the white-masked woman's entrance onto the aircraft. In the distance, positioned on either side of her, stands a platoon of combat soldiers. Behind them, smoke rises up from a city skyline. Once the woman is on board, the audience hears her backstory, witnesses her proficiency with a blade, and learns her name—Katana (Karen Fukuhara). After the commander in charge introduces her to the unsavory occupants of the transport, Katana's instinct is to draw her sword, to which the officer responds, "Whoa! Easy, cowgirl. This ain't that kind of mission." The details of the sequence serve to situate David Ayer's *Suicide Squad* (2016) in the western genre and pay homage to the film's source material.

With its comic book pedigree, bumping soundtrack, and penchant for visual excess, *Suicide Squad* seems far removed from the rolling hills of the frontier or the dusty streets of Tombstone, Arizona. Then again, *Suicide Squad* offers its own band of "misfits, loners, bullies, mavericks, and sociopaths," like those found in *The Magnificent Seven*, while muting its identity as a western and its faithfulness to the professional plot under the noise of its hyperstylized veneer (Mitchell 225). Thus, it is a more self-conscious version of the hyperreal, one rooted in the fiction of the western. Although it centers on genetically enhanced humans and urban vistas, the film is, in fact, a high-octane weird western, in which "cowboys" battle supernatural "Indians" to save a distressed damsel.[13] However, *Suicide Squad* is not about lone rangers, white and black hats, or good versus bad—it is about bad versus worse. The cavalry does not arrive in the nick of time, because "it ain't that kind of mission." Instead, the outlaws save the day and all of humanity along with it. The film upholds generic conventions through the juxtaposition of savagism and civilization and the ways its diverse characters seek to preserve the integrity of the family, even as they push against these same ideas.

Six cons, turned would-be heroes, are tasked with completing a rescue mission, turned termination, in the besieged city seen billowing with smoke behind Katana in the opening scene. Agent Amanda Waller (Viola Davis) finds this group of meta-human criminals with extraordinary abilities to combat a potential hostile alien invader—à la Superman except one who does not share the "values" of the US. The strike force, called Task Force X, under the direction of Colonel Rick Flag (Joel Kinnaman), a white man, is eventually pressed into national service to defend an attack on Midway City by the evil Enchantress (Cara Delevingne), a six-thousand-year-old meta-human with interdimensional abilities, and her equally powerful brother, Incubus (Alain Chanoine). Dubbed the Suicide Squad because they have explosive pellets injected into their necks that can be set off if they do not follow orders, the racially diverse group composed of Deadshot (Will Smith), Harley Quinn (Margot Robbie), Captain Boomerang (Jai Courtney), El Diablo (Jay Hernandez), Killer Croc (Adewale Akinnuoye-Agbaje), and Slipknot (Adam Beach), killed moments after his introduction, agree to the mission, not out of loyalty to country or love of the law but in exchange for reduced prison sentences. As hired guns, the Suicide Squad protects a city's population for personal gain, serving as the western village cleansers. The meta-human criminals in *Suicide Squad* abjure greater-good moral responsibility to battle meta-humans with abilities superior to their own, while still defending those in need. In keeping with the professional-western format, *Suicide Squad* culminates in a final battle in which the group members choose each other, rather than right or wrong, no matter the personal cost.

For no one is that cost higher than for Chato Santana. The limited-release, independent superhero/vigilante film *El Chicano* (2018) notwithstanding, Chato represents the only explicitly Latinx character among the countless live-action meta-humans, mutants, and other remarkable superheroes.[14] His characterization, even among a group of villains, as a homicidal cholo has its roots in a familiar western figure. Known on the streets as El Diablo, he easily fulfills the bandido role in its reimagined form as the gang member. Ramírez Berg argues that as a "second *bandido* variant," this particular character type reflects "only superficial changes to the external details of the stereotype; at their core these characters are the same inarticulate, violent, and pathologically dangerous *bandidos*" (*Latino Images* 68, 69). Agent Waller confirms and seeks to capitalize on this fact, introducing him as the "pyrokinetic homeboy" and later referring to him as an "L.A. gangbanger." A portion of the "Activity Report" on his criminal profile visible on-screen reads: ". . . born into a close family of Catholic Mexican immigrants in Boyle Heights and spent his early years under the watchful eye of his grandmother. . . . As he reached his teens, he was drawn into gang activity, moving up the ranks stealing cars, dealing drugs, and selling handguns." He is suspected of murdering more than fifteen men in Los Angeles.

When initially incarcerated, Diablo incinerates a sizable group of men in a prison riot. He is, in that moment, El Rey, the king of a toxic masculinity that is dependent on violence and destruction, cementing his place as a bad Mexican. "Even his powers, which allow him to generate and wield massive flames," as George Santos remarks, "can be read as invoking an ethnic stereotype—that of the fiery Latino—since he can only access his powers when he loses control of his emotions" (301). An immigrant Mexican criminal of the cinematic, cultural, and political imagination, Chato is covered in facial and body tattoos. His difference is not only remarked on but also marked in numerous ways throughout the

FIGURE 15. *A flashback to a family scene in the Santana household in* Suicide Squad. *Grace's white shirt, symbolizing her goodness, contrasts with Chato's black shirt, indicating his bad-guy status.*

film. Captain Boomerang asks when they first meet, "What's that crap on your face? Does it wash off?" Deadshot addresses Chato as "ese" (a slang term that means "dude" or "bro" but can also refer to gang ties) and with phrases such as "Hola, amigo."

Chato, however, possesses a duality that highlights a turning away from his former, bad self (figure 15). Perhaps in an effort to mitigate his deeply problematic representation, the film gives Chato a redemption arc that begins when Waller narrates a portion of his backstory. Set to War's "Slippin' into Darkness," a song about a descent into madness, scenes show Chato surrendering to police, instead of being apprehended, after losing control of his pyrokinetic power and setting fire to his house, accidentally killing his wife and two children. Waller references Chato's perceived position as El Rey brought low by his own hand: "This L.A. gangbanger thought he was king until he lost his queen." When the police slam Chato against the hood of the car to cuff him, a close-up shot reveals tears streaming down his face. His remorse becomes a tacit acknowledgment of his unchecked rage. The darkness that touches all the squad members, making them well suited to the role of urban cowboys, affects Chato differently. He has taken a vow to never again use his ability, making him analogous to Lee in *The Magnificent Seven*, who suffers from psychological trauma as the result of his experiences in the Civil War and can no longer fight. Stated another way, when approached about becoming a hired killer for the state, Chato refuses, even though doing so means that the conditions of his incarceration will stay the same. His skills are not for sale, at any price.

Chato's refusal places him in direct contrast with Deadshot, a character with whom he is uneasily aligned. Both men are fathers whose children, indirectly and directly, are responsible for their being in prison. Whereas Chato relinquishes himself to authorities after the accidental killing of his family, Deadshot is apprehended because his daughter Zoe, an eleven-year-old honors student, pleads with her daddy not to kill Batman. She even goes so far as to place herself between her father and the caped crusader. Murdering Batman would have allowed Deadshot to elude authorities, but instead he gives in to the angelic goodness of his daughter, dressed in a white parka that emphasizes her innocence. In doing so, he spares Zoe the experience of witnessing her beloved father use his lethal gift. In contrast to Chato's embracing a pacifist position, Deadshot unapologetically loves killing but agrees to do so for the state only under the condition that it will directly benefit Zoe's educational future. Cut off from his daughter, he tries to look after her welfare from prison, a prospect made available to him because he was able to check his worst impulse when it mattered. Chato's uncontrollable rage over his wife's decision to leave and take the children after she discovered the continuation of his criminal activities cost him his family, permanently. The film positions the two men of color in moral opposition. Chato is depicted as the devil, El Diablo; he even says, "I was born with the devil's gift." Deadshot, on the other hand, who according to his "Activity Report" started off as a vigilante, sees himself as an emissary of God. This idea is reflected through the quote that adorns his collar and the barrel of his gun: "I am the Light—the Way."[15] The oppositional positioning of Chato and Deadshot matters because one will be allowed to live, while the other will die. Either way, devil and angel share the same objective: to find a way back to their families, even if it means doing so through death.

Isolated from family and society at large in a Louisiana black-ops prison called Belle Reve, the squad members are denied rights of citizenship. As incarcerated individuals, they are the property of the state, in this case the federal government, and are exploited for their violent abilities. According to Lorrie Palmer, as westerns evolved, "[t]he cowboys themselves grew darker, more violent, and more divided within themselves . . ." (291). The Suicide Squad members' familiarity with what Deadshot calls "the dark places," along with their unpredictability, comes from living outside the boundaries of "civilization," the same society they are charged with protecting. Villages and towns have given way to a metropolis and planetary concerns. The members' status as criminals, in addition to their moral and in some cases mental instability, makes them unlikely protectors of civilization. However, the raised stakes of world-wide destruction warrant superoutlaws who excel at various forms of violence, skills honed through their extralegal endeavors:

> Stability is anathema to the real Western hero. And again the rejection of stability emphasizes the potential danger to society that the Western hero contains. He cannot be appealed to on the ground of normal citizenship. In a country where the whole idea of citizenship plays such an important role there is adulation of a hero who by definition rejects much that is a part of the citizen's role. As soon as the hero identifies himself entirely with a community his nature changes. (Calder 191)

The squad members *are* a danger to society; they cannot be convinced initially to do what is right on the basis of morality alone, which is why they are offered reduced sentences and forced into explicit compliance through electronic control measures. Regardless of whether they succeed in their mission they can never fully belong to the world they protect, for they are residents of a border, residing in a carceral condition both within and outside of the state. Elena dell'Agnese reminds us that "the same signifier (the 'border') can have different meanings," including "a barrier limiting the free movement of people and goods, a symbolic end of the nation-Self and/or an open frontier" (205). Cut off from all contact with their families and restricted from using their abilities, the meta-humans targeted by Waller experience a symbolic end to the use of the powers that defined them on the outside. Belle Reve ("Beautiful Dream") is a nightmare from which there is no immediate escape. In fact, the gates read "Till death do us part." The "special security barracks" exist as a place that technically does not exist. As Waller says, she put the prisoners "in a hole and threw away the hole." Even within these confines, Chato exists in the borderlands of nowhere, housed in a flood tank lest his pyrokinetic abilities get out of control. He is both one of and separate from the rest of the meta-human prisoners.

Throughout, the film never lets the audience forget the squad members' criminal histories and outsider status so as not to let convicts become "actual" heroes. Adhering to cultural standards of morality would make them no longer exceptional villains, which, more than their superhuman abilities, is what distinguishes the group from the rest of the population. What the outlaw heroes must do to rescue the damsel in distress further entrenches them beyond the boundaries of the social order, where they will remain separate. While this is true of most western heroes, from the titular character in *Shane*, directed by George Stevens, a film referenced throughout *Logan*, to Ethan Edwards in John Ford's *The Searchers*, the diverse racial and ethnic backgrounds of the squad members push them even further outside of "civilized" society and limit the roles they are allowed to occupy within the genre.

A pair of meta-human siblings of indigenous origins, Enchantress and Incubus, stand in opposition to the metropolitan outlaw heroes. In ancient times, Enchantress and Incubus were revered as gods, until they were trapped. Anthropologist Dr. June Moone (also played by Cara Delevingne), Colonel Flag's love interest, releases the Enchantress, who has been held captive in a clay vessel. While wandering in the South American or Central American jungle, Dr. Moone, a white woman, happens upon a pyramid of the Mesoamerican variety, falls into a cave (named either "Tres Osos Cave" or "Gobierno Cave"—the details on the printed page of the briefing are unclear), and purposely breaks open a clay totem, freeing the Enchantress. In addition to being a horrible anthropologist, Dr. Moone becomes the human host for this meta-human spirit, who takes possession of her body. The scenario calls to mind a captivity narrative. Dr. Moone's transformation into the Enchantress, an indigenous figure of Latin American origin, represents native corruption of the civilized individual. Eventually taking full control of her human host, the Enchantress becomes the Indian antagonist. In this way, the cowboys are charged with eliminating the Indians; the film, in other words, has the most basic western plot, one that involves the instrumentalization of indigeneity to secure the continuation of white cisgender heterosexuality through the reunion of Dr. Moone and Colonel Flag.

Given its adherence to generic conventions, *Suicide Squad* invites comparisons with other westerns. For example, the scene inside the Chinook as the squad rides into hostile territory brings to mind John Ford's *Stagecoach* (1939), starring John Wayne. Dr. June Moone and the Enchantress mirror, respectively, the virginal goodness of Amy Kane and the dangerous allure of Helen Ramírez in Fred Zinnemann's *High Noon* (1952). But *Suicide Squad* aligns most explicitly with *The Magnificent Seven*. Whereas the concerns of the squad are more global, Sturges's *Seven*, with its own eclectic group of gunslingers and opportunists, focuses on a local conflict. The Suicide Squad members possess abilities that correspond to the original seven, with the exception of Slipknot, who has no analogous figure because he plays no substantive role in the film. As the on-the-ground leader, Flag takes on the Chris Adams role, with the others corresponding as follows: Deadshot as Vin Tanner, Harley Quinn as Chico, Killer Croc as Britt, Captain Boomerang as Harry Luck, and Diablo as both Bernardo O'Reilly and Lee. Furthering the comparison, the Japanese character Katana, the model minority with a clear set of morals and values, is an homage to *The Magnificent Seven*'s source material, Kurosawa's *Seven Samurai*. Not officially one of the squad, she nevertheless leads the slow-motion "hero walk" to the climactic showdown.

Suicide Squad centralizes the fight of the professional western. The stakes of the final showdown could not be clearer. By defeating the extra-dimensional mystical Indigenous siblings and their mutant armies, the task force will safeguard millions of human families around the world. Many of the squad members' personal relationships to family, as a social institution, are both frustrated and aspirational. Deadshot is divorced and alienated from his daughter, who knows he does "bad things" but loves him anyway. Zoe writes to her father every day, but unbeknownst to Deadshot, the authorities withhold the letters to make him believe his daughter no longer wants contact with him, thereby deepening his punishment and isolation. Harley declares that she and the other squad members are not "normal," though her deepest desire, as revealed by the Enchantress, is to be just that, a "normal" wife and mother.[16] In her fantasy, Harley holds a child on her hip in a stark white kitchen bathed in light as the Joker, sans green pallor and dressed in a business suit, kisses her good morning and then turns his attention to a second child seated in a high chair. To no one in particular, she mutters, "He married me." The elusiveness of family does not diminish Deadshot and Harley's longing for it or the value they place on it. When Enchantress tries to delude Diablo with a vision of his own family restored, he sees the ruse for what it is. She is unaware that he possesses his own mystical ability—the power to see through delusion and enchantment, a capacity he has had his entire life. Refusing the illusion, Diablo confronts Enchantress, telling her, "You can't have them. These are my people here, right here." He lays claim to his fellow squad members and the bond he shares with them. Later he declares, "I lost one family. I'm not going to lose another." Chato goes back on his word and unleashes the full power of El Diablo. He sacrifices himself to save his "people," his criminal brethren. The squad members, who almost exclusively have taunted or mocked him, have replaced his dead wife and children.

Even more inexplicable is Chato's transformation from a tattooed, T-shirted homeboy into a skeletal Indian god, wearing a loincloth and headdress of quetzal feathers engulfed in flames. In this uncanny form, he

FIGURE 16. *Chato, fully transformed into a powerful pyrokinetic Aztec warrior god with a flaming headdress and loincloth, battling Incubus.*

speaks almost exclusively in Spanish. The unveiling of Chato's true identity, an Aztec-looking fire god, in his fight against Incubus further complicates his representation as a Mexican, or more precisely as a Mexican Indian. Now, as a mystical good Indian, he fights Incubus, a supernatural bad Indian, in a struggle to the death (figure 16). As the character most closely aligned with Bernardo in *The Magnificent Seven*, Chato dies in a similar situation: protecting others. His demise maintains the integrity of his surrogate family, who work in unison to vanquish Enchantress and save the damsel in distress. Chato gives his life so that Deadshot, Harley, and Flag can have the opportunity to be reunited with their loved ones. The remaining squad members defeat Enchantress, which allows Moone to escape and emerge fully restored. Born anew, she is free from any hint of corruption that might have occurred as a result of her experience. The reunion of the happy white couple, Flag and Moone, overshadows Chato's role as the true hero of the battle, his sacrifice quickly forgotten.

Suicide Squad satisfies the most basic conventions of the western: recover the girl and eliminate the Indigenous (albeit supernatural) threat to save civilization. Chato dies restoring whiteness, but he also helps bring about the reunion of Deadshot and his daughter, Zoe. After the squad saves the world, Waller tells the remaining members they will receive ten years off their prison sentences for the job they have successfully completed. Deadshot refuses, telling Waller "it's not enough." What he wants instead is to see his daughter, to which Waller agrees.[17] The scene cuts to Deadshot helping Zoe with her geometry homework as Flag watches from the hallway. Together they look at a diagram and Deadshot attempts to explain how to find the hypotenuse of a triangle. Zoe points to the image and asks, "So if you are up here, like in a building, and you shoot a man down here on the street, that's how far the bullet actually goes?" The scene not only represents the reunion between father and daughter, but it also hints at a key difference between Deadshot's and Chato's relationships with their families, as well as why one is reunited with his and the other is not. Chato's wife, Grace, whose prayers for his reform went unanswered, rejected who he was as a criminal and demanded that he abandon his gangster life. On the other hand, Zoe knows who and what her father is and does not care. In the moral landscape of the *Suicide Squad*, Zoe is "rewarded" and Grace and her children are punished. For the Black and Brown families in the film, the criminal fathers are a disappointment, but those feelings can be tempered by accepting their lawlessness.

Suicide Squad, at times, destabilizes the familiar conventions of a genre that centralizes white masculinity and regularly marginalizes or villainizes American Indian and Mexican characters. So although Flag serves as the field commander, he, like the other members of the crew, is exploited by Waller, who threatens his love interest. The film also features an actually diverse cast that includes Black, First Nations, Japanese, and Latinx actors. Women whose abilities match and exceed those of their male counterparts take on prominent roles, holding sway in each of the narrative arenas. For all of its progressive elements, the film still sacrifices Latinx and Native characters to uphold the value of heteronormative whiteness made evident when the distressed damsel is saved, a point punctuated by Flag and Moone's passionate embrace. Chato, as a heroic father figure, does what is necessary, by any means necessary, and then dutifully dies. Ultimately, the film depends on its diverse characters to reaffirm contemporary racial (and racist) paradigms and to quell anxieties about globalization.

Logan, on the other hand, concerns itself with the permeability of borders—racial, genetic, and geographic. Vulnerable populations of marginalized individuals, treated as property and weapons within the neoliberal economy, are, for the reluctant hero, people worth protecting. Although the film is named for its aging white male protagonist, *Logan* posits racially diverse children as the next generation of superheroes who need safeguarding, an idea far more progressive than any found in *Suicide Squad* or either version of *The Magnificent Seven*.

FAMILY AND *FRONTERAS*

The last installment of the Wolverine series, the stand-alone film *Logan* (2017), directed by James Mangold, engages directly with the western genre, both as a reference point and for narrative inspiration. Set in El Paso, along the US-Mexico border, in a world with a distinct post-apocalyptic visual aesthetic, the movie features an aged Logan (formerly Wolverine), who has become a limousine driver and caretaker for Professor Charles Xavier (Patrick Stewart), whose incredibly powerful mind is deteriorating and causing him to unintentionally harm others. The central conflict arises from Logan's reluctant relationship with a Spanish-speaking mutant girl named Laura (Dafne Keen), who shares abilities similar to his. Despite its senior superheroes and the corporate creation of patented weaponized children, the film immediately announces itself as a western.

Through geographic signposting and aesthetics, a frontier, or rather *frontera*, narrative emerges. *Logan* opens with the credits set against a black screen. Extradiegetic sounds slowly fade in: a car rumbling to a stop, Spanish-language music, and someone saying, "We get the wheels, we get la feria." The first image we see is a much-aged Logan being jostled awake in the back seat of his rocking limousine. He steps out of the car, feet twisted beneath him as he struggles to make his way around to the other side, where he discovers a group of cholos in the process of attempting to remove the front passenger-side tire. He does not try to stop them but just tells them they are wasting their time because the tires are not removable and are not as valuable as they appear. A particularly vicious-looking cholo fires his shotgun at Logan's chest, all while Spanish-language rap bumps in the background. The gang laughs, calling Logan a "pendejo" and a "cabron" and turning their backs on the presumably dead man. The camera moves to a medium shot of Logan from the waist up as he lies supine on the ground. Imposed above his arm, the film title slowly appears, letting the audience know that this is not the Wolverine of old. Distracted, the would-be thieves fail to notice as Logan slowly rises. He feebly warns them, "Guys, you don't want to do this." As they turn to attack, he raises his arms and closes his fists. In the frame behind Logan is an interstate sign that reads "WEST 62 El Paso." At this point, viewers familiar with the hero and former X-Men member Wolverine would expect Logan to extend his metal claws and quickly dispatch these amateur thieves. Instead, his infamous claws only half appear before one cholo connects with his jaw. The gang then attacks the elderly man with shouts of "Fuck him up!" and "Get that puto!" as if in confirmation of his diminished masculinity. On the ground, Logan's rage finally erupts, and Wolverine, although much changed, appears, cutting off one man's arm, impaling another beneath the chin, stabbing one through the top of his skull, and giving still another multiple stabs to the torso. The leader of the gang gets his throat slashed and falls to the ground as the remaining members flee. With bodies strewn everywhere, Logan gets into his limousine and drives away. As the vehicle exits the frame, "WEST 62 El Paso" looms prominently in the dark, illuminated by electric billboard signs across the highway.

The opening scene establishes a familiar scenario in a western—a stagecoach heist, demonstrated first through the iconic rocking of the vehicle interior, as if it were bucking along the trail, and then the violence of the outlaws. Logan, dressed in black and white, is the cowboy who confronts bandidos in a dystopian 2029. With his exemplary top-buttoned shirt, bandana, and general cholo style, the urban gang member, as Ramírez Berg argues, represents only a "superficial" change to the bandido type. The "[s]cars and scowls" of the men Logan confronts are part of what mark them as familiar signifiers of the violence that stands in opposition to moral stability:

> Behaviorally, [the bandido] is vicious, cruel, treacherous, shifty, and dishonest; psychologically, he is irrational, overly emotional, and quick to resort to violence. His inability to speak English or his speaking English with a heavy Spanish accent is Hollywood's way of signaling his feeble intellect, a lack of brainpower that makes it impossible for him to plan or strategize successfully. (Ramírez Berg, *Latino Images* 68)

This lack of intelligence explains why the Mexican criminals fail to comprehend that their robbery will result in failure and death. As suggested by the title superimposed over his body as he lies on the ground, the hero whom audiences once knew is now 197 years old, but still capable of dispatching outlaws. Logan has been brought down by age and as we later learn, illness. Gone are his supersized cigars, bravado, and swagger. Still, his abilities and rage are enough to allow him to defeat the attackers and steer his proverbial stagecoach (for what else is a limousine?), now riddled by buckshot, away from the scene.

Repeated visual placement of the highway sign reading "WEST 62 El Paso" during the confrontation situates the narrative in the borderlands, here characterized by danger and lawlessness. The prominence of "WEST," more than a directional indicator, marks the geography of the space—the west, or at the very least the frontier, where cowboys still battle bandidos. There is an additional key detail in the sign: "62," referring to US Route 62. It holds distinction as the only east-west numbered highway that connects Mexico and Canada, running from the border towns of El Paso, Texas, to Niagara Falls, New York. The nature of US Route 62 serves as foreshadowing for the movement of the narrative (south to north) and establishes borders and border crossings as prominent tropes in the film.

The film's border politics appear to uphold the idea of American superiority. The first passenger Logan transports is a cowboy, accessorized in a Stetson and a turquoise bolo tie. Next, a group of drunk, primarily white young men are seen hanging out of the sunroof shouting, "USA! USA!" as they drive through the border past security. Their behavior reflects both their fervent nationalism and their privilege, one that allows them to be chauffeured, without obstruction, across the border in luxury, a condition that is directly contrasted later in the film by Laura and the other children's movement north. But across the border into Mexico, Logan and his makeshift family, made up of what seem to be the last remaining mutants in the world (no mutant child has been born outside of a lab in the last twenty-five years), live in an abandoned, dilapidated smelting plant. There, he and Caliban, a light-sensitive mutant with extraordinary tracking abilities, house and care for Charles Xavier alone and undisturbed.[18] For them the border provides a place of safety and seclusion. As mutants on the margins, or a queer family of men in which Caliban is feminized through his domestic labor and Logan is masculinized as the breadwinner, Logan also assumes the role of caregiver for the man who has been like a father to him. These men constitute in the film one of at least four distinct iterations of family, an institution Logan has shunned for most of his life: (1) the X-Men members accidentally killed by Charles before the film begins; (2) Logan, Caliban, and Charles, the last surviving mutants; (3) the Munson family; and (4) the intergenerational family of Logan, Laura, and Charles.

From his initial introduction in the X-Men films, Logan is characterized as a loner. Through backstory provided in *X-Men Origins: Wolverine* (2009), audiences learn that as a boy, Logan witnessed the shooting of his father, John Howlett, by their family's groundskeeper, Thomas Logan. The incident activated Logan's mutation. He attacked Thomas, who before dying revealed he was the boy's actual father. Logan and his half-brother, Victor, flee the scene, a traumatic departure that leaves the two deracinated for much of their lives. After Logan crosses paths with Charles Xavier (aka Professor X), the man encourages him to take up residence with the other mutants in his home. In one way or another, Charles has served as a father figure to mutants as both the founder of the X-Men and the headmaster of his school for "gifted" children. The relationship between Charles and Logan is often strained, in large part because Logan resists forming long-term relationships that resemble something akin to family. In his own past, family has brought nothing but suffering: from the death of his mother, the killing of his father, the difficult relationship with his half-brother, and the death of his Blackfoot girlfriend, Kayla Silverfox. The latter tells him a story about the spirit Kuekuatsheu ("the Wolverine"), who was permanently separated from the woman he loved. After Kayla's death, Logan takes the name Wolverine in her honor. Charles persists, never giving up on the surly, solitary mutant. Late in life, the two switch places. Now, like a devoted son, Logan, who is in his own state of decline because the adamantium fused to his skeleton is deteriorating, takes care of a saltier, less refined Charles to prevent him from posing a danger to himself and others. It is Charles who initially communicates telepathically with a young mutant named Laura and who eventually helps Logan understand his connection to and foster a relationship with the eleven-year-old Mexican girl, once she comes into his orbit.

Through Laura, the plot of the professional western, the borderlands, and fatherhood intersect, beginning with a scene in which a woman approaches Logan in the cemetery, calling out to him in English, "Wolverine." She tells him she is in trouble and that "he's the only one who can help." The woman then switches to untranslated Spanish: "Necesito un héroe."[19] Logan turns his back on her, snapping, "Get the fuck away from me!" Her apparent desperation increases, as she shouts, "¿Qué demonio qué pasó de que te escondes?"[20] Unmoved by her pleas, Logan further ignores her. As the woman speeds away in her car, he sees a little girl looking out the back window. Later, he recognizes the same girl in the parking lot of the Liberty Hotel, where he has arrived after being pinged to pick up a group of clients. There he once again encounters the woman from the cemetery, Gabriela Lopez (Elizabeth Rodriguez), who offers him fifty thousand dollars (twenty thousand up front and thirty thousand more later) to drive her and her daughter to North Dakota so they can cross over into Canada. Gabriela explains that they are being hunted by her ex-boyfriend, who wants to take away Laura. Logan agrees to serve as a coyote so he can use the money to further his plan of buying a boat and living off-shore with Charles, but when he returns to transport the pair, Gabriela is dead and Laura is missing, though as Logan will discover later, she has stowed away in the trunk of his limousine. He retrieves Gabriela's phone from a hidden panel and finds a video on it telling the story of Laura and other children like her.

FIGURE 17. *A video Gabriela secretly filmed of imprisoned Mexican children who are being used for experimentation by Transigen Research in* Logan.

The film makes a narrative turn that seemingly incorporates stories of the missing women in Mexico, such as those in Ciudad Juarez, and the incarcerated children on the US side of the border who have been taken from their parents.[21] Charles and Logan watch as Gabriela explains in the video that for ten years she was a nurse for an American-owned company, Transigen Research, in Mexico City, where she took care of children who were born in the facility and never left (figure 17). As she narrates this portion of the story, images of children in cages or behind bars flash across the screen. "They have no birth certificates, no names, besides the names" given to them by the staff. She goes on to state, "They were raised in the bellies of Mexican girls, girls no one can find anymore." For these children, there will be no tearful reunions with either parent. The scene then cuts to a bloody delivery room, suggesting that these women whom Transigen inseminated with harvested mutant DNA were killed after they gave birth. Corporation employees, scientists, and security are directly responsible for the disappearance of Mexican women and for the experimentation being done on people in the American-owned facility.

The children of these women are then dehumanized through their incarceration at the facility, where they are assigned alphanumeric labels, such as X-23, instead of names. When the nurses who care for the children give them names and try to make their lives bearable, the director, Dr. Zander Rice (Richard E. Grant), admonishes them, telling a nurse named Maria, "Don't think of them as children. Think of them as things with patents and copyrights." Gabriela continues, "They thought we were too poor and stupid to understand.... This is business. They are making soldiers. Killers. . . . These are the babies of mutantes muertes." With dead mutant fathers, who were hunted down, captured, experimented on, and killed, and murdered Mexican mothers, the children are without families or advocates, making it easier for the company to experiment on and exploit them. Before the phone battery dies, an image of a bloodied Laura undergoing the same grafting of adamantium that Logan underwent appears on the screen. As Logan watches Laura from a distance, he asks, "What is she?" Charles responds, "She's your daughter."[22] Logan refuses to discuss any obligation to the girl. Danielle Orozco sees "Wolverine . . . as Laura's biological father via Laura's conception with his DNA" and as "an absent father and an aging patriarchy that has waned in its influence" (323). While the scene emphasizes the revelation of Laura's paternity, it also reveals another, equally notable truth: the next generation of mutant children is Mexican by birth. These children are literally undocumented, without papers to verify their existence.

Products of genetic experimentation, which as Gabriela explains is outlawed in the US and Canada, the very bodies of the children are illegal, forcing them in their escape to cross not one but two borders *sin papales*. The children also reflect the ethno-racial backgrounds of the mutants from whom genetic material was taken and as such represent a diverse, multiracial perspective of Mexican-ness. Seen another way, they are a manufactured version of José Vasconcelos's *raza cósmica*.[23] Relying on biological determinism and racist attributes he ascribed to particular groups, Vasconcelos's theory "deployed the idea of racial mixture in order to utilize the racial condition of Mexican society for the corporatist interest of the ruling party, the Partido Revolucionario Institucional (PRI)" (Pérez-Torres, *Mestizaje* 6). His perceived intent maps easily onto the other corporate interests depicted in the film, though the product, deemed unstable and uncontrollable, is targeted for termination. In other words, the corporation views racial mixing as a failed enterprise. The corporation euthanizes children in an act of corporate murder. Additional footage recorded by Gabriela shows employees tasing children and dragging them from their cages to be "put to sleep." As children scream in terror, the nurses, including Gabriela, band together to help as many of them escape as they can, including Laura. She and the other children are hunted down like animals to prevent them from reaching an alleged mutant safe haven called Eden, a location they have learned about from a comic book about the X-Men.

Once united with Charles and Logan, Laura exists for a time in a paternal environment that includes her genetic father and her adoptive grandfather. In the first half of the film, Charles is the only one who communicates with Laura, telepathically and through some Spanish, as well as a hodgepodge of French, English, and Spanish. However, Laura does not speak until the film's third act, first exclusively in Spanish and then in English, leading up to the final showdown, which deepens the divide between father and daughter. Despite or perhaps because of the fact that Laura shows a disposition and temper similar to Logan's, Charles is able to connect with her on an emotional level.

As he has done over the years with so many other young mutants, Charles cannot resist the urge to teach young Laura. Charles is the one who educates Laura about the western *Shane*, from which she gleans valuable information. In a Las Vegas hotel room, the former professor and the girl watch Jack Wilson (Jack Palance) shoot Stonewall Torrey (Elisha Cook, Jr.) after provoking him to draw his gun. Though the film is never named directly, it is immediately recognizable. Charles explains to Laura, "This is a very famous picture, Laura. It's almost a hundred years old." In the adjoining room, Logan laces up his combat boots, knocks over an assortment of empty alcohol bottles from the minibar, and coughs up blood. The scene crosscuts between Logan in a separate room and Laura and Charles together as they watch the movie.

Three additional scenes from *Shane* are included in the sequence. After Laura climbs into Charles's wheelchair to maneuver around the room, he discloses that he first saw the film when he was a boy about her age as they watch the townspeople sing at Stonewall's graveside and offer a prayer as he is laid to rest. Meanwhile, Logan rifles through Laura's belongings, discovering a file that identifies him as the source material for her DNA. Through the open door between the rooms, he watches Laura pull on a pair of combat boots identical to his, underscoring the visual connection between Logan and his daughter. He also finds her stash of *X-Men* comic books. Logan then walks into the room at the exact moment Shane shoots Jack Wilson dead. Logan confronts Laura about the comics and tells her they are "bullshit." He turns and leaves as Shane explains the necessity of his own departure to the boy Joey, who admires the gunslinger. Logan may want Laura to learn that the stories and feats of the superheroes featured in the comics are fiction, but one fictional text replaces another. As Charles and Laura watch, Shane delivers his final lines in the film: "A man has to be what he is, Joey. Can't break the mold. I tried it and it didn't work for me. Joey, there's no living with the killing. There's no going back from one. Right or wrong, it's a brand. A brand sticks. Now you run on home to your mother, and tell her everything's all right. There aren't any more guns in the valley." The scenes from *Shane* teach Laura, who has been separated from the outside world her entire life, valuable lessons: some people kill for the sake of killing and enjoy it; death involves rituals and provokes certain responses in individuals; a hero is the person who eliminates the villain and protects those unable to defend themselves; and finally, the person who does what others cannot or will not is often forced to live a separate existence. The final lesson also teaches her that some people cannot change despite their desire to do so, foreshadowing what she eventually comes to understand about her own father.

Logan engages in an intertextual dialogue with *Shane* in an effort to make the narratives of the two titular heroes parallel, namely, through their violence, isolation, and longing. Shane may yearn for a life different from that of a gunslinger, but from the outset, that film conveys the impossibility of this longing. In the title sequence, Shane enters the left-hand side of the frame and descends from the mountain. He is the god from on high who has come down from the heavens to save the valley folk. However, Shane's tenure as a laborer on the Starrett homestead reveals his desire for something more than killing, perhaps even for a family. The analogue in *Logan* occurs when the hero meets the Munson family. After Logan stops to help the Munson family push their truck out of a ditch, the two groups offer introductions. Logan identifies Laura as his daughter and Charles as his father. The Munsons extend the hospitality of a meal to the "Howlett" family, and over dinner, the two groups engage in lively banter about travel and school.[24] Logan tells the Munsons that Charles was a teacher; Charles says Logan was not a good student, which elicits laughter from the table, much to Laura's delight. While Charles, Logan, and Laura *act* like a family for the Munsons, they are also slowly *becoming* a family. Earlier, during an argument on the interstate, Logan tells Charles, "I know, Pop, I'm such a giant disappointment." After dinner Logan once again addresses Charles as Pop and then Dad. Repeatedly, Logan demonstrates his commitment to Charles, and Laura sees it. From a distance, she watches as Logan gently lifts Charles from his wheelchair to carry him to bed. The regard she has for both men is mirrored in the upward angle shot of the two ascending the stairs. Ever the teacher, Charles tells Logan, "This is what life looks like. A home, people who love each other. Safe place. You should take a moment and feel it." Logan may long for a life, inclusive of a home and family, but he will not let himself feel it, as Charles advises. Haunted by the death and violence that have always been part of his very long life, Logan does not believe he deserves a family.

The parallels between *Shane* and *Logan* become less clear when the Munson family is slaughtered by Transigen's new weapon, X-24, a genetic duplicate of Logan, who also kills Charles. Logan does not succeed in protecting the farmers or Charles but does manage to rescue Laura. *Logan* apparently works hard to establish a connection between itself and the psychological western *Shane*, not simply through intertextuality but also through the titular characters' similar experiences: the way death follows them wherever they go; their failure to protect vulnerable people; and their inability to have families of their own or to achieve a sustained sense of belonging. Despite these parallels to *Shane*, in the final tally *Logan* shows more explicit connections to Sturges's *Magnificent Seven*. For example, together, Charles, Logan, and Laura correspond to the members of the original magnificent seven: Charles takes on the Chris and Bernardo roles through his leadership as co-founder of the X-Men, as well as his connection to Laura and his commitment to her safety; Laura is a combination of the young fighter Chico and Vin; and finally Logan is an amalgam of the remaining members: Harry, the fortune hunter; Lee, the veteran with psychological distress; and Britt, the knife expert. So it is in the way the film, as a western, places narrative and emotional value on a vulnerable, racialized community that *Logan* best resembles the professional-western classic.

Without Charles to mediate between father and daughter, Logan and Laura are left alone to figure out the dynamics of their fragile relationship. Keeping Laura at a distance, Logan does not embrace the role of father in a way that Laura might like; nevertheless, he continues to look after the girl and agrees to drive her north, if only to disprove the fantasy of Eden and a community of mutants. During the drive, Logan discovers that Laura can talk and also that she can speak English. This new avenue of communication does little to improve their relationship. The two eventually arrive at the rendezvous point in North Dakota, which actually does exist and where the other mutant children have gathered in preparation to cross the border. Having safely delivered his daughter to the company of her companions, Logan decides to leave Laura, thus fulfilling the obligations of the professional plot. He also decides, in a curious move, to give back to the children the money he was paid for the job.

Logan's psychological struggle, externalized in the battle with his own clone, is with himself—between what he wants and what he believes he deserves. He sees himself as a killer, but as Laura points out, "I've hurt people too." Rather than see this shared experience as an opportunity to empathize with or console his daughter, Logan instead pushes Laura away. He tries to temper his comments, saying that "bad shit happens to people [he cares] about." Laura then tersely replies, "Then I'll be fine." The girl clearly yearns for a meaningful relationship with Logan; even after being reunited with her siblings of circumstance, she still wants a father—her father. Logan refuses this role, telling Laura, "I am not whatever it is you think I am." It is clear what Laura and the other mutant children in Eden think of Logan, based on the way they shave his beard, while he is sleeping, to make him look like the Wolverine of old: they want a hero.

Relinquishing the money does not free Logan from the professional plot. He must still eliminate the threat to the vulnerable population, and when he does, he becomes the hero his daughter and the other children long for him to be. As Jenni Calder notes, "Who, over and over again, rides in to save the villagers, aid the oppressed in their fight for freedom, rescue the girl, supply money, arms, technical skill to the scruffy bands who fight dictatorship but the American hero?" (199). Logan may resemble the prototypical American hero, except he is Canadian by birth and it is the country that represents safety for his daughter and the other mutant children. The border has shifted from south to north, but the stakes have not changed. After the children proceed to Canada as planned, Logan sees from a distance Transigen guards closing in on their location. Adrenalized with healing serum, Logan runs to the children's aid so they can successfully escape.[25] During the melee, Logan confronts Dr. Rice, who reveals that his original work involved "curing" mutants of their mutations.[26] Logan then shoots this eugenicist in the head. Instead of bringing about an end to the conflict, Logan is left to dispatch Dr. Rice's legacy—X-24. Yet, as a father within the western, Logan repeatedly demonstrates an intractability that *feels* autocratic, which means, as Bruzzi outlines, that the father and/or the "worst son" must die. If viewers think of the clone not simply as a copy of Logan but instead as a copy altered to enhance its capacity for violence, then his children, X-23 (Laura) and X-24, must battle it out to determine and inherit his legacy. To protect Laura and the other children, Logan orders them to flee. Laura, however, stays behind and shoots X-24 in the head with the adamantium bullet Logan has carried (which he was saving to use to kill himself) though not before X-24 impales him on a tree stump. In his final moments in the borderland between the US and Canada, he allows himself to feel, as Charles encouraged him to do earlier. Twice within his final moments, Laura calls him Daddy. Logan finally has the family he has always resisted. He protects his daughter and frees her from the violence that has marked her young life, telling her, "You don't have to fight anymore." In the final moments of

FIGURE 18. *Logan telling Laura as he dies, "Don't be what they made you." The final moments of his life allow him to feel what he has run away from since his childhood.*

his life, Logan gives Laura the father she has longed for (figure 18). Laura disrupts the masculinist legacy by dispatching her "sibling" and assumes her father's mantle but this time as a fully integrated member of a Mexican mutant family.

Logan's closing scene again links it to *Shane* and to the psychological western. Laura offers Shane's final lines to Joey as a graveside eulogy for her father, who died trying to protect her and the other Mexican mutant children against a cloned, more violent, rage-consumed, and weaponized version of himself. Before walking away, Laura takes the cross at the head of the grave and turns it on its side to form an *X*, marking the final resting place not simply of a man but of a hero, one of the X-Men. He has safeguarded the next generation of mutants and resolved the conflict within himself. Still, the film never abandons the professional-western plot. Logan's showdown with X-24 represents a battle of two equally matched individuals. Although refusing payment for delivering Laura to Eden seemingly negates the gun-for-hire element, Logan, like Bernardo in the original *Magnificent Seven*, dies defending the young *mutantes*, thereby extending and fulfilling his obligation to his daughter and the other children (figure 19). His legacy, as well as those of the other mutants, lives on in the children, symbolized by Laura and notably through the Wolverine action figure one of the mutant children carries as they make their way to the border and the safety that lies on the other side.

An uneasy parallel exists between Logan and Chato, despite their seeming racial differences. They are meta and mutant, so dangerous to the status quo that they are imprisoned and controlled (through genetics for Logan and subcutaneous explosives for Chato) to minimize their

FIGURE 19. *The next generation of* mutantes, *born of Mexican mothers and mutant fathers, watch as Laura mourns the death of her father.*

power. Both men are killers. Logan has killed historically as part of state-sanctioned violence—war, whereas Chato has killed for power and profit. As stand-ins for difference, the men inhabit a social liminality that is equated, for example, with race, which becomes complicated through Chato's actual race and ethnicity. The film depicts Chato's violence or penchant for destruction as innate and reified in fire. Chato showed greater devotion to power and criminality than to his wife and children. In other words, he failed his family spectacularly by burning them all down. Because his role is that of the bandido, a determined figure whose narrative capacity is predicated on his eventual demise, when he dies, no further mention is made of him in the narrative. He disappears as easily as his cholo brethren in *Logan*'s opening scene. Logan becomes both the dutiful son to Charles and the sacrificing father to his Mexican daughter and all her Mexican siblings so that they might have a better life. Therefore, Logan's success in delivering the children to safety is determined not only by his perceived normativity (nonmutant whiteness) but also by the western genre. Still, Chato and Logan both become reluctant heroes and save their families (adoptive and biological, respectively). However, both films make clear that, Brown or white, Chicanx or racial metaphor, the best thing a father can do for his Brown child, meta or mutant, is to die, and not even Terminators are immune to such a dark fate.

Postscript: In Terminator 2: Judgment Day *(1991), Sarah Connor (Linda Hamilton), while in Mexico, looks on from a distance as her son, future savior of the world John Connor (Edward Furlong), playfully interacts with a learning cyborg designed for the sole purpose of killing humans.*

The machine has been reprogrammed and sent back in time to protect John from assassination. Seeing them together, she offers the following extradiegetic thoughts: "Watching John with the machine, it was suddenly so clear. The Terminator would never stop. It would never leave him. And it would never hurt him. Never shout at him or get drunk and hit him. Or say it was too busy to spend time with him. It would always be there and it would die to protect him. Of all the would-be fathers who came and went over the years, this thing, this machine was the only one who measured up." Sarah realizes that, as the chosen one, John Connor needs a father as extraordinary as he to secure a future for humankind in the coming war with the machines. Even with the knowledge that machines would be responsible for human annihilation worldwide, Sarah still believes that a Terminator would make the best father for her son. Despite the fact that actor Edward Furlong's mother is Mexican, a detail not widely known and certainly not at the time, neither John nor the Terminator (Arnold Schwarzenegger) are coded as Mexican or Chicanx.[27]

Flash forward twenty-eight years to Terminator: Dark Fate *(2019), in which a Terminator who goes by the name Carl (Arnold Schwarzenegger) becomes a father to a Mexican boy.*[28] *But Carl is not just any slow, methodical, killing machine; he is the slow, methodical, killing machine that successfully assassinates a young John Connor and later reforms, settling down with a Mexican woman, Alicia, and her infant son, Mateo.*[29] *In other words, Sarah's vision was prophetic, it just did not involve her son. As an added detail, Alicia fled an abusive husband who was trying to kill their baby. Carl explains to Sarah, "Caring for this family gave me a purpose.... While raising Mateo, my son, I began to understand what I had taken from you." The film makes clear that a sentient, learning killing machine is a better father than a homicidal Mexican man because at least the former can change and "grow a conscience." In safeguarding his Brown family and protecting the future mother of the human revolution against the machines, Carl meets the same fate as Chato and Logan—he dies and will not "be back."*

PERSONAL NARRATIVE

FAMILY FICTIONS AND OTHER LIES ABOUT THE TRUTH

Growing up in our family, we could not walk ten feet without stumbling over a story. There were stories everywhere, like so many strewn toys one dances around while trying to cross a child's room, some worn to a gleam with love, some ignored without purpose, and still others handed down, again and again, welcomed in the widely outstretched arms of the next generation. Stories. In the kitchen, bedroom, bathroom, living room, garage, attic, in the crawl space, our clothes, shoes, socks, cars, everywhere we went, stores, schools, and restaurants. Stories, like smoke, so dense they could suffocate, block out even the sun, so thick they would get under our skin, saturating the pores, creating a lingering smell, like bacon, fried chicken, or tamales. We would wash and wash, scrub and scrub. All that scrubbing turned our bodies bright red, only making more stories, telling and being told, inescapable. They were like air, inhaled, exhaled, gasped for, even in dreams. Grand imaginings, large and small, populating the vastness of a landscape only our imaginations and Texas were big enough to hold. The Big Grandpa told such stories.

My brother once told me a story about morticians who break the legs on dead bodies too tall for normal-sized coffins. He confirmed the truth of his tale by explaining, "It's a fact. Not too many people know 'cause after they break the legs, they cover them up with dresses or pants. Then they stuff 'em in any old way. Why do you think only the top half of the coffin is opened at a funeral?"

Sensing my skepticism, he shrugged, "If you don't believe me, ask the Big Grandma." But I would not ask the Big Grandma. For although I could ask her and she would understand the question, her broken English would not be enough to dispel the horrific image my brother had unleashed.

Later that afternoon as my mother and I stood in the kitchen cleaning *frijoles*, I casually asked if she had ever heard of the people at funeral homes breaking the legs on dead bodies. Mami separated the stones and cracked *frijoles* with her left hand, leaving her right hand free to slide the whole beans across the linoleum countertop into the pot wedged between the counter and her stomach. She responded without breaking the hypnotic rhythm of her movement. "Who told you that?" As she looked down at me, I merely stared in reply. She waved her hand in the air as if to swipe away the question, but not before adding, "That's just an old wives' tale. You know, a story that was passed around *los ranchos*."

About that time my father, who had walked in through the back door, interjected. "You mean the ranches."

My mother turned and threw him a sideways look. "That's what I said. It doesn't really happen, not anymore."

I was thirteen when I picked out my grandfather's coffin. The Big Grandma had insisted. After a lengthy conversation in Spanish between the funeral director, my parents, and the Big Grandma, which I could understand only in part, my father tried to explain my grandmother's reasoning for the unusual request. In the end he could only say, "Because the Big Grandma says so."

As I wandered through the maze of coffins in Morales's funeral home, I carefully measured out each possibility, one foot in front of the other, the image of broken legs dictating the precision of my steps. I set my hopes on a mahogany casket with a forest green satin interior and brass handles, but it was short by one foot. The only one long enough in my sophisticated system of measurement was a dull blue, the color of disappointment, with a white taffeta lining. There were other coffins I know my father would have preferred I pick, though this was the only one to measure out six feet, four inches, exactly one inch taller than the Big Grandpa. My father looked disapprovingly at my grandmother, hoping to sway her in his direction. She did not budge.

No one was surprised when the Big Grandma asked Old Man Morales if his funeral home was in the habit of burying bodies *sin las cajas*. When I asked Mami about it later, she told me that in the old days it was believed that if someone did not stay to watch the gravediggers cover the coffin completely with earth, they would release a trap door on the bottom of the coffin, which each had, allowing the body to fall into the ground. The gravediggers would then bury the body and reuse the coffin. By selling the same caskets over and over again, the funeral homes could make much more money and the poor grieving families were never the wiser—which did not make sense considering so many people in my family knew about the practice. Only later did I understand why the Big Grandma stayed at the gravesite until her husband was buried deep in the earth of the Texas he loved more than his birthplace, Saltillo, Mexico.

Less than a week later, I sat half-dozing in Señora Jones's Spanish class. The lullaby droning of the murmuring voices seemed endless. Some of my fellow classmates were mumbling as they shuffled flash cards with vocabulary words, while others were taking turns quizzing each other in preparation for their time outside with the señora, the overly enthusiastic teacher who insisted we pronounce her last name "HO-niss" and had hardly spoken one word of English since the semester began. I never liked her, Señora Jones. On the first day of class as she had called roll, she had stopped a few times to utter phrases in Spanish to all the students with Latino-sounding surnames. When she got to my name, she rattled off a few phrases that I knew were questions by the way her voice raised at the end. I had sat there, stone faced and stiff tongued. Instead of moving on, she asked me again. When I did not respond a second time, she turned to the DeLeon twins, said something to them in Spanish, and then the three of them began to laugh.

Every once in a while during the oral exams, I overheard snippets of the conversations coming from the hallway, where the señora was posing questions over the parts of the body. Her voice, hollow and flat, felt far away. "¿Dónde está su nariz? Ah, muy bien. ¿Qué es la palabra por 'arm'? Dígame en español."

After about five minutes, a student would walk in looking relieved and sit down on the other side of the classroom. The rest of the class nervously waited for their names to be shouted from the hallway—everyone except me. I had purposely not studied for the test the night before because I was sure my parents would make me attend my grandfather's funeral. They had not. Still, I was not worried because my last name begins with a *P* and Señora HO-niss never reached the second half of the alphabet on the first day.

I folded my arms on the desk and lay down my head as "¿Qué es la palabra en inglés por piernas?" drifted into the class. At that moment Brent Owens stretched far back in his chair in front of mine, yawning the reply, "Legs. The answer is legs." I raised my head toward the sound of his voice, only to find that his outstretched arm, unusually brown, smelled warm like the earth. I suddenly thought about the Big Grandpa and realized that I had already started to forget how old he was when Pancho Villa rode into town. I could not remember how many hats he had and which ones went with which suits. I calmed myself by thinking, "I'll ask him the next time I see him. He won't mind that I can't remember."

My *familia* has lived in Tejas for more than five generations, but we have a tendency to wander. We get restless, imagining some great adventure awaiting us in Oklahoma, California, Nebraska, Alabama, Colorado, Germany, Japan, Iraq, or Saudi Arabia. So we go and see, staying months or years, long enough to prove that we have broken free of something, or found something that could not be had in Angleton, Beeville, Houston, Lockhart, Cuero, Yorktown, Ronge. Maybe it is the strain of an accordion through a broken speaker in a Mexican restaurant in Springfield, Illinois, where the salsa is from a jar, or the smell of fire splitting wood and releasing its smoky sweet perfume, or a burnt orange University of Texas Longhorns hat on a cab driver in Athens who repeatedly says "Hook 'em," UT's slogan, into the rearview mirror through a broad toothy grin, or a space shuttle above a cowboy riding high in his saddle on a license plate along the interstate. Some of us are unprepared for the rawness of a longing made manifest by happenstance. Others are forced to confront a purposely disregarded truth. At first, we may ignore the ache, though eventually we either plead or negotiate with it. In either case the outcome is the same. We pack our bags and head for the Lone Star on the horizon.

CONCLUSION

FATHERS AND FUTURITY

> We have to forge a future and a new identity, and that's not going to look like the past. We have to form a Latino identity that's looking toward the future. It's going to look very different than it has in the past.
>   Benjamin Alire Sáenz, "Benjamin Alire Sáenz"

Beginning as far back as *Bordertown* (1935), diasporic Mexican fathers in mainstream films have gone from absence to presence (as part of a unified family or as a single parent) and then back into absence, and so on, in a cycle that has continued for almost ninety years. Identifying where we are in the sequence at present depends on where we look. Films such as *Suicide Squad, Logan,* and *Terminator: Dark Fate* promote absence through the erasure of the violent father. These films, set in a fictional future, suggest that Brown fatherhood and futurity are incompatible. Even the nuanced offering of Latinx fatherhood found in the *Mandalorian* series intimates that the best thing Mando can do for Grogu is turn him over to a white Jedi. One could argue that as westerns, thinly veiled or otherwise, these films doom Brown fatherhood; it cannot exist in a genre that determines diasporic Mexican male characters in such a way as to uphold, not participate in, the status quo. These same films also offer up their violence and other forms of emotional excess as evidence as to why Brown men make bad fathers and therefore *should* be absent.

When fathers are present, even if the narrative is not about them, they often occupy considerable visual space or otherwise command attention, either physically or emotionally. In other words, they are characterized by an abundance of Brown feeling. From Alberto in *A Walk in the Clouds* and Ernesto in *Quinceañera* to Che in *La Mission* and Chato in *Suicide Squad*, fathers yell, rage, strut, and emote. "Feeling" Brown, as José Esteban Muñoz indicates, means to "navigate the material world on a different emotional register" ("Feeling Brown" 70). The excess helps to make them legible as outside of whiteness. Nowhere is the depiction of this excess more pronounced than in the animated feature films that include diasporic Mexican fathers: Eduardo Pérez in *Despicable Me 2* (2013), directed by Pierre Coffin and Chris Renaud; Carlos Sanchez in *The Book of Life* (2014), directed by Jorge R. Gutiérrez; and Héctor Rivera in *Coco* (2017), directed by Lee Unkrich and Adrian Molina.

The fathers in these mainstream films exhibit affective displays that heighten their racial difference and that demonstrate that their primary passion—for villainy, bullfighting, and mariachi, respectively—is responsible for the main source of conflict in their children's lives. Of the animated fathers present in these films, antagonist Eduardo Pérez (Benjamin Bratt) in *Despicable Me 2* (2013) embodies such an exemplary form of masculinity that it cannot be contained. Eduardo is an exaggerated visual representation of "the hot and spicy, over-the-top subjects who simply do not know when to quit" (Muñoz, "Feeling Brown" 70). As the owner of the Mexican restaurant Salsa & Salsa, he not only sells spicy deliciousness, he *is* spicy deliciousness. Outfitted in tight black pants, Cuban-heeled black dance shoes, and a red silk button-down shirt, complete with a gold chain that accentuates his hairy chest, Eduardo is a fat, balding man with a comb-over and a sleek Vandyke.[1] His sexual allure is so great that as he salsas across the dance floor, three women onlookers seated at a nearby table faint from his overwhelming seductive power. The desire of his son, Antonio (Moises Arias), to emulate his father results in a secondary conflict with the former super villain Gru. In *The Book of Life* Carlos Sanchez (Hector Elizondo), a renowned bullfighter, poses the greatest threat to his son, Manolo (Diego Luna), and Manolo's dreams of becoming a musician and singer. As the surviving patriarch of a family of bullfighters (including his mother), who is known for his killer instinct and ferocity in the ring, Carlos expects his son to participate in the family tradition. Carlos's *traje de luces*, the traditional bullfighting costume, which he wears proudly throughout the film, is a signifier of both his occupation and his masculinity, extending beyond the ring and into the everyday. Héctor Rivera (Gael García Bernal), father to the titular character in the movie *Coco*, is the only absent father in the three films. Héctor's objective is to return from the Land of the Dead to see his daughter, Coco, who believes he abandoned her for a career in music. Héctor crosses paths with his grandson, Miguel (Anthony González), who is searching for his musical idol, Ernesto de la Cruz (Benjamin Bratt), the man he believes to be his grandfather but who unbeknownst to the boy is responsible for his actual grandfather's (Hector's) death.

Notably, Eduardo and Carlos are single fathers to only children, sons Antonio and Manolo, respectively, whereas Héctor, at the time of his death, was married but also had an only child, Coco. However, the constitution of their families does not determine their success as fathers, and all exert considerable influence over their children. As an emerging Latin lover, Antonio performs the role notably, wooing and abandoning Margo (Amanda Cosgrove), Gru's oldest daughter; and Manolo repudiates hypermasculinity, one that is dependent on killing, to become a figure whose bravery comes from his devotion to friends, family, and music. By challenging narrow conceptions of Mexican masculinity, Manolo shows his father and audiences that the Sanchez family motto, "No retreat, no surrender," is about courage of conviction instead of Mexican masculine bravado. Coco, when of advanced age and suffering from dementia, still awaits her father's return. His perceived abandonment to pursue a career as a singer causes the surviving matriarch to ban all forms of music from the family, thereby creating the circumstances for Miguel's quest to find his grandfather. In the end, Coco and Miguel are the ones who save Héctor from "final death" and restore his place on the family altar.

Family is at the center of each of these films. *Despicable Me 2* continues the story of Gru and his daughters, Margo, Edith, and Agnes. Where *Despicable Me* (2010) is about the making of an unlikely family, the sequel focuses on the solidification of that family, to which Eduardo poses a direct threat. As the owner of the Salsa & Salsa restaurant, Eduardo announces himself on-screen and in the narrative with a "¡Buenos días!" A mariachi trumpet sounding out a few bars reminiscent of "La Virgen de Macarena," a traditional bullfighting song, underscores his arrival. Later in the same scene, he rips open his shirt to expose the Mexican flag tattooed across his chest and seductively makes his muscles undulate so that the flag appears to wave. His effect on white women is unmistakable. As a Latin lover, a type that, according to Charles Ramírez Berg, combines "eroticism, exoticism, tenderness tinged with violence and danger, all adding up to the romantic promise that, sexually, things could very well get out of control," Eduardo wields unbridled sexual power while pretending to exhibit restraint (*Latino Images* 76). When he closes his shirt or spins white women away from him and back to their husbands, he releases them from his thrall, alleviating the threat of miscegenation.

Conversely, Eduardo's evil alter ego, El Macho, is both a caricature and the embodiment of Mexican hypermasculine villainy. After Gru meets Eduardo, he concludes that Eduardo resembles El Macho, an unbelievably manly criminal he knew twenty years before and whose story Gru recounts. The narrated sequence takes place in a bar called El Bandido, signifying both the location and the familiar Latino trope, and begins with heavy percussion as a voice calls out, "¡El Macho!" Every visual aspect and character trait is meant to underscore his macho-ness. Seated at the bar, El Macho drinks a bottle of La Venganza del Escorpión, which has a skull-and-crossbones poison warning on the back. He breaks the bottle over his head, then prepares to chase that drink with a shot of rattlesnake venom from a snake he produces from beneath the bar. The shot glass begins to smoke and he picks it up and throws the whole thing into his mouth, chewing up the glass. Gru recalls, "He was ruthless. He was dangerous. And as the name implies, very macho." The drums and trumpet swell, as El Macho exits the bar by walking out through a wall instead of using the door. While the first portion of Gru's recollection establishes El Macho at the apex of masculinity, the second half secures his place as a bandido: he steps out into the street, stops an armored car with his body, and carries it away on his back. "He had a reputation for pulling off heists," according to Gru, "using only his bare hands." Gru then laments, "But ah, sadly, like all the greats, El Macho was gone too soon." His disappearance adds to the allure of his legacy.

Excess permeates the scene to elevate El Macho's masculinity to stratospheric levels. The tale concludes with Gru's recounting the most macho death of the most macho man in the most macho way possible: "riding on the back of a shark with 250 pounds of dynamite strapped to his chest into the mouth of an active volcano." Before doing so, El Macho is shown pulling the pins on the grenades he holds in each hand. The layering of phallic symbols is visually impressive, underscoring the manly nature of his exemplary masculinity. His depiction corresponds almost exactly to Américo Paredes's description of machismo: "the outrageous boast, a distinct phallic symbolism, the identification of the man with the male animal, and the ambivalence toward women," the latter of which is evinced in the portrayal of Eduardo (*Folklore* 215). The scene culminates with a metaphorical image of coitus, El Macho riding the bomb-laden shark into the volcano and both erupting in an on-screen explosion. Gru concludes the story by stating, "They never found his body. Only a pile of singed chest hair." Eduardo is indeed El Macho, who in the end, along with his pet chicken, Pollito (the perfect companion for his El Gallo personality), proves to be a formidable opponent. Gru successfully contains and neutralizes El Macho's Mexican hypermasculine excess, which was a danger to both Gru's family and the world.

Eduardo, nay, El Macho, is not Gru's only adversary. Eduardo's son, Antonio, serves as a secondary antagonist to the father of three, whose oldest daughter, Margo, becomes enamored with the junior Latin lover.

At the mall, Margo spots Antonio, a good-looking pre-teen bad boy in a leather jacket with cute hair, through the jutting fountains and against the backdrop of the Fit to be Bride shop, whose windows are shaped like hearts. Together these not-so-subtle details symbolize love at first sight, heteronormativity, arousal, and marriage. Ironically, Margo loses sight of him through the pulsating water. As she turns in circles searching for the mysterious stranger, she backs up against the fountain. Just as she is about to fall in, Antonio catches her with one arm. Gru later finds the couple in a corner of Salsa & Salsa and learns that Eduardo is Antonio's father. Eduardo is supportive of the couple, stating, "Young love is beautiful," and suggests that Antonio invite his "girlfriend" Margo and her family to their Cinco de Mayo party, at which point mariachis start to play and Antonio begins to dance around Margo. He then takes the tween girl by the hand and pulls her into his dance, twirling and dipping Margo in moves similar to those his father showed off earlier. Gru ultimately succeeds in neutralizing Antonio by literally shooting him with a freeze ray, but not before the boy causes Margo heartache. Gru's defeat of both father and son secures the safety of his white nuclear family.

Whereas Eduardo is largely indulgent of Antonio's aspiration to do nothing other than play video games professionally and woo girls, Carlos Sanchez in *The Book of Life* is of a singular mindset—that Manolo become not only a bullfighter but also the greatest Sanchez who ever lived. The film, set in the town of San Angel, Mexico, focuses on the relationships among and between Joaquin Mondragon (Channing Tatum), Maria Posada (Zoe Saldana), and Manolo, a trio of friends since childhood who are at the center of a wager between La Muerta (Kate del Castillo), ruler of the Land of the Remembered, and Xibalba (Ron Perlman), who presides over the Land of the Forgotten. Joaquin, whom Xibalba gifts with invincibility, is full of strength, bravado, and pride. His stand-and-fight attitude is in the service of becoming a hero, like his dead father. On the other hand, Manolo, outfitted in a *traje de luces* like his father, simply wants to play his guitar and become a musician. Carlos looks down on Manolo's musical talent and interests, seeing them as having no value, a point underscored by the fact that the town musicians are depicted as buffoons, illustrating another of Ramírez Berg's filmic types. Carlos's machismo and strength have made him a successful matador (which literally means "killer"). Square jawed and outfitted in a bright green *traje de luces* heavily adorned with gold appliqué and with two swords slung across his back, Carlos, as reflected in his sartorial excess, takes great pride in his family tradition. He also wants Manolo to uphold it, including killing a bull, an act that Manolo refuses to do because of a moral principle he shares with the animal lover Maria.

Manolo is being pushed toward the brutality of his family's traditional occupation when what he really wants is to pursue the creative expression of a musician, an aspiration supported by the woman he has loved since they were both children. At his first public bullfight, Manolo performs magnificently but refuses to "finish the bull." This pleases Maria, who has only recently returned from Spain, where she spent the remainder of her childhood after being sent away by her father when she was only a child. Before leaving, she had gifted Manolo with a guitar with the inscription "Always play from the heart." Playing music has allowed him to maintain his connection to Maria in her absence. Manolo emerges as a figure distinct from the Latino types that surround him: El Chacal, the town villain, is the bandido, exactly as Ramírez Berg describes the type—toothless, dirty, violent, dim-witted, and speaking in broken English (68); Joaquin, made arrogant by his invincibility, is the Latin lover (like Eduardo) who has a powerful effect on all the women of the town—except Maria; and as mentioned previously, the musicians are the buffoons. Manolo, however, does not easily fit into one of the three types. He rejects both his father's imperative to kill bulls for sport and Joaquin's need for violent conflict. Instead, the musician enacts a masculinity that is tender and full of thoughtful regard for others.

The Book of Life positions Joaquin, voiced by white actor Channing Tatum, as the film's hero, so when Manolo emerges as the film's true hero, the move is somewhat surprising. Illustrated through figures such as a pistol-packing rooster, talking Chihuahuas, and a fleet-footed mouse, animated Mexican male characters are rarely given the narrative development necessary to become anything more than cinematic Don Juans, sidekicks, or comic relief.[2] Manolo's decision to face his "greatest fear" makes the narrative's resolution possible. However, first Manolo must travel to the underworld and fight and kill not one bull, but every bull the Sanchez family has killed in its bull-fighting history, stretching back generations, to prove his commitment to the family tradition. The bulls, in a manifestation of bovine excess, merge into one mighty beast that looms over Manolo. Rather than take up his sword in an attempt to finish the monster, he pulls the guitar off his back. The young bullfighter does not defeat the colossus with brute strength or through violence. Instead, he does so with an *en serio*, an emotional song of apology, for all the violence and suffering his family has inflicted on bull-kind; only then does he succeed in vanquishing the beast. Carlos, who has joined the rest of the family in the Land of the Remembered after dying in an attack on the town, amazed by what Manolo has done, apologizes to his son for not being a better father. Manolo's actual greatest fear is then revealed as "not being himself." He returns to the town in time to save it, along with Maria and Joaquin, and in the process, through teamwork and selflessness, Manolo refashions conceptions of manhood and masculinity.

Fatherhood and affective excess appear the most subdued in *Coco*, of these three movies. Although Miguel's father, identified only as Papá (Jaime Camil), appears in the film, his role is to uphold his mother's authority and support the continuation of her family's shoemaking business while his mother, Abuelita, is the one who performs emotional excess through her vehement prohibition or mention of music. Because Héctor's wife and Coco's mother, Imelda (Alanna Ubach), believed that Héctor had abandoned his family, she refused to place a photo of him on the family's altar, a tradition passed down for generations. This means Héctor cannot return to the land of the living on the Día de Muertos. He spends decades trying to find a way back to his daughter and is thwarted at every turn until he crosses paths with Miguel, who agrees to take Héctor's picture back to the family altar. In the final confrontation with de la Cruz, who killed Héctor, stole his songs, and became famous, Miguel loses what is believed to be the only surviving photo of his grandfather. Miguel returns to the land of the living without it, even though it means for Héctor almost certain final death, from which there is no return. Reunited with his family in the land of the living, Miguel sings Coco the song her father used to sing to her when she was a girl, which miraculously brings her out of her dementia. Now lucid, she reveals that she secretly kept a photo of her father. Through her devotion, his place on the altar is restored. Flash forward to a year later and viewers find out that Héctor and Coco are reunited in death. The living and the dead join in on the Día de Muertos celebration, bringing together generations of *la familia*.

Embedded in this feel-good *familia* romance is a border crossing that should give audiences pause. To travel between the realm of the living and the Land of the Dead, *muertos* must pass through a border checkpoint and have their identities verified by a visual scanner to ensure that someone has placed a photo of them in remembrance on an altar. The narrative conceit is that all dutiful Mexican families have pictures of loved ones on display or, alternately, that those who are worth remembering have been photographed, both of which are materialist and classist. For those who have no such physical objects, their deceased loved ones are doomed to a final death. Reunifications also present other kinds of problems in *Coco*. Héctor has been trying for years to find a way across the border. His most recent effort involves attempting to sneak across disguised as Frida Kahlo, and when that fails, he makes a run for the bridge, is apprehended by border guards, and is dragged away. His prolonged separation from his daughter causes him great pain, and he refuses to abandon the effort to see Coco. The film reinforces the idea that even in death there are right and wrong ways for Mexicans to traverse the border. And without proper documentation, they might remain permanently separated from their families—in this life and the next.

All three films emphasize the importance of familial relationships, particularly those between fathers and their children. But all do so by relying on familiar themes and visual tropes—Latin lover, bandido, buffoon, macho, Aztexts (e.g., architecture, iconography, and gods), and Día de Muertos, to name only a few.[3] The stories that mainstream films tell about Brown families stick to established racial and perceived cultural scripts with little to no variation. Just before the titular character of *Logan* dies, he tells Laura, "Don't be what they made you." But popular films do not appear interested in making Brown characters outside of a narrow range of possibilities, all involving affective excess in some form. So while Laura may be a *mutante* and a future X-Men (*maybe*), her very existence makes her an outlaw. She is a lab-manufactured bandida—a killer who must learn to suppress her instincts toward violence and rage if she wants to change or be something more than an instrument that reinforces the superiority of the status quo.

Still, change is complicated. People are often open to the idea yet opposed to the practice. Others attempt to effect change and are met with obstacles, sometimes people or ideologies, advancing only in fits and starts. Gloria Anzaldúa's slow work illustrates the difficulties of change, to think beyond and through old ideas and toward something new. And there is slow, slower, too slow, and not slow at all. Depictions of Brown families, and of Latinx characters more broadly, have changed very little, in the whole of film history. Still, film is not the only medium that clings to particular kinds of or limited narratives about Brown fathers. Whether through Chicanismo, Indigeneity, or the concept of "El Rey" and other racialized masculinist scripts, the Mexican American and Chicanx authors that I include in *Fatherhood in the Borderlands: A Daughter's Slow Approach* demonstrate the power these narratives have on men and their relationships to and with their children, fictional relationships characterized most often by silence, pain, and frustration. Then again, it all depends on where we look.

Young adult fiction seems an unlikely place to find nuanced depictions of fathers, and it is. Most young adult fiction, aimed at readers twelve to eighteen years of age, focuses on protagonists similar to and/or near in age to the reader. Because the emphasis is on preteen and teen characters, parents are often absent, in the background, or obstacles to be overcome. In young adult fiction that features Mexican American, Chicanx, or Latinx protagonists, families and parents often play substantial roles in the narratives, most often with mothers instead of fathers as the parental figures featured, such as those found in Guadalupe Garcia McCall's *Summer of the Mariposas* (2012), Meg Medina's *Yaqui Delgado Wants to Kick Your Ass* (2013), Gabby Rivera's *Juliet Takes a Breath* (2016), Erika Sánchez's *I Am Not Your Perfect Mexican Daughter* (2017), Elizabeth Acevedo's *The Poet X* (2018), and Jennifer Mathieu's *The Liars of Mariposa Island* (2019), to name a few. Still it is always the exception that proves the rule.

The first time I sat down to read *Aristotle and Dante Discover the Secrets of the Universe* (2012), by Benjamin Alire Sáenz, I did so with the intention of reading a few chapters before heading off to bed. Hours later, I had read the novel straight through. In the early morning hours, as my family slept, I was full of many feelings and had no one with whom to discuss them. The novel was unlike any I had read, combining love stories with historical fiction and speculative futurism rooted in the real. It broke my heart and lifted me up. The Mexican American fathers and sons were complicated and diverse. So many things unspoken for so long, regarding the past, emotions, queerness, and mental health issues, that unfold slowly in the novel help establish a caring environment for the coming out of two teenage boys—Aristotle Mendoza and Dante Quintana—who experience violent homophobia, self-loathing, and alienation.

A quick search online told me, based solely on the fan art, that I was not alone in my feelings about the book. Set in 1987, the novel, which takes place in El Paso, Texas, focuses on the titular deuteragonists, who become friends and eventually fall in love with each other, though neither initially is out as queer. The novel highlights the diversity within Mexican American families and communities. For example, Aristotle, who goes by Ari, depicted as dark-skinned and bilingual, feels a growing anger and isolation, particularly about his parents' silence around his brother, Bernardo, who is in prison. Dante, on the other hand, "is *güero*, fair skinned. He doesn't speak Spanish" (Sáenz, "Benjamin" 212). Dante's lighthearted and easy manner further distinguishes him from Ari, who is quick tempered and often uses his fists to settle conflicts. But both boys love and respect their parents, even if they do not always understand them.

The Mexican American teens and their families at the center of the novel are ones not often represented in literature, or film for that matter, as Frederick Aldama notes in his interview with Sáenz. Because families play such a significant role in Aristotle's and Dante's lives, Sáenz knew he wanted to depart from previous depictions: "I did not want to give them the cliché Mexican American family, where the women are making tortillas. I didn't want the novel to perform a rarefied ethnicity. I wanted them growing up in urban communities" (Sáenz, "Benjamin" 211). Additionally, rather than the teens coming from working-poor backgrounds, each comes from a different class, a detail that was also important to Sáenz: "Ari's mom's a schoolteacher, and his dad's a mailman. He fought in the Vietnam War, and he's suffering from PTSD. Dante's dad is a professor, who teaches poetry.... His mother's a therapist. I wanted them to mirror a class that we don't see much of in Latino literature" (212). Despite their class difference, both families, and especially the fathers, are supportive of the boys before and after their coming out as queer.

The fathers' responses to their sons' queer identities defy convention in that neither explodes with rage, as Che does in *La Mission*, or alienates his child in a manner similar to Walter's in *Quinceañera*. Both Sam Quintano and Mr. Mendoza offer their sons acceptance and unconditional love. By doing so, according to Angel Daniel Matos, each father "disrupts patriarchal stereotypes by catalyzing and nurturing, rather than suppressing, his son's queerness" (45). Prior to coming out, Dante worries about telling his parents, his father in particular because he fears his disappointment. When Ari does not acknowledge his feelings for Dante, Mr. Mendoza, conversely, puts his son's feelings into words for him: "All of your instincts, Ari, all of them tell me something. You love that boy. . . . I think you love him more than you can bear" (*Aristotle and Dante* 349). The moment is heart-wrenching and problematic. Critics such as Amanda Haertling Thein and Kate E. Kedley argue that in naming his son's feelings, Mr. Mendoza prevents Ari from coming out on his own terms.[4] Yet Mr. and Mrs. Mendoza create for Ari a "holding environment," what William Kahn identifies as a place of security where people can work through their feelings, uncertainties, or anxieties.[5] Such a space allows Ari to act from a place of agency, where he can embody and eventually act on his feelings for Dante. It is important to note that Ari comes to a realization of his own about Dante, one that he expresses openly: "From the minute I'd met Dante, I had fallen in love with him. I just didn't let myself know it, think it, feel it. My father was right" (*Aristotle and Dante* 358–359). The holding environment helps Ari to feel safe so that he can proceed in a way that is best for him. However, the scene of acceptance is entirely unexpected, not necessarily within the novel but certainly within Chicanx literature more broadly. Mr. Mendoza's attempt to help his son put feelings into words is worth noting because too often these scenes end in violence and tragedy.

Through an "affective model reliant on love, support, and connection," the Mendozas and the Quintanas offer the family as a safe space for their queer sons (Matos 50). In doing so, the novel frames "*la familia* not as a force that drives queer characters away from the parameters of the home, but rather as a force of kinship and affinity that is capable of catalyzing and sustaining queer life" (48). One might imagine that Tío Tomas in *Quinceañera* wanted to provide such an environment for Carlos so that he could feel valued inside rather than outside of his home. *Aristotle and Dante* imagines a world where Brown families and fathers nurture and care for their queer sons, a world where Brown fathers love their sons more than they fear the ignorance and bigotry of others. In this way, as Matos states, the novel "is ultimately a narrative of a future past: a story fixated on a past that has not necessarily occurred, but on a past that could only achieve representation in a not-so-distant future" (52). And in that future Aristotle and Dante discover their love for each other, their love for their families, and other secrets of the universe.

I may not know the secrets of the universe, though I have made a number of discoveries about myself in the process of writing this book. Resisting the impulse to become knowledge laborers is difficult, especially when everything around us is telling us to speed up and go faster or get left behind. But "slow does not always mean slow," a statement that makes me think of Ralph Waldo Emerson and his idea of solitude, which one can keep even in the midst of a crowd (Honoré 15). In other words, slow is not about pace; instead it involves maintaining a set of practices even in situations that require timeliness. Carl Honoré in his book *In Praise of Slowness: Challenging the Cult of Speed* (2004), which is usually at the center of discussions about going slow, distinguishes between going fast and going slow: "Fast is busy, controlling, aggressive, hurried, analytical, stressed, superficial, impatient, active, quantity-over-quality. Slow is the opposite: calm, careful, receptive, still, intuitive, unhurried, patient, reflective, quality-over-quantity. It is about making real and meaningful connections—with people, culture, work, food, everything" (14–15). Completing this project has been a combination of both—stressful, yes, but also reflective, intuitive, still, and more than a little impatient.

The process and practice of writing has highlighted for me the different ways I already go slow in my life and my approach to work. For example, I have learned I am a foot dragger. I do this as a way to slow down making a decision or completing a task, to give myself additional time to think. The insight is valuable. It also tells me that I often feel like I cannot openly express myself, so I have devised other ways to create the conditions to get what I am unwilling to ask for. I also appreciate the slow intricacies of writing, of jotting down initial thoughts on napkins or scraps of paper and then typing them out followed by the adding of layer upon layer. And I also never met an endnote I did not love or that could not be a sentence or two longer. But in truth, endnotes are a writer's way to ask the reader to slow down, to stop briefly and participate in an aside or share a thought. Writing, even (especially?) academic writing, is a way to connect with ourselves and others. The Great Lakes Feminist Geography Collective reminds us: "Writing is a fundamental mark we make in the world as academics and should reflect values inherent in the life of the mind: rigor, engagement, nuance, critique, making a difference" (1252). The genre-bending knowledge production represented in and through this book encapsulates those values, while also creating additional knowledge about myself.

What I have discovered in the slow process of writing this book is that I am a storyteller and use research to tell a particular kind of story. This may not seem particularly insightful, though for me it is. I learned that the forms of expression I have allowed myself to use when crafting my research into a story have been limited. In an effort to meet the expectations of the academy and replicate acceptable (read: legible) forms of knowledge production, I have "been both oppressed and, in failing to resist," actively participated in my "own oppression," which in turn reinforces "institutional ideologies, values and practices we seek to critique and overturn" (Karkov 8). These forms constitute what Christopher González identifies in a different context as "narrative permissibility" (*Permissible Narratives* 2). Availing myself of various narrative techniques and forms has allowed me to convey confidently the process behind my thinking alongside the thinking itself. Personal reflection has been fundamental to these practices. Through my slow research, I have sought to close the illusory gap between subjective and objective thinking by consciously turning inward. By first understanding my own relationship to and investment in the intellectual project of the book, I was able to identify the stakes of the work and deepen my connection to it, making the writing and thinking more fulfilling. Parker J. Palmer reminds us that "we can reclaim our belief in the power of inwardness to transform our work and our lives" (20). But that turn inward also helped me to see what is yet missing from stories about fathers and fatherhood in the Mexican diaspora.

I am still searching for familiar Brown fathers on-screen and in the pages of books. I believe that fathers and futurity can coexist. I have seen outlines of it in the quotidian scenes throughout my life. The Brown fathers I knew gathered around the fire pit on Easter and the 4th of July. The Brown fathers I knew, and the imagined others, had an infectious laughter that ran through a room like electricity, wore boots with dress suits, smelled of Aramis cologne and peppermint, tickled their children's toes and tucked them into bed at night, never raised their voices, taught their foster children how to bake, coached their daughters' softball teams, twirled in princess costumes alongside their children in the front yard, spat from the gap between their front teeth, never missed a volleyball game, marched in the Pride parade, ironed their own shirts, used their children's correct pronouns, loved video games and rom-coms, drove us to breakfast in the early morning hours, had scratchy beards, showed us how to pitch a tent, and picked at the callouses that formed from holding the drafting pencil too tightly. So many Brown fathers whose lives, in all their multiplicities, are yet to be told.

The last movie my father and I saw together was Ridley Scott's *Black Rain* (1989). As we stood outside the fourplex, where we had seen *Raiders of the Lost Ark* (1981), *Blade Runner* (1982), *Dune* (1984), and countless others, the connection we had withered. Our familiar practice of dissecting the film into minute details to reassemble it again into an interpretation of our own making was abandoned for awkward small talk and an uncomfortable embrace and what would be a final goodbye.

PARTING SHOT

The moment comes too quickly. My son, standing outside of the dorms at Kenyon College, casually waving good-bye. For the next two weeks he will work on his novel and I will worry without him. Driving away, I see him as he once was so many summers ago. We are running hand in hand, my son and I. His laughter makes it difficult for him to keep up, so I attempt to shorten my stride. As we make our way down the long corridor, the world has simultaneously sped up and slowed down. I imagine how we must look, mother and child in an all-out sprint, blankets and comfort bears in tow, frantically searching the marquees above their heads as they go, participating in a scavenger hunt of their own making. At the far end of the hall, I spot what we are looking for. I try to jostle the blanket draped across my left arm to catch a glimpse of my watch. Judging from what I can see, we are not going to make it. Without breaking my stride, I bend down and scoop him up into my arms, causing his glee to bubble over in wheezy giggles. His arms tighten around my neck. In front of the heavy double doors at the end of the hall, I stop, pivot, and maneuver one free finger around the green oversized handle, giving it a firm yank. Locked in an embrace, we step into the darkness. A wall of digital sound greets us. We make our way down the hallway with its oversized angles toward the glow of the screen, then up the aisle to the first open seats available. My son bounces joyfully into his seat as we watch the opening of the movie that we finished seeing only minutes before at the other end of the cineplex. In this moment, my elation feels too big for this three-hundred-seat theatre, for I am fortunate enough to realize that I have just experienced one of the best moments of my life, not one that was planned, dreamed about, or worked toward, but one born simply of my child's wonder. That summer we would go on to see the film more than twenty times, and though by the end I practically knew the dialogue by heart, I would have seen it thirty, fifty times more, simply to watch him watch the film as if he were seeing it for the first time, every time. Such is the power of stories.

ACKNOWLEDGMENTS

When I was an undergraduate and I had a deadline looming, I would often pull an all-nighter. On these occasions, my mom would sleep on the couch in the living room while I worked at the kitchen table. Her presence on those long nights was her way of offering support in the only way she knew how. She never abandoned the practice, not even after my student days were long behind me. Since her passing in 2017, I miss her terribly, especially her exuberance for all my accomplishments and her quiet (though at times rousing) support. During COVID-19, while working from home, out of necessity, I set up an office in her old bedroom. I worked to complete this book in her former space. At times, late at night or in the early morning, I could feel her watching over and urging me on. Thank you, Mami, for always staying close.

    I want to thank Charlotte Canning, referred to in this book as my writing buddy, for reaching out, reading through multiple drafts of countless chapters and sections, and holding space for me and my work. I know this project would not have been jump-started without her help. Some of my favorite Saturdays were spent tussling about footnotes or laughing about my penchant for going down rabbit holes and wanting to pull the reader in with me. I am immensely grateful for our writing community of two.

    My sincerest thanks to Barbara Williamson, Cakes Stafford, Regina Marie Mills, and Rachel González-Martin for being my refuge, both intellectually and emotionally. I know that you will always answer my calls, respond to texts, and offer your support, whether from far away or in person. Your friendship and love keep me grounded to the things and people who matter most.

    As this book illustrates, knowledge production often does not happen in isolation, at least not for me. A number of people have helped me on the long journey to the realization of this book: Lydia CdeBaca, Kirby Brown, Sheela Jane Menon, Colleen Eils, and most recently, Brice Ezell, whose keen eye for detail proved invaluable. Each in her or his own way helped me think through this project. I am also indebted to Nicole Guidotti-Hernández for reading, what feels like several lifetimes ago, early drafts of what this project would eventually become.

And to all the people who stood by me during one of the most difficult periods of my professional life (and you know who you are), thank you. Your support and unwavering belief in me saw me through the worst of it and out the other side. In the words of Maya Angelou, "When someone shows you who they are, believe them the first time." This was a most difficult lesson, and I am the wiser for it.

I am so incredibly fortunate to have the support of the University of Texas Press. Ten years ago, Theresa May believed in the strength of my original proposal. Kerry Webb stuck with me and the project year after year, incarnation after incarnation. And Christopher González and Arturo J. Aldama were thoughtful, generous, and careful readers of the manuscript. I am pleased that they saw what I was attempting to achieve in both form and content.

I value the support of the University of Texas at Austin, namely, through the College Research Fellowship from the College of Liberal Arts and the Provost's Authors Fellowship from the Office of the Executive Vice President and Provost. I am especially thankful for my faculty fellows Tracie Matysik, Nassos Papalexandrou, Eric McDaniel, Akbar Hyder, and Luisa Nardini. Our monthly "therapy" meetings were an essential source of energy for me. I would also like to thank Martin Kevorkian for his fierce protection of my writing time and always having my back professionally. I appreciate Lisa Olstein's willingness to be a true ally and/or mentor, always on standby and at the ready for monster slaying. And without the Janky Slide Rules, the Zoom portions of this pandemic would have been intolerable.

My original analysis of Gloria E. Anzaldúa's concept of "new tribalism" appeared in "New Tribalism and Chicana/o Indigeneity in the Work of Gloria Anzaldúa," included in *The Oxford Handbook of Indigenous American Literature*, edited by James H. Cox and Daniel Heath Justice (Oxford University Press, 2014). I wish to extend my thanks to the editors and to Oxford for their vision in imagining (and bringing to fruition) this critical collection.

Earlier considerations of *The Magnificent Seven* (1960) and *Suicide Squad* (2016) are featured in my "Magnificence and Metas in Professional Westerns," in *Weird Westerns: Race, Gender, Genre*, edited by Kerry Fine, Michael K. Johnson, Rebecca M. Lush, and Sara L. Spurgeon (University of Nebraska Press, 2020). I include here parts of my original analysis of both films in a more developed form.

Portions of the chapter on *In Search of Snow* first appeared in "Of Myth and Men: Racialized Masculinities in Luis Alberto Urrea's *In

Search of Snow," featured in *Chiricú Journal*, vol. 3, no. 2, 2019. My thanks to Lee Bebout, who served as the special editor for the issue, and to Indiana University Press for its permission to include here a heavily revised and reimagined version of my original article.

Finally, and most importantly, I would like to thank James and Ewan for helping me to celebrate all victories, large and small. You are my home. Together we are enough, and that is everything.

NOTES

PREFACE. THE SLOW LOWDOWN

1. Members of Generation X (b. 1965–1980), wedged between the Baby Boomers (b. 1946–1964) and the Millennials (b. 1981–1996), were raised with minimal supervision and are often characterized by their resilience. The term comes from Douglas Coupland's novel *Generation X: Tales for an Accelerated Culture* (1991). According to the Pew Research Center, Gen Xers "were born during a period when Americans were having fewer children than in later decades" (Fry). As children, Gen Xers, along with their families, confronted "countless new movements and trends—feminism, sexual freedom, a divorce epidemic, fewer G-rated movies, child-raising handbooks telling parents to 'consider yourself' ahead of a child's needs, gay rights, Chappaquiddick, film nudity, a Zero Population Growth ethic, *Kramer vs. Kramer,* and *Roe v. Wade*," not to mention an HIV/AIDS epidemic (Howe and Strauss 123). Though Howe and Strauss's discussion is arguably skewed toward firmly middle-class families and above, it is noteworthy that they give equal weight to film alongside social and cultural movements, indicating the genre's generational impact on families.
2. The ABC Afterschool Special was a limited-anthology television series that ran from 1972 to 1997. The series was known for addressing timely, often controversial issues directly involving adolescents. Well-known actors, some very early in their careers, starred in a number of these films, including, for example, Jodie Foster in *Alexander* (1973), *Rookie of the Year* (1973), and *The Secret Life of T. K. Dearing* (1975); Rosanna Arquette in *Mom and Dad Can't Hear Me* (1978); Rob Lowe in *Schoolboy Father* (1980) and *A Matter of Time* (1981); River Phoenix and Joaquin Phoenix in *Backwards: The Riddle of Dyslexia* (1984); Viggo Mortensen in *High School Narc* (1985); Michelle Pfeiffer and Val Kilmer in *One Too Many* (1985); and Ben Affleck in *Wanted: The Perfect Guy* (1986) (Woolery).
3. For historicity and ideological context, I use the terms "Chicano," "Chicana," or "Chicanx" in keeping with usage by author, character, and/or time period.
4. In 1965, *Reader's Digest* published the article "Oak Island's Mysterious 'Money Pit,'" by David MacDonald, which has served as a touchstone for so many of us who would follow the hunt over the years. The Fox Mulder part of me "want[s] to believe" even though I suspect the Oak Island treasure either does not exist or was recovered ages ago by Samuel Ball, a formerly enslaved cabbage farmer who died an incredibly wealthy man. The mystery holds a special place for me because while reading the article, I learned about footnotes and what could be found in them—informational breadcrumbs that can lead to other opinions, sources, and research.
5. The design firm LEED Gold oversaw the award-winning remodel and expansion of the library, which was featured in *Architect: The Journal of the American Institute of Architects* ("Oak Forest Library").

INTRODUCTION. A SLOW APPROACH TO FATHERS AND OTHER FICTIONS

1. The photo was taken by award-winning photographer John Moore in McAllen, Texas, on 12 June 2018 as Sandra Sanchez, Yanela's mother, was being searched by Border Patrol agents.
2. Yanela's picture was used to tell a story that paradoxically was and was not true. The policy and its ongoing effects, ranging from trauma to death, are indisputably verifiable. However, Yanela and her mother were *not* separated at the border, and two weeks later, both were sent back to Honduras. The fact of the latter does not take away the truth from the former. *Vox* unpacked in detail the controversy surrounding Yanela's image and her story (Kirby).
3. The photo was taken by Kim Kyung-Hoon and circulated widely through various media outlets. See Gabe Gutierrez and Corky Siemaszko, "Photographer Reveals Story Behind Iconic Image of Fleeing Migrants at Mexico Border," in which Kim details how he captured the now iconic photo.
4. My use of "Brown" throughout this book aligns with that of José Esteban Muñoz, who expresses dissatisfaction with "Latina/o/@" and other "adjacent" designations: "Brownness is vast, present, and vital. It is the ontopoetic state not only of people who live in the United States under the sign of latinidad, but of a majority of those who exist, strive, and flourish within the vast trajectory of multiple and intersecting regimes of colonial violence" (*Sense of Brown* 120, 122).
5. In an interview, philosopher Isabelle Stengers, author of *Another Science Is Possible: A Manifesto for Slow Science* (2018), makes a distinction between a researcher and a scholar: "The idea that we learn to become a researcher, and not a 'scholar,' comes from the laboratory sciences, but today this has redefined everything else" (Stengers, "Care" 12). The result is the encroachment of publication and production standards based in the sciences into other academic fields and areas.
6. By "neoliberalism," I mean a free market approach, along with its inherently competitive structure, which has invaded our personal and professional lives.
7. The health (mental and physical) impact of knowledge labor in the academy, as the GLFGC points out, has disproportionately affected Black women: "*The Feminist Wire* (2012) reminds us that the academy has been deadly for legendary Black women like Audre Lorde, June Jordan, Barbara Christian, and Toni Cade Bambara" (1246).
8. A BIPOC colleague of mine filed a complaint about the sexism and gender discrimination she experienced. At the intake, the equity and inclusion representative told her that people of color cannot discriminate or harass other people of color and that clearly this was a cultural misunderstanding. The representative was also a person of color.
9. Derived from an anti-Mexican joke, Speedy Gonzales, "the Warner Bros. cartoon mouse[,] debuted in 1953 and immediately became a hit on both sides of the U.S.-Mexico border" (Arellano). Slowpoke Rodriguez appeared six years later (1959) in the Warner Bros. short "Mexicali Schmoes."
10. To date, *The Phantom Empire* remains one of two books that I have ever thrown across a room in frustration and/or disgust. The other was William Faulkner's *Absalom, Absalom!* (1936).
11. Mixed-genre or genre-bending works by Chicanx and Latinx authors include Sandra Cisneros, *The House on Mango Street* (1983); Cherríe Moraga, *Loving*

in the War Years: Lo Que Nunca Pasó por Sus Labios (1983); Ana Castillo, *The Mixquiahuala Letters* (1986); Roberta Fernández, *Intaglio: A Novel in Six Stories* (1990); Demetria Martínez, *Mother Tongue* (1990); Cristina García, *Dreaming in Cuban* (1992); Julia Alvarez, *In the Time of the Butterflies* (1994); Norma Elia Cantú, *Canícula: Snapshots of a Girlhood en la Frontera* (1995); Sheila Ortíz Taylor and Sandra Ortíz Taylor, *Imaginary Parents* (1996); Pat Mora, *House of Houses* († 1997); and Nina Marie Martínez, *¡Caramba! A Tale Told in Turns of the Card* (2004), to name but a few.

12. A Black man who was serving a life term for murder in Massachusetts, Horton was released on 6 June 1986 through a state weekend furlough program and did not return to prison. The following year, Horton "raped a white Maryland woman and bound and stabbed her boyfriend. Bush's campaign and supporters cited the case as evidence that his Democratic opponent, Gov. Michael S. Dukakis of Massachusetts, was insufficiently tough on crime" (Baker). While the ad was made by Republican campaign supporters, Bush, himself, did not hesitate to mention Horton and his actions as a failure on the part of Dukakis, who became known as "soft on crime."

13. In March 2017, Judge Curiel approved a $25 million settlement case against Trump University: "The settlement applies to three separate lawsuits—two class-actions and a fraud case. The $25 million deal includes payouts to more than 6,000 Trump U students who paid thousands of dollars for courses they describe as worthless" (Domonoske). Curiel later supported the Trump administration's border-wall project by making a favorable ruling against legal challenges to the wall that involved "environment waivers granted by the Department of Homeland Security" (Thomsen).

14. On 13–17 February 2021, winter storm Uri hit Texas with subfreezing temperatures, snow, and ice that placed a severe strain on the state's power grid as Texans tried to keep warm. Hundreds of thousands of residents across the state went without power and water for days or weeks. Many have taken to referring to the disaster within a disaster as Snovid-21. Online entrepreneurs began selling T-shirts that announce "I SURVIVED SNOVID-21."

15. In "*Bordertown*, the Assimilation Narrative, and the Chicano Social Problem Film," Ramírez Berg identifies the absent father as one of eight characteristics of the Chicano social-problem film.

16. Fregoso defines the *familia* romance as "an epic composed of memory traces triggered by familiar historical tropes and desires" in "The Chicano Familia Romance," chapter 4 of her *meXicana Encounters: The Making of Social Identities on the Borderlands* (2003; p. 71), which offers a detailed critique of *familia* romances, focusing on the intersection of patriarchy and nationalism.

17. I am incredibly grateful to Frederick Aldama for sharing with me an early copy of *Decolonizing Latinx Masculinities*. It has shaped and continues to shape my thinking about fatherhood and masculinity.

18. "That's why I struggled so hard to get here." All translations are mine unless otherwise noted.

19. President James Monroe, in an address to Congress on 2 December 1823, offered the "United States' policy on the new political order developing in the rest of the Americas and the role of Europe in the Western Hemisphere." Briefly outlined, "[t]he three main concepts of the [Monroe Doctrine]—separate spheres of influence for the Americas and Europe, non-colonization, and non-

intervention—were designed to signify a clear break between the New World and the autocratic realm of Europe" ("Monroe Doctrine, 1823").
20. In the episode "Chapter 8: Redemption," Din Djarin (aka Mando) recounts his experience with the child (who is of the same species as Jedi Master Yoda but is not actually Yoda) to the Armorer of their secret society, and "the Armorer declared Grogu to be a foundling. As such, Djarin was from then on seen as Grogu's father, until he could train him or otherwise return him to his kind. The Armorer declared Djarin and Grogu to be a clan of two" ("Grogu").
21. For example, prior to the release of *Star Wars: Episode I—The Phantom Menace* (1999), audiences took note of certain racialized stereotypes in the movie trailers among the different species, most notably Jar Jar Binks, a member of the Gungan Tribe who has been likened to the notoriously racist minstrel caricature Stepin Fetchit, performed by Lincoln Theodore Monroe Andrew Perry, most popularly in the late 1920s to mid-1930s. Additionally, "Nute Gunray, the evil Viceroy of the Federation, seems based on Asian stereotypes. And Watto, young slave Anakin Skywalker's sleazy owner, strikes some viewers as an offensive caricature of an Arab. In addition, the Gungan Tribe . . . is ruled by a fat, buffoonish character, seemingly a caricature of a stereotypical African chieftain" (Harrison).

PART I. SOURCING AUTHORITY

1. A guinea refers to a unit of currency that equals one pound and one shilling. According to Theodore Dalrymple, retired physician, author, and senior fellow at the Manhattan Institute, "Even in Woolf's day, no guinea coin or guinea banknote actually existed. It was purely a notional unit, used for transactions of superior social status, such as the purchase of art at auction, the payment of surgeons, or, as in [*Three Guineas*], the giving of charitable contributions."
2. Relatively few women had access to Woolf's level of privilege, and many women outside of her immediate circle may have disagreed with her point of view. One literary critic, who did not align herself with feminist ideologies or practices, took issue with the limited scope of Woolf's advocacy. Q. D. Leavis, in her scathing review of the essays in *Three Guineas*, cited a number of the works' shortcomings, focusing on three main areas: class, gender, and experiential knowledge. Most, if not all, of Leavis's negative appraisal originates in objections to Woolf's class privilege. Leavis sees Woolf as "quite insulated by class" and critiques the author for equating "propertied people" with "the educated class" (203).
3. Upon closer reflection, Leavis's and Woolf's ideas about structural transformation are more similar than the former would have readers believe: both make crucial points about women, education, and access. Leavis's explicit concerns about class and the problems with critiquing men exclusively make Woolf's argument richer. Rather than see these points of intersection or the relationality of their individual concerns, Leavis proves Woolf's point about women taking on the "pugnacious," or in this case, the pugilistic, approaches of men by beating down what she perceives as an oppositional perspective.
4. One appeal made for a donation from Woolf was to help prevent war and protect culture; how to avoid war is a thread that runs through the collection.
5. In *The Idea of the Modern in Literature and the Arts* (1968), Irving Howe identifies nine characteristics of modernism, one of which includes the idea of aban-

doning the aesthetic order (such as form). Woolf's stream-of-consciousness style of narration in her fiction represents its own innovation within literary modernism.

6. "One could say," Stengers observes, "that the research career was designed for men, and even specifically for men who benefit from the support of women at home—bringing up children, taking care of practical matters, allowing them to do all-nighters at the laboratory and go off on numerous training workshops or on the kind of overseas trips expected in a research career" (*Another Science* 25).

7. Woolf advocated in behalf of "qualified" white and Black women, without acknowledging barriers to educational or professional access based on race: "You shall swear that you will do all in your power to insist than any woman who enters any profession shall in no way hinder any other human being, whether man or woman, white or black, provided that he or she is qualified to enter that profession, from entering it" (66). Alice Walker, in *In Search of Our Mothers' Gardens: Womanist Prose* (1983), makes a similar critique of Woolf's "A Room of One's Own."

FILM: *ANCIANOS* NOT *ABUELOS*

1. My college uses this transactional term, "down payments," to describe a form of labor assurance that faculty will continue to produce as knowledge workers beyond tenure (or promotion).
2. Folklorist Américo Paredes refers to the Mexican diaspora on both sides of the US-Mexico border as "Greater Mexico" (*Texas Mexican* xiv).
3. Ramírez Berg identifies the status quo in film as being "the best of all worlds ... one that is safe, peaceful, and prosperous. But it is also one that is white, upper-middle-class, Protestant, English-speaking, one that conforms to Anglo norms of beauty, health, intelligence, and so forth" (67).
4. See Chon A. Noriega, ed., *Chicanos and Film: Representation and Resistance*; Gary D. Keller, *Hispanics and United States Film: An Overview and Handbook* and *A Biographical Handbook of Hispanics and United States Film*; and Christine List, *Chicano Images: Refiguring Ethnicity in Mainstream Film*.
5. Ramírez Berg offers the following as examples of the ways in which stereotypes of Latinxs have been circumvented or subverted: "studio-made films that went against the stereotyping grain, stars who managed to portray Latinos with integrity despite a filmmaking system heavily reliant on stereotyping, and more recently, a growing number of Latino filmmakers who began consciously breaking with the stereotyping paradigm of classical Hollywood" (66).
6. According to film scholar Allen Woll, beginning in the silent film era, the Mexican (singular because there was only one variant) constituted the "most vile of the screen's villains. He robbed, murdered, pillaged, raped, cheated, gambled, lied and displayed virtually every vice that could be shown on the screen. This image flowered in a series of 'greaser" films, such as 'Tony the Greaser' (1911), 'Bronco Billy and the Greaser' (1914), and 'The Greaser's Revenge' (1914)."
7. For example, in one of the most memorable scenes from *Giant*, an old Mexican man enters Sarge's Place with his family. After Sarge refuses them service, the Brown man, with a pained, almost apologetic look on his face, "holds out to Sarge a wad of dollar bills proving his ability to pay ... [and] his worth" (Pérez-Torres, "Chicano Ethnicity"). Incapable of securing one of the most basic needs for his family, the Mexican man can only watch as Jordan "Bick" Benedict (Rock

Hudson), an Anglo with a Mexican American daughter-in-law, champions the elder man's cause by using physical violence to challenge Sarge's authority.

8. The film, referred to as *My Family* or *My Family/Mi familia*, stars Chicanx and Latinx mainstays, including Edward James Olmos, Jimmy Smits, Esai Morales, Jennifer Lopez, Constance Marie, Jenny Gago, and the inestimable film treasure Lupe Ontiveros, whose scene-stealing performance in the 1980s classic *The Goonies* (1985) remains memorable to this day. Though given very little to work with as a Spanish-speaking maid in *The Goonies*, Ontiveros's character saves the families from being evicted from their homes on the "Goondocks" and is, thus, the unsung heroine of the film.

9. Nava believed that "actors raised in such houses" could bring authenticity to his film (Britt). While insisting that Latinx actors be cast in Latinx roles does not appear radical today, two years before the release of *My Family*, white actors Winona Ryder, Glenn Close, and Jeremy Irons starred as Chileans in *The House of the Spirits* (1993), based on the novel by Isabel Allende, and two years later, Marisa Tomei and Anjelica Huston were cast as Cubans in *The Perez Family* (1995).

10. The film's budget was $5.5 million; its total domestic gross (it did not receive worldwide release) was approximately $11 million. Released 3 May 1995, in its first week the film ranked sixth behind *French Kiss*, *While You Were Sleeping*, *Friday*, *Bad Boys*, and *Panther* ("Weekend Domestic"). The last three films focused on and featured Black characters.

11. For Coppola, *The Godfather* was a family chronicle that "envisioned the Corleone family" as "a symbol of America" (Benshoff and Griffin 86). Italians, who were outside the category of white Anglo-Saxon Protestants, were historically racialized, so Coppola's film writes the Corleones into the nationalist idea about family while also highlighting how they resort to extralegal means to achieve the American Dream. With Coppola as *My Family*'s executive producer, his name and association with the project serves as a tacit endorsement of the film, inviting comparisons between it and the family drama *The Godfather*. The fact that both films open with a large family wedding furthers this comparison. Both focus on ethnically and racially diverse multigenerational families, disrupting the privileging of and narrative emphasis on the cinematic status quo.

12. Romantic or idealized images of *la familia* are not exclusive to film. They are found in other cultural productions such as visual art and served as the central image of Chicano nationalism from the 1960s through the 1980s. See Richard T. Rodríguez, *Next of Kin: The Family in Chicano/a Cultural Politics* (2009).

13. Here, Mirandé means Chicano researchers and their analyses, which he later cites. Mirandé also provides the following overview of previous sociological studies that condemn Mexican American families: "In comparison to the Anglo-American family, the Mexican-American family is perceived as a tangle of pathology for many social scientists. It propagates the subordination of women, impedes individual achievement, engenders passivity and dependence, stifles normal personality development, and on occasion can even give rise to incestuous feelings among siblings" (749).

14. Mirandé explicitly acknowledges the diversity of Mexican American families: "Just as there is no one uniform Anglo-American family, there is no one Chicano family but a number of family types that vary according to region, recentness of

migration to the United States, education, social class, age, and urban-rural locale" (751).
15. Fregoso identifies the defense of *la familia* as a central mission of Chicano cultural politics and chronicles the rise of more affirming views that were meant to counter the "culture of poverty" and other negative assessments offered by the social sciences (*meXicana Encounters* 81). These efforts, as put forth by Mirandé and others, emphasized structure over agency: "Yet, informed as it was by this logic or reversal, by the transformation of the negative into the positive, the new orthodoxy of structuralism set into motion an equally myopic logic of valorization: an uncritical celebration of the Chicano familia with a singular focus on only the 'positive' aspects of culture" (*meXicana Encounters* 84).
16. The film is narrated by Paco (Edward James Olmos), whose "voice-over narration," as Carmen Huaco-Nuzum asserts, "sets the patriarchal tone of the film" (265).
17. Todd McCarthy of *Variety* called it "corny but good-hearted," and he, too, cited the "ambitious" nature of the film and its director. Roger Ebert also positively reviewed the film, declaring, "Few movies like this get made because few filmmakers have the ambition to open their arms wide and embrace so much life." The need, in all three instances, including James's review, to cite the ambitious nature of the film and its filmmaker may speak simply to the management of a broad range of characters and the epic narrative; on the other hand, it can also be seen as condescending, as if Nava, in telling the lives of Latinx characters and taking up so much film to do so, has "overreached."
18. Rodríguez's critique of *My Family* focuses on its "advocacy of a heteropatriarchal vision of *la familia* that aims to appease authoritarian ideologies coded as American" (16).
19. *My Family* never states explicitly how José and El Californio are related, but the two have kin in common. El Californio becomes a father figure to José and later a grandfather figure to his children. When the old man dies, he leaves his house and property to José. He also leaves specific instructions indicating that he wanted to be buried in the backyard because he did not want anything to do with the "pinche Church or the pinche government." Pérez remarks that "El Californio's rejection of anything having to do with the Church and state and his lack of heterosexual indicators make him a quintessential queer character," adding "it suffices to say that he does not engage in heteronormative practices and, therefore, he is queer" (99–100).
20. An *abuelo* is not the same as the folkloric figure "el abuelo," also known as "el coco" or "el cucuy," the US/Mexico transnational bogeyman who threatens to whip or spirit away naughty children. According to Rafaela G. Castro, el abuelo is "more known in northern New Mexico than in other parts of the Southwest. He appeared at Christmastime to test and discipline children who did not know their catechism or prayers. He was a scary figure, dressed to terrify children with a black cape and a mask with large horns, and always carrying a whip." The whip signifies his authority as a disciplinarian and when taken together with the horns and cape makes him a horrific figure (R. Castro 1).
21. Each appeared in the wake of *My Family*, which was expected to usher in a new wave of Latinx-themed films. Similar expectations arose a decade earlier following the release of Luis Valdez's biopic *La Bamba* (1987), about the 1950s Los

Angeles teenage rocker Ritchie Valens, which grossed more than $54 million. Released during the latter part of the 1980s, toward the end of what the film industry dubbed "the Decade of the Hispanic," *La Bamba*, along with *Born in East L.A.* (1987), *The Milagro Beanfield War* (1988), and *Stand and Deliver* (1988), represented a focused effort on the part of studios to appeal to Spanish-speaking audiences. The latter three films together did not gross as much as Valdez's *La Bamba*, so studios' attention to and investments in Latinx-themed projects and audiences waned. The three movies grossed, respectively, $17.3 million, $13.8 million, and $13.9 million, for a total of $45 million (*"Born in East L.A."*; *"Milagro Beanfield War"*; *"Stand and Deliver"*). A few years later, Nava's modest hit ushered in a second wave of mainstream Latinx-themed projects that helped to pave the way for generations of Latinx actors and directors, such as Benjamin Bratt, Alfonso Cuarón, Benicio del Toro, Guillermo del Toro, Salma Hayek, Alejandro González Iñárritu, Oscar Isaac, Jennifer Lopez, Michael Peña, Michelle Rodriguez, Robert Rodriguez, and Zoe Saldana, among others.

22. Magical Negro characters, such as John Coffey (Michael Clark Duncan) in *The Green Mile* (1999) and God (Morgan Freeman) in *Bruce Almighty* (2003), are nurturers or self-sacrificing teachers, who help to perpetuate Anglo superiority in popular film. Earlier portrayals of magical Negro characters include Aunt Delilah (Louise Beavers) in *Imitation of Life* (1934) and Noah Cullen (Sidney Poitier) in *The Defiant Ones* (1958). Delilah suddenly appears in Bea's life, and her pancake recipe makes them both rich. While Bea's socioeconomic status improves, Delilah wants nothing more than to continue to serve her white boss, so she refuses her percentage of the profits from the business. Noah is a convict who escapes with the white man to whom he is chained, Joker Johnson, after a bus crash. In spite of the fact that Joker is a racist, when the two men face being captured, Noah sacrifices his freedom so Joker can escape. For additional films that include magical Negroes and further discussion of the issue, see Kempley and Okorafor-Mbachu.

23. The term "magical Negro" includes all BIPOC people, and it emphasizes sameness at the expense of the distinct colonial histories of individual ethnic groups, setting aside the way mainstream Hollywood productions regularly limit Black and Latinx characters through certain roles—bandido, homeboy, drug addict, terrorist, etc.—to perpetuate mythologies about Anglo heroic exploits.

24. Later Victoria complains to her mother and grandmother, "He wants me to marry some man in Mexico I have never even met just because he has the right bloodline. I'm not a horse, Mama. It's my choice, not his." Her refusal to be treated as chattel, in addition to her graduate education, is meant to establish her as a proto-feminist.

25. When first learning of Victoria's marriage to Paul Sutton, Pete responds, "Victoria Sutton, I like the sound of it." In other words, he approves of her marriage to an Anglo and, as his *anciano* demonstrates, is wise to do so.

26. "Please sit down" because "Ana has something she wants to tell you."

27. "From this day forward, everything will be different."

28. "Nothing will be different."

PERSONAL NARRATIVE: "NO, I AM YOUR FATHER"

1. According to *Cinema Houston*, when it opened the Alabama was only the "tenth theatre in the Houston area." The others included "the Metropolitan, Majes-

tic, Kirby, Delman, Eastwood, North Main, Tower, Bluebonnet, and the Yale" (Welling).
2. True "event films," roadshow features were meant to replicate the look and feel of live theatre. Premiering in big cities (such as New York, Chicago, and Los Angeles), these films involved advance tickets sales, usually at higher prices, reserved seating, and a souvenir program. Martin B. Hart of the American Wide-Screen Museum identifies the following distinct features of roadshows: they have a musical overture, followed by part one of the feature, end of part one, intermission, entre acte music, part two of the feature, and, finally, walk-out music (Hart).
3. Born in Dallas, Texas, Bill Paxton would later be featured in such blockbuster films as *Aliens* (1988), *Tombstone* (1993), *Twister* (1996), and *Titanic* (1997). Generationally, he is perhaps best known for his *Aliens* role, in which, as Private Hudson, he delivers the memorable lines "We're all gonna die, man!" and "That's it, man. Game over, man. Game over!" In 2012, Trader Joe's took over the site of the old theatre. The owners of the property, Weingarten's Reality, restored the original towering sign, which still remains, to its former grandeur before renting the space to Trader Joe's. Many of the building's exterior details stayed intact, but the only interior remnants of the Alabama are the yellow spirals inside the entrance, a small portion of the balcony, and the ceiling medallions, including the central, illuminated one that frames the auditorium on the top and sides. Faux movie posters, such as ones for "The Cod Father" and "Planet of the Grapes," are a commercial nod to the building's history.
4. "Luke, I am your father" is incorrect but has become iconic. Mark Hamill, who played Luke, revealed in 2020 that when the company was shooting the film, Vader said a different line: "The cast & crew first learned of it when they saw the finished film. When we shot it, Vader's line was 'You don't know the truth, Obi-Wan killed your father.' Only Irvin Kershner, George Lucas & I knew what would be dubbed in later. Agony keeping that secret for over a year [before the film's release]!" (Hamill). The line was dubbed in the final cut to reveal the true relationship between Vader and Luke.
5. Before I headed off to college, my father offered me three pieces of advice: (1) Always park under a light at night; (2) Always carry your keys in your hand; and (3) No matter what, don't become an English major. Two years later at our kitchen table, I looked him in the eye and told him my truth in direct defiance of no. 3. He stormed away from the table without saying a word. Later that night, he told my mom he was "proud" about how I handled myself and the situation, even if he did not agree. The path he thought was a "bad idea" has now become my profession.

LITERATURE: FATHERS AND RACIALIZED MASCULINITIES IN LUIS ALBERTO URREA'S *IN SEARCH OF SNOW*

1. Lee Bebout in "Troubling White Benevolence: Four Takes on a Scene from *Giant*" (2011) makes a case that Turk and by extension Mike could be Mexican (32). While I think this is true for Mike, as I will later argue, I do not think it is necessarily the case for Turk.
2. The Apache man's surname is the same as one of the seven dwarfs who shelter Snow White in the fairy tale. Although the narrative provides no explanation for the origin of his name, more than one joke is made about Sneezy and the dwarfs.

However, the association between Sneezy and whiteness is explicit in both the fairy tale and Delbert's relationship with Turk.

3. My article "Of Myth and Men: Racialized Masculinities in Luis Alberto Urrea's *In Search of Snow*," which serves as the basis for this chapter, includes an analysis of the McGurk father-son relationship. In his nonfiction, Urrea has written about his relationship with his own father, including an account of his death in *Across the Wire*, which details traveling to collect his father's body in Mexico. Regarding the latter, Urrea states that the metafictional account in "Father Returns from the Mountain" represents "the only fiction . . . that is utterly true" (*Six Kinds of Sky* 143).

4. Although Mexican male masculinity is a frequent theme or issue addressed in Urrea's writings, the short stories "Taped to the Sky" and "Bid Farewell to Her Many Horses," in his *Six Kinds of Sky: A Collection of Short Fiction* (2002), directly engage with intersectional masculinities, namely, white and American Indian, and the influence of popular culture forms on ethnic or racial identity.

5. Leah Sneider, in "Complementary Relationships: A Review of Indigenous Gender Studies," "trace[s] the conversation in Indigenous gender studies regarding complementarity—as social balance and the responsibility and power to act—as a means to understanding the ways in which Indigenous gender studies as scholarly and practical modes also depend on complementarity" (62–63). The chapter brings into conversation a number of threads regarding ongoing scholarship in Indigenous gender studies.

6. Connie McGurk dies of consumption when Mike is seven years old. The circumstances surrounding her death allow for the possibility that she left Turk under the guise of illness because Mike has a distinct memory from when he was a boy of "the night [Turk] punched his wife" (*In Search of Snow* 24). The likelihood of her having fled from an abusive marriage is underscored when Turk tells Mike, "You're not the only abandoned pup in the desert . . ." (89).

7. The narrator states that "when Carroll's drinking finally burned its way through his esophagus, killing him in a geyser of blood that emptied him in a minute flat, Mr. Sneezy had delivered Turk to the train station to ride home alone. Turk was ten" (32). The two appear to have reconnected after Turk bought the gas station in Arizona.

8. Turk uses the term to describe Walt Whitman and a professor who stops at the gas station (47, 20). The disparagement of education represents a vein of anti-intellectualism that Turk harbors.

9. For example, later in this same dialogue, Mike narrates an incident in which he claims to have been involved that mirrors the Bick Benedict and Sarge scene in *Giant*. As Mike explains, after he went into a diner one time, "these Mexicans came in and [the owner] threw 'em out. And I said something about it, and the next thing I knew, we were at it" (174).

10. Mike's observation conflates three different Chicanx types: zoot-suiter, "greaser," and pachuco, each of which, in the white imaginary, is associated with violence.

11. In his essay "Pachucos and the Taxicab Brigade," José Antonio Burciaga offers a number of origins for the pachuco, citing the work of Cary McWilliams, Jorge Acevedo, and Octavio Paz. However the figure emerged, in Burciaga's view, "[t]he pachuco has enjoyed a cultural aura, complete with a stylistic pathos. He was both a tragic and heroic figure—a mythical creation" (*Spilling the Beans* 63). The zoot suit often worn by pachucos served as a focal point for racial vio-

lence perpetuated against young Chicanxs by white servicemen in 1943. The attacks escalated into what became known popularly, though inaccurately, as "the Zoot Suit Riots," for "it was not Mexican American youths who rioted but the military" (63).
12. Bobo's name calls to mind the Lone Ranger's companion Tonto, whose name in Spanish means "stupid" or "foolish." Both Bobo and Tonto demonstrate repeatedly that they are much smarter than the men they eventually accompany.
13. Bobo's experiences bear a striking resemblance to those Urrea documents in "Whores."
14. The theme is particularly prevalent, along with the negotiation of his own cultural hybridity, in *Nobody's Son* (1998).
15. *The Adventures of Kit Carson*, featuring Bill Williams in the titular role and Don Williams in brownface as El Toro, centered on the frontier scout and his trusty sidekick riding to aid those in need. Of additional note, Carson rode a horse called Apache. The show glossed over Carson's history as a federal Indian agent and known Indian killer. *The Cisco Kid* starred Romanian actor Duncan Renaldo in brownface as the lead and the self-identified Spanish actor Lee Carillo as Pancho, his trusty companion. The series about the Mexican hero was part of a larger storytelling universe that included radio shows, films, and comic books that reinforced, on the surface, ideas about the power relations between Anglos, or rather white cowboy heroes, and their ethnic sidekicks.
16. Horn facilitated and participated in the deaths of Mexicans and Indians throughout his career, but he was hanged in Cheyenne, Wyoming, for killing a fourteen-year-old white boy, Willie Nickell, in Colorado.
17. Before committing an act of violence, Ramses "offered his actions to the ancestors, to the grandfathers—except Grandfather Sneezy, who had beat him up, then gone to Disneyland" (240).
18. Delbert's trip to Disneyland inspires Mike and Bobo to visit the theme park, and Delbert agrees to return with them. His initial visit, therefore, is reminiscent of a scouting trip of westward territory. Before departing on their trip together, Delbert tells Mike, "You're the leader. We're your soldiers" (254). Replicating his service to Carroll McGurk, Delbert places himself in Mike's service. I have never understood this turn in the novel, but it does confirm my earlier theory about Delbert's choosing white (presenting) men over other Apaches.

PART II. INSTRUMENTALIZING INDIGENEITY

1. Rutger Hauer famously rewrote portions of Roy's elegy to better reflect the character's sentiments about his own passing: "I've seen things you people wouldn't believe. Attack ships on fire off the shoulder of Orion. I watched C-beams glitter in the dark near the Tannhäuser Gate. All those moments will be lost in time, like tears in rain. Time to die." Hauer's invented Tannhäuser Gate was also mentioned in the Kurt Russell film *Soldier* (1998), a film considered *Blade Runner*-adjacent, meaning existing in the same universe.
2. The opening crawl of *Blade Runner* does not clearly delineate between robot and human: "Early in the 21st Century, THE TYRELL CORPORATION advanced Robot Evolution into the NEXUS phase—a being virtually identical to a human—known as a *Replicant*." In *Blade Runner 2049* (2017), directed by Denis Villeneuve, the opening inter-title sequence makes clear that Replicants are "bio-engineered humans." Despite their presentation as white, the Replicants

are coded, through their labor, their lack of rights, and the criminality of their existence on Earth (i.e., they are "illegal immigrants"), similarly to historically enslaved laborers.

3. The lack of empathy is the only means of distinguishing Replicants from their non-engineered counterparts. Replicants are outlawed on Earth because of their involvement in a bloody uprising on an off-world colony. Punishment for their presence on Earth is "retirement," a euphemism Blade Runners and other police use for execution.

4. I recognize that humans are considered biological machines by scientists.

5. Berg and Seeber use a similar example in their advocacy for going to the library as a means for academics to slow down, as opposed to relying on sources available or found exclusively through online searches.

6. Here, I am referring to those colleagues who either opt out of service because they have some real or perceived privilege or do not have to pay a cultural or racial tax in the form of service.

7. This ability often unsettles friends and colleagues, who say with some frequency, "I can't believe you remember that story."

8. In an interview with Inés Hernández-Ávila, Gloria Anzaldúa cites two conferences where Native women leveled accusations of cultural and spiritual appropriation on the part of Chicanas: the Violence against Women of Color conferences in Santa Cruz in 2000 and in Chicago in 2002 (Anzaldúa, "Quincentennial").

9. Olmos was instrumental in the development of Gaff as a character, including his style of dress, blue eyes, and the literalization of his City-Speak language—a patois of "Spanish, French, Chinese, German, Hungarian, and Japanese" (Sammon 115). In the theatrical release and in notes related to the film, Gaff's language is also referred to as "gutter talk," which indicates his racialization and social standing, particularly among the other Blade Runners, who are white.

10. The action of the film begins in the Pyramid of the Sun, when Leon shoots Blade Runner Dave Holden in the Tyrell Corporation headquarters. Batty's murder of Eldon in the Pyramid of the Moon bookends the narrative initiated by Leon's actions and sets up the final confrontation with Deckard.

11. John Morán González, in "Aztlán @ Fifty: Chican@ Literary Studies for the Next Decade" (2010), includes a brief analysis of *Blade Runner*. González sees the film as reflective of "white flight to the off-world colonies," leaving behind "[a] culturally hybrid, biologically mestizo working class . . . to deal with the toxic mess as best it can" (175).

12. The scholarship on American Indian representation is vast. Pauline Turner Strong notes that it "first emerged in the fields of literary and intellectual history, notably with the publication in 1953 of Roy Harvey Pearce's *The Savages of America* (better known under its 1965 title, *Savagism and Civilization: A Study of the Indian and the American Mind*)" (5). Countless books on the subject, such as *The White Man's Indian* (1978), by Robert Berkhofer; *Indians in Unexpected Places* (2004), by Philip Deloria (Dakota); *Tribal Television: Viewing Native People in Sitcoms* (2014) and *Cinematic Comanches:* The Lone Ranger *in the Media Borderlands* (2022), both by Dustin Tahmahkera (Comanche); and Strong's *American Indians and the American Imaginary: Cultural Representation across the Centuries* (2013), to name only a few, document and critically assess depictions of Indians historically in various mass-produced forms.

13. Saldaña-Portillo's transnational study focuses on how Indigenous identities get constituted on both sides of the border. Mexico venerates the Indian at the center of the national imaginary while living tribal communities are subject to all forms of local and state violence, and the US recognizes Indigenous populations through their colonial histories and other documented forms of existence.

PERSONAL NARRATIVE: NOBODY EVER SAID WE WERE AZTECS

1. Despite being a regular part of conquistador iconography, "pumpkin pants," popular during the Elizabethan era, did not come into vogue until the late 1500s and are, therefore, anachronistic for Spaniards in Mexico.
2. "You look like an Indian."
3. I discuss my complicated maternal family dynamics in "A Familial Legacy of MeXicana Style" (2020). To briefly sum up, the people I called my grandparents were actually my great-grandparents. When my mother's mom, Eugenia, died, the three youngest siblings were sent to live with the parents who had disowned her. The four oldest siblings, all boys, were taken to work on the migrant trail with their father, Eduardo. The two groups did not reunite until later in life.

FILM: FATHERHOOD, CHICANISMO, AND THE CULTURAL POLITICS OF HEALING IN *LA MISSION*

1. Bratt's statement is ironic given that he went on to play Jonathan Pangborn in *Doctor Strange* (2016), which is part of the Marvel Cinematic Universe that includes the *Iron Man* films.
2. When Peter Bratt was trying to secure funding for the film, white backers were not interested because "the 'gay thing' had already been done," he says. Conversely, he explains, "when we tried to rally support from within the Latino and Native community, we were sometimes met with resistance, shame, or straight-up hostility. One relative asked me, 'Why do you have to make the son a faggot, can't he be a drug addict instead?'" (P. Bratt). Black and Brown communities are not more or less homophobic than other communities, but in Bratt's view, they do not as openly discuss homosexuality. At screenings, Bratt also notes that among the "*veteranos* and homies coming in huge numbers to see the film . . . some, when they first hear about it, [express] reservations—'Hey, I heard this is about *jotos*.' I've even been confronted with some hostility by some *veteranos*. Then when they see it, they have a whole different take. Like, 'Wow, we need to get this to the barrio and to the prisons'" (B. Bratt et al.).
3. Whenever possible, I draw examples from early work and collected editions (inclusive of literature and culture) on Mexican Americans and Chicanos that inform Che's brand of Chicanismo, which the film critiques: *The Chicano: From Caricature to Self-Portrait* (1971), edited by Edward Simmen; *The Proud Peoples: The Heritage and Culture of Spanish-Speaking Peoples in the United States* (1972), by Harold J. Alford; *Yearnings* (1972), edited by Albert C. Chavez; *Chicanos: Our Background and Our Pride* (1972), by Nephtalí De León; *Songs and Dreams* (1972), edited by Joseph A. Flores; *El espejo—The Mirror: Selected Chicano Literature* (1969), edited by Octavio Ignacio Romano-V. and Herminio Rios C.; *Aztlan: An Anthology of Mexican American Literature* (1972), edited by Luis Valdez and Stan Steiner; *We Are Chicanos: An Anthology of Mexican-American Literature* (1973), edited by Philip D. Ortego; and *Canto y grito mi liberación: The Liberation of a Chicano Mind* (1971), by Ricardo Sánchez.

4. IAT sought ownership of Alcatraz Island for Indian use, basing its claim on the success in similar cases of the Oglala, Miniconjou, and Brulé bands of Lakota people, "whose Fort Laramie Treaty of 1868 granted the tribe surplus federal land." The island had been closed and abandoned by the government because of the high maintenance costs and deteriorating conditions of the prison (Smith and Warrior 10).
5. "The Bay Area Indian Community," according to Paul Chaat Smith and Robert Allen Warrior, "was one of the largest in the nation, and that was no accident." Smith and Warrior cite the fact that the "American government developed programs during the 1950s to move Indian people from reservations to cities, to assimilate them as quickly as possible, and to undermine reservation life" (6). San Francisco, though not an original site of relocation, was included by 1957. It was also home to the United Bay Area Council of American Indian Affairs, Incorporated, aka the United Council, which was made up of "existing social clubs," including "the Navajo Club, the Haskell Alumni, the Haida Tlingit Club, and the Four Winds Club" (9).
6. In the first section of Luis Valdez and Stan Steiner's *Aztlan: An Anthology of Mexican American Literature* (1972), titled "Where Are the Roots of Men? The Origins of Mexico," the editors commingle Aztec, Mayan, and other Mesoamerican beliefs and traditions. In their introduction they do name "Toltecs, Mixtecs, Totonacs, Zapotecs," along with "hundreds of other tribes," though they are ultimately set aside for the Aztecs, who are seen as Chicano "ancestors" (xvii).
7. Jesse reads a picture book to his cousin called *Storm Boy* (1995), which draws from nonspecific Pacific Northwest Native traditions and Haida-inspired art.
8. According to the Kateri shrine website, the first group of Indian nuns in Mexico had prayed for her canonization: "Their prayers were answered on October 21, 2012," when Kateri was canonized ("Kateri's Pathway"). Her shrine is located in Montgomery County, New York.
9. The line is a shout-out to a scene in *Animal House* (1978) where a group of Black men approach a table of white fraternity brothers to request a dance with their dates. The call and response represent a way to express racial difference and brotherhood.
10. Ten Bears shares kinship, if not familial ties, with Che and Jesse. He also has the same name as the Comanche Chief Ten Bears, principal chief of the Yamparika Comanches from 1860 to 1872. A Comanche chief named Ten Bears appears in *The Outlaw Josey Wales* (1976), played by Will Sampson (Creek), and in Michael Blake's novel *Dances with Wolves* (1988) and the 1992 Kevin Costner film by the same name. The Ten Bears in the latter, played by Floyd "Red Crow" Westerman, was Lakota, which is ironic because the historical Ten Bears was orphaned as a child when his family was killed by Lakotas, purportedly.
11. The back of Che's lowrider includes an image that reads "A mother's love never dies." Lena, the neighbor with whom Che has sex and whose body is marked with scars, represents an earth-mother figure, particularly through her Buddhist practices, the goddess imagery that adorns her house, and her work at the women's shelter. Che also includes an image of the goddess Tonantzín (the antecedent of the Virgen de Guadalupe) on the back of the lowrider he builds for Jesse. One could easily argue that women are as instrumentalized in this film as Indigeneity.

12. Denise Michelle Sandoval states in the section of her chapter where she gives an abbreviated history of lowriders, "Low riding as a cultural form is part of an American mode of expression through both its materialist ideology and its classifications of aesthetics. Low riders emerged out of the post–World War II socioeconomic context" (183). Sandoval goes on to discuss the cultural expression as a particularly gendered and racialized form: "As an extension of car culture fascination within the United States, low riding began as an inherently masculine activity. Moreover, the car also began to be tied to a particular cultural identity—an expression of a Mexican American self" (184).
13. Alberto distinguishes between Indigeneity and indigenism: "Culture became the terrain on which the Chicano nation was elaborated and indigenism became the topography of that terrain. Indigeneity, in the form of [Chicano] indigenism and through the logic of nationalism, functioned as succor for Chicanos within a U.S. ethnoracial framework that had enacted a long history of violence against Mexican Americans, including mass deportation, lynching, quotidian racism, land dispossession, language elimination, nativism, and police abuse" (110).
14. Numerous stories recount the tale of Popocatépetl and Ixtaccíhuatl, who are depicted in the painting *La leyenda de los volcanes*. The artist narrator in Sandra Cisneros's short story "Bien Pretty" describes wanting to update the "Prince Popocatépetl/Princess Ixtaccíhuatl volcano myth, that tragic love story metamorphosed from classic to kitsch calendar art, like the ones you get at Carnicería Ximénez or Tortillería la Guadalupanita. Prince Popo, half-naked Indian warrior built like Johnny Weissmuller, crouched in grief beside his sleeping princess Ixtaccíhuatl, buxom as an Indian Jayne Mansfield. And behind them, echoing their silhouettes, their namesake volcanoes" (*Woman Hollering Creek* 144).
15. According to Elisa Diana Huerta, Azteca-Mexica ancestry "remains a dominant narrative within many communities" (6).
16. The mapping of Aztlán, as Saldaña-Portillo notes, "was produced not only through the melancholic and manic representational incorporation of lost indigeneity but also through the figurative incorporation of indigenous territoriality" (*Indian Given* 197).
17. Rodolfo "Corky" Gonzales, in his epic poem *I Am Joaquín* (1967), identifies alongside both the Aztec and Mayan princes "Yaqui/Tarahumara/Chamala" and "Zapotec" Indians, but it is Aztlán and the Aztecs that endure.
18. In Melero's poem "Mi Gente," the narrator tells the reader, "My people were the Bronze-skinned warriors whose courage was beyond compare" (20). De León's "Of Bronze the Sacrifice," which the poet describes as an "epic poem written for an interpretive dance," includes references to the Aztec kingdom and "Bronze warriors," as well as to Aztec gods and mythic figures including Huitzilopochtli, Coatlicue, Tlaloc, Princess Ixta, and Quetzalcóatl ("Of Bronze" 155; 157).
19. In the introduction to their section "Madre," Valdez and Steiner offer the following: "On the hill where Juan Diego, the humble *indio*, saw his vision of La Virgen de Guadalupe, there had been a temple to Tonantzin, the goddess of fertility. The *indios* of Mexico often still call their patron saint Guadalupana-Tonantzin" (265).
20. Latinas in the film occupy roles similar to those found in Gonzales's *I Am Joaquín*, which details the origins of the Chicano nation through a mythopoetic history of the Spanish, Indigenous, and mestizos in Mexico. The poem references three women figures: the Virgen de Guadalupe; Tonantzín; and the black-

shawled woman (a symbol of mourning and devotion). The Virgen de Guadalupe/Tonantzín appears throughout in murals, graffiti, and home altars. By extension, her role as mother is a prominent one for women in *La Mission*, as mentioned in a previous note. The black-shawled mother, an image taken directly from *I Am Joaquín*, attends the street vigil to mourn her son Smoke, Jesse's shooter who himself became the victim of violence.
21. Rene is shown, at one point, reading a copy of the magazine *Biodiesel Smarter*.
22. The Aztec pantheon provides Anzaldúa with inspiration. For example, Coatlicue was a powerful earth mother, a goddess of "birth and death" for the Mexica. She serves as a significant archetype for Anzaldúa, who sees "*Coatlicue* states" as those activities that "disrupt the smooth flow (complacency) of life" but also as "what propel the soul to do its work: make soul, increase consciousness of itself.... The *Coatlicue* state can be a way station or a way of life" (*Borderlands* 46). Similarly, Coyolxauhqui, the moon, whose severed head was thrown into the night sky by her brother and whose body parts were scattered across the land, is a powerful idea and image for Anzaldúa and led to her definition of the Coyolxauhqui imperative as "an ongoing process of making and unmaking" ("Let Us Be the Healing of the Wound" 312).

LITERATURE: NEW TRIBALISM AND CHICANA/O INDIGENEITY IN THE WORK OF GLORIA ANZALDÚA

Author's note: A few years ago, a colleague asked me to visit her graduate class to discuss my research. She suggested that I pick two pieces of my writing that the students would read in advance of my visit. I chose one about film and the other, "New Tribalism and Chicana/o Indigeneity in the Work of Gloria Anzaldúa," focused on literature and theory. In my narrative that preceded our discussion, I mentioned that the chapter had originally appeared in *The Oxford Handbook of Indigenous American Literature* (2014) but was being reprinted in *The Routledge Handbook of Chicana/o Studies* (2019). My colleague turned to me and asked, "How did you pull that off? Satisfying both disciplines is not easy." Part of my academic training was in comparative ethnic literatures with an emphasis on American Indian and Chicanx literatures, so, in my thinking and training, the two have always been in conversation, though not always amicably. But I have always tried to position myself in a place where I could listen critically and learn from both sides. The strength of the chapter, why it found audience in both Indigenous and Chicanx studies, reflects that practice.

The decision to include the chapter in *Fatherhood in the Borderlands* was not an easy one. I was not sure how it fit or what more I could add to my thoughts about the work. But I believe that in the context of this book, the piece takes on a different valence. More than analyzing the unfolding of Anzaldúa's new tribalism as an emerging idea, I also see my work as an inquiry into how she disrupts the heteropatriarchal nationalism in Chicanismo through new tribalism. The concept decenters Chicanos who saw themselves as fathers of a social movement. New tribalism is a way to find identity and community that are not focused on the father, whether biological (a shared genetic contributor), religious (priest), political (the men who positioned themselves at the head of the Chicano civil rights movement), or cultural (e.g., Joaquín Murieta). Anzaldúa's theory of new tribalism represents the slowness of emerging and transformative thought. Her emphasis on transformation, as found in her additional theories, such as the Coatlicue state or *conocimiento*, demonstrates the slow work of thinking from the self toward ways of social and cultural belonging. Throughout her works, Anzaldúa talks openly about the process of her writing, of getting "stuck" when trying to develop an idea, and of revisiting her own work to add a little more here and there. She lays bare both the methods behind and the outcomes of her dynamic knowledge production, though nowhere more powerfully than in her essay titled "Now Let Us Shift . . . the Path of Conocimiento . . . Inner Work, Public Acts." Instead of reproducing my original chapter, I have updated portions, made changes to phrases and word use I did not particularly care for, expanded the conclusion, and most significantly, embedded a contrapuntal discussion of the various imaginings and instantiations of tribalism as a way to demonstrate how Anzaldúa's new tribalism shares similar objectives to those found in popular and mainstream culture.

1. In the early part of *Survivor*'s history, the "tribal" names assigned to the four competing groups were meant to reflect the culture in geographic proximity to the exotic locale that served as the setting for each season's "castaway" experience. Aspects of Indigenous cultures, such as history and food, were woven into the shows, but this practice was abandoned. In light of the show's history, however, the current meaning of "tribe" as used on the show most readily reflects a temporary and contrived home group. The only shared experiences of the group are in the competition against other tribes for resources, such as food, fire, or comfort items like showers, and protection from elimination. As such, participants must transcend their "tribes" or home groups to "win" the game. The show represents an artificial journey from civilization into primitivism and back out again, where the "survivor," whose life was never in actual jeopardy, is rewarded with a million-dollar cash prize. But the real prize, and one that also serves as definitive evidence of successfully casting off the tribal identity, is celebrity—the ultimate expression of individuality.
2. The show drew widespread criticism for this format, and that same season, major advertisers, including General Motors, Procter & Gamble, Coca-Cola, Home Depot, United Parcel Service, and Campbell's Soup, withdrew their spots from the show. However, GM insisted the main reason was "cost effectiveness" rather than the show's decision to include a race-based format (Wyatt and Elliot).
3. Four Hispanics, one African American, and one Asian were voted off in the first six weeks. But Yul Kwon—of South Korean descent—from Flushing, New York, was the season's winner.
4. Valdez's films *Zoot Suit* (1981) and *La Bamba* (1987) also include Mesoamerican iconography and themes, such as the use of the colors red and black (also discussed in the previous chapter), explicitly associated in Valdez's work with the god Tezcatlipoca ("Smoking Mirror"); instruments such as flutes and rattles; and philosophical principles including In Lak'ech, the Mayan precept that equates self and other. Rosa Linda Fregoso provides a detailed analysis of both films, as well as a critique of heteropatriarchy, in *The Bronze Screen: Chicana and Chicano Film Culture* (1993). Both the play and the film *Zoot Suit*, which emphasizes father-son relationships, have inspired volumes of criticism.
5. Sarah Chohan in "What Are Tribes (and Why Should You Be Targeting Them)?" outlines a strategy that businesses should use to target these highly specialized populations, stating that individuals "identify with one another through their collective interests and behaviors, rather than their demographic traits. This

could be anything from eco-friendly fashion, fairtrade goods, pets, sexual orientation, and music preference to dietary requirements and health issues."

6. Neo-tribalism as theorized by Maffesoli is not associated with the neo-tribalists inspired by Daniel Quinn's novel *Ishmael* (1992), who see a correlation between agricultural, sociological, and economic problems, for example, and the decline of "tribes" in the modern era. These devotees seek to reproduce Indigenous practices and organizing principles in their own daily lives. Neo-tribalists have been criticized for holding romantic, Luddite, and Malthusian beliefs. The latter refers specifically to Thomas Malthus's beliefs on sustainable development, first published in *An Essay on the Principle of Population* (1798) in response to the ideas of Jean-Jacques Rousseau and William Godwin. His idea was that populations cannot grow beyond the limit of their food supplies. If this happens, and some catastrophic natural disaster on a wide scale does not intervene, starvation will likely occur.

7. This is now the very definition of a social influencer: an individual (though often a group or a company) who uses social media to promote their favorite brands to their followers or "tribes" in order to boost personal and brand recognition and sales. These positions often include financial or material compensation.

8. Pitts points to specific tribal customs enacted by modern primitives, including "the Native American O-Kee-Pa, the Tamil Hindu kavadi ritual (wearing a frame of spears which poke the body), the Sadhu ball dancing ritual (dancing with weighty items sewn into the skin), and many other indigenous practices" (125). Although modern primitives, as Pitts notes, "believe that their practices are antithetical to racism, colonialism, and the negative effects of globalization," their ritualized practices appear entirely dependent on acts of cultural taking and/or appropriation (137). These include the use of "sage, cedar, grass, smoke, incense, feathers, bones, stones, thorns, spears, and fire, and use prayer, meditation, ritual bathing, dancing, and drumming" and a lexicon filled with references to "vision quests, spirits, spirit guides, totems, and talismans" (125).

9. In *Black Looks: Race and Representation* (1992), bell hooks argues, "White racism, imperialism, and sexist domination prevail by courageous consumption. It is by eating the Other . . . that one asserts power and privilege" (36).

PART III. *FANTASMAS* AND *FRONTERAS*

1. The following represent a few examples of the strangeness of pandemic time: "Why Time Feels So Weird Right Now," by Emily VanDerWerff; "Why Does Time Feel So Weird Right Now?," by Sadaf Ahsan; "Why Time Feels So Weird in 2020," by Fielding Cage; and "Congratulations, Our Sense of Time Has Been Off for a Year," by Natalie Gontcharova.

2. Cummins tweeted on 29 May 2019 images from a celebration hosted by her publisher, Flatiron Books, that included floral centerpieces wrapped in barbed wire. Prior to the publication of her novel, Cummins had mentioned her Puerto Rican grandmother, but identified as white. González, in "The Problem with *American Dirt*, Part 4: Slow Violence," conducts an analysis of Cummins's and Urrea's narration of the boy being crushed by a truck in one of the garbage dumps of Tijuana and notes that the "similarities" are striking. González also directs readers to David J. Schmidt's article "'American Dirt' Isn't Just Bad—Its Best Parts Are Cribbed from Latino Writers" (2019) for additional instances of "borrowing" on the part of Cummins. Not even our pain is our own. And regarding the author's

advance, on 25 May 2018 *Publishers Weekly* announced, "After a nine-house auction spanning three days, Flatiron Books' Amy Einhorn won *American Dirt*, a novel by Jeanine Cummins. Einhorn paid seven figures for the book" (Deahl).
3. As stated on its website, Dignidad Literaria "believes in the social and political power of wholly authentic Latinx voices and that it is the duty of the publishing industry and literati to use their full power and privilege to elevate these voices" (Dignidad Literaria).

LITERATURE: FATHERS, SONS, AND OTHER (SHORT) FICTIONS

1. John Morán González in *Border Renaissance: The Texas Centennial and the Emergence of Mexican American Literature* (2009) offers a detailed analysis of masculinity and the "demise of patriarchal anticolonialism" in Paredes's *George Washington Gómez* (127). Arturo J. Aldama and Frederick Luis Aldama state in the introduction to *Decolonizing Latinx Masculinities* (2020) that Arturo Islas offers an "interrogation of toxic masculinities" in his poetry, short fiction, and novel (9). Frederick Aldama provides a more comprehensive analysis of Islas's work in *Dancing with Ghosts: A Critical Biography of Arturo Islas* (2004).
2. In response to his mother's emerging proto-feminism later in the novel, Richard concludes that "a family could not survive when the woman desires to command" (134).
3. Mary Madison, a white Protestant classmate, befriends Richard and decides that she will one day marry him. Mary, who speaks with "self-assurance" and a "matter-of-fact" tone, is one of the very few women, though still a girl, not subject to Richard's abusive behaviors (137).
4. Rodriguez self-identifies as "Latin." The somewhat antiquated term has been used throughout film history, most notably in 1939–1943, during the Good Neighbor Policy years, in which, as Ana M. López notes, "Latin America was the only foreign market available for exploitation" (407).
5. Comcast, the largest cable provider in the US with over twenty-two million subscribers, agreed to carry several "minority-backed channels" in an effort to win government approval for acquiring a controlling interest in NBC Universal. In 2012, Comcast solicited proposals for ten new networks (four channels and six stations). Rodriguez was one of three high-profile male celebrities, along with basketball legend Magic Johnson and music artist/producer and designer Sean "Diddy" Combs, selected to develop new networks from more than one hundred proposals. Johnson's Atlanta-based Aspire TV, which launched on 27 June 2012, aims to deliver "enlightening, entertaining and positive programming to African-American families" and to appeal to multiple generations, all while focusing on people "reach[ing] for their dreams." Combs's Los Angeles–based Revolt TV launched on 21 October 2013 and features a "robust social media component" in its showcasing of "music and pop culture programming" (Guthrie).
6. The language in an article about El Rey by Luke Bouma for *Cord Cutters News*, "Sling TV Is Moving the El Rey Network," parallels the original "About" description of El Rey that once appeared on the network's website but is there no longer.
7. An additional motivation for the network, as Rodriguez stated in an exclusive interview with Fox News Latino, was his family: "I have five children of my own. They are bilingual, like most second and third generations. . . . But they speak primarily in English and they couldn't find anything on television that represented who they are in this country" (Rodriguez).

8. On 30 August 2012, the band El Chingon, started by Rodriguez, performed at the Paramount Theatre in Austin and the set included the song "El Rey," which appears on the *Machete* soundtrack. Rodriguez, who plays guitar, introduced the song and explained that it is "one of his favorites" and is one that guys sing when they are drinking or drunk and "want to feel good about themselves.... It's about Latin pride, which is why I named the network [El Rey]" ("Chingon"). Rodriguez fails to acknowledge the gender politics and male claim to power that permeate the song's lyrics.
9. Fernández came into popularity after the passing of icons Jorge Negrete (1953), Pedro Infante (1957), and Javier Solis (1966), who were associated with *ranchera* music and whose deaths created an opening that Fernández filled with his talent and persona. Fernández, like his predecessors, performs in a *traje de charro*, the style and dress of the traditional Mexican cowboy.
10. "With or without money, I will always get my way and my word is the law."
11. According to the Pew Research Center, as of 2019, Mexican-origin peoples were the largest population of Latinos in the US, numbering 36.6 million (Noe-Bustamante).
12. Charles Ramírez Berg gives a description of this type of performance: "Jorge Negrete, a virile singing charro . . . defined machismo for a generation with films like *La Madrina del diablo* (*The Devil's Godmother*, 1937, Ramón Peón), *¡Ay Jalisco . . . no te rajes!* (*Oh, Jalisco . . . Don't Back Down!*, 1941, Joselito Rodríguez), and the remake of *Allá en el Rancho Grande* ([*Out on the Big Ranch*], 1948, . . . by Fernando de Fuentes)" (Ramírez Berg, Introduction 16).
13. In defining *comedia ranchera*, Ramírez Berg describes *Allá en el Rancho Grande* as "[p]art romantic melodrama, part comedy, part musical" and notes that "it originated the *comedia ranchera*, a uniquely hybrid genre that has become a staple of Mexican cinema for decades" (*Classical Mexican Cinema* 88).
14. The editors of *Global Mexican Cinema: Its Golden Age* (2013), Robert McKee Irwin and Maricruz Castro Ricalde, claim that this period "runs for about two decades . . . during which Mexico's film industry became one of the most productive in the world, exercising a decisive influence on constructions of national culture and identity in Mexico" (2).
15. In addition to the lyrics of the song El Rey is named for, the network's early emphasis on grindhouse productions, a form that takes its name from the burlesque theatres where pornographic, slasher horror, and other exploitation films notorious for the brutalization and/or subjugation of women were shown, also suggests that El Rey intentionally skewed initially toward men and did not include much family fare.
16. As Laurie Kenney originally reported in 2014, *The Boy Kings of Texas* was optioned for an HBO series. Salma Hayek and Jerry Weintraub were set to serve as executive producers with Martinez as the scriptwriter. The project never materialized.
17. Martinez notes that "Grampa's brothers' wives were horrified that he had married a widow with a child, married below his station, as head of their clan . . ." (52).
18. During one of Mingo's disastrous attempts to connect with his son, he asks about the boy's favorite place. In exchange, Mingo reveals that his is "inside a nice warm pussy" (11). Martinez thinks, "I simply cannot run far enough away from this man. His mustachioed upper lip curls when he forms the word *warm*,

and for a moment his mouth becomes vulvular, creating the image of a female pudenda, and I think I might try to turn gay to get as far away from my Dad as possible" (12). The incident is but one in a lifetime of masculine performances from which Martinez seeks to distance himself.

19. *Circling the Tortilla Dragon* (2002), Gonzalez's collection of gritty "short-short" fictions teeming with less enlightened views, includes a number of stories that reference patriarchs or fathers specifically: "Bowling Alley," "The Baby," "Man on the Wall," "Frogs," "Blue Butterflies," "The Ghost," and "Clapping." In one of the longer short-shorts, "Joey's Diablo," the protagonist fires "two shots into his father, one in the back and one in the head," killing the abusive, adulterous man and replicating the familial violence (106). Fathers appear and disappear spectrally throughout the collection, which makes it feel even more haunted than *The Ghost of John Wayne and Other Stories*.

20. According to Muñoz Martínez, "The violence on the Texas-Mexico border took many forms. Ethnic Mexicans were intimidated, tortured, and killed by hanging, shooting, burning, and beating. Nearly all the known victims were adult men, though a few women and children suffered the same vicious wrath" (7).

21. When complete, *The Alamo* was meant to reflect Wayne's position on Vietnam: "In the mind of superpatriot John Wayne, whenever and wherever America fought, it was a just fight for American values, regardless of circumstances" (Schoenberger 153). Of note, John Wayne played characters that fought in every major US war from the Civil War to World War II. The private citizen John Wayne fought in none, which some believe pushed him to overcompensate for this fact through his hyperpatriotism.

22. According to "Foods That Make You Hallucinate," by Sam Dean, hot peppers create an "endorphin rush from the pain caused by the hotness of the chile."

23. The father's much-belated health disclosure parallels Gonzalez's discovery that his father had a heart attack he failed to mention at the time to any of his children. Gonzalez's uncle is the one who passes on the information in the form of a question: "Did you know that Ray had a heart attack in 1988?" ("My Literary Fathers" 182).

24. The source of the quote is found in "Jerry Fuentes." The protagonist, George, tells his wife, Anna, "Don't believe anything he tells you," to countermand Jerry's insistence that they need expensive end-of-life planning (151).

25. Mr. Sanchez says to Marcelo in "Charro," "They found [the dog] over there in the park. They say he was lost" (117).

26. Still, Julie Avril Minich's "Disabling la Frontera: Disability, Border Subjectivity, and Masculinity in 'Big Jesse, Little Jesse' by Oscar Cásares" (2010) gave me pause, especially since her analyses of borders, masculinity, and disability flow together seamlessly. Minich has conducted the most extensive scholarship to date on Cásares's *Brownsville*, which includes a chapter in her award-winning book *Accessible Citizenships: Disability, Nation, and the Cultural Politics of Greater Mexico* (2013) and her essay "'The Emotional Residue of an Unnatural Boundary': *Brownsville* and the Borders of Mental Health" (2017). A rush of exhilaration followed those initial feelings. So I did something else that we do not do nearly enough: I wrote to say thanks for her scholarship. Although our analyses overlap concerning how masculinity is narrated and performed in the story, my attention is drawn to a specific narrative locus.

27. Minich points to a parallel between attitudes about disability and queerness: "Crucially, Jesse laments that his son was born *this way*, a phrase often used as an ostensibly polite but nonetheless homophobic euphemism for queer identities, suggesting that what pains Jesse is his son's refusal to comply with gender norms, a refusal that may be related to his disability but is not necessarily reducible to it" ("Disabling" 42).
28. "Fuck him up!"
29. The father says, "Like that, Junior, like that" (110); and, as quoted in text, "Ya déjalo, Junior" (111).

FILM: META AND MUTANT FATHERS

1. *Shang-Chi and the Legend of the Ten Rings* (2021) and *Eternals* (2021), the twenty-fifth and twenty-sixth films in the MCU, trouble this pattern but only slightly: the former focuses exclusively on an Asian Pacific Islander character and the latter features cosmic beings that appear in human forms, a number of which include ethno-racialized bodies, though early indicators suggest that a white-presenting, cisgender, heterosexual male Eternal is the main focus of the story.
2. While both categories refer to genetically evolved people, meta-humans appear in DC Comics publications and movies and mutants are in those from Marvel Comics.
3. Earlier examples include *Battle Beyond the Stars* (1980), *Outland* (1981), *Blade Runner* (1982), and the *Star Trek* film series of fourteen films as of 2020.
4. Colonel Rick Flag utters this line before the group leaves for its mission.
5. In my original chapter "Magnificence and Metas in Professional Westerns," in *Weird Westerns: Race, Gender, Genre* (2020), edited by Kerry Fine et al., I attribute this citation to Lee Clark Mitchell, *Westerns: Making the Man in Fiction and Film*. These four types do appear in Mitchell's work; however, he is citing from Wright's *Sixguns and Society*. The misattribution is now amended.
6. Bruzzi goes on, "The prevalence of this model is demonstrated by its appearance in A-features and B-features alike" (62). She cites as examples such films as *The Furies* (1950), *Broken Lance* (1954), *The Halliday Brand* (1957), *The Big Country* (1958), and *Gunman's Walk* (1958).
7. The bandido, in his racialization and limited narrative capacity, does not have access to the same avenues of power as white male fathers. In other words, the stories are not about the bandido, as men or fathers. Morally and ideologically, he is a narrative tool in the service of whiteness and the masculinist status quo.
8. Anthony Quinn, born Antonio Rodolfo Quinn Oaxaca, brought the idea to adapt *Seven Samurai* to Yul Brynner. Quinn was set to star in the film and Brynner to direct. The extensive delay in getting the production off the ground and a number of other issues, including Quinn's poster-billing demands and questions around his ability to carry the project, influenced the production company, which Brynner owned, to sell the rights to the film. Later the project went forward with John Sturges as director, and Sturges cast Brynner in the lead. Quinn sued, claiming ownership of the idea, but lost. We are left to imagine what Quinn in the lead role could have done for a film that was redrawing generic boundaries.
9. According to Jenni Calder, "*The Magnificent Seven* was hailed in 1961, by many who are not Western enthusiasts, as something new and real from the West. The

10. fact that it is a direct reworking of Kurasawa's [sic] *The Seven Samurai* is hardly relevant to its character as a Western, for it failed to utilize so much that is subtly distinctive in the original" (199).
10. This scene represents a change from the original, in which the villagers went looking to hire men. As Hannan explains, in the revised version, "[t]hey planned to buy guns to defend themselves against bandits. It was now pure accident that brought them into the orbit of the gunslinger Chris. Crucially, the suggestion to hire gunmen originated not from the villagers but from Chris. That left Chris to claim, illogically, that men were cheaper than guns" (Hannan 88).
11. The Travis County War may refer to the Coke-Davis controversy concerning the gubernatorial election of 1873, when the Travis Guard and Rifles, a small policing force, were called in to protect Coke but turned into a posse that protected Davis (Bishop). From 1869 to 1873, Agustín Salinas, Sr., while serving as mayor of Laredo, Texas, hired an extra police force allegedly to quell political unrest in the town, though it is generally believed he did so to intimidate his opponents (L. Mora). And the Yaqui Wars in Mexico began in 1887 and lasted until 1910. Given the location of the town, the wars would have impacted the villagers far more than a bandit. Considering the dates of these events, the film is set somewhere between 1875 and 1886. The 2016 remake is explicitly identified as taking place in 1879, which is consistent with this proposed dating of the 1960 version.
12. Leah Williams, in her review of the 2016 *Magnificent Seven* remake, reminds readers that "people of color were not only present at the inception of the Wild West—but they were also its primary architects."
13. In their introduction to *Weird Westerns: Race, Gender, Genre* (2020), editors Kerry Fine, Michael K. Johnson, Rebecca M. Lush, and Sara L. Spurgeon identify "weird westerns" as "texts that utilize a hybrid genre format, blending canonical elements of the western with either science fiction, fantasy, horror, or some other component of speculative literature" (2).
14. Michael Peña, who has appeared as Luis in the *Ant-Man* films (2015; 2018), does not possess an explicit superhero ability. Also, Afro-Latinx movie-goers might identify with the Wakandan hero Black Panther, but he is not identified as Latinx. Featured in *Doctor Strange in the Multiverse of Madness* (2022), Xochitl Gomez as America Chavez is the first Latine LGBTQ character in the MCU.
15. The line parallels John 14:6 from the Bible: "I am the way, and the truth, and the life. No one comes to the Father except through me."
16. After Chato tearfully recounts the story of how he accidentally killed his wife and children, Harley responds sharply, "What'd you think was going to happen? Huh? What, you were just thinking you could have a happy family and coach little league and make car payments? Normal is a setting on the dryer. People like us don't get normal."
17. In comparison to Deadshot's request, what the others ask for seems frivolous: Killer Croc asks for the BET (Black Entertainment Network) channel on the TV in his cell, and Harley Quinn asks for an espresso machine. Captain Boomerang, who threatens Waller, gets nothing.
18. When Caliban first appears on-screen, he is dressed in a poncho that brings to mind the iconic costuming of Clint Eastwood in Sergio Leone's *A Fistful of Dollars* (1964). Later, Transigen uses Caliban for his tracking skills, as Indian scouts sometimes betrayed other Native people by helping whites, such as the Pawnee scouts who help the cavalry track the Lakotas in *Dances with Wolves*.

19. "I need a hero." The spoken Spanish in the film is not translated via subtitles.
20. "What the hell happened to you that made you hide?"
21. From 1993 to 2005, more than five hundred women were reported missing, and many of those were found dead, in Ciudad Juarez, Mexico, located across the border from El Paso, Texas, where the film's opening is set. More recently, from 2018 to 2021, "the city has recorded 491 homicides where women were the victims" (Resendiz).
22. Earlier Charles hints at the connection between the two after Logan watches Laura dispatch almost an entire team of federales, telling him, "She's a mutant like you. Very much like you."
23. Vasconcelos, a philosopher and minister of education under President Eulalio Gutiérrez Ortiz, argued that a cosmic race would one day emerge: "[T]he various races of the earth tend to intermix at a gradually increasing pace, and eventually will give rise to a new human type, composed of selections from each of the races already in existence" (3).
24. Logan tells the Munsons that his family's name is Howlett, the surname of his nonmutant father. His use of this name, particularly given that the Munsons are a Black family, creates an interesting dialogue about the marginality of mutants, their historical positioning in conversations about civil rights, and passing as nonmutants.
25. Helping the children reach safety serves as a callback to *X-Men Origins: Wolverine* (2009), in which Logan frees caged children who are being experimented on by the US government.
26. What Transigen really wanted to accomplish was to eliminate the randomness of the mutation and the resulting superhuman abilities. Once the mutant population fell into decline, Dr. Rice then selected and genetically engineered particular abilities that would be beneficial for military or other commercial purposes. In other words, he sought to monetize mutants while demonstrating a complete disregard for their lives.
27. Tony Castro of *La Opinión* notes, "Had it been common knowledge that the dreamy-eyed Furlong was Mexican on his mother's side, Hispanics who helped make the 'Terminator' franchise a worldwide blockbuster would have been hailing him as the American Latino major Hollywood star who might open the gates in Tinseltown."
28. *Dark Fate*, directed by Tim Miller, is the sixth film in the series that includes *The Terminator* (1984) and *Terminator 2: Judgment Day* (1991), directed by James Cameron; *Terminator 3: Rise of the Machines* (2003), directed by Jonathan Mostow; *Terminator Salvation* (2009), directed by McG; and *Terminator Genisys* (2015), directed by Alan Taylor.
29. Of note, Schwarzenegger's professional and personal lives appear to have crossed paths in this kind of role: in his career he also appeared alongside Latina leads Maria Conchita Alonso in *The Running Man* (1987), Elpidia Carrillo in *Predator* (1987), and Rachel Ticotin in *Total Recall* (1990), and in real life he fathered a child with his housekeeper, Mildred Baena, from Guatemala.

CONCLUSION. FATHERS AND FUTURITY

1. In light of his pet chicken and his characteristic preening, Eduardo calls to mind a *gallo*, a familiar Mexican and Mexican American male type identified in early work conducted by Anglo researchers about Mexican and Mexican American

families. In 1972, anthropologist William Madsen associated *el gallo* with machismo: "The Latin thinks of a true man as being proud, self-reliant, and virile. He is jokingly compared to a rooster" (22). Sociologist Alfredo Mirandé directly refuted this particular kind of oversimplified interpretation of men's roles within Mexican and Mexican American families ("A Reinterpretation" 474). However, it is important to note that these attitudes about Latino men prevailed and that the men themselves willingly took up this position, which found a place even in artistic expression. Virginia Raymond notes that the *gallo* is a "significant and enduring masculine symbol that appears frequently in Chicana/o visual art" (381). The *gallo* represents a stand-and-fight attitude most often associated with bravado, machismo, pride, virility, flamboyance, and strength.

2. Panchito is depicted as a revolutionary-era rooster in *The Three Caballeros* (1944); Papi serves as the Mexican Chihuahua love interest of the titular *Beverly Hills Chihuahua* (2008); and the mouse Speedy Gonzales of Warner Bros. cartoon fame debuted in an early iteration of the character in 1953. *Puss in Boots* (2011) features a suave romantic outlaw cat, *Turbo* (2013) includes Tito Lopez as sidekick to a supercharged snail, and Ramon, a lowrider, serves as comic relief in *Cars* (2006).

3. Only *Spider-Man: Into the Spider-Verse* (2018), featuring the main character Miles Morales (Shameik Moore), breaks from this formula, with its Afro-Latinx protagonist. Miles's father is a Black police officer and his Afro-Latinx mother is a nurse.

4. For Thein and Kedley's complete analysis of Mr. Mendoza's outing of Ari, see "Out of the Closet and All Grown Up: Problematizing Normative Narratives of Coming-Out and Coming-of-Age in Young Adult Literature."

5. For additional information on Kahn's concept, including implementation and effects, see his article "Holding Environments at Work."

WORKS CITED AND CONSULTED

Alberto, Lourdes. "Nations, Nationalisms, and Indígenas: The 'Indian' in the Chicano Revolutionary Imaginary." *The Journal of Critical Ethnic Studies*, vol. 2, no. 1, 2016, pp. 107–127.

Alcalde, M. Cristina. "What It Means to Be a Man? Violence and Homophobia in Latino Masculinities On and Off Screen." *The Journal of Popular Culture*, vol. 47, no. 3, 2014, pp. 537–553.

Alcoff, Linda Martín. "The Unassimilated Theorist." *PMLA*, vol. 121, no. 1, 2006, pp. 255–259.

Aldama, Arturo J., and Frederick Luis Aldama, editors. *Decolonizing Latinx Masculinities*. U of Arizona P, 2020.

Aldama, Frederick Luis. *Brown on Brown: Chicano/a Representations of Gender, Sexuality, and Ethnicity*. U of Texas P, 2005.

Alexie, Sherman. *Reservation Blues*. Atlantic Monthly, 1995.

Alford, Harold J. *The Proud Peoples: The Heritage and Culture of Spanish-Speaking Peoples in the United States*. The New American Library, 1972.

Alfred, Taiaiake. "Reimagining Warriorhood: A Conversation with Taiaiake Alfred." *Masculindians: Conversations about Indigenous Manhood*, edited by Sam McKegney, East Michigan State UP, 2014, pp. 76–86.

Alvarez, Julia. *In the Time of the Butterflies*. Algonquin, 1994.

Alves, Julio. "Unintentional Knowledge: What We Find When We're Not Looking." *The Chronicle of Higher Education*, 23 June 2013, www.chronicle.com/article/unintentional-knowledge/.

Anaya, Rudolfo. *Bless Me, Ultima*. 1972. Grand Central, 1999.

———. "'I Am the King': The Macho Image." *Muy Macho: Latino Men Confront Their Manhood*, edited by Ray Gonzalez, Anchor Books, 1996, pp. 57–73.

Anaya, Rudolfo A., and Francisco Lomelí, editors. *Aztlán: Essays on the Chicano Homeland*. U of New Mexico P, 1989.

Angelou, Maya [@DrMayaAngelou]. "When someone shows you who they are, believe them the first time." *Twitter*, 12 June 2015, twitter.com/drmayaangelou/status/609390085604311040?lang=en.

Anzaldúa, Gloria. *The Borderlands/La Frontera: The New Mestiza*. Aunt Lute, 1987.

———. "Daughter of Coatlicue: An Interview with Gloria Anzaldúa." By Irene Lara. *EntreMundos/AmongWorlds: New Perspectives on Gloria Anzaldúa*, edited by AnaLouise Keating, Palgrave, 2008, pp. 41–56.

———. "Doing Gigs: Speaking, Writing, and Change." Interview by Debbie Blake and Carmen Abrego. 1994. *Interviews/Entrevistas/Gloria Anzaldúa*, edited by AnaLouise Keating, Routledge, 2000, pp. 211–234.

———. "Let Us Be the Healing of the Wound: The Coyolxauhqui Imperative—La Sombra y el Sueño." *The Gloria Anzaldúa Reader*, edited by AnaLouise Keating, Duke UP, 2009, pp. 303–317.

———. "Now Let Us Shift . . . the Path of Conocimiento . . . Inner Work, Public

Acts." *This Bridge We Call Home: Radical Visions for Transformation*, edited by Gloria E. Anzaldúa and AnaLouise Keating, Routledge, 2002, pp. 540–578.

———. "Quincentennial: From Victimhood to Active Resistance." Interview by Inés Hernández-Ávila. 1991. *Interviews/Entrevistas/Gloria Anzaldúa*, edited by AnaLouise Keating, Routledge, 2000, pp. 177–194.

———. "(Un)natural Bridges, (Un)safe Spaces." Preface. *This Bridge We Call Home: Radical Visions for Transformation*, edited by Gloria E. Anzaldúa and Ana-Louise Keating, Routledge, 2002, pp. 1–5.

Anzaldúa, Gloria E., and Simon J. Ortiz. "Speaking across the Divide." Interview by Inés Hernández-Ávila and Domino Renee Perez. *Studies in American Indian Literatures*, ser. 2, vol. 15, nos. 3/4, fall 2003/winter 2004, pp. 7–22.

Arellano, Gustavo. "Why Do So Many Mexicans Defend Speedy Gonzales?" *Los Angeles Times*, 17 Mar. 2021, www.latimes.com/california/story/2021-03-17/speedy-gonzales-cancelled-hollywood-mexican-americans.

Associated Press. "US NY Reunited Families." *AP Archive*, 11 Jul. 2018, www.aparchive.com/metadata/youtube/93126069009754f992122f90bd00f203.

Baker, Peter. "Bush Made Willie Horton an Issue in 1988, and the Racial Scars Are Still Fresh." *New York Times*, 3 Dec. 2018, www.nytimes.com/2018/12/03/us/politics/bush-willie-horton.html.

Ballí, Cecilia. "Bard of the Border." *Texas Monthly*, Mar. 2003, pp. 100–103, 124.

Bataille, Gretchen M., editor. *Native American Representations: First Encounters, Distorted Images, and Literary Appropriations*, U of Nebraska P, 2001.

Bates, Daniel, and Karen Ruiz. "'They're Together and Safe': Father of Honduran Two-year-old Who Became the Face of Family Separation Crisis Reveals Daughter Was Never Separated from Her Mother, But the Image of Her in Tears at U.S. Border Control 'Broke His Heart.'" *Daily Mail*, 21 June 2018, www.dailymail.co.uk/news/article-5869829/Father-two-year-old-face-child-separation-crisis-speaks-out.html.

Baudrillard, Jean. *Simulacra and Simulation*. Translated by Sheila Faria Glaser, U of Michigan P, 1994.

Bebout, Lee. "Troubling White Benevolence: Four Takes on a Scene from *Giant*." *MELUS: The Journal of the Society for the Study of the Multi-Ethnic Literature of the United States*, vol. 36, no. 3, 2011, pp. 13–36.

———. *Whiteness on the Border: Mapping U.S. Racial Imagination in Brown and White*. New York UP, 2016.

Benshoff, Harry M., and Sean Griffin. *America on Film: Representing Race, Class, Gender, and Sexuality in the Movies*. 2nd ed., Wiley-Blackwell, 2009.

Berg, Maggie, and Barbara K. Seeber. *The Slow Professor: Challenging the Culture of Speed in the Academy*. New ed., U of Toronto P, 2016.

Berkhofer, Robert. *The White Man's Indian*. Knopf, 1978.

Beydoun, Khaled. "More than Thugs: The Case of Richard Sherman and Other Men of Colour." *Al Jazeera Online*, 29 Jan. 2014, www.aljazeera.com/indepth/opinion/2014/01/more-than-thugsthe-case-richar-2014125134532950282.html.

Bishop, Curtis. "Coke-Davis Controversy." *Handbook of Texas Online*, www.tshaonline.org/handbook/entries/coke-davis-controversy.

Blade Runner. Directed by Ridley Scott, performances by Harrison Ford, Rutger Hauer, and Edward James Olmos, Warner Bros., 1982.

Blade Runner 2049. Directed by Denis Villeneuve, performances by Ryan Gosling, Harrison Ford, Jared Leto, and Robin Wright, Warner Bros., 2017.

Blanchard, Marc. "Post-Bourgeois Tattoo: Reflections on Skin-Writing in Late-Capitalistic Societies." *Visualizing Theory: Selected Essays from V.A.R. 1990–1994*, edited by Lucian Taylor, Routledge, 1995, pp. 287–300.

The Book of Life. Directed by Jorge R. Gutiérrez, performances by Diego Luna, Channing Tatum, and Hector Elizondo, 20th Century Fox, 2014.

"Born in East L.A. (1987)." *The Numbers*, 2021, www.the-numbers.com/movie/Born-in-East-L-A#tab=summary.

Bouma, Luke. "Sling TV Is Moving the El Rey Network." *Cord Cutters News*, 16 May 2017, www.cordcuttersnews.com/sling-tv-moving-el-rey-network/.

Bratt, Benjamin, et al. "Benjamin Bratt and Cast of 'La Mission' on Machismo, Lowriders, and Love." Interview by A. J. Miranda. *Austin Vida*, 21 May 2010, www.austinvida.com/entertainment/2010/bratt-la-mission-interview/.

Bratt, Peter. "Peter Bratt, *La Mission*: Patriarch, Homosexual and Change." *Indiewire*, 4 Jan. 2009, www.indiewire.com/2009/01/peter-bratt-la-mission-patriarch-homosexual-and-change-71016/. Interview.

Bratt, Peter, and Benjamin Bratt. "Bratt Brothers and *La Mission*." Interview by Lydia Chavez. *Mission Local*, 16 Apr. 2010, missionlocal.org/2010/04/bratt-bros-and-la-mission/.

Britt, Donna. "The Struggle of *My Family*." *Washington Post*, 28 July 1995, www.washingtonpost.com/archive/local/1995/07/28/the-struggle-of-my-family/2463a287-f0cc-48a7-b008-2e4b281314c1/.

Bruzzi, Stella. *Bringing Up Daddy: Fatherhood and Masculinity in Post-War Hollywood*. BFI, 2005.

Burciaga, José Antonio. *Spilling the Beans: Lotería Chicana*. Odell, 1995.

Calder, Jenni. *There Must Be a Lone Ranger: The American West in Film and in Reality*. Taplinger, 1975.

Cantú, Norma Elia. *Canícula: Snapshots of a Girlhood en la Frontera*. U of New Mexico P, 1995.

Cásares, Oscar [*published as* Oscar Casares]. *Brownsville: Stories*. Back Bay, 2003.

Castillo, Ana. *The Mixquiahuala Letters*. Bilingual Press/Editorial Bilingue, 1986.

Castro, Rafaela G. *The Dictionary of Chicano Folklore*. Oxford UP, 2000.

Castro, Tony. "Edward Furlong: The Unknown Latino Badboy of Hollywood." *La Opinión*, 24 Nov. 2014, laopinion.com/2014/11/24/edward-furlong-the-unknown-latino-badboy-of-hollywood/.

Ceseña, María Teresa. "Creating Agency and Identity in Danza Azteca." *Dancing across Borders: Danzas y Bailes Mexicanos*, edited by Olga Nájera-Ramírez et al., U of Illinois P, 2009, pp. 80–94.

"Chapter 8: Redemption." *The Mandalorian*, created by Jon Favreau, season 1, episode 8, Disney+, 2019.

"Chapter 16: The Rescue." *The Mandalorian*, created by Jon Favreau, season 2, episode 8, Disney+, 2020.

Chavez, Albert C., editor. *Yearnings*. Pendulum, 1972.

"Chingon—El Rey." *YouTube*, 4 Nov. 2012, www.youtube.com/watch?v=sZXSTVwZMrc.

Chohan, Sarah. "What Are Tribes (and Why Should You Be Targeting Them)?" *Linkfluence*, n.d., www.linkfluence.com/blog/what-are-tribes-and-why-you-should-be-targeting-them.

"Chow Shepherds." *Dogtime.com*, n.d., dogtime.com/dog-breeds/chow-shepherd#/slide/1.

Cisneros, Sandra. *The House on Mango Street*. Arte Público, 1983.
———. *Woman Hollering Creek and Other Stories*. Random House, 1991.
Coco. Directed by Lee Unkrich and Adrian Molina, performances by Gael García Bernal and Benjamin Bratt, Walt Disney, 2017.
Cordova, Cary. *The Heart of the Mission: Latino Art and Politics in San Francisco*. U of Pennsylvania P, 2017.
Cummins, Jeanine. *American Dirt*. Flatiron, 2019.
——— [@jeaninecummins]. "Incredible way to kick off #BookExpo2019 last night with the @Flatironbooks party and a bookseller dinner in honor of AMERICAN DIRT. I'm overwhelmed with gratitude." *Twitter*, 29 May 2019, twitter.com/jeaninecummins/status/1133697703685361664?lang=en.
Curiel, Tony. Introduction. *Luis Valdez—Early Works: Actos, Bernabé, and Pensamiento Serpentino*, by Luis Valdez. Arte Público, 1994, pp. 3–5.
Dabney, Courtney. "It Took a Global Pandemic, but Generation X Is Finally Getting Love." *Paper City*, 26 Mar. 2020, www.papercitymag.com/culture/generation-x-earns-respect-conronavirus-pandemic-stay-home/.
Dalrymple, Theodore [Anthony Malcolm Daniels]. "The Rage of Virginia Woolf." *City Journal*, 2002, www.city-journal.org/html/rage-virginia-woolf-12371.html.
Darren, Liana. "How to Write a Literature Review." *Grammarly*, 9 Dec. 2020, www.grammarly.com/blog/how-to-write-a-literature-review/.
Deahl, Rachel. "Book Deals: Week of May 28, 2018." *Publishers Weekly*, 25 May 2018, www.publishersweekly.com/pw/by-topic/industry-news/book-deals/article/76994-book-deals-week-of-may-28-2018.html.
Dean, Sam. "Foods That Make You Hallucinate." *Bon Appétit*, 10 Jan. 2013, www.bonappetit.com/trends/article/foods-that-make-you-hallucinate.
de la Garza, Rudolphe O., et al. *Chicanos and Native Americans: The Territorial Minorities*. Prentice Hall, 1973.
de la Mora, Sergio. *Cinemachismo: Masculinities and Sexuality in Mexican Film*. U of Texas P, 2006.
De León, Nephtalí. *Chicanos: Our Background and Our Pride*. Trucha Publications, 1972.
———. "Of Bronze the Sacrifice." *We Are Chicanos: An Anthology of Mexican-American Literature*, Washington Square Press ed., edited by Philip D. Ortego, Pocket Books, 1973, pp. 155–162.
dell'Agnese, Elena. "The US-Mexico Border in American Movies: A Political Geography Perspective." *Geopolitics*, vol. 10, 2005, pp. 204–221.
Deloria, Philip. *Indians in Unexpected Places*. UP of Kansas, 2004.
Despicable Me 2. Directed by Pierre Coffin and Chris Renaud, performances by Steve Carell and Benjamin Bratt, Universal, 2013.
Dignidad Literaria. "#DignidadLiteraria Press Conference." *Dignidad Literaria*, n.d., dignidadliteraria.com/.
Domonoske, Camila. "Judge Approves $25 Million Settlement Of Trump University Lawsuit." *NPR*, 31 Mar. 2017, www.npr.org/sections/thetwo-way/2017/03/31/522199535/judge-approves-25-million-settlement-of-trump-university-lawsuit.
Eating Raoul. Directed by Paul Bartel, performances by Mary Woronov, Paul Bartel, and Robert Beltran, Twentieth Century Fox International Classics, 1982.
Ebert, Roger. Review of *My Family*, directed by Gregory Nava. *RogerEbert.com*, 3 May 1995, www.rogerebert.com/reviews/my-family-1995.

El Plan Espiritual de Aztlán. Papeles of the National Chicano Youth Liberation Conference, Denver, Mar. 1969. Available at M.E.Ch.A., University of Arizona, clubs.arizona.edu/~mecha/pages/PDFs/ElPlanDeAtzlan.pdf.

Emerick, Laura. "Coming of Age: How 'Quinceañera' Ushered a Couple of Hollywood Outsiders into the Mainstream." *Chicago Sun-Times*, final ed., 6 Aug. 2006, p. D5.

Esquibél, Catrióna Rueda. "Velvet Malinche: Fantasies of 'the' Aztec Princess in the Chicana/o Sexual Imagination." *Velvet Barrios: Popular Culture and Chicana/o Sexualities*, edited by Alicia Gaspar de Alba, Palgrave, 2003, pp. 295–307.

Estrada, Gabriel S. "Two-Spirit Mexica Youth and Transgender Mixtec/Muxe Media: *La Mission* (2009), *Two Spirit: Injunuity* (2013), and *Libertad* (2015)." *Journal of Religion & Film*, vol. 21, no. 1, art. 38, 2017, pp. 1–50, digitalcommons.unomaha.edu/jrf/vol21/iss1/38/.

Estrella, Sara. "Soy Chicana de Aztlán." *Aztecas del Norte: The Chicanos of Aztlán*, edited by Jack D. Forbes, Fawcett, 1973, pp. 319–320.

Faludi, Susan. *Stiffed: The Betrayal of the American Man*. Harper, 1999.

Fantina, Richard. *Ernest Hemingway: Machismo and Masochism*. Palgrave, 2005.

Fawaz, Ramzi. *The New Mutants: Superheroes and the Radical Imagination of American Comics*. New York UP, 2016.

Fernández, Roberta. *Intaglio: A Novel in Six Stories*. Arte Público, 1990.

Fine, Kerry, et al., editors. *Weird Westerns: Race, Gender, Genre*. U of Nebraska P, 2020.

Flores, Joseph A., editor. *Songs and Dreams*. Pendulum, 1972.

Flores Niemann, Yolanda, et al., editors. *Presumed Incompetent II: Race, Class, Power, and Resistance of Women in Academia*. Utah State UP, 2020.

Forbes, Jack D., editor. *Aztecas del Norte: The Chicanos of Aztlán*. Fawcett, 1973.

Foster, David William. "*La Mission*." Review of *La Mission*, directed by Peter Bratt. *Chasqui*, vol. 29, no. 2, 2010, pp. 249–250.

Fregoso, Rosa Linda. *The Bronze Screen: Chicana and Chicano Film Culture*. U of Minnesota P, 1993.

———. *meXicana Encounters: The Making of Social Identities on the Borderlands*. U of California P, 2003.

Fry, Richard. "Millennials Overtake Baby Boomers as America's Largest Generation." *Pew Research Center*, 28 Apr. 2020, www.pewresearch.org/fact-tank/2020/04/28/millennials-overtake-baby-boomers-as-americas-largest-generation/.

Fuller, Stephanie. "'Filmed Entirely in Mexico': *Vera Cruz* (1954) and the Politics of Mexico in American Cinema." *Journal of Popular Film and Television*, vol. 41, no. 1, 2013, pp. 20–30.

Fusco, Coco. *English Is Broken Here: Notes on Cultural Fusion in the Americas*. New Press, 1995.

García, Cristina. *Dreaming in Cuban*. Ballantine, 1992.

Garroutte, Eva Marie. *Real Indians: Identity and the Survival of Native America*. U of California P, 2003.

Gerhard, Susan. "SFIFF52: Peter Bratt's *La Mission*." *SF360*, San Francisco Film Society, 23 Apr. 2009, sf360.org.mytempweb.com/page/12042.

Giant. Directed by George Stevens, performances by Elizabeth Taylor, Rock Hudson, and James Dean, Warner Bros., 1956.

Gomez-Peña, Guillermo. *The New World Border: Prophecies, Poems and Loqueras for the End of the Century*. City Lights, 1996.

González, Christopher. *Permissible Narratives: The Promise of Latino/a Literature.* Ohio State UP, 2017.

———. "The Problem with *American Dirt*, Part 4: Slow Violence." *Christopher González*, 31 Jan. 2020, thechrisgonzalez.com/problem-with-american-dirt-part-4/.

González, John Morán. "Aztlán @ Fifty: Chican@ Literary Studies for the Next Decade." *Aztlán: A Journal of Chicano Studies*, vol. 35, no. 2, 2010, pp. 173–176.

———. *Border Renaissance: The Texas Centennial and the Emergence of Mexican American Literature.* U of Texas P, 2009.

Gonzalez, Ray. *Circling the Tortilla Dragon: Short-Short Fictions.* Creative Arts, 2002.

———. *The Ghost of John Wayne and Other Stories.* U of Arizona P, 2001.

———. *The Heat of Arrivals.* BOA Editions, 1996.

———. "An Interview with Ray Gonzalez." By Alex Lemon. *Indiana Review*, vol. 28, no. 1, 2006, pp. 121–127.

———, editor. *Muy Macho: Latino Men Confront Their Manhood.* Anchor, 1996.

———. "My Literary Fathers." *Muy Macho: Latino Men Confront Their Manhood*, edited by Gonzalez, Anchor, 1996, pp. 165–185.

Gonzales, Rodolfo. *I Am Joaquín/Yo soy Joaquín.* 1969. Bantam, 1972.

"Good, Clean and Fair: The Slow Food Manifesto for Quality." "Our Philosophy," *Slow Food*, n.d., www.slowfood.com/about-us/our-philosophy/#:~:text=Slow %20Food% 20envisions%20a%20world,%3A%20good%2C%20clean%20and %20fair.

Gordon, Avery. *Ghostly Matters: Haunting and the Sociological Imagination.* 1997. 2nd ed., U of Minnesota P, 2008.

Gorov, Lynda. "A Walk in the Park; With Clever Casting, Partners Make Indie Film 'Quinceanera' A Neighborly Labor of Love." *The Boston Globe*, 6 Aug. 2006, 3rd ed., p. N11.

Gradante, William. "Low and Slow, Mean and Clean." *Natural History*, vol. 91, no. 4, 1982, pp. 28–38.

Great Lakes Feminist Geography Collective (GLFGC). "For Slow Scholarship: A Feminist Politics of Resistance through Collective Action in the Neoliberal University." *ACME: An International E-Journal for Critical Geographies*, vol. 14, no. 4, 2015, pp. 1235–1259.

"Grogu." *Wookieepedia: The Star Wars Wiki*, n.d., starwars.fandom.com/wiki /Grogu#cite_note-Chapter_8-6.

Guidotti-Hernández, Nicole. *Unspeakable Violence: Remapping U.S. and Mexican National Imaginaries.* Duke UP, 2011.

Gurba, Myriam. "Pendeja, You Ain't Steinbeck: My Bronca with Fake-Ass Social Justice Literature." Review of *American Dirt*, by Jeanine Cummins. *Tropics of Meta: Historiography for the Masses*, 12 Dec. 2019, tropicsofmeta.com /2019/12/12/pendeja-you-aint-steinbeck-my-bronca-with-fake-ass-social-justice -literature/?fbclid=IwAR3LqdyMZCvuWKhlu-0cf6Kx3cx78EeGYLoghB5zNwz HuFmSuc_n_xhsEg4.

Guthrie, Marisa. "Comcast to Launch Networks Backed by Sean Combs, Magic Johnson and Robert Rodriguez." *The Hollywood Reporter*, 21 Feb. 2012, www .hollywoodreporter.com/news/general-news/comcast-sean-combs-magic -johnson-robert-rodriquez-293119/.

Gutierrez, Gabe, and Corky Siemaszko. "Photographer Reveals Story Behind Iconic Image of Fleeing Migrants at Mexico Border." *NBCNews*, 26 Nov. 2018, www

.nbcnews.com/news/us-news/photographer-reveals-story-behind-iconic-photo-fleeing-migrants-mexico-border-n940271.

Gutiérrez, Jessica Marie. "The Tejano Monument on TX Capitol Grounds: A Testimony of Spanish-Mexican Heritage Influenced in Present Day Texas Culture." *The Hispanic Blog*, 30 Mar. 2012, thehispanicblog.com/2012/03/30/the-tejano-monument-on-tx-capitol-grounds-a-testimony-of-spanish-mexican-heritage-influenced-in-present-day-texas-culture/#:~:text=The%20Tejano%20Monument%20was%20created,in%20present%2Dday%20Texas%20culture.

Gutiérrez y Muhs, Gabriella, et al., editors. *Presumed Incompetent: The Intersections of Race and Class for Women in Academia*. Utah State UP, 2012.

Gwaltney, Marilyn. "Androids as a Device for Reflection on Personhood." *Retrofitting* Blade Runner: *Issues in Ridley Scott's* Blade Runner *and Philip K. Dick's* Do Androids Dream of Electric Sheep?, edited by Judith B. Kerman, U of Wisconsin P, 1997, pp. 32–39.

Halberstam, J. Jack. *Gaga Feminism: Sex, Gender, and the End of Normal*. Beacon Press, 2012.

Halberstam, Judith. *Female Masculinity*. Duke UP, 1998.

Hamill, Mark [@HamillHimself]. "The cast & crew first learned of it . . ." *Twitter*, 24 May 2020, twitter.com/HamillHimself/status/1264661085459628032.

Hannan, Brian. *The Making of* The Magnificent Seven: *Behind the Scenes of the Pivotal Western*. Kindle ed., McFarland, 2015.

Harrison, Eric. "A Galaxy Far, Far Off Racial Mark?" *Los Angeles Times*, 26 May 1999, www.latimes.com/archives/la-xpm-1999-may-26-ca-40965-story.html.

Harry Potter and the Deathly Hallows: Part 2. Directed by David Yates, performances by Daniel Radcliffe, Rupert Grint, Emma Watson, and Warwick Davis, Warner Bros., 2011.

Hart, Martin B. "Roadshow." *The American WideScreen Museum*, 2002, www.widescreenmuseum.com/widescreen/roadshow_presentation2.htm.

Harwood, Sarah. *Family Fictions: Representations of the Family in 1980s Hollywood Cinema*. St. Martin's, 1997.

Hearne, Joanna. *Native Recognition: Indigenous Cinema and the Western*. State U of New York P, 2012.

Heide, Markus. "Learning from Fossils: Transcultural Space in Luis Alberto Urrea's *In Search of Snow*." *Literature and Ethnicity in the Cultural Borderlands*, edited by Jesús Benito and Anna María Manzanas, Rodopi, 2002, pp. 115–25.

Hernández, David Manuel. "Confronting or Confounding Masculinities?" Review of *Muy Macho: Latino Men Confront Their Manhood*, edited by Ray Gonzalez. *American Quarterly*, vol. 51, no. 1, 1999, pp. 203–211.

Hernández, Leandra H. "Paternidad, Masculinidad, and Machismo: Evolving Representations of Mexican American Fathers in Film." *Deconstructing Dads: Changing Images of Fathers in Popular Culture*, edited by Laura Tropp and Janice Kelly, Lexington, 2016, pp. 247–272.

Hinojosa, Rolando. *The Valley*. 1973. Arte Público, 2014.

Hokowhitu, Brendan. "Taxonomies of Indigeneity: Indigenous Heterosexual Patriarchal Masculinity." *Indigenous Men and Masculinities: Legacies, Identities, Regeneration*, edited by Robert Alexander Innes and Kim Anderson, U of Manitoba P, 2015, pp. 80–95.

Honoré, Carl. *In Praise of Slowness: Challenging the Cult of Speed*. HarperCollins, 2004.

hooks, bell. *Black Looks: Race and Representation*. South End, 1992.

———. *Reel to Real: Race, Sex, and Class at the Movies*. Routledge, 1994.

Howe, Irving, editor. *The Idea of the Modern in Literature and the Arts*. Horizon, 1968.

Howe, Neil, and William Strauss. *Millennials Rising: The New Great Generation*. Vintage, 2000.

Huaco-Nuzum, Carmen. "*Orale* Patriarchy: *Hasta Cuando Corazón* Will You Remain *el Gallo Macho* of *Mi Familia*?" *The Chicana/o Cultural Studies Reader*, edited by Angie Chabram-Dernersesian, Routledge, 2006, pp. 261–268.

Huerta, Elisa Diana. "Embodied Recuperations: Performance, Indigeneity, and *Danza Azteca*." *Dancing across Borders: Danzas y Bailes Mexicanos*, edited by Olga Nájera-Ramírez et al., U of Illinois P, 2009, pp. 3–18.

Huerta, Jorge. *Chicano Drama: Performance, Society, and Myth*. Cambridge UP, 2000.

Hutton, Paul Andrew. *The Apache Wars: The Hunt for Geronimo, The Apache Kid, and the Captive Boy Who Started the Longest War in American History*. Broadway, 2016.

Innes, Robert Alexander, and Kim Anderson, editors. *Indigenous Men and Masculinities: Legacies, Identities, Regeneration*. U of Manitoba P, 2015.

Irwin, Robert McKee, and Maricruz Castro Ricalde. *Global Mexican Cinema: Its Golden Age*. Palgrave, 2013.

James, Caryn. "A Mexican-American Journey of Generations." Review of *My Family/Mi familia*, directed by Gregory Nava. *New York Times*, 3 May 1995, www.nytimes.com/1995/05/03/movies/film-review-a-mexican-american-journey-of-generations.html.

Johnson, Reed. "Peter and Benjamin Bratt Are on a Mission." *Los Angeles Times*, 10 Apr. 2010, www.latimes.com/archives/la-xpm-2010-apr-10-la-et-bratt10-2010apr10-story.html.

Jung, Ryan. "HD 720 Isaias Mata '500 Years of Resistance.'" *YouTube*, 6 May 2013, www.youtube.com/watch?v=r7XG0pjqMAk.

Justice, Daniel Heath. "'Go Away, Water!': Kinship Criticism and the Decolonization Imperative." *Reasoning Together: The Native Critics Collective*, edited by Craig S. Womack et al., U of Oklahoma P, 2008, pp. 147–168.

Kahn, William A. "Holding Environments at Work." *The Journal of Applied Behavioral Science*, vol. 37, no. 3, 2001, pp. 260–279.

Kallio, Galina, and Eeva Houtbeckers. "Academic Knowledge Production: Framework of Practical Activity in the Context of Transformative Food Studies." *Frontiers in Sustainable Food Systems*, vol. 4, 2020, pp. 1–12.

Karkov, Catherine E., editor. *Slow Scholarship: Medieval Research and the Neoliberal University*. New ed., Boydell and Brewer, 2019. *JSTOR*, www.jstor.org/stable/j.ctvktrxwz.

"Kateri's Pathway to Sainthood." *Saint Kateri Tekakwitha National Shrine and Historic Site*, 2016, www.katerishrine.com/st-kateri.

Keating, AnaLouise, editor. *Interviews/Entrevistas/Gloria Anzaldúa*, Routledge, 2000.

Keller, Gary D. *A Biographical Handbook of Hispanics and United States Film*. Bilingual Review/Press, 1997.

———. *Hispanics and United States Film: An Overview and Handbook*. Bilingual Review/Press, 1994.

Kempley, Rita. "Movies' 'Magic Negro' Saves the Day—But at the Cost of His Soul." *The Black Commentator*, 13 Oct. 2006, www.blackcommentator.com/49/49 _magic.html.

Khoury, Noura. "Iconic Mural, Symbol of Resistance, Is Reborn." *El Tocolote*, 10 May 2013, eltecolote.org/content/iconic-mural-symbol-of-resistance-is-reborn/.

Kimmel, Michael. *Manhood in America: A Cultural History*. 1998. 3rd ed., Oxford UP, 2012.

King, Gayle. "Father Shares Family Reunification Story as Lawyers Search for Parents of More than Five Hundred Children." *CBS This Morning*, CBS News, 2 Mar. 2021, www.cbsnews.com/video/father-shares-family-reunification-story-as -lawyers-search-for-parents-of-more-than-500-children/#x.

King, Thomas, editor. *All My Relations: An Anthology of Contemporary Canadian Native Fiction*. U of Oklahoma P, 1992.

———. *The Truth about Stories: A Native Narrative*. CBC Massey Lectures, House of Anansi, 2003.

Kenney, Laurie. "HBO Options *The Boy Kings of Texas*." *Lyons Press*, 9 Jan. 2014, lyonspress.wordpress.com/2014/01/09/hbo-options-the-boy-kings-of-texas -hayek-weintraub-to-produce/.

Kirby, Jen. "*Time*'s Crying Girl Photo Controversy, Explained." *Vox*, 22 June 2018, www.vox.com/policy-and-politics/2018/6/22/17494688/time-magazine-cover -crying-girl-photo-controversy-family-separation.

Kolata, Gina. "Kati Kariko Helped Shield the World from the Coronavirus." *New York Times*, 8 Apr. 2021, www.nytimes.com/2021/04/08/health/coronavirus -mrna-kariko.html.

Lake Placid. Directed by Steve Miner, performances by Bill Pullman, Bridget Fonda, Brendan Gleeson, Oliver Platt, and Betty White, 20th Century Fox, 1999.

Lawrence, John Shelton, and Robert Jewett. *The Myth of the American Superhero*. William B. Eerdmans, 2002.

Leavis, Q. D. "Caterpillars of the Commonwealth Unite!" *Scrutiny*, vol. 7, no. 2, 1938, pp. 203–214.

Lee, Spike. "Thinking about the Power of Images." Interview by Gary Crowdus and Dan Georgakas. *Cinéaste*, vol. 26, no. 2, 2001, pp. 4–9.

Lewis, Paul Owen. *Storm Boy*. Beyond Words, 1995.

Lindemann, Mary. "Slow History." *The American Historical Review*, vol. 126, no. 1, 2021, pp. 1–18.

List, Christine. *Chicano Images: Refiguring Ethnicity in Mainstream Film*. Garland, 1996.

Logan. Directed by James Mangold, performances by Hugh Jackman, Patrick Stewart, and Dafne Keen, 20th Century Fox, 2017.

López, Ana M. "Are All Latins from Manhattan? Hollywood, Ethnography, and Cultural Colonialism." *Unspeakable Images: Ethnicity and the American Cinema*, edited by Lester D. Friedman, U of Chicago P, 1991, pp. 404–424.

Lux, Guillermo, and Maurilio E. Vigil. "Return to Aztlán: The Chicano Rediscovers His Indian Past." *Aztlán: Essays on the Chicano Homeland*, edited by Rudolfo A. Anaya and Francisco Lomelí, U of New Mexico P, 1989, pp. 93–110.

Madsen, William. *Mexican-Americans of South Texas*. 2nd ed., Holt, Rinehart and Winston, 1972.

Maffesoli, Michel. *The Time of the Tribes: The Decline of Individualism in Mass Society*. 1988. Translated by Don Smith, Sage, 1996.

The Magnificent Seven. Directed by John Sturges, performances by Yul Brynner and Steve McQueen, United Artists, 1960.

The Magnificent Seven. Directed by Antoine Fuqua, performances by Denzel Washington, Chris Pratt, Ethan Hawke, Manuel Garcia-Rulfo, Lee Byung-hun, Vincent D'Onofrio, and Martin Sensmeier, Sony, 2016.

Martell, Luke. "The Slow University: Inequality, Power, and Alternatives." *Forum Qualitative Sozialforschung/Forum: Qualitative Social Research*, vol. 15, no. 3, 2014, www.qualitative-research.net/index.php/fqs/article/view/2223.

Martínez, Demetria. *Mother Tongue*. Harper Collins, 1990.

Martinez, Domingo. *The Boy Kings of Texas: A Memoir*. Lyons, 2012.

Martínez, Nina Marie. *¡Caramba!: A Tale Told in Turns of the Card*. Knopf, 2004.

Matos, Angel Daniel. "A Narrative of a Future Past: Historical Authenticity, Ethics, and Queer Latinx Futurity in *Aristotle and Dante Discover the Secrets of the Universe*." *Children's Literature*, vol. 47, no. 1, 2019, pp. 30–56.

McCarthy, Todd. Review of *My Family/Mi familia*, directed by Gregory Nava. *Variety*, 29 Jan. 1995, variety.com/1995/film/reviews/my-family-mi-familia-1200439914/.

McKegney, Sam, editor. *Masculindians: Conversations about Indigenous Manhood*. East Michigan State UP, 2014.

McNickle, D'Arcy. *Native American Tribalism: Indian Survivals and Renewals*. Oxford UP, 1973.

Meeuf, Russell. *John Wayne's World: Transnational Masculinities in the Fifties*. U of Texas P, 2013.

Melero, Apolinar. "Mi Gente." *Yearnings*, edited by Albert C. Chavez, Pendulum, 1972, pp. 19–22.

Merchant, Nomaan, and Elliot Spagat. "Nine Parents Separated from Families Return to Children in US." *AP News*, 23 Jan. 2020, apnews.com/article/donald-trump-us-news-ap-top-news-az-state-wire-immigration-e22c6f494ec9017648dd402d9e47a54e.

Metcalf, Stephen. "How John Wayne Became a Hollow Masculine Icon." *The Atlantic*, Dec. 2017, www.theatlantic.com/magazine/archive/2017/12/john-wayne-john-ford/544113/.

"*The Milagro Beanfield War* (1988)." *The Numbers*, 2021, www.the-numbers.com/movie/Milagro-Beanfield-War-The#tab=summary.

Minich, Julie Avril. *Accessible Citizenships: Disability, Nation, and the Cultural Politics of Greater Mexico*. Temple UP, 2013.

———. "Disabling la Frontera: Disability, Border Subjectivity, and Masculinity in 'Big Jesse, Little Jesse' by Oscar Casares." *MELUS: The Journal of the Society for the Study of the Multi-Ethnic Literature of the United States*, vol. 35, no. 1, 2010, pp. 35–52.

———. "'The Emotional Residue of an Unnatural Boundary': *Brownsville* and the Borders of Mental Health." *Symbolism 17: Latina/o Literature*, edited by Rüdiger Ahrens et al., 2017, pp. 123–142.

Miranda, Carolina A. "Border Drones and Labor-Bots: Alex Rivera's Prescient 'Sleep Dealer.'" *Los Angeles Times*, 2 Aug. 2014, www.latimes.com/entertainment/arts/miranda/la-et-cam-alex-rivera-sleep-dealer-prescient-border-drones-20140801-column.html.

Mirandé, Alfredo. "The Chicano Family: A Reanalysis of Conflicting Views." *Journal of Marriage and the Family*, vol. 39, no. 4, 1977, pp. 747–756.

———. *Hombres y Machos: Masculinity and Latino Culture.* Westview, 1997.

———. "A Reinterpretation of Male Dominance in the Chicano Family." *The Family Coordinator*, vol. 28, no. 4, 1979, pp. 473–479.

La Mission. Directed by Peter Bratt, performances by Benjamin Bratt, Jesse Borrego, Jeremy Ray Valdez, and Talisa Soto Bratt, Global Cinema Distribution, 2009.

Mitchell, Lee Clark. *Westerns: Making the Man in Fiction and Film.* U of Chicago P, 1996.

"Monroe Doctrine, 1823." Office of the Historian, United States Department of State, n.d., history.state.gov/milestones/1801-1829/monroe.

Mora, Lilia R. "Salinas, Agustín, Sr." *Handbook of Texas Online.* www.tshaonline.org/handbook/entries/salinas-agustin-sr.

Mora, Pat. *House of Houses.* Beacon Press, 1997.

Moraga, Cherríe. *The Last Generation: Prose and Poetry.* South End, 1993.

———. *Loving in the War Years: Lo Que Nunca Pasó por Sus Labios.* South End, 1983.

———. "The Salt That Cures: Remembering Gloria Anzaldúa." *A Xicana Codex of Changing Consciousness: Writings, 2000–2010*, Duke UP, 2011, pp. 116–130.

Moraga, Cherríe, and Gloria Anzaldúa, editors. *This Bridge Called My Back: Writings by Radical Women of Color.* Persephone, 1981.

Muñoz, José Esteban. "Feeling Brown: Ethnicity and Affect in Ricardo Bracho's *The Sweetest Hangover (and Other STDs).*" *Theatre Journal*, vol. 52, no. 1, 2000, pp. 67–79.

———. *The Sense of Brown.* Edited by Joshua Chambers-Letson and Tavia Nyong'o. Duke UP, 2020.

Muñoz Martínez, Monica. *The Injustice Never Leaves You: Anti-Mexican Violence in Texas.* Harvard UP, 2018.

My Family/Mi familia. Directed by Gregory Nava, performances by Edward James Olmos, Lupe Ontiveros, and Jimmy Smits, New Line Cinema. 1995.

Nava, Gregory. "Filming the Chicano Family Saga." Interview by Dennis West. *Cinéaste*, vol. 21, no. 4, 1995, pp. 26–28.

Nieves, Santiago, and Frank Algarin. "Two Film Reviews: *My Family/Mi Familia* and *The Perez Family.*" *Latin Looks: Images of Latinas and Latinos in the U.S. Media*, edited by Clara B. Rodriguez, Routledge, 1997, pp. 221–224.

Nixon, Rob. *Slow Violence and the Environmentalism of the Poor.* Harvard UP, 2011.

Noe-Bustamante, Luis. "Key Facts about U.S. Hispanics and Their Diverse Heritage." *Pew Research Center*, 16 Sept. 2019, www.pewresearch.org/fact-tank/2019/09/16/key-facts-about-u-s-hispanics/.

Noriega, Chon A., editor. *Chicanos and Film: Representation and Resistance.* U of Minnesota P, 1992.

"Oak Forest Library." *Architect: The Journal of the American Institute of Architects*, 28 June 2012, www.architectmagazine.com/project-gallery/oak-forest-library-196.

O'Brien, Geoffrey. *The Phantom Empire: Movies in the Mind of the Twentieth Century.* Norton, 1993.

Okorafor-Mbachu, Nnedi. "Stephen King's Super-Duper Magical Negroes." *Strange Horizons*, 25 Oct. 2004, www.strangehorizons.com/2004/20041025/kinga.shtml.

Orozco, Danielle Alexis. "Laura Kinney as X-Treme Niña." *Latinx Ciné in the

Twenty-First Century, edited by Frederick Luis Aldama, U of Arizona P, 2019, pp. 312–332.
Ortego, Philip D., editor. *We Are Chicanos: An Anthology of Mexican-American Literature*. Washington Square Press ed., Pocket Books, 1973.
Ortíz Taylor, Sheila, and Sandra Ortíz Taylor. *Imaginary Parents*. U of New Mexico P, 1996.
Palmer, Lorrie. "The Punisher as Revisionist Superhero Western." *The Superhero Reader*, edited by Charles Hatfield et al., U of Mississippi P, 2013, pp. 279–294.
Palmer, Parker J. *The Courage to Teach: Exploring the Inner Landscape of a Teacher's Life*. 20th Anniversary ed., Jossey-Bass, 2017.
Paredes, Américo. *Folklore and Culture on the Texas-Mexican Border*, edited by Richard Bauman, U of Texas P, 1993.
———. *George Washington Gomez: A Mexicotexan Novel*. Arte Público, 1990.
———. *A Texas Mexican Cancionero: Folksongs of the Lower Border*. Urbana: U of Illinois P, 1976.
———. *"With His Pistol in His Hand": A Border Ballad and Its Hero*. 1958. U of Texas P, 1971.
Pearce, Roy H. *Savagism and Civilization: A Study of the Indian and the American Mind*. Johns Hopkins UP, 1967.
Pérez, Daniel Enrique. *Rethinking Chicana/o and Latina/o Popular Culture*. Palgrave, 2009.
Perez, Domino Renee. "A Familial Legacy of MeXicana Style." *MeXicana Fashions: Politics, Self-Adornment, and Identity Construction*, edited by Aída Hurtado and Norma E. Cantú, U of Texas P, 2020, pp. 109–133.
———. "Magnificence and Metas in Professional Westerns." *Weird Westerns: Race, Gender, Genre*, edited by Kerry Fine et al., U of Nebraska P, 2020, pp. 174–196.
———. "New Tribalism and Chicana/o Indigeneity in the Work of Gloria Anzaldúa." *The Oxford Handbook of Indigenous American Literature*, edited by James H. Cox and Daniel Heath Justice, Oxford UP, 2014, pp. 489–502.
———. "Of Myth and Men: Racialized Masculinities in Luis Alberto Urrea's *In Search of Snow*." *Chiricú Journal*, vol. 3, no. 2, 2019, pp. 77–93.
Pérez-Torres, Rafael. "Chicano Ethnicity, Cultural Hybridity, and the Mestizo Voice." *American Literature*, vol. 7, no. 1, 1998, p. 159.
———. *Mestizaje: Critical Uses of Race in Chicano Culture*. U of Minnesota P, 2005.
Pina, Michael. "The Archaic, Historical and Mythicized Dimensions of Aztlán." *Aztlán: Essays on the Chicano Homeland*, edited by Rudolfo A. Anaya and Francisco Lomelí, U of New Mexico P, 1989, pp. 14–48.
Pitts, Victoria. *In the Flesh: The Cultural Politics of Body Modification*. Palgrave Macmillan, 2003.
Quinceañera. Directed by Richard Glatzer and Wash Westmoreland, performances by Emily Rios, Jesse Garcia, and Chalo González, Sony Pictures Classics, 2006.
Quinn, Daniel. *Ishmael*. Bantam/Turner, 1992.
Raheja, Michelle H. *Reservation Reelism: Redfacing, Visual Sovereignty, and Representations of Native Americans in Film*. U of Nebraska P, 2011.
Ramirez, Michael. "'My Dog's Just Like Me': Dog Ownership as a Gender Display." *Symbolic Interaction*, vol. 29, no. 3, 2006, pp. 373–391.
Ramírez Berg, Charles. "*Bordertown*, the Assimilation Narrative, and the Chicano Social Problem Film." *Chicanos and Film: Representation and Resistance*, edited by Chon A. Noriega, U of Minnesota P, 1992, pp. 29–46.

———. *The Classical Mexican Cinema: The Poetics of the Exceptional Golden Age Films.* U of Texas P, 2015.

———. Introduction. *Cine Mexicano: Posters from the Golden Age 1936–1956,* by Rogelio Agrasanchez, Chronicle, 2001, pp. 8–24.

———. *Latino Images in Film: Stereotypes, Subversion, and Resistance.* U of Texas P, 2002.

Raymond, Virginia. *Mexican Americans Write towards Justice in Texas, 1973–1982.* 2007. U of Texas at Austin, PhD dissertation. Texas ScholarWorks, repositories.lib.utexas.edu/handle/2152/6260.

Real Women Have Curves. Directed by Patricia Cardoso, performances by America Ferrera, Lupe Ontiveros, Felipe de Alba, and Jorge Cervera, Jr., Newmarket Films, 2002.

Reel Injun. Directed by Neil Diamond, Catherine Bainbridge, and Jeremiah Hayes, National Film Board of Canada, 2009.

Reeser, Todd W. *Masculinities in Theory.* Wiley-Blackwell, 2010.

Reilly, Katie. "Here Are All the Times Donald Trump Insulted Mexico." *Time,* 31 Aug. 2016, time.com/4473972/donald-trump-mexico-meeting-insult/.

Reitsma, Richard. "Quo Vadis, Queer Vato? Queer and Loathing in Latino Cinema." *LGBT Transnational Identity and the Media,* edited by Christopher Pullen, Palgrave, 2012, pp. 231–241.

"Replicant." *Off-World, the Blade Runner Wiki.* 15 Feb. 2021, bladerunner.fandom.com/wiki/Replicant.

Resendiz, Julian. "Juarez Reports Nearly Five Hundred Women Murdered in Past 3 Years." *KXAN,* 31 Aug. 2021, www.kxan.com/%20border-report/juarez-reports-nearly-500-women-murdered-in-past-3-years/.

Review of *The Phantom Empire,* by Geoffrey O'Brien. *Kirkus,* 15 Aug. 1993, www.kirkusreviews.com/book-reviews/geoffrey-obrien/the-phantom-empire/.

Review of *The Phantom Empire,* by Geoffrey O'Brien. *Publishers Weekly,* 1993, www.publishersweekly.com/978-0-393-03549-0.

Rieff, David. "Professional Aztecs and Popular Culture." *New Perspectives Quarterly,* vol. 8, no. 1, 1991, pp. 42–46.

Rivera, Tomás. *And the Earth Did Not Devour Him.* 1971. Translated by Evangelina Vigil-Piñón, Arte Público, 1995.

Robinson, Cecil. "The Extended Presence: Mexico and Its Culture in North American Writing." *MELUS: The Journal of the Society for the Study of the Multi-Ethnic Literature of the United States,* vol. 5, no. 3, 1978, pp. 3–15.

Rochlin, Margie. "Not Fat, Not Greek, Not a Wedding, but What a Party." *New York Times,* 23 July 2006, late ed., sec. 2, p. 18.

Rodríguez, Richard T. *Next of Kin: The Family in Chicano/a Cultural Politics.* Duke UP, 2009.

Rodriguez, Robert. "Robert Rodriguez Wants You for New Network Channel." Interview by Alexandra Gratereaux. *Fox News,* 21 Feb. 2012, www.foxnews.com/entertainment/robert-rodriguez-wants-you-for-new-network-channel.

Romano-V., Octavio Ignacio, and Herminio Rios C., editors. *El espejo—The Mirror: Selected Chicano Literature.* 1969. Quinto Sol, 1972.

Rosaldo, Renato. *Culture and Truth: The Remaking of Social Analysis.* 1989. Beacon Press, 1993.

Sáenz, Benjamin Alire. *Aristotle and Dante Discover the Secrets of the Universe.* Simon and Schuster, 2012.

———. "Benjamin Alire Sáenz." Interview by Frederick Luis Aldama. *Latino/a Children's and Young Adult Writers on the Art of Storytelling*, edited by Aldama, U of Pittsburgh P, 2018, pp. 207–213.
Saldaña-Portillo, María Josefina. *Indian Given: Racial Geographies across Mexico and the United States*. Duke UP, 2016.
———. "Who's the Indian in Aztlán? Re-Writing Mestizaje, Indianism, and Chicanismo from the Lacandón." *The Latin American Subaltern Studies Reader*, edited by Ileana Rodríguez, Duke UP, 2001, pp. 402–423.
Saldívar-Hull, Sonia. *Feminism on the Border: Chicana Gender Politics and Literature*. U of California P, 2000.
Sammon, Paul M. *Future Noir: The Making of Blade Runner*. Harper, 1996.
Sánchez, Ricardo. *Canto y grito mi liberacíon: The Liberation of a Chicano Mind*. 1971. 2nd ed., Anchor, 1973.
Sandoval, Denise Michelle. "Cruising through Low Rider Culture: Chicana/o Identity in the Marketing of Low Rider Magazine." *Velvet Barrios: Popular Culture and Chicana/o Sexualities*, edited by Alicia Gaspar de Alba, Palgrave, 2003, pp.×179–196.
Santos, George. "Latinx-Men: Logan's Undocumented Voices Speak." *Latinx Ciné in the Twenty-First Century*, edited by Frederick Luis Aldama, U of Arizona P, 2019, pp. 299–311.
Schlesinger, Lisa. "Towards a Slow Theatre." *Innovation in Five Acts: Strategies for Theatre and Performance*, edited by Caridad Svich, Theatre Communications Group, 2015, pp. 64–70.
Schmidt, David J. "'American Dirt' Isn't Just Bad—Its Best Parts Are Cribbed From Latino Writers." Huffington Post, 1 Jan. 2020, www.huffpost.com/entry/american-dirt-book_n_5e2a11e8c5b6779e9c2fd79f.
Schoenberger, Nancy. *Wayne and Ford: The Films, the Friendship, and the Forging of an American Hero*. Anchor, 2017.
Sehra, Rohina Katoch. "Twenty-three Indigenous Fashion Brands: Clothing, Jewelry, Accessories and Shoes." Huffington Post, 27 July 2020, www.huffpost.com/entry/indigenous-fashion-designers-brands_l_5f11d1f4c5b619afc400ea87.
Shapiro, Lila. "Blurbed to Death." *Vulture*, 5 Jan. 2021, www.vulture.com/article/american-dirt-jeanine-cummins-book-controversy.html.
Shields, Rob. "Foreword: Masses or Tribes?" *The Time of the Tribes: The Decline of Individualism in Mass Society* (1988), by Michel Maffesoli, translated by Don Smith, Sage, 1996, ix–xii.
Simmen, Edward, editor. *The Chicano: From Caricature to Self-Portrait*. New American Library, 1971.
Sloss, Pete Silva. "One Spark Can Start a Prairie Fire." *Aztecas del Norte: The Chicanos of Aztlán*, edited by Jack D. Forbes, Fawcett, 1973, pp. 171–173.
Slotkin, Richard. "Gunfighters and Green Berets: *The Magnificent Seven* and the Myth of Counter-Insurgency." *Radical History Review*, vol. 1989, no. 44, 1989, pp. 65–90.
Smith, Paul Chaat, and Robert Allen Warrior. *Like a Hurricane: The Indian Movement from Alcatraz to Wounded Knee*. New Press, 1996.
Sneider, Leah. "Complementary Relationships: A Review of Indigenous Gender Studies." *Indigenous Men and Masculinities: Legacies, Identities, Regeneration*, edited by Robert Alexander Innes and Kim Anderson, U of Manitoba P, 2015, pp. 62–79.

"Stand and Deliver (1988)." *The Numbers*, 2021, www.the-numbers.com/movie/Stand-and-Deliver#tab=summary.

Star Wars: Episode I—The Phantom Menace. Directed by George Lucas, performances by Liam Neeson, Ewan McGregor, and Natalie Portman, 20th Century Fox, 1999.

Star Wars: Episode IV—A New Hope. Directed by George Lucas, performances by Mark Hamill, Carrie Fisher, and Harrison Ford, 20th Century Fox, 1977.

Star Wars: Episode V—The Empire Strikes Back. Directed by George Lucas, performances by Mark Hamill, Carrie Fisher, and Harrison Ford, 20th Century Fox, 1980.

Stengers, Isabelle. *Another Science Is Possible: A Manifesto for Slow Science*. 2013. Translated by Stephen Muecke, Polity, 2018.

———. "The Care of the Possible." Interview by Eric Bordeleau. *Scapegoat: Architecture/Landscape/Political Economy*, vol. 1, 2011, pp. 12–13, 16–17, 27.

Strong, Pauline Turner. *American Indians and the American Imaginary: Cultural Representation across the Centuries*. Paradigm, 2013.

Suicide Squad. Directed by David Ayer, performances by Will Smith, Margot Robbie, Jai Courtney, Cara Delevingne, Viola Davis, Adewale Akinnuoye-Agbaje, Jay Hernandez, Adam Beach, and Karen Fukuhara, Warner Bros., 2016.

Tahmahkera, Dustin. *Cinematic Comanches:* The Lone Ranger *in the Media Borderlands*. U of Nebraska P, 2022.

———. *Tribal Television: Viewing Native People in Sitcoms*. U of North Carolina P, 2014.

Tallbear, Kim. *Native American DNA: Tribal Belonging and the False Promise of Genetic Science*. U of Minnesota P, 2013.

Thein, Amanda Haertling, and Kate E. Kedley. "Out of the Closet and All Grown Up: Problematizing Normative Narratives of Coming-Out and Coming-of-Age in Young Adult Literature." *Beyond Borders: Queer Eros and Ethos (Ethics) in LGBTQ Young Adult Literature*, edited by Darla Linville and David Lee Carlson, Peter Lang, 2016, pp. 3–20.

Thomsen, Jacqueline. "Mexican-American Judge Who Trump Attacked Rules in Favor of Border Wall." *The Hill*, 27 Feb. 2018, thehill.com/regulation/court-battles/375875-mexican-american-judge-that-trump-attacked-rules-in-favor-of-trumps.

Tremmel, Michelle. "Forget Formulas: Teaching Form through Function in Slow Writing and Reading as a Writer." *Composition Studies*, vol. 45, no. 2, 2017, pp. 113–129.

United States Census Bureau. "The American Indian and Alaska Native Populations: 2010." GPO, 2012.

Urrea, Luis Alberto. "Amazing Grace: Story and Writer An Afterword." *Six Kinds of Sky: A Collection of Short Fiction*, Cinco Puntos, 2002, pp. 129–146.

———. "Bid Farewell to Her Many Horses." *Six Kinds of Sky: A Collection of Short Fiction*, Cinco Puntos, 2002, pp. 115–125.

———. *In Search of Snow*. U of Arizona P, 1994.

———. "Whores." *Muy Macho: Latino Men Confront Their Manhood*, edited by Ray Gonzalez, Anchor, 1996, pp. 99–110.

Valdez, Luis. "Notes on Chicano Theatre." *Luis Valdez—Early Works: Actos, Bernabé, and Pensamiento Serpentino*, Arte Público, 1994, pp. 6–10.

Valdez, Luis, and Stan Steiner, editors. *Aztlan: An Anthology of Mexican American Literature.* Vintage, 1972.

Varon, Alberto. *Before Chicano: Citizenship and the Making of Mexican American Manhood, 1848–1959.* New York UP, 2018.

Vasconcelos, José. *The Cosmic Race/La raza cósmica.* 1925. Translated by Didier T. Jaén, Johns Hopkins UP, 1997.

Vasquez, Richard. *Chicano.* 1970. HarperCollins, 2009.

Vick, Karl. "A Reckoning after Trump's Border Separation Policy: What Kind of Country Are We?" *Time,* 21 June 2018, https://time.com/5318229/donald-trump-border-separation-policy/.

Villarreal, José Antonio. *Pocho.* Anchor, 1959.

Vizenor, Gerald. *Manifest Manners: Narratives on Postindian Survivance.* U of Nebraska P, 1999.

Walker, Alice. *In Search of Our Mothers' Gardens: Womanist Prose.* Harcourt Brace Jovanovich, 1983.

A Walk in the Clouds. Directed by Alfonso Arau, performances by Anthony Quinn, Giancarlo Giannini, Keanu Reeves, and Aitana Sánchez-Gijón, 20th Century Fox, 1995.

Watson, Elwood, and Marc E. Shaw, editors. *Performing American Masculinities: The Twenty-first-Century Man in Popular Culture,* Indiana UP, 2011.

"Weekend Domestic Chart for May 5, 1995." *The Numbers,* 2021, www.the-numbers.com/box-office-chart/weekend/1995/05/05.

Welling, David. "Alabama Theatre." *Cinema Houston,* 2016, www.cinemahouston.info/about.shtml.

Williams, Leah. "How Hollywood Whitewashed the Old West." *The Atlantic,* 5 Oct. 2016, www.theatlantic.com/entertainment/archive/2016/10/how-the-west-was-lost/502850/.

Wills, Bob, and His Texas Playboys. "Roly-Poly." Written by Fred Rose. Columbia, 1946.

Woll, Allen. "How Hollywood Has Portrayed Hispanics." *New York Times,* 1 Mar. 1981, www.nytimes.com/1981/03/01/movies/how-hollywood-has-portrayed-hispanics.html.

Woolery, George W. *Children's Television: The First Thirty-five Years, 1946–1981,* pt. 2, *Live, Film, and Tape Series.* Scarecrow Press, 1983.

Woolf, Virginia. *Three Guineas.* Harcourt, 1938.

Wright, Will. *Sixguns and Society: A Structural Study of the Western.* U of California P, 1975.

Wyatt, Edward, and Stuart Elliot. "G.M. Drops 'Survivor' but Says Racial Format Isn't the Reason." *New York Times,* 31 Aug. 2006, www.nytimes.com/2006/08/31/business/media/31adco.html#:~:text=GENERAL%20MOTORS%2C%20which%20has%20accounted,will%20be%20based%20on%20race.

Zitkála-Šá [*published as* Gertrude Simmons Bonnin]. "Impressions of an Indian Childhood." *Atlantic Magazine,* vol. 85, 1900, pp. 37–47.

———. "School Days of an Indian Girl." *Atlantic Magazine,* vol. 85, 1900, pp. 185–194.

INDEX

Note: For film and TV titles, the year is included in parentheses; for titles of written works, the author in included in parentheses.

ABC Afterschool Special (1972–1997), 5, 275n2
absence: *Blade Runner* (1982), 117; *The Book of Life* (2014), 262; *Coco* (2017), 258; cycle of absence-presence-absence, 257; *Logan* (2017), 223, 244, 257; *The Magnificent Seven* (1960), 223; *La Mission* (2009), 75, 133; representation of fathers and families and, 21, 49, 53, 257, 277n15; *Star Wars* (1977), 75; *Suicide Squad* (2016), 223, 257; *Terminator: Dark Fate* (2019), 257; Urrea's *In Search of Snow*, 105, 108; young adult fiction and, 265
abuelo figure, 54, 55, 281n20
academic culture: BIPOC scholars and, 16, 21, 109, 276n8; CV, updating, 27–29; instrumentalism and person as machine, 111–114; knowledge labor, impact of, 276n7; literature reviews, 30–33; neoliberalism and, 16; personal truth, distrust of, 115; slow scholarship and research, 8–9, 15–19, 39–43, 112–114; writing and publication, 20–21, 46–47, 268, 276n5
Acevedo, Elizabeth, 265
Acevedo, Jorge, 284n11
Across the Wire (Urrea), 284n3
The Adventures of Kit Carson (1951–1955), 98, 285n15
affective excess, Latinx: *Despicable Me 2* (2013), 260; *The Mandalorian* (2019–present), 35–36; Muñoz on whiteness and affective normativity, 34–35; narrative of, 34–35, 257–258
Alabama Theater, Houston, 77–78
The Alamo (1960), 195–196, 224, 295n21

Alberto, Lourdes, 140, 289n13
Alcalde, M. Cristina, 130
Alcatraz occupation, 131–132, 288n4
Alcoff, Linda Martín, 155–156, 165–166
Aldama, Arturo J., 32–33, 195, 293n1
Aldama, Frederick Luis, 32–33, 186, 195, 266, 293n1
Alexie, Sherman, 167–169
Alfred, Taiaiake, 102
Aliens (1988), 283n3
Alurista, 144
Alves, Julio, 112
American Dirt (Cummins), 177–180, 292n2
American Me (1992), 50
Amigoland (Cásares), 204
Anaya, Rudolfo, 143–144, 184, 190–191, 197, 200–201
ancianos: *la familia* image, history of, 48–49; family-drama and *la familia* romance genres and, 50–54; female protagonists and, 56–57; as figure, 48, 54–59; *Quinceañera* (2006), 55–58, 70–75; *Real Women Have Curves* (2002), 55–58, 65–70; *A Walk in the Clouds* (1995), 55–65
Anders, Allison, 58
Anderson, Kim, 88
Anderson, Wallace "Mad Bear," 131
And the Earth Did Not Devour Him (Rivera), 184
Animal House (1978), 288n9
animated feature films, 257–264, 299n2
Ant-Man (2015), 83, 297n14
Ant-Man and the Wasp (2018), 83, 297n14
Anzaldúa, Gloria: about, 154–155; on accusations of appropriation, 286n8;

INDEX

on Aztec pantheon and Coatlicue states, 160, 162, 290n22; on Aztec red and black ink, 148; *The Borderlands/La Frontera*, 19–21, 154, 156, 160–161, 173, 186; critiques of, 155–156, 161–163; interviews, 165–166; *mestizaje* theorization, 154–156, 161, 162–165, 171–172; on new tribalism, 134, 161–167, 169–173, 290–291; "Now Let Us Shift . . . the Path of Conocimiento . . . Inner Work, Public Acts," 291; orange tree metaphor, 164–165; slow work and, 264; *This Bridge Called My Back*, 156, 173; *This Bridge We Call Home*, 164, 166–167, 169, 173
Aquaman (2018), 217
Arau, Alfonso, 55, 57
Aristotle and Dante Discover the Secrets of the Universe (Sáenz), 265–267
Austen, Jane, 93
authority: *Quinceañera* (2006), 70–71, 75; *Real Women Have Curves* (2002), 68–70; Urrea's *In Search of Snow*, 97; Villarreal's *Pocho*, 185; *A Walk in the Clouds* (1995), 59–65
Ayer, David, 230
Aztec culture and iconography: Anzaldúa on colors in, 148; Anzaldúa on pantheon and Coatlicue states, 160, 290n22; Chicanismo and, 116–117, 140; *danza azteca*, 149–151; *La Mission* (2009), 140–145, 148–152
"Aztext," 158, 162, 264
Aztlán, 116, 123, 143–144, 147, 159–160, 289nn16–17

Ballí, Cecilia, 205
La Bamba (1987), 49, 281n21, 291n4
Banda, Eldy, 131–132
bandido figure: about, 48; *Despicable Me 2* (2013), 259–260; *Logan* (2017), 240, 250, 264; *The Mandalorian* (2019–present), 35–36; as narrative tool of whiteness and masculinism, 296n7; *Quinceañera* (2006), 73; *Suicide Squad* (2016), 231; in western genre, 220–221, 224
Bataille, Gretchen M., 117

Baudrillard, Jean, 223
Bebout, Lee, 85, 94–95, 97, 283n1
Before Chicano (Varon), 186
Berg, Maggie, 46–47, 113–114, 286n5
A Better Life (2011), 49
Beverly Hills Chihuahua (2008), 299n2
The Big Country (1958), 296n6
"Big Jesse, Little Jesse" (Cásares), 204, 208–212
BIPOC (Black, Indigenous, and people of color): academic culture and, 16, 21, 109, 276n8; character stereotypes, 47–48, 49, 57–58; research, criticism of, 17–18; slow living and culture, 10
Black Panther (2018), 217, 297n14
Black Rain (1989), 269
Blackwell, Maylei, 160
Blade Runner (1982), 82, 111, 117, 269, 285n1–286n3, 286nn10–11
Blade Runner 2049 (2017), 285n2
Blanchard, Marc, 141
Bless Me, Ultima (Anaya), 184
Blood In, Blood Out (1993), 50
Bonnin, Gertrude Simmons (Zitkála-Šá), 9–10, 41
The Book of Life (2014), 258, 261–263
border family separations, 13, 33–35
The Borderlands/La Frontera (Anzaldúa), 19–21, 154, 156, 160–161, 173, 186
border policies, U.S., 13–14, 23
border politics, in *Logan* (2017), 241
Bordertown (1935), 49, 257
border wall, 23
Born in East L.A. (1987), 50, 282n21
Borrego, Jesse, 128
The Boy Kings of Texas (Martinez), 188–191, 206–207, 294n16
The Brady Bunch (1969–1974), 23
Bratt, Benjamin, 128–129, 133–134, 142, 287n1
Bratt, Peter, 128, 130–133, 136, 146, 150, 287n2. See also *La Mission* (2009)
Bringing Up Daddy (Bruzzi), 32
Broken Lance (1954), 296n6
brownface, 51, 223, 285n15
Brownness: feeling, Brown, 257; meaning of, 276n4; *La Mission* (2009),

Brownness (*continued*)
144–145, 257; public appetite for Brown pain, 177–178; "re-Browning of America," 144–145
Brown on Brown (Aldama), 186
Brownsville (Cásares): about, 184; "Big Jesse, Little Jesse," 204, 208–212; "Chango," 204; "Charro," 204, 208, 212–215, 295n25; "Mr. Z," 204–208
Bruce Almighty (2003), 282n22
Bruzzi, Stella, 32, 220–221, 225, 248, 296n6
Brynner, Yul, 225, 296n8
Buchholz, Horst, 223
buffoon type, 48, 261
Burciaga, José Antonio, 284n11
Bush, George H. W., 23
By the Lake of Sleeping Children (Urrea), 179

Calder, Jenni, 225–226, 234, 248, 296n9
Captain Marvel (2019), 217
Cardoso, Patricia, 55
Cars (2006), 299n2
Cásares, Oscar: about, 186, 204–205; *Amigoland*, 204; *Where We Come From*, 204. See also *Brownsville*
Castillo, Debra A., 155
Castro, Rafaela G., 281n20
Castro, Tony, 298n27
Castro Ricalde, Maricruz, 294n14
"Chango" (Cásares), 204
"Charro" (Cásares), 204, 208, 212–215, 295n25
charros, 187–188, 212–215, 294n12
Chateaubriand, François-René de, 40
Chicanismo and Chicano nationalism: Anzaldúa on "Chicano" vs. "Mexican American," 166; *danza azteca* and, 149; feminist critique of, 159–160; Indigeneity, instrumentalizing of, 115–116, 131; Mexica identification and, 142; *La Mission* (2009), 131, 133–134, 140–143, 145–147; new tribalism and, 290
Chicano (Vasquez), 184
El Chicano (2018), 231
The Chicano (Simmen), 184–185

Chicano civil rights movement (*el movimiento*), 157–160
"The Chinese Restaurant" (Gonzalez), 198–199
El Chingon (band), 294n8
Chohan, Sarah, 291n5
Circling the Tortilla Dragon (Gonzalez), 295n19
The Cisco Kid (1950–1956), 98, 285n15
Cisneros, Sandra, 289n14
civilization: of Aztlán, 159; role in transforming environments, 41–42; *Suicide Squad* (2016), 230, 233–234, 237; *Survivor* (2000–present) and, 291n1
Coco (2017), 49, 75, 258–259, 263–264
Coffin, Pierre, 258
Coke-Davis controversy, 297n11
Comcast, 293n5
comedia ranchera genre, 188, 294n13
communitas, 170
Conrad, Joseph, 40
Convoy (1978), 125
Coppola, Francis Ford, 52, 280n11
Cordova, Cary, 131, 132
Cotera, María Eugenia, 160
Cottage Grove, TX, 1
COVID-19 pandemic, 7–8, 11, 23–24
cowboy characters. *See* meta-human/mutant fathers and the western
cowboy/Indian dynamic: *Suicide Squad* (2016), 230, 235; Urrea's *In Search of Snow*, 90, 101–102, 195
Cowboys & Aliens (2011), 218
Crazy Horse, 103, 104
cultural tourism and appropriation, 167–169
Cummins, Jeanine, 177–180, 292n2
Curiel, Gonzalo, 23, 277n13
Curiel, Tony, 158
curriculum vitae (CVs), updating, 27–29
The Curse of La Llorona (2019), 49
The Curse of Oak Island (2014–present), 7–8

Dalrymple, Theodore, 278n1
Dances with Wolves (1990), 224, 288n10, 297n18
Dances with Wolves (Blake), 288n10

danza azteca, 149–151
Darren, Liana, 30
The Day After (1983), 7
DC Comics, 296n2
Deadpool (2016), 217
Deadpool 2 (2018), 217
Dean, James, 92–93
Decolonizing Academia (Rodríguez), 20–21
Decolonizing Latinx Masculinities (Aldama and Aldama), 32–33
The Defiant Ones (1958), 282n22
de la Mora, Sergio, 187–188
De León, Nephtalí, 144, 147, 289n18
Desperado (1995), 50
Despicable Me (2010), 259
Despicable Me 2 (2013), 258–261
Devotions upon Emergent Occasions (Donne), 107
Dickens, Charles, 93
Dickinson, Emily, 182
Dignidad Literaria, 180, 293n3
disability: Cásares's *Brownsville*, 205, 209–212; *La Mission* (2009), 137; queerness and, 296n27; Urrea's *In Search of Snow*, 94
DNA: *Logan* (2017), 218, 243–245; Martinez's *The Boy Kings of Texas*, 188; testing, 125–126
Donne, John, 107
Dora and the Lost City of Gold (2019), 83
Down Argentine Way (1940), 49
Dune (1984), 82, 269

East of Eden (1955), 92
East Side Sushi (2014), 49
Eastwood, Clint, 297n18
Eating Raoul (1982), 6–7
Emerson, Ralph Waldo, 267
emotional excess. *See* affective excess, Latinx
The Empire Strikes Back (*Star Wars Episode V*) (1980), 24, 77–82
Espinoza, Dionne, 160
Esquibél, Catrióna Rueda, 140
Estrada, Gabriel S., 130, 139, 151
Estrella, Sara, 143
Eternals (2021), 296n1

E.T. the Extra-Terrestrial (1982), 82
excess, emotional. *See* affective excess, Latinx

Faludi, Susan, 98–99
familia romance genre, 53–54, 59, 263
families, Brown (*la familia*). *See specific works and themes, such as* authority
family-drama genre, 51–52
family genealogies, complications of, 120–127
family separations at the border, 13, 33–35
Fantina, Richard, 93
fathers. *See specific works and themes, such as* masculinities
"Fathers" (Gonzalez), 193–194, 203
Fernández, Vicente, 187, 294n9
Ferretis, Jorge, 224
Fine, Kerry, 297n13
"Fishing" (Gonzalez), 201–203, 215–216
A Fistful of Dollars (1964), 145, 297n18
500 Years of Resistance (Mata), 132–133
Flying Down to Rio (1933), 49
Follow Me Home (1996), 128
Fools Rush In (1997), 49, 75
For Whom the Bell Tolls (Hemingway), 107
Foster, David William, 151
Fregoso, Rosa Linda, 32, 52, 54, 185, 277n16, 281n15, 291n4
From Prada to Nada (2011), 75
Frozen (2013), 13–14
Fuller, Stephanie, 223–224
Fuqua, Antoine, 228–229
The Furies (1950), 296n6
Furlong, Edward, 250–251, 298n27
Fusco, Coco, 168
futurity, 53, 107, 206, 257, 267, 269

Gaga Feminism (Halberstam), 20–21
el gallo figure, 260, 298n1
gangbanger figure, 231–232
García, Alma M., 159–160
Gardner, Chris, 114
Garroutte, Eva Marie, 142–143
genealogies, complicated, 120–127
Generation X, 8, 275n1
Gerhard, Susan, 132

Geronimo, 101, 103, 104, 106
Ghostbusters (1984), 82
The Ghost of John Wayne and Other Stories (Gonzalez): background on John Wayne, 194–196; "The Chinese Restaurant," 198–199; "Fishing," 201–203, 215–216; "The Ghost of John Wayne," 196–197; "The Grandfather Horse," 199–201; "Jalapeño Contest," 197–198; overview, 183–184, 192, 194
ghosts and haunting: Cummins's *American Dirt* and, 177–180; Dickinson's "One need not be a chamber to be haunted," 182; Gonzalez's "The Grandfather Horse," 199–201; Gordon on, 176–177, 179, 182; slowness and, 175–177
Giant (1956), 49, 279n7, 284n9
Glatzer, Richard, 55, 58
globalization, 165–166
The Godfather (1972), 52, 145, 280n11
Gomez-Peña, Guillermo, 96
Gonzales, Rodolfo "Corky": *I Am Joaquín/Yo soy Joaquín*, 116, 157–160, 289n17, 289n19; National Chicano Youth Liberation Conference and, 159
González, Christopher, 178–180, 268, 292n2
González, Genero, 184
González, John Morán, 286n11
González, Jovita, 183
Gonzalez, Ray: about, 186, 191–193; *Circling the Tortilla Dragon*, 295n19; "Fathers," 193–194, 203; *The Heat of Arrivals*, 193–194; *Muy Macho*, 87. See also *The Ghost of John Wayne and Other Stories*
The Goonies (1985), 280n8
Gordon, Avery, 176–177, 179–180, 182
"The Grandfather Horse" (Gonzalez), 199–201
Great Lakes Feminist Geography Collective (GLFGC), 15–18, 25–26, 28, 42–43, 113, 181, 268, 276n7
The Green Mile (1999), 282n22
Guardians of the Galaxy (2014), 218
Guevara, Che, 145–146

Guidotti-Hernández, Nicole, 155, 162–163
Gunman's Walk (1958), 296n6
Gurba, Myriam, 177–180
Gutiérrez, Jorge R., 258
Gutiérrez Ortiz, Eulalio, 164

Hackford, Taylor, 50
Halberstam, J., 20–21, 85–86, 188–189
The Halliday Brand (1957), 296n6
Hamill, Mark, 283n4
Hannan, Brian, 222–223, 225, 228, 297n10
Harry Potter and the Deathly Hallows: Part 2 (2011), 26
Hart, Martin B., 283n2
Harwood, Sarah, 51
Hauer, Rutger, 285n1
hauntings. *See* ghosts and haunting
Hearne, Joanna, 133
Heide, Markus, 85
Helguera, Jesús, 140
Hemingway, Ernest, 93–94, 107
Hernández, David Manuel, 87
Hernández, Leandra H., 129, 130
Hernández, Yanela, 13, 34, 276n2
Hernández-Ávila, Inés, 165
Herrera-Sobek, Maria, 155
Heston, Charlton, 223
Hidalgo, Miguel, 133
higher education. *See* academic culture
High Noon (1952), 49, 235
Hinojosa, Rolando, 184
Hokowhitu, Brendan, 104
homosexuality, queerness, and homophobia: disability and queerness, 296n27; *La Mission* (2009), 129–130, 136, 138, 147, 266; *Quinceañera* (2006), 70–74, 266, 267; Sáenz's *Aristotle and Dante Discover the Secrets of the Universe*, 265–267; as taboo subject, 130, 287n2; Urrea's *In Search of Snow*, 91; *A Walk in the Clouds* (1995), 65
Honoré, Carl, 267
hooks, bell, 58, 170, 292n9
Horn, Tom, 106, 285n16
Horton, Willie, 23, 277n12
The House of the Spirits (1993), 280n9

INDEX   321

Houtbeckers, Eeva, 17, 21, 114, 172
Howe, Irving, 278n5
Huaco-Nuzum, Carmen, 53, 185, 281n16
Huerta, Elisa Diana, 149, 289n15
Huerta, Jorge, 158–159
Hurtado, Aída, 185
hybridity, 155–156, 165–166

I Am Joaquín (1969), 157–159
I Am Joaquín/Yo soy Joaquín (Gonzales), 116, 157–160, 289n17, 289n19
I Am Not Your Perfect Mexican Daughter (Sánchez), 265
"I Am the King" (Anaya), 190–191, 200–201
I Like It Like That (1994), 50
Imitation of Life (1934), 282n22
imperialist nostalgia, 10
Indians of All Tribes (IAT), 131–132, 288n4
Indigeneity: Aztec culture and iconography, 116–117, 140–145, 148–152; "Aztext," 158, 162, 264; Aztlán, 116, 123, 143–144, 147, 159–160, 289nn16–17; *Blade Runner* (1982), 111; Chicanismo and Chicanx instrumentalizing of, 115–118, 139–142; colonial histories and, 88; cowboy/Indian dynamic, 101–102; detribalization, 127, 154; DNA testing and complications, 125–126; dynamic masculinity and, 104; family genealogies, complications of, 120–127; healing practices and *danza azteca*, 147–151; IAT occupation of Alcatraz, 131–132, 288n4; indigenism vs., 289n13; the "masculindian," 88, 103; Mexican aggression against Apaches, 101; *La Mission* (2009), 131–134, 139–153, 288n11; the pan-*humano*, 134; *Suicide Squad* (2016), 235–238; Tonto figure, 57, 285n12; Urrea's *In Search of Snow*, 101–107. *See also* tribalism
Indigenous Men and Masculinities (Innes and Anderson), 88
Infante, Pedro, 294n9
In Praise of Slowness (Honoré), 267
In Search of Snow (Urrea): Bobo and Mike as interracial duo, 98–99; Bobo as outsider, 96–97; cowboy/Indian dynamic, 101–102; Delbert, 90, 105–107; gas station blown up, 107; Indigeneity, instrumentalization of, 117–118; Mike as father to Umbelinda, 107–108; Mike's racial lineage, 97–98; *La Mission* (2009) compared to, 136, 138–139; Ramses and Indian masculinity, 101–107; relational dynamics and racialized triangle, 88–91; source materials for masculinity, 91–94; veteran status in, 91–92; visit to García home and transculturation, 99–101; John Wayne and, 195; whiteness and Mike's racialization of Mexicans, 94–96
Instructions not Included (2013), 49
Irwin, Robert McKee, 294n14
Isaac, Oscar, 82
Ishmael (Quinn), 292n6
Islas, Arturo, 183, 293n1

"Jalapeño Contest" (Gonzalez), 197–198
Jewett, Robert, 219
Jiménez, José Alfredo, 187, 188
Johnson, Michael K., 297n13
Johnson, Reed, 131
Juliet Takes a Breath (Rivera), 265
Justice, Daniel Heath, 104

Kahn, William, 266
Kallio, Galina, 17, 21, 114, 172
Kariko, Katalin, 39
Karkov, Catherine E., 15–16, 17, 39, 177, 268
Keating, AnaLouise, 166
Kedley, Kate E., 266
Kimmel, Michael, 86, 89, 108, 196
King, Thomas, 115, 153
knowledge production: Anzaldúa on, 291; Chicanx culture as site and source of, 11; CV and, 27–28; demands on time and labor, 112–113; genre-bending, 268; keeping quiet and, 33; self-reflection and, 114–115; as sites of wounding, 21; slow research and, 17–18, 39–40, 109; writing and, 181–182
Kurosawa, Akira, 222, 236, 297n9

latchkey kids, 2–5
Latin lover type: about, 48; *The Book of Life* (2014), 262; *Despicable Me 2* (2013), 259, 260–261; *Quinceañera* (2006), 73
Latino Images in Film (Ramírez Berg), 32
Lawrence, John Shelton, 219
Leavis, Q. D., 278nn2–3
Lee, Spike, 57
Leone, Sergio, 297n18
Lewis, Paul Owen, 137
La leyenda de los volcanes (Helguera), 140, 152, 289n14
The Liars of Mariposa Island (Mathieu), 265
Life on the Mississippi (Twain), 91
Lindemann, Mary, 181
literature reviews, 30–33
La Llorona, 173, 176–177
Logan (2017), 217–222, 238–250, 257, 264
Lomelí, Francisco, 143–144
The Lone Ranger (1949–1957), 98
Lone Star (1996), 49
López, Ana M., 293n4
lowrider culture: *La Mission* (2009), 134–139, 146–147, 152; Sandoval on, 289n12; slow culture and, 10–11
Luna, Diego, 82
Lush, Rebecca M., 297n13
Lux, Guillermo, 141–142, 145

Machete (2010), 49, 75, 186
machismo. *See* masculinities
Madsen, William, 299n1
Maffesoli, Michel, 160–161, 171, 292n6
magical Negro character, 57–58, 282nn22–23
The Magnificent Seven (1960), 220, 222–229, 232, 235–237, 247, 249
The Magnificent Seven (2016), 228–229, 297n12
Malthus, Thomas, 292n6
Mambo Kings (1992), 50
Man About Town (1939), 77
A Man Called Horse (1970), 224

The Mandalorian (2019–present), 35–36, 257
Mangold, James, 238–239
El Mariachi (1992), 186
Martell, Luke, 19, 47, 175
Martinez, Domingo, 188–191
Martínez, Javier Garrido, 14
Marvel Cinematic Universe (MCU), 217, 296n1
Mary Poppins Returns (2018), 83
Masculindians (McKegney), 88
masculinities: Aldama and Aldama's *Decolonizing Latinx Masculinities*, 32–33; Anaya's "I Am the King," 190–191, 200–201; *The Book of Life* (2014), 263; Cásares's *Brownsville*, 206–215; competition and, 197; critical scholarship on, 87, 185–186; *Despicable Me 2* (2013), 258, 259–260; female, 188–189; feminist critiques, 159–160; Gonzalez's *Muy Macho*, 87; Gonzalez's *The Ghost of John Wayne and Others Stories*, 196–197, 200–204; Halberstam on, 85–86, 188–189; *Logan* (2017), 241; Martinez's *The Boy Kings of Texas*, 188–191; *La Mission* (2009), 134–139; *My Family/Mi familia* (1995), 51, 53; paternalism and, 56; performance of, as dynamic, 90; *Quinceañera* (2006), 73; El Rey and, 187–188; Rodríguez's "On Macho," 84; *Suicide Squad* (2016), 231; Villarreal's *Pocho*, 184–185; John Wayne and, 194–195, 203; western genre and, 221. *See also* Chicanismo and Chicano nationalism; *In Search of Snow* (Urrea)
Mata, Isaias, 133
Mathieu, Jennifer, 265
Matos, Angel Daniel, 266, 267
McCall, Guadalupe Garcia, 265
McFarland, USA (2015), 49
McKegney, Sam, 88, 103
McNickle, D'Arcy, 116
McWilliams, Cary, 284n11
Medina, Meg, 265
Meeuf, Russell, 195
Melero, Apolinar, 144, 289n18

Melville, Herman, 93
mestizaje: Anzaldúa's theorization of, 154–156, 162–165, 171–172; Pérez-Torres on, 157
meta-human/mutant fathers and the western: *Logan* (2017), 217–222, 238–250, 257, 264; *The Magnificent Seven* (1960), 220, 222–229, 232, 235–237, 247, 249; *The Magnificent Seven* (2016), 228–229; Palmer on evolution of westerns, 233; professional-western plots, 220, 236, 242, 247–249; *Shane* (1953), 221, 227, 235, 245–247, 249; *Suicide Squad* (2016), 217–222, 229–238, 249–250, 257; superhero genre and, 217–218; *Terminator 2: Judgment Day* (1991) and *Terminator: Dark Fate* (2019), 250–251; village cleansers myth, 219; "weird western" subgenre, 230, 297n13; the western film genre, 217, 218–222
Metcalf, Stephen, 196
Mexica: Anzaldúa on, 160, 162; *La Mission* (2009), 128–130, 141–145, 151–152
Mexico, in Hollywood films, 223–224
Meza, Maria, 13, 34
"Mi Gente" (Melero), 289n18
The Milagro Beanfield War (1988), 50, 282n21
Million Dollar Movie (1972–1992), 3
Minich, Julie Avril, 209, 211–212, 295n26–296n27
Miranda, Lin-Manuel, 83
Mirandé, Alfredo, 52–54, 59, 185, 280n13–281n15, 299n1
missing women, 243, 298n21
La Mission (2009): absent mother in, 75; Anzaldúa's new tribalism and, 172; Brown feeling in, 257; Chicano Indigeneity and tattoo iconography in, 139–147; end credits and "All My Relations" message, 152–153; healing practices, Indigenous, 147–152; homophobia in, 129–130, 136, 138; lowrider culture and heterosexual masculinity in, 134–139, 146–147; Mission District setting, new tribalism, and the pan-*humano*, 131–134; overview, 128–131; Sáenz's *Aristotle and Dante* compared to, 266; screening event, 128; title sequence and opening credits, 148–149; Urrea's *In Search of Snow* compared to, 136, 138–139

Mission District, San Francisco, 131–132
Mi Vida Loca (1993), 50, 58
modernism, 278n5
modern primitives, 169, 292n8
modern tribalism, 165, 170–171
Molina, Adrian, 258
Monroe Doctrine, 34, 277n19
Montiel, Miguel, 185
Moraga, Cherríe, 116, 139, 155, 159, 171–172
Morales, Miles, 83, 299n3
Mortuary (1983), 77
"Mr. Z" (Cásares), 204–208
Muñoz, José Esteban, 34–35, 257, 276n4
Muñoz Martínez, Monica, 194, 295n20
Murieta, Joaquín, 157
mutant fathers. *See* meta-human/mutant fathers and the western
Muy Macho (Gonzalez), 87
My Family/Mi familia (1995), 49, 50–54, 280n8, 281nn18–19, 281n21

National Chicano Youth Liberation Conference, first (Denver, 1969), 159
nationalism. *See* Chicanismo and Chicano nationalism
Nava, Gregory, 49, 50–53, 75, 280n9
Negrete, Jorge, 294n9, 294n12
neoliberalism, 15–16, 276n6
new tribalism. *See under* tribalism
Nixon, Rob, 178–179
Nobody's Son (Urrea), 285n14
El Norte (1993), 50
Nyong'o, Lupita, 82

Oak Forest Library, Houston, 4
Oak Island, 7–8, 275n4
O'Brien, Geoffrey, 20–21
"Of Bronze the Sacrifice" (De León), 289n18

Olmos, Edward James, 50
"One need not be a chamber to be haunted" (Dickinson), 182
"On Macho" (Rodríguez), 84
Ontiveros, Lupe, 280n8
Orozco, Danielle, 244
Ortiz, Simon J., 168
Our Family Wedding (2010), 49, 75
The Outlaw Josey Wales (1976), 288n10

pachuco persona, 95–96, 284n11
Padron, Rangel, 121
Palmer, Lorrie, 233
Palmer, Parker J., 115, 268–269
pan-humanism, 134, 153, 171
Paredes, Américo, 183, 184, 260, 279n2
Partido Revolucionario Institucional (PRI), 244
patriarchal institutions, critiques of, 37–38, 41
patriarchs. See *ancianos*
patriarchy: Halberstam on masculinity and, 86; Indigenous men and, 88; La Llorona and, 176–177; masculinist narratives and, 53; *La Mission* (2009), 146; *A Walk in the Clouds* (1995), 63, 69; the western genre and, 221; Woolf on, 37
patrimony, cultural, 21–22
Paxton, Bill, 77, 283n3
Paz, Daniel, 33–34
Paz, Octavio, 284n11
Peña, Michael, 83, 297n14
Pérez, Daniel Enrique, 53, 185
The Perez Family (1995), 280n9
Pérez-Torres, Rafael, 146, 157
The Phantom Empire (O'Brien), 20–21
The Phantom Menace (*Star Wars Episode I*) (1999), 278n21
Pina, Michael, 143
Pitts, Victoria, 169, 292n8
El Plan Espiritual de Aztlán, 116, 143–144, 159
Pocho (Villarreal), 184–185
The Poet X (Acevedo), 265
power: the *anciano* and, 54–59; autonomy and, 47; knowledge production and, 33; of names, 22–23; *Real Women Have Curves* (2002), 65–66, 68–69; slow approach and, 19; source and, 40; Urrea's *In Search of Snow*, 94; Villarreal's *Pocho*, 184–185; *A Walk in the Clouds* (1995), 59, 62, 65; white savior narrative and, 14–15; Woolf on, 38, 41–42
Predator (1987), 298n29
pregnancy: *Quinceañera* (2006), 70, 73–74; Urrea's *In Search of Snow*, 100; *A Walk in the Clouds* (1995), 59–60
Price of Glory (2000), 49, 75
primitives, modern, 169, 292n8
"Professional Aztecs and Popular Culture" (Rieff), 161–162
The Professionals (1966), 220
publishing industry, slow violence of, 178–180
Puss in Boots (2011), 299n2

queerness. See homosexuality, queerness, and homophobia
Quinceañera (2006), 55–58, 62, 70–75, 257, 266, 267
Quinn, Anthony, 222, 296n8
Quinn, Daniel, 292n6

racist stereotypes. See stereotypes and tropes
Raheja, Michelle H., 133
Raiders of the Lost Ark (1981), 269
Raleigh, Eve, 183
Ramirez, Michael, 189–190
Ramírez Berg, Charles, 32, 47–49, 82, 221, 231, 240, 259, 277n15, 279n3, 279n5, 294n12, 294n13
Raymond, Virginia, 299n1
raza cósmica (cosmic race), 164, 244, 298n23
Real Women Have Curves (2002), 55–58, 62, 65–70, 129
Rebel without a Cause (1955), 92
Rebolledo, Tey Diana, 155
redface, 168
Reeser, Todd W., 86, 89, 93, 94, 96
Reitsma, Richard, 130, 134
Renaud, Chris, 258
René (Chateaubriand), 40
Reservation Blues (Alexie), 167–169, 178

INDEX

"El Rey" (song; Jiménez), 187–188, 190–191
El Rey Network, 187–188, 293n6, 294n15
Ridge, John Rollin, 157
Rieff, David, 161–162, 165
The Ring (1952), 49
Rivera, Alex, 79, 82
Rivera, Diego, 145–146
Rivera, Gabby, 265
Rivera, Tómas, 184
roadshow pictures, 77, 82, 283n2
Robinson, Cecil, 94
Rodríguez, Clelia O., 20–21
Rodríguez, Luis J., 84
Rodríguez, Richard T., 53, 185, 281n18
Rodriguez, Robert, 186–188, 293nn4–5, 293n7–294n8
Rogue One: A Star Wars Story (2016), 82–83
Rojas, Gonzalo, 193
"A Room of One's Own" (Woolf), 38
Rosaldo, Renato, 10
Rubio, Richard, 195
Ruiz de Burton, María Amparo, 183
The Running Man (1987), 298n29

sachem character, 57–58
Sáenz, Benjamin Alire, 257, 265–267
Saldaña-Portillo, María Josefina, 117, 144, 155, 160, 162–163, 287n13, 289n16
Saldívar-Hull, Sonia, 32
Salinas, Agustín, Sr., 297n11
Salt of the Earth (1954), 49
Sánchez, Erika, 265
Sandoval, Denise Michelle, 289n12
Santos, George, 231
Say Anything (1989), 26–27
Schatz, Thomas, 217
Schlesinger, Lisa, 9, 16, 18, 21
Schoenberger, Nancy, 195
Schwarzenegger, Arnold, 251, 298n29
science, gender of, 41
Scott, Ridley, 111, 269
The Searchers (1956), 50, 224
Seeber, Barbara, 46–47, 112, 113–114, 180
Sehra, Rohina Katoch, 9

Selena (1997), 49
Serenity (2005), 218
Seven Samurai (1954), 222, 236, 296n8–297n9
Shane (1953), 221, 227, 235, 245–247, 249
Shang-Chi and the Legend of the Ten Rings (2021), 296n1
Shaw, Marc E., 90
Silko, Leslie Marmon, 22
Simmen, Edward, 184–185
Sinha, Mrinal, 185
Six Kinds of Sky (Urrea), 284n4
Sloss, Pete Silva, 142
Slotkin, Richard, 224–225, 227, 228
slowness: autonomy and, 47; balance and, 177; BIPOC cultures and, 9–11; change and, 264; COVID-19 pandemic and, 11; ghosts, haunting, and, 175–177; instrumentalization vs. caring culture and practices, 112–115; joy of scholarship and, 177; libraries and, 286n5; *La Mission* (2009), 134; new tribalism and, 172, 290–291; personal reflection and power of inwardness, 268–269; scholarship and research, slow, 8–9, 15–19, 39–43; "slow does not always mean slow," 267–268; Slow Fashion movement, 9; Slow Food movement, 9, 18; unpacking, 180–181; writing as slow work, 181
Slowpoke Rodriguez, 19, 276n9
Slow Scholarship (Karkov), 39
Smith, Paul Chaat, 288n5
Smits, Jimmy, 82–83
Smokey and the Bandit (1977), 125
Sneider, Leah, 284n5
Soldier (1998), 285n1
Solis, Javier, 294n9
"Soy Chicana de Aztlán" (Estrella), 143
Spare Parts (2015), 49
Speedy Gonzales, 19, 276n9, 299n2
Spider-Man: Into the Spider-Verse (2018), 83, 299n3
Spurgeon, Sara L., 297n13
Spy Kids series (2001; 2002; 2003), 49, 54, 186
Stagecoach (1939), 235

Stand and Deliver (1988), 50, 282n21
Star Wars storyverse: *The Empire Strikes Back* (*Episode V*) (1980), 24, 77–82; Latinx actors in, 82–83; *The Mandalorian* (2019–present), 35–36, 257; *The Phantom Menace* (*Episode I*) (1999), 278n20; as roadshow pictures, 82; *Rogue One: A Star Wars Story* (2016), 82–83; *Star Wars* (*Episode IV—A New Hope*) (1977), 79, 81–82, 218
Steinbeck, John, 94
Steiner, Stan, 288n6, 289n19
Stengers, Isabelle, 38–42, 177, 276n5, 279n6
stereotypes and tropes: affective excess, Latinx, 34–36, 257–258, 260; brownface, 51, 223, 285n15; the buffoon, 48, 261; cultural patrimony and, 21–22; *el gallo* figure, 260, 298n1; gangbanger figure, 231–232; media images of Brown families, 14–15, 34–35, 48–49, 52–53; pachuco persona, 95–96, 284n11; positive and romanticized, 52–53; publishing industry and, 178–179; redface, 168; Simmen on evolution of, 184–185; six prevailing stereotypes, 48; slowness and, 19; Speedy Gonzales and Slowpoke Rodriguez, 19, 276n9, 299n2; subversion of, 279n5; Tonto figure, 57, 285n12; U.S. presidents, villainizing of Mexicans by, 23. See also *bandido* figure
Storm Boy (Lewis), 137, 147, 288n7
storytelling, 114–115, 252–254, 268
Sturges, John, 220, 228, 296n8
Suárez, Mario, 184
Suicide Squad (2016), 217–222, 229–238, 249–250, 257
Summer of the Mariposas (McCall), 265
superhero genre. *See* meta-human/mutant fathers and the western
Survivor (2000–present), 156–157, 291nn1–3

tattoos: *La Mission* (2009), 139–147; *Suicide Squad* (2016), 231–232
El Teatro Campesino, 158

Tejano monument, Austin, Texas, 119
Tekakwitha, Kateri, 133, 288n8
Teotihuacán, Mexico, 117
Terminator 2: Judgment Day (1991), 250–251
Terminator: Dark Fate (2019), 250–251, 257, 298n28
Thein, Amanda Haertling, 266
There Was a Woman (Perez), 26
This Bridge We Call Home (Anzaldúa), 164, 166–167, 169, 173
The Three Amigos (1986), 50
The Three Caballeros (1944), 299n2
Three Guineas (Woolf), 37–41
Titanic (1997), 283n3
Tombstone (1993), 283n3
Tonantzín, 145, 152, 157, 289n19
Tonto, 57, 285n12
Tortilla Soup (2001), 75
Total Recall (1990), 298n29
Touch of Evil (1958), 50, 223
toxic masculinity. *See* masculinities
trauma porn, 178
Treasure of the Sierra Madre (1948), 49
tribalism: Chicano civil rights movement and, 157–160; consumption and, 170–171; cultural tourism, appropriation, and, 167–172; detribalization, 127, 154, 169; hybridity and, 155–156, 165–166; Maffesoli's *The Time of the Tribes*, 160–161; modern, 165, 170–171; neo-tribalism, 161, 165, 292n6; new tribalism, 134, 160–167, 169–173; *Survivor* (2000–present) and, 156–157, 291nn1–3; urban, 165, 169; US popular imagination, "tribe" in, 170
Trump, Donald, 13, 23
Turbo (2013), 299n2
Turner, Victor, 170
Twain, Mark, 91, 93
Twister (1996), 283n3

United Bay Area Council of American Indian Affairs, 288n5
Unkrich, Lee, 258
unpacking, 180–181
Urrea, Luis Alberto: *Across the Wire*, 284n3; "Bid Farewell to Her Many

Horses," 284n4; *By the Lake of Sleeping Children*, 179; critical attention to, 85; *Nobody's Son*, 285n14; "Taped to the Sky," 284n4; "Whores," 87, 285n13. See also *In Search of Snow*
U.S. border policies, 13–14, 23

Valdez, Luis: *Aztlan* (with Steiner), 288n6; *La Bamba* (1987), 49, 281n21, 291n4; *I Am Joaquín/Yo soy Joaquín* (1969), 158–159; Reiff's critique of, 161–162; on Tonantzín, 289n19; *Zoot Suit* (1981), 291n4
The Valley (Hinojosa), 184
Varela Hernández, Denis Javier, 14
Varon, Alberto, 186
Vasconcelos, José, 164, 244, 298n23
Vasquez, Richard, 184
Vera Cruz (1954), 220, 224
viejito figure, 54
Vigil, Maurilio E., 141–142, 145
Villa, Pancho, 76
Villarreal, José Antonio, 184–185
violence: affection shown through, 90; *The Book of Life* (2014), 262; Cásares's *Brownsville*, 207–212, 214–215; dominance as contextual, 96; Gonzalez's "Fathers," 194; Gonzalez's *The Ghost of John Wayne and Others Stories*, 198–200; Indigenous peoples and experience of, 88; Latinx emotional excess and, 257; *Logan* (2017), 245–250; *The Magnificent Seven* (1960), 224–225; *La Mission* (2009), 151; Muñoz Martínez on borderlands violence, 194, 295n20; publishing industry, slow violence of, 178–180; *Shane* (1953), 221, 245–247; Urrea's *In Search of Snow*, 89–90, 95–96, 101–104, 106–107
Virgen de Guadalupe, 141, 144–145, 157, 289nn19–20
virgin/whore dichotomy, 74
¡Viva Zapata! (1952), 49
Vizenor, Gerald, 133

A Walk in the Clouds (1995), 55–65, 257
Walkout (2006), 49
Wallach, Eli, 223

War Games (1983), 7
Warrior, Robert Allen, 288n5
warrior persona: "bronze-skinned warriors," 144, 289n18; colonial violence and, 88; *Suicide Squad* (2016), 237; Urrea's *In Search of Snow*, 101–108
Watson, Elwood, 90
Wayne, John, 194–196, 235, 295n21. See also *The Ghost of John Wayne and Other Stories* (Gonzalez)
westerns. See meta-human/mutant fathers and the western
Westmoreland, Wash, 55, 58
Where We Come From (Cásares), 204
whiteness and white masculinity: the bandido and, 296n7; Bebout on, 94–95; *Blade Runner* (1982), 117; Brown feeling and, 257; Brown pain, white appetite for, 177–178; cultural appropriation and, 168; family dramas and, 51–52; Indigeneity and, 58; *Logan* (2017), 250; Muñoz on affective normativity and, 34–35; *Quinceañera* (2006), 75; *Suicide Squad* (2016), 237–238; Urrea's *In Search of Snow*, 86, 90, 91, 93–95, 98, 99, 118; *A Walk in the Clouds* (1995), 65; western genre and, 221–222, 235
white savior narrative: *The Magnificent Seven* (1960), 226; power and, 14–15; superhero films and, 217–218; *A Walk in the Clouds* (1995), 59
Whitman, Walt, 284n8
The Wild Bunch (1969), 50, 220
Williams, Leah, 297n12
Winterhawk (1975), 125
Woll, Allen, 279n6
Womack, Craig, 156
women, Latina: in film history, 48–49; media narratives of the "bad mother," 34; missing, 243, 298n21; sacred place of, in *La Mission* (2009), 136–137, 288n11; virgin/whore dichotomy, 74
Wonder Woman (2017), 217
Woolf, Virginia: ghosts and, 177; privilege and, 278n2, 279n7; "A Room of One's Own," 38; Stengers and, 38–

Woolf, Virginia (*continued*)
    42; *Three Guineas*, 37–41, 278n2;
    The Years, 38
Wright, Will, 219–220
A Wrinkle in Time (2018), 83
writing buddies, 24–26. *See also* academic culture

X-Men series, 217; *Deadpool* (2016), 217; *Deadpool 2* (2018), 217; *Logan* (2017), 217–222, 238–250, 257, 264; *X-Men Origins: Wolverine* (2009), 241, 298n25
Xol, David, 14

Yaqui Delgado Wants to Kick Your Ass (Medina), 265
Yaqui Wars, 297n11
The Years (Woolf), 38
young adult fiction, 264–267

Zinn, Maxine Baca, 185
Zinnemann, Fred, 235
Zitkála-Šá (Gertrude Simmons Bonnin), 9–10, 41
Zoot Suit (1981), 291n4
zoot suiters, 284n11
Zoot Suit Riots, 285n11